CIVIL WAR

Peter Ackroyd

THE HISTORY OF ENGLAND
Volume III
CIVIL WAR

MACMILLAN

First published 2014 by Macmillan
an imprint of Pan Macmillan, a division of Macmillan Publishers Limited
Pan Macmillan, 20 New Wharf Road, London N1 9RR
Basingstoke and Oxford
Associated companies throughout the world
www.panmacmillan.com

ISBN 978-0-230-70641-5 HB
ISBN 978-1-4472-6070-7 TPB

3 5 7 9 8 6 4 2

A CIP catalogue record for this book is available from the British Library.

Typeset by Palimpsest Book Production Ltd, Falkirk, Stirlingshire
Printed and bound by CPI Group (UK) Ltd, Croydon, CR0 4YY

Contents

List of illustrations

1. James I of England and James VI of Scotland (John de Critz the Elder / Mary Evans Picture Library)
2. Anne of Denmark, James's spouse (c.1605–10, Gheeraerts, Marcus (c.1561–1635) (attr. to)) / Woburn Abbey, Bedfordshire, UK / Bridgeman Images)
3. James in front of his lords, temporal and spiritual (Mary Evans Picture Library / Everett Collection)
4. The title page of the King James Bible (© Photo Researchers / Mary Evans Picture Library)
5. The title page of John Milton's *Areopagitica* (Mary Evans Picture Library)
6. George Villiers, 1st duke of Buckingham (Mary Evans / Iberfoto)
7. Henry, prince of Wales (Oliver, Isaac (c.1565–1617) / Fitzwilliam Museum, University of Cambridge, UK / Bridgeman Images)
8. The future Charles I, as prince of Wales (Royal Armouries, Leeds, UK / Bridgeman Images)
9. Elizabeth, daughter of James I (Private Collection / Bridgeman Images)
10. Charles I and his wife, Henrietta Maria (Alinari Archives, Florence – Reproduced with the permission of Ministero per I Beni e le Attivit . . . Cu)
11. Three out of seven of Charles I's children, painted by Anthony Van Dyck (Alinari Archives, Florence – Reproduced with the permission of Ministero per I Beni e le Attivit . . . Cu)
12. A disapproving illustration of the Rump Parliament (Interfoto / Sammlung Rauch / Mary Evans Picture Library)

1

A new Solomon

Sir Robert Carey rode furiously from London to Edinburgh along the Great North Road, spending one night in Yorkshire and another in Northumberland; he arrived at Holyrood Palace, 'be-bloodied with great falls and bruises' after a journey of more than 330 miles. It was late at night on Saturday 26 March 1603. He was ushered into the presence of King James VI of Scotland and, falling to his knees, proclaimed him to be 'King of England, France and Ireland'. He gave him as testimony a sapphire ring that his sister, Lady Scrope, had thrown to him from a window at Richmond Palace immediately after the death of Elizabeth I. 'I have', he told his new sovereign, 'a blue ring from a fair lady.'

'It is enough,' James said. 'I know by this you are a true messenger.' The king had previously entrusted this ring to Lady Scrope in the event of the queen's death.

A body of prelates and peers had already met Sir Robert Cecil, the principal councillor of the old queen, at Whitehall Gate before they proceeded with him to the cross at Cheapside where Cecil proclaimed James as king; bonfires and bells greeted the news of the swift and easy succession. Cecil himself declared that he had 'steered King James's ship into the right harbour, without cross of wave or tide that could have overturned a cock-boat'. The councillor had entered a secret correspondence with James before Elizabeth's death; he had urged the Scottish king to nourish 'a heart of adamant in a world of feathers'.

On 5 April James left Edinburgh to travel to his new realm. He had been the king of Scotland for thirty-six years, ever since he had assumed the throne at the age of thirteen months after the forced abdication of his mother Mary Queen of Scots. He had been a successful if not a glorious monarch, managing to curb the pretensions of an argumentative clergy and of a fractious nobility. From his earliest years the restive and combative spirit of the Scottish lords ensured that, in the words of the French ambassador, he had been nourished in fear. Yet he had by guile and compromise held on to his crown. Now, as he told his followers, he was about to enter the Land of Promise. He had already written to the council at Westminster, asking for money; he did not have the funds to finance his journey south.

The king did not perhaps expect so effusive and jubilant a welcome from his new subjects. He recalled later how 'the people of all sorts rid and ran, nay rather flew to meet me'. They came to gaze at him, since none of them had experienced the rule of a male monarch. He himself was impressed by the prosperity of the land and by the evident wealth of its rulers. He said later that the first three years of his reign were 'as a Christmas'. It took him a month to reach London, largely because he wished to avoid the funeral of his predecessor. He had no great fondness for Elizabeth; she had prevaricated over his right to the succession and, perhaps more significantly, had ordered the execution of his mother.

He reached York by the middle of April, where Cecil came to greet him. 'Though you be but a little man,' the king told him, 'we shall surely load your shoulders with business.' At Newark-on-Trent he gave orders that a cutpurse, preying upon his retinue, should summarily be hanged; he had not properly been informed on the provisions of English common law. It is an indication that he was still, in many important respects, a foreigner. At Burghley-by-Stamford he fell from his horse and broke his collar bone. Slowly he made his way to London. For three or four days he rested in Hertfordshire at Robert Cecil's country home, Theobalds House, at which seat he took pleasure in creating many knights.

He was so generous with titles that he was accused of improvidence. The reign of Elizabeth witnessed the creation of 878 knights; in the first four months of the king's rule, some 906 new men were awarded that honour. The queen had knighted those whom she considered to be of genuine merit or importance; James merely considered knighthood to be a mark of status. He was said to have knighted a piece of beef with the words 'Arise, Sir Loin'. On another occasion he did not catch the name of the recipient and said, 'Prithee, rise up, and call thyself Sir What Thou Wilt.' Other titles could be purchased with cash. The diminution in the importance of honour marks one of the first changes to the old Tudor system.

Those who were permitted into the king's presence may not have been entirely impressed. He was awkward and hesitant in manner; his legs were slightly bowed and his gait erratic, perhaps the consequence of rickets acquired in childhood. One admittedly hostile witness, Sir Anthony Weldon, also described him as forever 'fiddling about his codpiece'.

He was a robust and fluent conversationalist, who rather liked to hear the sound of his own voice, but the effect upon his English audience was perhaps impaired by the fact that he retained a broad Scots accent. If he was eager to talk, he was also quick to laugh. He could be witty, but delivered his droll remarks in a grave and serious voice. His manners were not impeccable, and he was said to have slobbered over his food and drink. He paid little attention to his dress, but favoured thickly padded doublets that might impede an assassin's dagger; ever since his childhood he had lived in fear of assault or murder. He was said to have a horror of naked steel. He had a restless, roving eye; he paid particular notice to those at court who were not known to him.

On 7 May he rode towards London, but was greeted 4 miles outside the city by the lord mayor and innumerable citizens. He lodged at the Charterhouse for four nights, and then made his way to the Tower, where he remained for a few days. While staying in the royal apartments he began an excited tour of his capital, 'secretly in his coach and by water', as one contemporary put it; he was particularly struck by the sight of the crown jewels, held at the palace in Whitehall. Here was the glittering and unmistakable evidence of his new-found wealth.

Yet London was not a pleasure-dome. Even as he approached it, the plague began its secret ministry in the streets and alleys; by the end of the summer it had claimed the lives of 30,000 citizens. A grand state entry had been planned for 25 July, the day of the coronation, but the fear of infected crowds curtailed the ceremony; there would be a crowning, but no state procession.

Even in these early months of the reign conspiracies began to mount against his throne. A group of gentlemen, among them Sir Walter Raleigh and Henry Brooke, Lord Cobham, were suspected of a scheme to depose James and to replace him with his cousin Arabella Stuart; like most conspiracies it was plagued by rumour, indecision and premature disclosure. Raleigh was arrested and consigned to the Tower, where two weeks later he attempted suicide; at his subsequent trial he was denounced by the attorney general, Sir Edward Coke, as 'a spider of hell'.

Raleigh: You speak indiscreetly, barbarously and uncivilly.
Coke: I want words sufficient to express thy viperous
    treasons.
Raleigh: You want words, indeed, for you have spoken the
    one thing half a dozen times.

This was the end of what was called 'the Main Plot'. A 'Bye Plot' was also discovered, whereby the king was to be kidnapped by priests and forced to suspend the laws against Roman Catholics. It came to nothing, of course, except for the deaths of the principals engaged in it.

The time had come for the formal, if subdued, coronation of the king; the archbishop of Canterbury performed the ceremony expeditiously in the sight of an invited audience. James's consort, Anne of Denmark, agreed to receive her crown from the archbishop; as a Catholic, however, she refused to partake of Protestant communion. Being of a complaisant and gregarious disposition she caused very little trouble for the rest of her husband's reign. Her chaplain once remarked that 'the king himself was a very chaste man, and there was little in the queen to make him uxorious; yet they did love as well as man and wife could do, not conversing together'. After the ceremony the royal family left pestilential London for the healthier air of the country. James and Anne made their first 'progress' in the August of the year, making their way to Winchester and Southampton before turning north into Oxfordshire; in this, they were following the fashion of the king's illustrious predecessor.

James had already established, however, the foundations of his court and council. In particular he took care to reward his Scottish nobles with the most prominent positions in his personal retinue. The centre of his rule lay in the royal bedchamber, which was almost wholly staffed by the entourage that had followed him from his native land. This was a source of much discontent and disquiet among the English courtiers; it was said that the Scottish lords stood like mountains between the beams of the king's grace and themselves. Yet a new privy chamber was also established, half of Scots and half of English; the king revelled in his role as 'the pacifier', and this equal pairing evinced his moderation.

Among the English councillors the palm was awarded to Sir Robert Cecil and to the Howards. Henry Howard, earl of Northampton, was appointed as lord warden of the cinque ports at the beginning of 1604 and, a year later, lord privy seal; in the previous reign he had sent what James called 'Asiatic and endless volumes' of advice to Edinburgh. Thomas Howard, earl of Suffolk, was lord chamberlain. Cecil, soon to become Viscount Cranborne and then earl of Salisbury, was in fact pre-eminent; he was very small, with a hunched back, but he stood above the others. The king had told him that 'before God I count you the best servant that ever I had, albeit you be but a beagle'. He often addressed him as 'my little beagle'. Cecil managed parliament, and the revenues; he supervised Ireland and all foreign affairs. He was forever industrious, highly efficient and always courteous; he had borne with patience all the humiliating remarks about his appearance and physique. He was the ultimate civil servant and his cousin, Francis Bacon, once said of him that he might prevent public affairs getting worse but could not make them any better. That is perhaps too harsh; Cecil had so great a political intelligence that he may qualify as a statesman. Snapping at his heels, however, was Henry Howard.

Elizabeth's council had comprised some thirteen members; James soon doubled its size, but took great pleasure in avoiding its meetings. He favoured private deliberations, in the seclusion of his bedchamber, where he could then delegate responsibility. He preferred intimate meetings where his wit and common sense could compensate for his lack of dignity. He did not particularly like London in any case, and always preferred to go hunting in the countryside beyond; from this vantage James once wrote a complacent letter to his councillors, imagining them to be 'frying in the pains of purgatory' upon royal business. Yet he made quick and sudden visits to the capital, when his presence was deemed to be indispensable; he said that he came 'like a flash of lightning, both in going, staying there, and returning'.

The palace of Whitehall was a straggling complex of some 1,400 rooms, closets and galleries and chambers huddled together. It was a place of secrets and of clandestine meetings, of staged encounters and sudden quarrels. This is the proper setting for John Donne's satires as well as for Ben Jonson's two Roman plays on the nature of ambition and corruption. It is also the setting for the great age of the masque. A ball, or a comedy, was staged every other day.

Yet the court is also the most significant context for the collection of Thomas Howard, earl of Arundel, which came to include the architectural drawings of Palladio as well as the work of Holbein, Raphael and Dürer. The great lords and courtiers also built elaborate houses at Audley End, Hatfield and elsewhere. The earl of Northampton furnished his house in the Strand with Turkish carpets, Brussels tapestries and Chinese porcelain; he also owned globes, and maps of all the principal nations. This is the burgeoning world of Jacobeanism.

On his progress to London from Edinburgh, at the beginning of his reign, the king was given a petition; it was an appeal from his puritan subjects that became known as the 'millenary petition', bearing the signatures of 1,000 ministers of religion. In moderate terms it suggested to the king that the sign of the cross should be removed from the baptismal ceremony and that the marriage ring was unnecessary. The words 'priest' and 'absolution' should be 'corrected', and the rite of confirmation abolished. The cap and the surplice, the vestments of conformity, were not to be 'urged'.

The king himself liked nothing so much as doctrinal discussion, in which he could display his learning. The first important act of his reign, therefore, was to bring together a small number of clerics at his palace of Hampton Court where they might debate matters of religious policy and religious principle. Five distinguished and learned puritan ministers were matched against the leading ecclesiastics of the realm, among them the archbishop of Canterbury and eight bishops.

This was an age of religious polemic, perhaps prophesying the civil wars of the succeeding reign. On the side of the bishops were those generally satisfied with the doctrines and ceremonies of the established Church; they were moderate; they espoused the union of Church and state. They put more trust in communal worship than in private prayer; they acknowledged the role of custom, experience and reason in spiritual matters. It may not have been a fully formed faith, but it served to bind together those of unclear or flexible belief. It also suited those who simply wished to conform with their neighbours.

On the side of the puritans were those more concerned with the exigencies of the private conscience. They believed in the natural depravity of man, unless the sinner be redeemed by grace. They abhorred the practice of confession and encouraged intensive self-examination as well as self-discipline. They did not wish for a sacramental priesthood but a preaching ministry; they accepted the word of Scripture as the source of all divine truth. They took their compass from the stirrings of providence. Men and women of a puritan tradition were utterly obedient to God's absolute will from which no ritual or sacrament could avert them. This lent them zeal and energy in their attempt to purify the world or, as one puritan theologian put it, 'a holy violence in the performing of all duties'. Sometimes they spoke out as the spirit moved them. It was said, unfairly, that they loved God with all their soul and hated their neighbour with all their heart.

They were not at this stage, however, rival creeds; they are perhaps better regarded as opposing tendencies within the same Church, and their first formal confrontation took place at Hampton Court in the middle of winter. The proceedings of the first day, 14 January 1604, were confined to the king and his ecclesiastics. James debated with his bishops the changes suggested in the 'millenary petition'. On the second day the puritan divines were invited to attend. John Reynolds, the first to be called, argued that the English Church should embrace Calvinist doctrine. The bishop of London, Richard Bancroft, quickly intervened. He knelt down before the king and demanded that 'the ancient canon might be remembered', by which he meant that '*schismatici*' should not be permitted to speak against the bishops. James allowed the discussion on specific matters to continue.

In the subsequent debate the king seems to have been shrewd and judicious. He did not accede to the puritans' demand for Calvinism, but he did accept their proposal for an improved translation of the Bible. This request bore magnificent fruit in the King James translation published later in the reign. The delegates then discussed the problem of providing a learned ministry, and the difficulties of dealing with issues of private conscience. The king was willing to concede certain matters to the puritans, in the evident belief that a middle way would encourage unity within the Church. In the bitter weather the fires of Hampton Court roared, while the king sat in his furs; the bishops, and even the puritan delegates, were also clad in fur cloaks.

All seemed to be proceeding without much incident until Reynolds recommended that the bishops of the realm should consult with the 'presbyters'. At this, the king bridled. 'Presbyter', the term for the elder or minister of a Christian church, had for him unfortunate connotations. He had previously been outraged by the Presbyterian divines of Scotland, who did not always treat His Majesty with appropriate respect; they inclined towards republicanism and even egalitarianism. One of them, Andrew Melville, had called him to his face 'God's silly vassal'.

James now told Reynolds and his colleagues that they seemed to be aiming 'at a Scottish Presbytery which agreeth with monarchy as well as God and the devil'. He added that it would mean 'Jack and Tom, and Will and Dick, shall meet, and at their pleasure censure me and my council and all our proceedings'. He concluded with advice to Reynolds that 'until you find that I grow lazy, leave it alone'. His motto from this time forward would be 'no bishop, no king'. He observed, as the puritan delegates left his presence, that 'if this be all they have to say, I shall make them conform themselves, or I will harry them out of the land, or else do worse'.

Two days later the king summoned the bishops for a further conference. He then called back the puritans, and ordered them to conform to the whole of the orthodox Book of Common Prayer reissued forty-five years before. The conference was over. The impending translation was the greatest benefit of the proceedings but, altogether, the conference cannot be counted a great success. It had now emerged that there was perhaps not one national Church, after all, but at least two Churches with different meanings and purposes.

The king was, as ever, delighted with his performance at Hampton Court. 'I peppered them soundly,' he said. 'The bishops had told him that he had spoken with the power of inspiration. 'I know not what they mean,' Sir John Harington wrote to his wife, 'but the spirit was rather foul-mouthed.' The king had said, at one point, 'A turd for this argument. I would rather my child were baptized by an ape as by a woman.' He also chastised the puritans by remonstrating 'Away with your snivelling!'

He was, however, in many respects a learned man. All his life he had argued, and debated, with his Scottish clergy. He delighted in theological controversy, and according to an early observer 'he apprehends clearly, judges wisely and has a retentive memory'. The king also believed himself to be a master of the written word and composed volumes on demonology, monarchy, witchcraft and smoking. On his accession medal he is crowned with a laurel wreath, a sure sign of his literary pretensions. He even replied to 'rayling rhymes' published against him with his own doggerel verse. In 1616 he collected all of his prose writings into a folio volume, the first English monarch ever to do so. So he became known, sometimes sarcastically, as 'the British Solomon'.

John Whitgift, archbishop of Canterbury, now close to death, realized that the conclusion of the Hampton Court conference was by no means the end of religious controversy. He knew well enough that parliament, about to meet, contained many lords and gentlemen of a puritan persuasion. The king had decided to ride in state through the capital four days before the opening of parliament on 19 March 1604. Now that the threat of plague had lifted it was declared that people from every 'county, borough, precinct, city, hamlet' had flocked to give praise to the new monarch. Seven triumphal arches, in the style of imperial Rome, were erected along the processional route from the Tower to Whitehall. Yet magnificence did not necessarily command assent.

It was a large parliament, eager to take the measure of James I. In his opening speech the king made some remarks upon the state of religion and admonished the puritans for 'being ever discontented with the present government'. When it became clear that the Commons were more concerned with various matters of privilege and grievance, James rebuked them 'as a father to his children'. Further causes of contention soon emerged.

A dispute had arisen over the election of a member for Buckinghamshire and the ensuing argument pitched king against parliament. On 5 April the Speaker delivered a message from James that he desired 'as an absolute king' that there might be a conference between the Commons and the judges. No monarch had spoken to parliament in that manner for years. Silence and amazement followed this peremptory request, whereupon one member stood up and said that 'the prince's command is like a thunderbolt; his command upon our allegiance like the roaring of a lion; to his command there is no contradiction'.

That was not necessarily the case. In the middle of April it was proposed that James should assume the title of king of Great Britain, with the union of his kingdoms; it might have been deemed a mere formality under the circumstances. But the Commons were not so easily to be persuaded. What kind of union was being proposed? Economic? Constitutional? By what laws will this 'Britain' be governed? There might be a flood of Scots taking up all posts and honours. How could the common law of England be consistent with the legal traditions of Scotland or even with the customs of Ireland?

The king himself was adamant. 'I am the husband,' he said, 'and all the whole isle is my lawful wife; I am the head and it is my body.' Did they wish him to be a polygamist with two separate wives? The debate lingered into the succeeding year with what the king called 'many crossings, long disputations, strange questions, and nothing done'. He had a vision of a united kingdom with one law, one language and one faith; yet the practicalities of the period rendered the ambition useless. The English demanded, for example, that the Scots be taxed at the same rate as themselves; the Scots demurred, pleading poverty. The Commons had already agreed that since 'we cannot make any laws to bind *Britannia* . . . let us proceed with a leaden foot'. The king's enthusiasm for the project was as great as his anger against the opponents of union.

Parliament then turned its attention to matters of religion, and in particular to the work of the Hampton Court conference. It was here, as we have seen, that Archbishop Whitgift sensed trouble from the great puritan gentry who had already taken their seats. By the end of May the Commons had brought in two bills, one of which was directed against pluralists and non-residents; these men, who held more than one clerical living or were keen to relegate their duties, included some of the most prominent members of the established Church. The bias of the Commons was clear enough. The second bill expressed the desire for 'a learned and godly ministry', a request tantamount to a demand for puritanism.

The king was vexed, and by way of justification a parliamentary committee drew up a 'form of apology and satisfaction', read to the Commons on 20 June, in which were defended such rights as freedom of speech and freedom from arrest. It was declared that 'our privileges and liberties are our true right and due inheritance, no less than our lands and goods'. It was a parliamentary way, perhaps, of introducing a Scottish king to the peculiar constitution of England. Another section stated that 'your majesty should be misinformed if any man should deliver that the kings of England have any absolute power in themselves either to alter religion . . . or to make any laws covering the same'. The 'form of apology' was never presented to the king; it may have been rejected by a majority as too extreme.

Without doubt, however, James came to hear of it; he resented its implication and was angered at its impudence. He came down to prorogue parliament on 7 July, where in the course of his speech he berated some of its members for being 'idle heads, some rash, some busy informers'. He said that in Scotland he was heard with respect whereas here there was 'nothing but curiosity from morning to evening to find fault with my propositions'. In Scotland 'all things warranted that came from me. Here all things suspected.' He added that 'you have done many things rashly, I say not you meant dis-loyally'. Then, at the conclusion, he advised that 'only I wish you had kept a better form. I like form as much as matter.'

He was perhaps waiting for the assistance of Richard Bancroft, newly installed as archbishop of Canterbury, who was a firm upholder of the royal prerogative and no lover of puritans. Even then Bancroft was steering the convocation of senior clergy towards a statement of general religious conformity; the canons of 1604 gave nothing to the puritans but demanded that they submit to the Book of Common Prayer and to the Thirty-Nine Articles. The sectarian ministers must conform or be deprived. The more draconian penalties were in truth rarely applied, but the measures marked the first schism in the history of the reformed English Church.

So the king had prorogued parliament with a very bad grace, little or nothing having been achieved by it. He stated at a later date that it was a body without a head. 'At their meetings,' he is reported to have said, 'nothing is heard but cries, shouts and confusion. I am surprised that my ancestors should ever have allowed such an institution to come into existence.' His opinion may have been shared by others. In the winter of 1604 Thomas Percy subleased a house beside the Palace of Westminster and, with the assistance of Guy Fawkes and other conspirators, began to excavate a tunnel.

2

The plot

In these early years the king was proclaimed as a Caesar, a David, a Noah, a Joash and even a Homer. He was a second Augustus, a true Josiah, a wise and religious sovereign. It is difficult to know what this bewildering wealth of parallels might signify, but one virtue soon became predominant. He was '*rex pacificus*' or '*Jacobus pacificus*'. Blessed was the peacemaker. His was the reign of the fig tree and the vine.

Others were not so satisfied by the pleasures of peace. 'Na, na,' James is supposed to have said after his coronation, 'we'll not need papists now.' He had wooed them in case of trouble, but could now afford to discard them. In February 1604, the Jesuit priests who owed all their obedience to Rome were banished from the realm. It was a sensible precaution, perhaps, but for fervent Catholics it was an ominous sign.

Among these was Thomas Winter, or Wintour, who had unsuccessfully appealed to Philip III of Spain for aid on behalf of the faithful. In the same month of February 1604, he visited his cousin, Robert Catesby, at Lambeth. Catesby was possibly a convert from Protestantism and therefore one in whom the Roman fire burned ever more brightly. It was he, rather than Guy Fawkes, who led what became known as the 'powder plot'. Catesby informed his cousin of his grand plan to blow up parliament with gunpowder,

but of course he needed allies in the work. In April Winter travelled
to Flanders from which place he brought back Fawkes himself. We
may now refer to them as conspirators. 'Shall we always, gentlemen,
talk,' Thomas Percy said, 'and never do anything?' In the following
month an oath of secrecy was sworn before they made their way to
a house behind the church of St Clement Eastcheap, where they
met a Jesuit by the name of Gerard who administered to them the
Holy Sacrament.

It was now agreed that a dwelling conveniently close to parliament
must be found, but it was not until the beginning of December that
a suitable property became available. On the 11th of the month they
entered the house, carrying with them a stock of hard-boiled eggs and
baked meats. By Christmas Eve the conspirators had dug their way
down and, in the words of Thomas Winter, 'wrought under a little
entry to the wall of the parliament house and underpropped it as we
went with wood'. They believed that the next session would begin in
February 1605, but now they learned that it was prorogued until the
following October. They had more time. The gunpowder was being
stored at Catesby's lodgings in Lambeth but, under conditions of great
secrecy and security, it was brought to the house at Westminster. They
had already made some progress in penetrating the 9-foot wall, but
their work was impeded by the influx of water.

One day, soon after the gunpowder had been acquired, they
heard a rustling sound above their heads. Fawkes went out of doors
and cautiously investigated. He was met by Ellen Bright, coal
merchant, who informed him that she was leaving the premises;
it so happened that her cellar or vault ran under the parliament
house itself. The deal was quickly settled; Thomas Percy, another
conspirator, secured the lease of the space. An iron gate between
the basement of the conspirators' house and Mrs Bright's cellar was
opened, and Fawkes was able to smuggle some thirty-six barrels of
gunpowder into the neighbouring vault. There was enough powder
to destroy many thousands of people.

By September fresh barrels of gunpowder were acquired in order
to replace those affected by damp. Funds were running low, however,
and it was deemed advisable to bring in three other conspirators
with money or property. Thirteen men were by this time apprised
of the secret, leaving thirteen ways for the secret to be betrayed.

One of the newly recruited conspirators, Francis Tresham, pleaded strongly that his brother-in-law, Lord Monteagle, should be spared the general conflagration. Monteagle was a staunch Catholic who had already defended his Church in the House of Lords. The others demurred at the exception, however well meant. Monteagle was sitting down for dinner on 26 October, at his house in Hoxton, when a letter was brought to him by a messenger. He glanced at it and then requested one of his gentlemen to read it aloud.

'My lord, out of the love I bear to some of your friends, I have a care of your preservation. Therefore I would advise you, as you tender your life, to devise some excuse to shift of your attendance at this parliament . . . ' So it began. The correspondent then went on to warn that 'they shall receive a terrible blow this Parliament, and yet they shall not see who hurts them'. Monteagle immediately set out for Whitehall with the letter in his hand. He came upon Robert Cecil, now the newly created earl of Salisbury, sitting down to supper with some other members of the privy council.

Monteagle took Salisbury into an adjoining room, and showed him the document. Salisbury was at first inclined to dismiss the matter as a false alarm but, on his consulting his colleagues, the possibility of gunpowder as a 'terrible blow' was discussed. The lord chamberlain, the earl of Suffolk, knew intimately the interior of parliament; in particular he was aware of the damp and capacious cellars beneath the building. He, and other privy councillors, agreed that they should be searched before the beginning of the session that had been further postponed to 5 November; but they did not wish to act too precipitately for fear of scaring away the plotters.

The king had been hunting at Royston and, on his return to London at the beginning of November, the letter was shown to him. Instantly he agreed that it suggested 'some stratagem of fire and powder'. On the afternoon of Monday 4 November, Suffolk and Monteagle began their search on the excuse that they were looking for some property belonging to the king. Guy Fawkes opened the door of the cellar.

Suffolk: To whom do these coals and faggots belong?
Fawkes: They belong to Mr Thomas Percy, one of his
 majesty's gentlemen pensioners.

Thomas Percy was of course a known Catholic, at a time when there was some fear of Catholic disaffection. The king now ordered a further and more thorough search. At eleven o'clock that night a Westminster magistrate, Sir Thomas Knyvett, went down to the cellar with certain soldiers. The door was once more opened by Guy Fawkes. Knyvett then began to brush aside the coals and the bundles of wood only to discover the barrels of gunpowder. Fawkes made no attempt at flight or combat. He admitted that he intended to blow up the king and the two houses of parliament on the following morning. It seems that he was prepared to light a slow match and then to make his way to Wapping where he would take boat to Gravelines in France. When he was asked later, in formal questioning by the council, the reason for procuring so much gunpowder he replied that he wanted 'to blow the Scottish beggars back to their native mountains'. The king was informed of Fawkes's capture, and gave thanks for his miraculous deliverance.

It was, perhaps, not a miracle at all. Francis Tresham and Lord Monteagle may have conspired in the production of the letter, as a device to gain the favour of the king. It has also been suggested that Salisbury himself was aware of the conspiracy but allowed it to proceed as a way of catching out the Catholics; this is highly unlikely, but not wholly impossible.

News of the arrest, and the intended treason, soon spread. Robert Catesby and the other conspirators fled from London, hoping to create the conditions for a Catholic rising; but the Catholic gentlemen were not about to commit suicide. The principal fugitives then took refuge in Holbeche House, on the borders of Staffordshire, where a lighted coal or stray spark ignited the gunpowder they were carrying with them. Two or three were injured, and were inclined to see in the accident a sign of divine displeasure. One of them cried out, 'Woe worth the time that we have seen this day!' They then knelt in prayer before a picture of the Virgin. The sheriff of Worcester was on their track; his men surrounded the house and fired on its occupants. Some were killed, while the wounded were taken back to London; Catesby was among those shot dead.

Other conspirators were found in hiding over the next few days. On 27 January 1606, Guy Fawkes and seven others were brought for trial to Westminster Hall where all but one of them pleaded innocence. They were executed a few days later. The Jesuits, who had condoned if not connived in the plot, were soon enough taken to the scaffold. So ended 'the powder plot'. Seven years later the study of Robert Cotton, librarian and antiquarian, was found to contain certain sainted relics of the plotters, including a finger, a toe and a piece of a rib.

The king himself, despite his miraculous survival, was not comforted. The Venetian ambassador reported that 'the king is in terror, he does not appear nor does he take his meals in public as usual. He lives in the innermost rooms with only Scotsmen about him.' James seemed subdued and melancholy, occasionally giving vent to his anger against the Catholics. 'I shall most certainly be obliged to stain my hands with their blood,' he said, 'though sorely against my will.' It did not come to that.

The members of the Commons had continued their ordinary business on the day they were meant to be destroyed; a committee on Spanish trade was established, and a petition was discussed from a member asking to be excused on account of gout. Yet by the end of May 1606, they had passed an Act 'for the better discovering and repressing of popish recusants'; one of its provisions was an oath of allegiance, drawn up by Archbishop Bancroft, which acknowledged James to be the lawful king beyond any power of the pope to depose him. Catholics were obliged to attend the services of the established Church and to receive holy communion at least once a year; the penalties included fines or the impropriation of property. No recusant was to come within 10 miles of London, and a statute of the previous reign was revived prohibiting any recusant from travelling further than 5 miles from his or her home. No recusant could practise as an attorney or as a doctor.

These measures did not bring about the demise of the old faith. The Catholics merely withdrew from political activity during the reign of James and largely remained quiet or quiescent. Most of them were willing to accept the oath of allegiance in order to secure both peace and property; only the Jesuitically inclined were still eager to support the pretensions of the pope. James himself said of the oath that he wished to make a distinction between the doctrinaire Catholics and those 'who although they were otherwise popishly affected, yet retained in their hearts the print of their natural duty to their sovereign'. The previous sanctions against the puritans had been only hesitantly or partially imposed; the same policy of caution was now pursued against the Catholics. James had no wish to make martyrs out of his subjects. It was in any case far easier, in the early seventeenth century, to make laws than to enforce them.

The court of James I, its excesses having already become public knowledge, was now notorious for its laxity; drunkenness and dissimulation, venality and promiscuity, were its most significant characteristics. Freedom of manners was the only rule. The earl of Pembroke was believed to have a horror of frogs, so the king put one down his neck. The king himself had an aversion to pigs, and so Pembroke led one into the royal bedchamber. One courtier took into the palace at Whitehall 'four brawny pigs, piping hot, bitted and harnessed with ropes of sausages, all tied to a monstrous pudding'. The sausages were hurled about the room while the fools and dwarves of the court began leaping on one another's shoulders.

In *Sejanus, His Fall*, a play performed in the first year of the king's reign, Ben Jonson alluded to courtiers when he wrote that:

> We have no shift of faces, no cleft tongues,
> No soft and glutinous bodies that can stick
> Like snails on painted walls . . .

'If I were to imitate the conduct of your republic,' the king told the Venetian ambassador, 'and begin to punish those who take bribes, I should soon not have a single subject left.'

When the king of Denmark arrived in the summer of 1606 the courtiers of Whitehall were said by Sir John Harington 'to wallow in beastly delights' while the ladies 'abandon their sobriety and are seen to roll about in intoxication'. A great feast was held for the two sovereigns, in the course of which was shown a representation of Solomon and the Queen of Sheba. The lady who played the queen carried various gifts to the two kings 'but forgetting the steps arising to the canopy overset her caskets into his Danish majesty's lap and fell at his feet . . . His Majesty then got up and would dance with the Queen of Sheba, but he fell down and humbled himself before her, and was carried to an inner chamber and laid on a bed of state.'

Other actors in the pageant, such as Hope and Faith, 'were both sick and spewing in the lower hall'. Harington concluded that 'the gunpowder fright is got out of all our heads' and 'I ne'er did see such lack of good order, discretion and sobriety, as I have now done'. He yearned for the days of his godmother, the Virgin Queen, when a certain stateliness and severity touched the atmosphere of the court.

There could be no doubt that the new court differed markedly from its predecessor. The king was known to be devoted to his pleasures rather than what were considered to be his duties. He attended the fights of the Cockpit in Whitehall Palace twice a week, and, like his predecessor, loved to ride or hunt every day. When James rode up to the dead hart he dismounted and cut its throat with dispatch; he then sated the dogs with its blood before wiping his bloodied hands across the faces of his fellow horsemen.

It soon became clear that he did not enjoy the company of spectators at his sports. Quite unlike his predecessor he disliked and even detested crowds. When the people flocked about him he would swear at them and cry out, 'What would they have?' On one occasion he was told that they had come in love and reverence. To which he replied, in a broad Scots accent, 'God's wounds, I will pull down my breeches and they shall also see my arse.' He would bid 'A pox on you!' or 'A plague on you!' As a result of outbursts of anger such as this he became, in the words of the Venetian ambassador, 'despised and almost hated'.

He justified his exertions at the hunt on the grounds that his vigour was 'the health and welfare of them all', no doubt meaning both the court and the nation. Let his officers waste away in closets or at the council table. He must be strong and virile. In any case, he said, he could do more business in an hour than his councillors could manage in a day; he spent less time in hunting than other monarchs did in whoring. One day a favourite dog, Jowler, disappeared from the pack. On the following morning it reappeared with a note tied around its neck. 'Good Mr Jowler we pray you speak to the king (for he hears you every day and so doth he not us) that it will please his majesty to go back to London, for else the country will be undone.' When eventually James did return to Whitehall he feasted and played cards, at which sport he lost large sums of money.

James was continually and heavily in debt. He had thought to come into a realm of gold, but soon found his purse to be bare. Or, rather, he emptied it too readily. He bought boots and silk stockings and beaver hats in profusion. Court ceremonial was more lavish with the arrival of ever more 'gentlemen extraordinary'. There was a vogue at court for 'golden play' or gambling. The king loved masques and feasts, which were for him a true sign of regality. He wished to have a masque on the night of Christmas, whereupon he was told that it was not the fashion. 'What do you tell me of the fashion?' he enquired. 'I will make it a fashion.'

The king also purchased plate and jewels, which he then proceeded to distribute among his followers. It was said that he had given to one or two men more than his predecessor had given to all of her courtiers during the whole of her reign. The earl of Shrewsbury remarked that Elizabeth 'valued every molehill that she gave . . . a mountain, which our sovereign now does not'. His generosity to favourites and to courtiers was by the standard of any age in English history exceptional.

One particular favourite emerged in the spring of 1607. Robert Carr, twenty-one, was a model of affability and deportment; he was also exceptionally handsome. He took part in a tournament in the king's presence, but he was thrown from his horse and broke his leg. The king was much affected and ordered his own doctor to take charge of the young man; Carr was carried to the hospital at Charing Cross, where the king visited him every day. The patient was placed on a choice diet and, at the insistence of James, was surrounded by surgeons. It was clear to the courtiers that here was a man worth flattering. 'Lord!' one contemporary, Sir Anthony Weldon, wrote, 'how the great men flocked to see him, and to offer to his shrine in such abundance . . .' James had become infatuated with him and, by the end of the year, Carr had been knighted and appointed as a gentleman of the bedchamber. The king decided to educate as well as to promote him. He himself gave Carr lessons in Latin grammar and in the politics of Europe. And of course he lavished gold and jewels upon him. It was observed that the king 'leaneth on his arm, pinches his cheek, smoothes his ruffled garments . . .'

Sir John Harington was still seeking preferment at court after a lifetime of service to Elizabeth. Thomas Howard, earl of Suffolk, took him aside and offered some advice. He was told that the king 'doth wonderfully covet learned discourse' and 'doth admire good fashion in cloaths'. He was instructed to 'get a new jerkin well bordered, and not too short; the king saith, he liketh a flowing garment; be sure it be not all of one sort, but diversely coloured, the collar falling somewhat down, and your ruff well stiffened and bushy'. Eighteen courtiers had already been dismissed for not conforming to the king's taste in male attire.

Suffolk suggested to Harington that in his conversation he should not dwell too long on any one subject, and touch only lightly on the topic of religion. Never say that 'this is good or bad' but modestly state that 'if it were your majesty's good opinion, I myself should think so and so'. Do not ask questions. Do not speak about the character or temperament of anyone else at court. Remember to praise the king's horse, a roan jennet. You must say that the stars are bright jewels fit for Robert Carr's ears, and that the roan jennet surpasses Bucephalus and is worthy to be ridden by Alexander.

Suffolk also advised Harington that 'silence and discretion should be linked together, like dog and bitch'. The previous sovereign had always spoken of her subjects' 'love and good affections', but James preferred to talk of their 'fear and subjection'. Why did Harington wish to come to court in the first place? 'You are not young, you are not handsome, you are not finely.' So he must rely upon his learning, which the king would admire.

Soon enough James took Harington aside, and questioned him in his private closet. He quizzed him on Aristotle and other philosophers; he asked him to read out a passage from Ariosto, and praised his elocution. He then posed a series of questions to him. What do you think pure wit is made of? Should a king not be the best clerk [the most learned] in his own country? Do you truly understand why the devil works more with ancient women than with others? He told Harington that the death of his mother, Mary Queen of Scots, had been foretold and that at the time of her execution a bloody head was seen dancing in the air; he dilated on the powers of prophecy and recommended several books on the matter. The king concluded by discussing 'the new weed', tobacco, and declared that 'it would, by its use, infuse ill qualities on the brain'. So ended the audience. Harington passed through the court 'amidst the many varlets and lordly servants who stood around'. Yet he had passed the test, and was appointed as tutor to the young Prince Henry.

Reasons other than favouritism can be adduced for the king's indebtedness. The steady rise in prices, and the reluctance of land-owners to pay further taxation, all contributed to the rise in the expenditure of the court above its income. The cost of an extended royal household, complete with wife and three children, was also very high. Queen Anne was extravagant and devoted to the delights of fashionable London; her husband had proposed that she might confine herself to the 3,000 dresses in the previous queen's wardrobe, but she did not care for some of the old fashions. She would appear at court in the guise of a goddess or a nymph, an Eastern sultana or an Arab princess.

James was perpetually surprised by his debts, and continually promised to be more economical; yet it was not in his nature to be thrifty. 'My only hope that upholds me,' he told Salisbury, 'is my good servants, that will sweat and labour for my relief.' But where was the money to be found? Certain taxes had been levied 'time out of mind', or at least since the latter years of the fourteenth century. 'Tonnage' was the duty levied on each 'tun' or cask of wine; 'poundage' was the tax raised on every pound sterling of exported or imported goods. James decided to revise the book of rates, however, and to impose new levies that came to be known as 'impositions'.

A merchant by the name of John Bate refused to pay. He drove a cartload of currants from the waterside before the customs officials had the opportunity to tax them; he was brought before the council, where he declared that the 'imposition' was illegal. His became a test case before the court of the exchequer which ruled that the king had absolute power in the matter; in all aspects of foreign trade, his prerogative was assured.

Nevertheless opposition arose in parliament, where there was talk of money being poured into bottomless coffers. In October 1607 James addressed his council on the pressing problems con-cerning 'this eating canker of want'. He promised to abide by any 'cure' they prescribed and to accept 'such remedies and antidotes as you are to apply unto my disease'. The case was not an easy one. Salisbury tried various expedients for raising money, by fining for long-forgotten transgressions or by extorting as many feudal 'aids' to the king as he could find.

Yet the Commons were not impressed by the measures. It was an ancient principle that the sovereign of England should 'live of his own'; he should maintain his estate, and bear the cost of government, out of his own resources. It was also universally believed that taxation was an extraordinary measure only to be raised in time of war. The first parliament of James I was summoned for five sessions from March 1604 to February 1611, and in that long period it acquired the beginning of a corporate identity largely lacking during the reign of Elizabeth. More business was enacted, and parliament sat for longer. In 1607, for example, the Commons instituted a 'committee of the whole house'. This committee could elect its own chairman, as opposed to the Speaker chosen by the sovereign, and could debate freely for as long as it wished. It was at the time seen as a remarkable innovation, and might be considered the harbinger of strife between court and parliament.

A group of disparate and variously inclined parliamentarians was not necessarily on the king's side. Francis Bacon wrote to the king that 'that opposition which was, the last parliament, to your majesty's business, as much as was not *ex puris naturalibus* but out of party, I conceive to be now much weaker than it was'. This did not yet embody the partisanship of later struggles, or the creation of 'parties' in the modern sense, but it suggests a change in national affairs. Some of the disputatious details have been recorded. Sir Edward Herbert 'plops' with his mouth at Mr Speaker. John Tey complains that Mr Speaker is 'clipping him off' and proceeds to threaten him.

The king had another doughty opponent. A legal dispute had arisen. Was there a distinction between those Scots born before James's accession to the English throne and those born after it? The king argued that those born after his accession were naturalized by common law and, therefore, could hold office in England. James turned to the judges whom he assumed to take his part. One of them refused to do so. Sir Edward Coke had been chief justice of the common pleas since 1605, and was an impassioned exponent of English common law. James had no real conception of common law, having been educated in the very different jurisprudence of Scotland. Coke believed, for example, that both sovereign and subject were accountable to a body of ancient law that had been conceived in practice and clarified by usage; it represented immemorial general custom, but it was also a law of reason. This was not, however, the king's opinion. He had already firmly stated that 'the king is above the law, as both the author and the giver of strength thereto'. From this it could be construed that the king possessed an arbitrary authority. James alleged, for example, that he could decide cases in person. Coke demurred: a case could only be judged in a lawcourt. Coke's own report tells the story of bad blood.

James: I thought the law was founded on reason. I and
  others have reason as well as the judges.
Coke: Although, sir, you have great endowments of nature,
  yet you are not learned in the laws of England. Causes
  are not to be decided by natural reason but by the
  artificial reason and judgment of law.

More debate followed.

James: So then I am under the law? It is treason to affirm
  that!
Coke: Bracton has said that the king should not be under
  man but under God and the law.

An observer noted that 'his majesty fell in that high indignation as the like was never known in him, looking and speaking fiercely with bended fist, offering to strike him, which the Lord Coke perceiving fell flat on all fours . . .' Coke might yield and beg for mercy, but over succeeding years the debate between the Crown and the law continued with ever greater volume and seriousness.

The manoeuvres of the court were never still. The favourite, now Sir Robert Carr, needed land to complement his title. By Carr's great good fortune Sir Walter Raleigh, still incarcerated, had forfeited his interest in the manor of Sherborne; he thought that he had conveyed it to his son, but the king's council believed otherwise. It was given to the favourite. Lady Raleigh, accompanied by her two sons, was admitted into the king's presence where she threw herself at his feet. 'I maun have the land' was his only reply. 'I maun have it for Carr.' This is the true voice of the king.

3

The beacons

In 1605 one of the king's 'learned counsel' presented him with a treatise that summoned up the spirit of a new age. Francis Bacon's 'Of the Proficience and Advancement of Learning Divine and Human' is better known to posterity as *The Advancement of Learning*; it can justifiably be said to have changed the terms of human understanding and the nature of knowledge. Bacon had been a royal servant for some years under the patronage of his uncle, Lord Burghley, and had been first enlisted in the court of Elizabeth. But the advent of a new king promised more tangible rewards and, soon after the accession, Bacon provided James with texts of advice on such matters as the union of Scotland with England and ecclesiastical polity.

Yet *The Advancement of Learning* was a work in quite another key, and one that helped to create the climate of scientific rationalism that characterized the entire seventeenth century. Bacon had first to clear away the clutter of inherited knowledge. In the early pages of the treatise 'the first distemper of learning' is denounced as that by which 'men study words and not matter'. Yet words, and not matter, had been the foundation of traditional learning for innumerable centuries, whether in the rhetorical humanism of the Renaissance or in the scholastic theology of the Middle Ages. Bacon declared, however, that 'men have withdrawn themselves too much from the

26

contemplation of nature, and the observations of experience, and
have tumbled up and down in their own reasons and conceits'.
It was time to look at the world.

He further observed that:

> this kind of degenerate learning did chiefly reign amongst the
> schoolmen, who having sharp and strong wits, and abundance
> of leisure, and small variety of reading, but their wits being
> shut up in the cells of a few authors (chiefly Aristotle their
> dictator) as their persons were shut up in the cells of monas-
> teries and colleges, and knowing little history, either of nature
> or of time, did out of no great quantity of matter, and infinite
> agitation of wit, spin out unto us those laborious webs of
> learning which are extant in their books . . . cobwebs of learn-
> ing admirable for the fineness of thread and work, but of no
> substance or profit.

The clarity and cogency of his prose are the perfect instruments
for his attack upon the ornateness and excessive ingenuity of the
old learning. That is why Shelley cited Plato and Bacon as the two
most influential of all the poet-philosophers.

Bacon was assaulting the methods and principles of previous
human learning in favour of experiment and observation, which he
believed to be central to true natural science. He was suggesting
that the scholars and experimenters of the time should confine
themselves 'to use and not to ostentation' and to 'matters of common
sense and experience'. He warned that 'the more you remove yourselves from particulars, the greater peril of error you do incur'. At
a later date this would be described as the 'scientific' disposition.

The purpose of all learning was, for Bacon, to promote the
benefit and prosperity of humankind. The material world is to be
understood and mastered by means of 'the laborious and sober
inquiry of truth' which can be pursued only by 'ascending from
experiments to the invention of causes, and descending from causes
to the invention of new experiments'. This was a revolutionary
statement of intent that places Bacon, and the Jacobean period, at
the opening of the modern age.

Bacon desired an institutional, as well as an epistemological,
change; he suggested that universities, colleges and schools be

directed 'by amplitude of reward, by soundness of direction, and by
the conjunction of labours'. We may see here the origin of the
attitude that was to guide the Royal Society and to inform the inventive energies that emerged in the first years of the Industrial
Revolution. Bacon himself was of a puritan disposition. He believed
in the power of individual agency above the manifold allures of
tradition and authority; he believed in observation rather than contemplation as the true instrument of practical reason. The beacons
of utility and progress were always before him.

Bacon hoped that by their bright light 'this third period of time
will far surpass that of the Grecian and Roman learning'. It would
be fair to say that he helped to change the pace and the direction
of that new learning. He entitled a later work *Instauratio Magna*,
'the great innovation' or foundation; the frontispiece of that book
shows a ship sailing through the two Pillars of Hercules that traditionally signified the limits of knowledge as well as of exploration.
It is an emblem of a journey of discovery in defiance of the motto
'*nec plus ultra*', nothing further beyond. The reign of James I, therefore, can be said to mark the beginning of a voyage through strange
seas of thought.

4

The god of money

The treasury was bare; the officers of the Crown were demanding their salaries, but there was no money to be found. Parliament was reluctant to vote taxes, and local officials in the counties were not zealous in collecting the proper revenues from their neighbours; much of the money raised on custom duties was diverted into the pockets of those who collected it.

When parliament reassembled in February 1610, it was in a fractious mood. Salisbury outlined the financial woes of the nation, but the members were more concerned to arrest the prodigal spending of the court rather than to vote new taxes. One of them, Thomas Wentworth, argued that it would be worse than useless to grant new moneys to the king if he refused to reduce his expenditure. He asked, 'To what purpose is it to draw a silver stream into the royal cistern, if it shall daily run out thence by private cocks?' Salisbury was not impressed. It was his understanding that the Commons had a duty to supply the needs of the king, after which their grievances might be addressed. The members, on the other hand, demanded that their complaints be answered before turning to the demands of the king.

A conference was called in which Salisbury put forward a long-meditated plan that became known as the 'great contract'. The king would give up his feudal dues and tenures in exchange for a

guaranteed annual sum; the Commons offered £100,000, only half
of the amount James required. Parliament still seemed to believe
that he should and could be as economical, or as parsimonious, as
his predecessor. The negotiations were suspended.

On 21 May the king summoned both houses of parliament
into his presence and upbraided them for sitting fourteen weeks
without relieving his necessities. He would listen to what they had
to say about increased taxation, but he would not be bound by their
opinions. They must not question the royal prerogative in such
matters. The members answered that, if this were the case, then the
king might lawfully claim all that they owned. A deputation, armed
with a petition of right, met James at his palace in Greenwich.
Realizing that he had perhaps gone too far, he welcomed them and
explained that he had been misunderstood. He always knew when
to draw back from confrontation, a lesson never learned by his two
more earnest sons.

The debate on the great contract resumed on 11 June, with the
concomitant issues of supplies, revenues, grievances and impositions.
When the grievances were presented to the king on a long roll of
parchment, he remarked that it might make a pretty piece of tapestry.
Concessions were yielded on both sides, but there was no end in
sight. On 23 July James prorogued the parliament, and the members
dispersed to their constituencies where the details of the great
contract would further be discussed. Naturally enough the towns
and counties were more concerned with their injuries than with the
poverty of the king. The whole debate had served only to demonstrate the gulf between king and country, between court and realm.

The king was irate at the lack of progress. He resolved that he
would never again endure 'such taunts and disgraces as have been
uttered of him'. If they came back and offered him all he wished,
he would not listen to them. James had in any case already made
a speech which rendered the political situation infinitely worse.
In March 1610 he had assembled at Whitehall the Lords and the
Commons. 'The estate of monarchy', he proclaimed, 'is the supremest
thing upon earth: for kings are not only God's lieutenants upon
earth, and sit upon God's throne, but even by God himself they are
called Gods.' He went on to claim that kings 'exercise a manner or
resemblance of divine power on earth'. The sovereigns of the world

can 'make and unmake their subjects; they have power of raising
and casting down; of life and death; judges over all their subjects
and in all causes, and yet accountable to none but God only'. He
admonished them that 'you cannot so clip the wing of greatness.
If a king be resolute to be a tyrant, all you can do will not hinder
him.' Did they really want him to be a mere doge of Venice?

James's sentiments were not necessarily very welcome to the
members of parliament. A contemporary news-writer, John
Chamberlain, noted that they were 'so little to their satisfaction that
I hear it bred generally much discomfort'. If the parliament acqui-
esced in this bravura statement of kingship, 'we are not like to leave
to our successors the freedom we received from our forefathers'.

James did not understand common law, as his confrontations
with Coke had suggested, and seemed to be unaware that the principle of absolute sovereignty was not one the English would even
remotely entertain. It was noted that 'the king speaks of France and
Spain what they may do'. He did not realize, or pretended not to
realize, that the sovereigns of those two countries were in a position
very different from his own. He maintained the theory of divine
right without any clear understanding of how it would operate in
the context of parliamentary authority and the common law.

He may have adopted his position for less theoretical reasons.
His hatred of the Presbyterian elders of Scotland derived from the
fact that they directly challenged his authority. The nobility of that
country, also, had been inclined to treat him as if he were one among
equals. So his statements about his own powers are likely to have
been in part a response to his difficult and sometimes dangerous
position as king of Scotland. He had once observed that 'the highest
bench is the sliddriest to sit upon'.

He might also have been acutely aware that his temperament
and behaviour were not always impeccably regal; he slobbered and
walked at an odd angle; he kissed and slavered over his handsome
favourites. In compensation for his apparent weaknesses, therefore,
he may have been all the more eager to maintain the doctrine of
divine right.

Yet in truth his theoretical understanding was very different from
his practical grasp of political realities. He never did behave like an
absolute prince, and with rare exceptions took care to remain within

the fabric of the laws; he was neither arbitrary nor erratic in his exercise of power. In return no serious attempt was made by the parliament to undermine his authority or to question his sovereignty.

The fate of kings was also an immediate concern. On 14 May 1610, Henri IV of France was assassinated in Paris by a Catholic zealot who believed regicide to be his religious duty. Ever fearful for his own life, James responded with a kind of panic. On hearing the news, according to the French ambassador, James 'turned whiter than his shirt'.

In the following month Prince Henry, the king's oldest son, was formally invested as prince of Wales. He was of an heroic or militant character, and a fierce proponent of Protestantism. Francis Bacon remarked that his face was long 'and inclining to leanness . . . his look grave, and the motion of his eyes rather composed than spirited, in his countenance were some marks of severity'. Henry's court eschewed the prodigality and drunkenness condoned by his father; it was a model of formality and propriety, where the sentence for swearing was a fine. At a time when the morals and manners of the king's court were known to be in decline, many believed that he was a true Christian prince who might save the nation for righteousness.

Henry was surrounded by men of a military bent, men of action; he had a keen interest in maritime affairs, and in the progress of colonial exploration. He immensely admired Sir Walter Raleigh, still incarcerated in the Tower, and remarked aloud that 'none but my father would keep such a bird in a cage'. He had an equally keen dislike of his father's bosom companions. Of Carr himself he is supposed to have stated that 'if ever he were king, he would not leave one of that family to piss against the wall'. If ever he were king . . . that was the overwhelming question for the country. Henry IX would no doubt have followed the martial example of Henry V. James, noting the popularity of his son's court, is supposed to have asked, 'Will he bury me alive?' When the king's fool, Archie, remarked that James looked upon Henry as a terror rather than as a comfort the king burst into tears.

Another royal imbroglio, albeit of a minor kind, emerged in the weeks after Henry's investiture. Arabella Stuart was the cousin of the king, and for the first six years of his reign she had enjoyed all the comforts and considerations of the court. She had even been considered as a replacement for James himself, by Raleigh and others, but she had taken no part in the plot. It was still of the utmost importance that she married wisely and well. At the beginning of 1610, however, she came to a pre-contractual arrangement with William Seymour, who by indirect and circuitous route had some small claim to the throne. This always aroused the horror of princes.

The couple agreed to renounce their plans but, in June, they took part in a secret ceremony of marriage at Greenwich. On hearing the news, the king raged. Seymour was instantly confined to the Tower while Arabella was taken to Lambeth before it was decided to send her further north to Durham. En route, at Barnet, she planned her escape. She disguised herself, according to a contemporary chronicler, John More, 'by drawing a pair of great French-fashioned hose over her petticoats, putting on a man's doublet, a man-like peruke, with long locks over her hair, a black hat, black cloak, russet boots, with red tops, and a rapier by her side'. She took ship for France at Leigh, but was overtaken by a vessel sent from Dover to arrest her. She was escorted to the Tower, where her reason gave way under the oppression of her trials, and she died insane four years later. It is a sad story of the perils and perfidies that attended anyone of high estate.

When a new session of parliament opened in the autumn of the year it was clear to everyone that Salisbury's idea of a 'great contract' between the king's necessities and the country's generosity was not to be obtained by any means. The Commons abandoned discussions on the matter by 8 November, with repeated animadversions against 'favourites' and 'wanton courtiers'. The Scots were also attacked as men with open mouths. The king was in a fury, and told the privy council that 'no house save the house of hell' could match the House of Commons. He went on to say that 'our fame and actions have been daily tossed like tennis balls amongst them'. He was inclined to blame Salisbury for putting too much trust in a parliament which he dubbed 'this rotten reed of Egypt'; he continued in biblical mode when he told him that 'your greatest error hath been that you ever expected to draw honey out of gall'. He adjourned and then dissolved parliament within a matter of weeks.

The economic woes of the king were not all of his own making. The fiscal system of England had to a large extent been formulated in the fourteenth century, and it could not deal with the problems attendant upon the seventeenth century. It simply did not work, especially in times of warfare, and all manner of fiscal expedients had to be found. Thus in the spring of the following year James offered to sell hereditary titles to any knights or esquires who desired them. The title of baronet could be purchased for £1,080 in three annual payments, but the overall gain to the exchequer of approximately £90,000 was not enough to balance the profusion of the king's expenditure. Peerages were put on the market four years later. When in 1616 Sir John Roper made over the sum of £10,000 to become Lord Teynham, he was given the nickname of Lord 10m. A seventeenth-century historian, Arthur Wilson, remarked that the multiplicity of titles 'made them cheap and invalid in the vulgar opinion; for nothing is more destructive to monarchy than lessening the nobility; upon their decline the commons rise and anarchy increases'.

The king had another scheme to raise money. It was proposed to him that his oldest son might be pleased to accept the hand of the Infanta Maria Anna, daughter of Philip III of Spain; at once James sent one of his envoys to Madrid. Robin Goodfellow in Ben Jonson's *Love Restored*, performed at court on Twelfth Night 1612, complained "tis that impostor, PLUTUS, the god of money, who has stolen love's ensigns; and in his belied figure, reigns in the world, making friendships, contracts, marriages and almost religion'.

In the spring of that year James joined the Protestant Union that had been established four years earlier with the coalition of German states such as Brandenburg, Ulm, Strasbourg and the Palatinate; in this matter he was following the sympathies of his people. At the same time he agreed formally that his daughter, Elizabeth, should be engaged to Frederick V of the Palatinate. This was a large territory in the valley of the Rhine, and included cities such as Heidelberg and Düsseldorf; it had been a centre of Protestantism since the middle of the sixteenth century, and Frederick himself was the leading Calvinist in all of Europe. It seemed, therefore, to be an expedient union for a king of England who believed that he himself might become the champion of Protestantism.

He had the appropriate credentials. The King James version of the Bible had emerged in the previous year; it was the fruit of the Hampton Court conference of 1604, and quickly supplanted the Geneva Bible and the Bishops' Bible. Indeed it still remains for many the key translation of the Scriptures and the model of seventeenth-century English prose. It also became a touchstone for English literary culture: in 'On Translating Homer', Matthew Arnold remarked that there is 'an English book, and one only, where, as in the *Iliad* itself, perfect plainness of speech is allied with perfect nobleness; and that book is the Bible'. Its influence can be traced in the work of Milton and Bunyan, of Tennyson and Byron, of Johnson and Gibbon and Thackeray; the power of its cadence is to be found everywhere. The King James Bible invigorated the consciousness of the nation and inspired some of its most eloquent manifestations.

It also prompted a great wave of religious publications in English and, as Robert Burton said in his preface to *The Anatomy of Melancholy*, of books of divinity there was no end. 'There be so many books in that kind, so many commentaries, treatises, pamphlets, expositions, sermons, that whole teams of oxen cannot draw them.' There was also a glut of cheap religious pamphlets that espoused the wonders of God's providence and the evil fate of His enemies.

James consolidated his Protestantism with another measure. In the spring of 1611 George Abbot had been appointed archbishop of Canterbury in succession to Richard Bancroft. His principal qualification for the post, after the assassination of Henri IV, was his persistent and rigorous opposition to Roman Catholicism; he had already taken a leading role in the prosecution of two priests who were subsequently executed at Tyburn.

So it was that in the early spring of 1612 the last two persons convicted for heresy were condemned to death. Edward Wightman published his belief that Christ was 'a mere creature, and not both God and man in one person', and that he himself was the Messiah of the Old Testament. Bartholomew Legate had preached against the rituals and beliefs of the established Church, and had admitted to the king that he had not prayed for seven years. The king kicked out at him. 'Away, base fellow! It shall never be said that one stayed in my presence that hath never prayed to our Saviour for seven whole years together.' Legate was taken to the stake in Smithfield in March 1612, while Wightman followed him to the fire at Lichfield one month later. Wightman had the distinction, if it can be so called, of being the last heretic burned in England.

Another enemy of the state, or at least of convention, may be mentioned here. John Chamberlain relates that in February 1612, Moll Cutpurse, 'a notorious baggage that used to go in man's apparel', was brought to Paul's Cross 'where she wept bitterly and seemed very penitent; but it is since doubted that she was maudlin drunk, being discovered to have tippled three quarts of sack before she came to her penance'. It is an apt vignette of Jacobean London.

5

The angel

In the summer of 1612 King James went on a 'progress' of a month's duration, taking in Leicester, Loughborough, Nottingham and Newark. All around him he could see evidence of a prosperous and tranquil nation. A peace with Spain, and a commercial treaty with France, had encouraged trade while a series of good harvests maintained that happy condition. Dairy produce flowed into London from Essex, Wiltshire and Yorkshire; wool for export arrived at the ports from Wiltshire and Northamptonshire; cattle from North Wales and Scotland, sheep from the Cotswolds, were herded to the great market of Smithfield.

Other trades were also rising. 'Correct your maps,' the poet John Cleveland wrote, 'Newcastle is Peru.' Coal, in other words, was as plentiful and valuable as silver; its production was rising rapidly each year, and the coal traders bargained noisily at the Exchange in Billingsgate. In the hundred years from 1540, the production of iron also increased fivefold. From the port at Bristol sailed cutlery from Sheffield and tin from Cornwall in exchange for sugar and cereals from America and the Indies. Norwich was a safe haven for exiled weavers from France or Germany, while Chester dominated trade with Ireland.

The struggle against monopolies, begun late in the reign of Elizabeth, played its part in the economy of the country. A declaration of the House of Commons, in 1604, stated that 'merchandise being the chief and richest of all others, and of greater extent and import-ance than all the rest, it is against the natural right and liberty of the subjects of England to restrain it into the hands of some few'. Yet patents were still given for such activities as the draining of the fens, the manufacture of paper, the making of salt from sea water, the production of sword blades, and the production of iron without charcoal. The wealth of the monopolies testifies, if nothing else, to the variety of new products and techniques.

The yeomen were constructing bigger and better dwellings, while the poor left their huts of reed or wood and built cottages of brick or stone. Kitchens and separate bedrooms were introduced, while stairs replaced ladders and chairs took the place of benches; the vogue for more comfortable living continued after the reign of Elizabeth with the taste for crockery rather than wooden platters, and eventually for knives and forks rather than daggers and spoons. It is unwise to exaggerate the general prosperity of the country; areas of the direst poverty still existed, especially among the class of landless agricultural labourers and the wandering workmen of the cities. But the conditions of social and commercial life continued to improve.

One minister had no part in the king's progress of 1612. Robert Cecil, earl of Salisbury, died towards the end of May from an illness of unknown cause; his infirmity might perhaps have been compounded with his knowledge of the king's displeasure at his failure to improve the royal finances. He had preserved among his papers a letter, written in Italian, which compared those who loved the great and the powerful to the heliotrope 'which while the sun shines looks towards it with flowers alive and open, but when the sun sets closes them and looks another way'. In the end he longed for his life, 'full of cares and miseries', to be dissolved. In any case he was not mourned for long. The London news was that, even if he had lived, he had already lost all authority and credit. He had no friends left. Ben Jonson dismissed Salisbury by saying that he 'never cared for any man longer than he could make use of him'.

With the death of any great administrator, there was always a scramble for place and office. Francis Bacon was one who hoped that the demise of Salisbury would prove a blessing. The king himself was not unhappy to have been freed from the yoke of his councillor; he could now, as it were, rule for himself. He could be his own principal secretary. In the following year he discovered, much to his disgust, that Salisbury had for a long time been in the paid employment of Spain. Whom could James ever trust?

Robert Carr, now created Viscount Rochester, was the king's confidant while Henry Howard, the earl of Northampton, had become the principal minister of the new administration. Howard gathered about him a group of peers and other noblemen, some of whom were secret Catholics and almost all of whom favoured the Spaniards. Against them, in the counsels of the king, was a Protestant and anti-Spanish party under the nominal leadership of Lord Chancellor Ellesmere. With the balance of these divided counsels James might be able to steer the nation forward. Different men were given different responsibilities. John Chamberlain wrote, in the summer of 1612, that the king 'hath found the art of frustrating men's expectations, and holding them in suspense'.

Another death occurred at court. All had seemed well with the heir to the throne. Prince Henry was an assertive and athletic young man who excelled in masques as well as martial sports. But at the end of October 1612, he fell sick. He was playing cards with his younger brother, Charles, and a bystander, Sir Charles Cornwallis, noticed that 'his highness for all this looked ill and pale, spake hollow, and somewhat strangely with dead sunk eyes'. A doctor was called but over the next eleven days could do nothing to curb the slow invasion of a disease that has since been tentatively diagnosed as porphyria or, perhaps, typhoid fever.

A dead pigeon was put on the prince's head, and a dead cock at his feet, both freshly killed and still warm, to draw out the noisome humours. He died raving, to the authentic dismay and dejection of the court. He had been the emblem of England's future destiny and had promised an age of heroic adventure in the Protestant cause. Queen Anne wept alone, and a year later it was still not safe to mention her son to her; James mourned aloud with 'Henry is dead! Henry is dead!' The crown was now destined for Charles, a silent, shy and reserved prince quite unlike his brother.

A strange incident occurred soon after when, in the words of John Chamberlain, 'a very handsome young fellow, much about his age, and not altogether unlike him, came stark naked to St James's, while they were at supper, saying he was the prince's ghost, come from heaven with a message to the king'. He was questioned, to no effect, and was deemed to be either mad or simple. After two or three lashes of the whip, he was dismissed.

The king was temperamentally averse to protracted mourning, and had a natural distaste for a gloomy court. In February 1613, he celebrated with great splendour and spectacle the marriage of his only surviving daughter, Elizabeth, to Frederick V of the Palatinate. No one beneath the rank of baron was admitted to the ceremony, and the members of the royal family were stiff with the jewels embroidered onto their clothing. Twenty-five diamonds glittered from the king's velvet hatband. The crown jewels were also on display, among them a pendant of rubies and pearls known as the 'Three Brothers' and a 'great and rich jewel of gold' called 'the Mirror of Great Britain'. The princess herself seemed to mar the solemnity of the occasion by indulging in a low titter that eventually became a loud laugh. She was, perhaps, overwhelmed. On the following day the king visited the newly wedded couple and asked them what had happened in their ornate bed. It is believed that Shakespeare introduced the masque into the fourth act of *The Tempest* in order to celebrate their union.

A more sinister marriage was about to take place. In the middle of April 1613, Sir Thomas Overbury was committed to the Tower of London. This was on the face of it surprising since Overbury had been the close companion and confidant of the king's favourite, Viscount Rochester. It was reported, however, that Overbury had been confined on the king's realization that it was 'a dishonour to him that the world should have an opinion that Rochester ruled him and Overbury ruled Rochester'.

Yet there was more to it than that. Rochester had become enamoured of the young countess of Essex, Frances Howard, but was thwarted by the inconvenient fact that the lady had been married for seven years to Robert Devereux, 3rd earl of Essex. She had been a child bride who now regretted her early union. They had in any case always been a reluctant and resentful pair; with the prospect of Rochester before her, she grasped at the chance of freedom. She asked that her marriage be declared null and void on the grounds that Essex was physically incapable of siring a son. Her father, Thomas Howard, 1st earl of Suffolk, enthusiastically took her part; his daughter's marriage to the king's favourite could only raise his already high standing at court.

Essex was naturally aggrieved that his manhood had been questioned, especially since it might affect his chances of finding another wife. So it was intimated that, although Essex had not been successful with his first partner, he suffered from no disability that might prevent him from marrying again. A solemn commission was established to test the case and, like most solemn commissions, it took the easiest way out.

The king was in favour of the divorce, not least because it would delight and satisfy Viscount Rochester. When Frances Howard declared that her husband's impotence might have been a bewitchment, James was altogether on her side; had he himself not written a tract on witchcraft? The archbishop of Canterbury objected. But James had packed the commission. One churchman asked Essex 'whether he had affection, erection, application, penetration, ejaculation' to prove the consummation of the marriage; the hearings were filled with what one contemporary called 'indecent words and deeds'. A jury of twelve matrons examined Lady Frances herself for evidence of her virginity; the lady wore a veil throughout the proceedings, and it was suspected that a true virgin had taken her place. The divorce was of course granted according to the wishes of the sovereign. It was considered to be a notable instance of court corruption, and one that was widely noted and condemned.

Sir Thomas Overbury now enters the plot. As Rochester's close companion he despised the idea of this marriage, no doubt in part because he might lose his friend to the Howard cause at court. When it was believed that Overbury might know some infamous secret about Frances Howard, the king intervened. He asked Overbury to become one of his envoys in Russia, effectively banishing him from England. Overbury refused to take up the appointment, and was committed to the Tower; although in poor health, he was to be kept in close confinement until the marriage itself had been celebrated. That, at least, seems to have been the plan.

Frances Howard was of a different mind, however, and had determined to murder Overbury even before he stepped out of the

Tower. She had an accomplice, Mrs Turner, who was skilled in the management of poisons; Mrs Turner had a servant, Richard Weston, who by means of influence or bribery was appointed to be the keeper of the prisoner. Rochester was in the habit of sending wine, tarts and jellies to Overbury; it has been suggested, but not proved, that a poison was included in the sweet provisions. It is more likely that, with the connivance of Weston, the unfortunate man was slowly fed quantities of sulphuric acid or 'oil of vitriol'. Whatever the method of dispatch Overbury died at the beginning of autumn 1613, and was buried in the Tower. John Chamberlain wrote that 'he was a very unfortunate man, for nobody almost pities him, and his own friends speak that indifferently of him'. It was reported that all was calm and quiet at court; the talk was of masques and feasts and coming noble marriages.

On 26 December Frances Howard and Robert Carr, created earl of Somerset in the previous month, were united in marriage. This was four months after the death of Overbury, and no suspicion of malfeasance had emerged to trouble their marital bliss. At the ceremony the new countess of Somerset appeared with her long hair flowing down her shoulders as a token of virginity; she was, in the phrase of the time, 'married in her hair'. The king and the archbishop of Canterbury were among the congregation in the Chapel Royal, and rich gifts were showered upon the newly married couple. Soon enough, however, the revelation of their conduct would excite the greatest scandal of the king's reign.

It was time to summon a new parliament. The parlous state of the king's finances demanded it. All the departments of government were in urgent need of money; the ambassadors had not been paid their salaries, and the sailors of the fleet pleaded in vain; even the fortifications of the nation were in a state of disrepair. The councillors were voluble with suggestions and recommendations, but they were irresolute and uncertain. The nobles and lords around the king determined to ensure that court candidates were returned to parliament; they became known as the 'undertakers' but suspicion about their activities meant that few constituencies were willing to take their advice. They sent missives to the various towns and regions, but the practice became known as 'packing'. The constituencies wanted new men, untainted by connection to the court, and in fact two-thirds of the Commons were elected for the first time. This did not bode well for the king.

James opened the proceedings on 5 April 1614, with a conciliatory speech that promised reform while requesting more revenue. The Commons chose to ignore the message and instead complained that the 'undertakers' had violated freedom of election and the privileges of parliament. They did not wish to vote supplies to the king but preferred instead to challenge the king's right to levy 'impositions' or special taxes on imports and exports. In a second speech three days later James asked for a parliament of love; he wished to demonstrate his affection for his subjects, while the Commons must manifest their devotion to their sovereign. Yet the Commons were in restless and unyielding mood, full of hissing and jeering. One member, Christopher Neville, declared that the courtiers were 'spaniels to the king and wolves to the people'. There had never been a more disorderly house. It was compared to a cockpit and a bear-garden; the members were called 'roaring boys', street hooligans.

When the members refused James's order to debate supplies alone, he quickly dissolved parliament and committed five members to the Tower of London. The session had lasted less than three months and not one bill had received the royal assent. Thus it became known as the Addle or Addled Parliament. No assembly met again for seven years.

Supplies had not been granted to the king and, in his need for revenue, he redoubled his matrimonial negotiations with both Spain and France; the prize on offer to both parties was Charles, prince of Wales. Yet business of that nature takes time and, in the interim, he approached the City for a large loan; the City refused, on the indisputable grounds that the Crown was not worthy of credit. Thomas Howard, earl of Suffolk, was now appointed lord treasurer and immediately began to raise money by whatever means available; he levied fines, for example, on any new buildings erected within 7 miles of London.

At the time of the dissolution of parliament some of the bishops and great lords brought to the Jewel House of the Tower their best pieces of plate, for the purposes of sale, and the king determined that their example should be followed by the whole nation. So he requested a 'benevolence' from every county and borough in the land. The results, however, were not encouraging. Oliver St John, a gentleman of Marlborough, refused to send the king money on the grounds that the 'benevolence' was contrary to Magna Carta. He was brought before the Star Chamber and committed to the Tower. Eventually he was sentenced to a fine of £5,000 and imprisonment at the king's pleasure.

In the absence of parliament all eyes turned towards the court as the proper centre of affairs. The earl of Somerset, the favourite, was still the cynosure. He had been appointed lord chamberlain in 1614 and was in constant attendance upon the king; correspondence with the ambassadors and other worthies passed through his hands, and he controlled the vast machinery of patronage that acted as the engine of the court. Yet his association with the Howards through his marriage earned him the enmity of many courtiers, and it was widely rumoured that the rule of one man over the king was improper and undesirable.

It was time to introduce to the king another fair-faced minion. In the summer of 1614 a young man of twenty-two was presented to James. George Villiers, the son of a knight, had already been trained as a courtier; he had become practised in the arts of dancing and of fencing. He had also spent three years in France, where he had acquired a good manner further to adorn what was called 'the handsomest-bodied man in all of England'. He also had powerful allies, among them Archbishop Abbot and the queen. Abbot supported him in the hope of diminishing the influence of Somerset and the Howards, who favoured Catholic Spain. The queen, influenced by Abbot, pressed her husband to show favour to the young man. Villiers was accordingly appointed to be the royal cup-bearer, in constant attendance upon his sovereign, and in the spring of 1615 was knighted as a gentleman of the bedchamber.

Somerset, sensing a rival, protested. He alienated the king still more by constant complaint and insolent argument, leading James to remonstrate with him. 'Let me never apprehend that you disdain my person', the king wrote, 'and undervalue my qualities (nor let it not appear that your former affection is cold towards me).' He rebuked him for his 'strange streams of unquietness, passion, fury and insolent pride' as well as his 'long creeping back and withdrawing yourself from lying in my chamber, notwithstanding my many hundred times earnestly soliciting you to the contrary'. It is a strange letter for a sovereign to write to a subject, reflecting as it does the once extraordinary intimacy between them.

Villiers may already have interposed himself between the two men. In the summer of 1615 James travelled to Farnham Castle, home of the bishop of Winchester, where he was joined by his new gentleman of the bedchamber. At a later date Villiers questioned the king 'whether you loved me now . . . better than at the time which I shall never forget at Farnham, where the bed's head could not be found between the master and his dog'. It is an ambiguous reference, but it is at least open to an interesting interpretation.

Sir Francis Bacon, observing the workings of the Jacobean court, once wrote that 'all rising to great place is by a winding stair: and if there be factions, it is good, to side a man's self, whilst he is in the rising'. Bacon therefore attached himself to Villiers. He told him that, as the king's favourite, he should 'remember well the great trust you have undertaken. You are as a continual sentinel, always to stand upon your watch to give him true intelligence.'

In the summer of this year Somerset, sensing numerous plots rising against him, drew up a general pardon for himself for offences which he may or may not have committed. It was said by his enemies, for example, that he had purloined some of the crown jewels. At a meeting of the council, held on 20 July, the king ordered the lord chancellor, Francis Bacon himself, to seal the pardon 'at once, for such is my pleasure'. Bacon fell to his knees and begged him to reconsider. 'I have ordered you to pass the pardon,' James said as he walked out of the council chamber, 'and pass it you shall.' But as always he was hesitant and irresolute; the queen and other councillors argued against the decision which would allow Somerset to keep any of the jewels or other goods he might have taken from the king. It would set an unfortunate precedent. Eventually James left Whitehall without forming any certain decision.

This was only the beginning of Somerset's woes. In the early autumn of 1615 reports began to emerge that Sir Thomas Overbury had been poisoned in the Tower. One of the minor accomplices, an apothecary's boy, had fallen gravely ill and confessed to his part in the affair. It did not take long before the secret plot began to unravel. The lieutenant of the Tower was questioned. It was discovered that Richard Weston had been procured as the keeper of the prisoner. It was then revealed that he had been a servant of Mrs Turner. The trail now led in turn to Frances Carr, countess of Somerset, and to her husband.

The king, now thoroughly alarmed at a turn of events that might even touch the throne, asked his lord chief justice, Edward Coke, to make out a warrant against Somerset. Somerset remonstrated with James about this insult to his name and family. 'Nay, man,' the king exclaimed, 'if Coke sends for *me*, I must go.' He was supposed to have added, as the quondam favourite left his presence, 'The devil take thee, I will never see thee mair.'

Coke conducted a thorough investigation, and eventually reported to the king that Frances Carr had in the past used sorcery both to estrange her previous husband, the earl of Essex, and to inveigle her new lover. He further revealed that she had procured three different types of poison to be administered to Overbury.

On 24 May 1616, the countess of Somerset stood in front of the grand jury at Westminster; she was dressed all in black, except for ruff and cuffs of white lawn. Some of her letters were read out in court, apparently of an obscene character; when the crowd of spectators pressed forward to gaze at the magic scrolls and images she had employed in the course of her secret work, a large 'crack' was heard from the wooden stage. The crowd now believed that the devil himself had come into the court and that the noise signalled his anger at the disclosure of his wiles. Panic and confusion followed that could not be quelled for a quarter of an hour. Witches and demons were still in the Jacobean air.

The countess pleaded guilty to the charge of murder, perhaps on the understanding that the king always favoured clemency to the members of the nobility. Her husband appeared on the following day and declared himself to be not guilty of the crime, but his judges did not believe him. Man and wife were sentenced to death. They were spared the final penalty on the orders of the king, and instead were taken to the Tower where they remained for almost six years. The exposure of their fraud and betrayal, their profligacy and hypocrisy, served only further to undermine the court and the status of the king whose intimate associates they once had been. Mrs Turner, condemned to death for her part in the poison plot, said of the king's courtiers that 'there is no religion in the most of them but malice, pride, whoredom, swearing and rejoicing in the fall of others. It is so wicked a place as I wonder the earth did not open and swallow it up.'

At the beginning of the spring of this year the heir apparent, Charles, in the garden of Greenwich Palace, turned a water-spout 'in jest' upon Villiers. The favourite was much offended. Whereupon in an unusual show of anger the king boxed his son's ears, exclaiming that he had 'a malicious and dogged disposition'. Villiers was now known to his sovereign as 'Steenie', a babyish rendition of St Stephen; the reference was to the fact that those who looked upon the face of the saint declared it to be the countenance of an angel. The angel would soon be in charge.

6

The vapours

The most colourful and compelling account of early Jacobean London can be found in *The Seven Deadly Sins of London*, published in 1607. It is a work, little more than a pamphlet, written by Thomas Dekker in a period of seven days with all the vivacity and immediacy of swift composition. Dekker himself was a playwright and pamphleteer of obscure life and uncertain reputation, but in these respects he does not differ from most writers of the time.

He announces, to the city, that 'from thy womb received I my being, from thy breasts my nourishment'; in which case London must be judged a harsh nurse or mother. He complains that of all cities it is 'the wealthiest, but the most wanton. Thou hast all things in thee to make thee fairest, and all things in thee to make thee foulest.' At the time of James's accession it had been the 'only gallant and minion of the world' but 'hadst in a short time more diseases (than a common harlot hath) hanging upon thee'.

He paints the scene of the capital at midday where

> in every street, carts and coaches make such a thundering as if the world ran on wheels: at every corner, men, women and children meet in such shoals, that posts are set up of purpose to strengthen the houses, lest with jostling one another they should shoulder them down. Besides, hammers are beating in

one place, tubs hooping in another, pots clinking in a third, water tankards running at tilt in a fourth: here are porters sweating under burdens, there merchants' men bearing bags of money, chapmen (as if they were at leap-frog) skip out of one shop into another, tradesmen (as if they were dancing galliards) are lusty at legs and never stand still: all are as busy as country attorneys at an assizes.

Yet the city takes on a different aspect at night. Dekker has a vision of London by candlelight, the companion 'for drunkards, for lechers, and for prodigals'. This was the time when 'mercers rolled up their silks and velvets: the goldsmiths drew back their plate, and all the city looked like a private playhouse when the windows are clapped down, as if some nocturnal or dismal tragedy were presently to be acted before all the tradesmen'. The bankrupt and felon had kept indoors for fear of arrest but, at night, 'began now to creep out of their shells, and to stalk up and down the streets as uprightly, and with as proud a gait, as if they meant to knock against the stars with the crowns of their heads'.

The prosperous citizen who in the day 'looked more sourly on his poor neighbours than he had drunk a quart of vinegar at a draught' now sneaks out of doors and 'slips into a tavern where either alone, or with some other that battles their money together, they so ply themselves with penny pots [of ale] . . . that at length they have not an eye to see withall, not a good leg to stand upon'. They reel into the night, have an altercation with a post on the way and end up in the gutter. Their apprentices, despite the oath of their indentures, 'make their desperate sallies out and quick retires in' with their pints. The three nocturnal pursuits of the city are drinking, dancing and dicing.

The prose of Thomas Dekker is crisp, strenuous and elliptical. He observes the Londoners at a bookstall in St Paul's Churchyard 'looking scurvily (like mules chomping upon thistles) on the face of a new book, be it never so worthy: and go (as ill favouredly) mewing away'. He notices the fact that the brothels of London have painted posts before them, and that their keepers always serve stewed prunes to their customers. He reports that the lattices for the windows of the alehouses are painted red. He observes the hackney men of Coleman Street, the butchers of Aldgate and the brokers of Houndsditch.

The dress of the Londoner 'is like a traitor's body that hath been hanged, drawn and quartered, and is set up in several places: his codpiece is in Denmark, the colour of his doublet and the belly in France: the wing and narrow sleeve in Italy: the short waist hangs over a Dutch butcher's stall in Utrecht; his huge slops [hose for the legs] speaks Spanish: Polonia gives him the boots'. It is a typical complaint concerning London's variegated fashions.

Dekker observes the disagreeable habits of other citizens. He alludes to the various 'tobacconists, shuttle-cock makers, feather-makers, cobweb lawn weavers, perfumers' as manifesting the qualities of 'apishness'; each one is 'a fierce, dapper fellow, more light-headed than a musician: as fantastically attired as a court jester: wanton in discourse: lascivious in behaviour; jocund in good company: nice in his trencher, and yet he feeds very hungrily on scraps of songs'.

Dekker abhors the common practice of marrying a young bride to a rich old man, 'though his breath be ranker than a muck-hill, and his body more dry than a mummy, and his mind more lame than Ignorance itself'. He complains about London landlords 'who for the building up of a chimney, which stands them not above thirty shillings, and for whiting the walls of a tenement, which is scarce worth the daubing, raise the rent presently (as if it were new put into the subsidy books) assessing it at three pounds a year more than ever it went for before'. This has all the bitterness of personal experience. Welcome to the world of Jacobean London.

Greed and avarice were also much on the mind of another Londoner. Ben Jonson's *Bartholomew Fair* was first performed in the Hope Playhouse at the end of October 1614; it was a long play, of some three hours, and began at two in the afternoon. On that stage the essence of London was quiddified. The Hope was also used for bear-baiting, on which occasions the stage was removed, and in the induction Jonson compares the theatre to the venue of the fair itself, 'the place being as dirty as Smithfield and as stinking every whit'. The stench of the dead or dying animals still lingered. The hazel nutshells and apple-cores might not have been swept away. *Bartholomew Fair* has the soul and substance of the Jacobean city somewhere within it. Its characters are the flesh and bone of London, in which all the people are merely players.

Canvas booths have been erected on the stage to give a simulacrum of the fair. A character comes on, and is soon joined by another, and then another, until a concourse of citizens is visible. They jeer, they swear, they laugh. They fight. They are obscene. They piss. They vomit. They cheat one another. A couple of them burst into song. Various plots and stories emerge only to fall back into the swelling tumult of the fair. Prostitutes and cutpurses rub against ballad-singers and tapsters.

Some of the characters adopt disguise, but in the end their true identities are revealed and their pretensions crossed or crushed. All authority is reviled. That is the way of the city. There is no real power except that of money, and no real considerations other than those of aggression and appetite. 'Bless me!' someone calls out. 'Deliver me, help, hold me! The Fair!' Mousetraps and ginger bread, purses and pouches, dolls and puppies, all are for sale. 'What do you lack, gentlemen? What is't you buy?' All the world's a fair. 'Buy any new ballads? New ballads?' A puppet show brings a conclusion to the play that has revealed London to be a panoply and a pageant, a prison and a carnival.

One of the guardian spirits of the fair is Ursla, the fat seller of ale and roast pig who is also a part-time bawd.

> *Ursla:* I am all fire and fat, Nightingale, I shall e'en melt
> away to the first woman, a rib, again, I am afraid.
> I do water the ground in knots as I go, like a great
> garden-pot, you may follow me by the Ss I make.

She has also a firm line in abuse.

> *Ursla:* You look as you were begotten atop of a cart in
> harvest-time, when the whelp was hot and eager. Go
> snuff after your brother's bitch, Mistress Commodity.

In the words of the play, she has a hot coal in her mouth.
The other great character of the fair is Jonson's parody of the puritan, Zeal-of-the-Land-Busy.

> *Busy:* Look not towards them, hearken not. The place is
> Smithfield, or the field of smiths, the grove of hobby
> horses and trinkets . . . They are hooks and baits, very

baits, that are hung out on every side to catch you, and
to hold you, as it were, by the gills, and by the nostrils,
as the fisher doth . . .

He turns out to be, of course, an arrant voluptuary and hypocrite, amply confirming the suspicions that some people conceived of the godly in this period.

Jonson had said that he wished to present 'deeds and language, such as men do use'. He knew of what he wrote. By his own report he was 'brought up poorly' in London and when his mother took a second husband, a master bricklayer, the small family moved to a house in a lane off the Strand. He attended an elementary school in the neighbourhood before Westminster School and may have been about to attend a college at Cambridge; shortage of funds, however, did not permit the move. Instead he took up his stepfather's business of bricklaying, in which trade he laboured intermittently for some years. He later saw service in the Low Countries and, on his return to London, entered the world of theatre. So he was a child of the city, and *Bartholomew Fair* is his tribute to its teeming life.

Here are your 'pretenders to wit! Your Three Cranes, Mitre and Mermaid men.' These three taverns were the haunt of poetasters and men of supposed good taste. 'Moorfields, Pimlico Path or the Exchange' are mentioned a few moments later as places of resort for tired Londoners. In the puppet play at the close of the proceedings, the myth of Hero and Leander is set in the city.

> *Littlewit:* As, for the Hellespont, I imagine our Thames
> here; and then Leander I make a dyer's son, about
> Puddle Wharf; and Hero a wench o' the Bankside,
> who going over one morning to Old Fish Street,
> Leander spies her land at Trig Stairs.

It is remarkable that ordinary Londoners were supposed to be wholly familiar with the old story, perhaps from Marlowe's poem published sixteen years earlier.

Many of the play's allusions are lost to us, and many of the words are now strange or unfamiliar. A 'hobby-horse' was a prostitute. An 'undermeal' was a light snack. To 'stale' was to urinate.

When one character discloses that 'we were all a little stained last night', he means that they were drunk. 'Whimsies' were the female genitalia. A 'diet-drink' was a medicine. A Catholic recusant was derided as 'a seminary'.

The visitors to the fair often refer to 'vapour' or 'vapours' that can mean anything or nothing. To vapour is to talk nonsense or to brag; a vapour is a frenzy or a passing mood or a mad conceit of the town. In the popular 'game of vapours' each participant had to deny that which the previous speaker had just said. London seethed with vapours.

> *Quarlous:* Faith, and to any man that vapours me the lie,
> I do vapour that. [*Strikes him*].

It is in a sense like watching a foreign world, except that there are still flashes of recognition and understanding. And then once more we are part of the Jacobean city.

7

What news?

The trial of Somerset and his wife marked the beginning of a deterioration at court, where it was believed that the king had become both more cunning and more cowardly; his learning had once been praised but now behind his back he was called a pedant. His new fancy for Villiers provoked scorn, jealousy and even disgust. His own health also showed signs of decline. His doctor wrote subsequently that 'in 1616 pain and weakness spread to knees, shoulders and hands, and for four months he had to stay in a bed or in a chair'. He became impatient and morose and bad-tempered. The doctor went on to say that 'he is extremely sensitive, most impatient of pain; and while it tortures him with violent movements, his mind is tossed as well, thus augmenting the evil'.

James drank frequently and immoderately. He perspired heavily, and caught frequent colds; he was always sneezing. His face had become red; he was growing fat, and his hair was turning white. At the age of fifty, he was rapidly ageing. He was still averse to business and preferred to hunt, but now he rode more slowly and allowed his horse to be guided by grooms.

So the eyes of aspirants turned more often to the heir. Charles, at the age of fifteen, had acquired many of the virtues of a prince. He was a champion at tennis and at tilting; he delighted in horses and in masques; he was already a connoisseur of art and music. Yet he was also pious and reserved; he was silent and even secretive; he blushed at an indelicate word. He was 5 feet 4 inches in height, and had a pronounced stutter.

The Venetian ambassador reported that his chief endeavour 'is to have no other aim than to second his father, to follow him and do his pleasure and not to move except as his father does. Before his father he always aims at suppressing his own feelings.' So Charles grew to be uncertain and hesitant, apt to cling to the few maxims that he had already imbibed. He was too modest for his own good, perhaps stunned by the loquacity of his father and the beauty of Villiers. When he did try to act forcefully, in later life, he often descended into rash action without any thought of the consequences. His piety, and sense of divine mission, also rendered him humourless and strict.

In the summer of the year the king turned upon his judges. Edward Coke, the chief justice of the king's bench, had often angered James by his continual assertion of common law over the claims of royal power. The king called the judges before him in June 1616, and accused them of insubordination; they fell on their knees, pledging their loyalty and obedience. The king then asked each of them in turn whether they would consult with him before pronouncing on matters of the prerogative. All assented, with the notable exception of Coke himself, who simply answered that he would behave in a manner fitting for a high judge. The king turned upon him, calling him a knave and a sophist. James proceeded to the Star Chamber a few days later, where he delivered a long speech on his zeal for justice. 'Kings are properly judges,' he told his councillors, 'and judgement properly belongs to them from God . . . I remember Christ's saying, "My sheep hear my voice", and so I assure myself, my people will most willingly hear the voice of me, their own shepherd and king.' It was not the most modest of his pronouncements.

Coke was not destined to remain in the king's service for much longer. He was removed from the privy council and ordered to desist from his summer circuit of the kingdom; he was told to revise his law reports 'wherein (as his Majesty was informed) there were many exorbitant and extravagant opinions'. Five months later, in November 1616, he was dismissed from office. He was, in a phrase of the time, 'quite off the books'. The king had rid himself of a turbulent judge but, in the process, he had turned Coke into a martyr for the rule of law and the liberties of the people.

The nature and the character of the 'people', however, could be understood in a multitude of ways. The population itself was growing rapidly until 1620, with the consequence that the number of the poor also began to rise. As late as 1688 it was reported that over half of the population, both rural and urban, were below the level of subsistence. The purchasing power of the wages of agricultural labourers or minor craftsmen was in relative terms at its lowest point for generations. In 1616 it was recorded that in Sheffield, out of a population of little over 2,000, 725 persons were 'not able to live without the charity of their neighbours'; they were all 'begging poor'. There were 160 others who 'are not able to abide the storm of one fortnight's sickness but would thereby be driven to beggary'. Their children 'are constrained to work sore to provide them necessaries'.

The inequalities of society were such that, in this same period of want, the prosperity of the rural gentry and the wealthier citizens increased dramatically; this in itself may help to account for the great period of building and rebuilding that culminated in the Jacobean country house with its elaborate ornamentation and astonishing skyline.

It also became plain that, as the gentry increased in wealth and status, so the members of the old aristocracy lost some of their authority. The rise of the country gentleman in turn materially affected the power and prestige of the Commons, of which they were the most considerable element; it was said that they could buy out the Lords three times over. In a later treatise, *Oceana*, James Harrington stated that the work of government was 'peculiar unto the genius of a gentleman'. The decline in the fortunes of the old lords, in favour of the rising gentry, has been variously explained. It had to do with the loss of wealth and territory; but it was also the natural consequence of diminished military power. The king in any case had been selling peerages and the new baronetcies for cash, thus diminishing the honourable worth of any title.

As the gentry rose in influence, so there was a corresponding increase in what might be called the professional classes. The number of lawyers rose by 40 per cent between 1590 and 1630, in a period when doctors and surgeons also multiplied. The merchant class, too, was now thriving and was no longer considered to be a demeaning connection; the younger sons of squires were happy to become apprentices with the hope of an eventual rise to partnership. The division between rich and poor had been sharpened while, at the same time, the wealthier elements of society were drawing together.

The gentry now also controlled the machinery of local government. The lords-lieutenant and deputies, the sheriffs and justices of the peace, were indispensable for the order and safety of the country; the king and his council wholly relied upon them for such matters as the collection of taxes, the regulation of trade and the raising of troops for any foreign war. In turn a form of local government grew up at the quarter sessions, where the most important men of the county or borough met to discuss the business of the community. They were collectively known as the commission of the peace, and their clerk was called the clerk of the peace. Their authority filtered down to the high constables in the hundred and to the petty constables, the churchwardens and overseers of the poor in the parish.

The country gentry had also in large part taken against the court. In a local election of 1614 both candidates claimed to represent 'the country' and denied charges of 'turning courtier'. Soon enough 'court' and 'country' factions would manifest themselves. The ways of Whitehall were already deeply suspect. The king's extravagance required higher taxation. The practice of purveyance, by which the court could effectively seize goods and services for royal use, had become iniquitous. Rumours of the king's homosexual passions also circulated through the nation. At the beginning of 1617 George Villiers, now Viscount Villiers, was created earl of Buckingham and appointed Master of the Horse. His lands were extensive, his income immense, but he had also acquired a monopoly of patronage. Any aspirant for office had to transact his business with the earl, and Buckingham insisted that all his clients acknowledged him as their only patron. Lucy Hutchinson, a memoirist of puritan persuasion, wrote that he had risen 'upon no merit but that of his beauty and prostitution'.

An office was considered to be a family property. The great officials were permitted, and expected, to appoint their successors;

of course they made their choice after an appropriate fee was exacted. Negotiations took place between the incumbent of the office, the favourite for the post and the various aspiring candidates. Some officials were the private employees of other officials. All that mattered was who you knew and how rich you were. When the chancellorship of the duchy of Lancaster fell vacant in 1618, forty-three competitors vied for the post which was being sold for approximately £8,000. The administrators of the navy were particularly corrupt, taking bribes, appointing private servants as public officials, diverting supplies, paying themselves double allowances, ordering inferior material and pocketing the difference in cost, employing ships for merchant journeys and charging accordingly.

All transactions under the aegis of the Crown – gratuities and perquisites, annuities and pensions – came at a price. Samuel Doves wrote that 'on the 2nd of February last past, I had a hearing in the Court of Chancery and for that hearing, there stood one in the crier's place; to whom being demanded, I gave him eight shillings . . . and two men more which kept the door would have eight shillings more, which I paid. And when I was without the door, two men stayed me and would have two shillings more, which I paid.' You paid to have a stall in the marketplace; you paid for the right to sell or manufacture cloth. When a group of monopolists was granted the maintenance of the lighthouse at Dungeness, being rewarded with the tolls on all shipping that passed by, they provided only a single candle.

What's the news abroad? *Quid novi*? 'It were a long story to tell all the passages of this business,' John Chamberlain wrote, 'which hath furnished Paul's and this town very plentifully the whole week.' 'Paul's' was the middle aisle of the cathedral where gossips and men known as 'newsmongers' met to discuss all the latest rumours. It was customary for the lords and the gentry, the courtiers and the merchants, as well as men of all professions, to meet in the abbey at eleven and walk in the middle aisle till twelve; they met again after dinner, from three to six, when they discoursed on politics and business or passed on in low voices all the rumours and secrets of the town. A purveyor of court secrets was called 'one of our new principal verbs in Paul's, and well acquainted with all occurrents'. So the busy aisle became known as the 'ears' brothel' and its interior was filled with what a contemporary observer, John Earle, called 'a strange humming or buzz mixed of walking, tongues and feet'.

It was said that one of the vices of England was the prattling of the 'busie-body', otherwise known as an 'intelligencer'. Joseph Hall, in *Characters of Virtues and Vices* (1608), describes one such creature. 'What every man ventures in Guiana voyage, and what they gained, he knows to a hair. Whether Holland will have peace he knows and on what conditions . . . If he see but two men talk and read a letter in the street he runs to them and asks if he may not be partner of that secret relation.'

So we might read that 'the world is full of casting and touching Fabritio's great affair' or 'at the worst, the world is of opinion, that if they should come to jostle, both of them are made of as brittle metal, the one as the other'. The world says this; the world thinks that. 'Now-a-days what seems most improbable mostly comes soonest to pass.' 'There is a speech, of the king's going to Royston.' 'It is current in every man's mouth.' 'We were never at so low an ebb for matter of news, especially public, so that we are fain to set ourselves at work with the poorest entertainment . . .' 'There is some muttering of the change of officers . . . by which you may smell who looks and hopes to be lord chancellor.' The watermen regaled their customers with the news; the humble citizen sitting in the barber's chair heard the news. Some men made their living by sending manuscript newsletters into the country. Rumour could travel at a speed of 50 miles per night.

And so what news of court? The king travelled north in March 1617. He told his privy council in Scotland that 'we have had these many years a great and natural longing to see our native soil and place of our birth and breeding'; he called it, charmingly, a 'salmon-like instinct'. On his slow journey he was attended by many hundreds of courtiers who ate their way through the land like locusts before their arrival at Edinburgh in the middle of May. No one was sure how the visit was to be financed, and those on his route feared the worst. No English king had come this way for hundreds of years. When James reached the border he dismounted and lay on the ground between the two countries, proclaiming that in his own person he symbolized the union between Scotland and England.

Many of his councillors and nobles had not wanted to accompany James to his erstwhile home. They took no interest in, and had no happy expectations of, Scotland. For them it was an uncouth and even savage land. The queen herself declined to go with her husband, pleading sickness. One English courtier, Sir Anthony Weldon, wrote that this foreign country 'is too good for those that possess it, and too bad for others . . . there is a great store of fowl – as foul houses . . . foul linen, foul dishes and pots . . . The country, although it be mountainous, affords no monsters but women.'

The king brought with him candles and choristers as well as a pair of organs; he was intent upon making the Scottish Kirk conform to the worship of the Church of England, but he had only limited success. The Scottish ministers were wary of these 'rags of popery'. 'The organs are come before,' said one Calvinist divine, 'and after comes the Mass.' James also alienated many members of the Scottish parliament. In his speech at the opening of the session James expatiated on the virtues of his English kingdom; he told his compatriots that he had nothing 'more at heart than to reduce your barbarity to the sweet civility of your neighbours'. The Scots had already learned from them how to drive in gay coaches, to drink healths and to take tobacco. This could not have been received warmly.

And what other news? In the summer of 1617 Sir Walter Raleigh, newly released from the Tower for the purpose, sailed to Guiana in search of gold. The king had expressly ordered him not to injure the Spanish in any way; he was still seeking the hand of the infanta for his son. When Raleigh eventually reached the mouth of the Orinoco he sent a lieutenant, Lawrence Keymis, up the river to determine the location of a fabled mine of gold. On his way, however, Keymis attacked the Spaniards who held San Thome and, after an inconsequential combat in which Raleigh's son was killed, he was eventually forced to return to the main fleet. There was now no possibility of reaching the mine and Raleigh made an ignominious return to England. Keymis killed himself on board ship. The wrath of the king was immense and, sometimes, the wrath of the king meant death. James believed that he had been deliberately deceived by Raleigh on the presence of gold and that the unlucky explorer had unjustifiably and unnecessarily earned for him the enmity of Spain.

The Spanish king of course made angry complaints, through the agency of his notorious ambassador, the count of Gondomar. As a measure of conciliation or recompense, James sent Raleigh to the scaffold in the Old Palace Yard at Westminster. It was commonly believed that he had sacrificed him for the honour of the king of Spain. 'Let us dispatch,' Raleigh told his executioner. 'At this hour my ague comes upon me. I would not have my enemies think I quaked from fear.' On viewing the axe that was about to destroy him he is supposed to have said that 'this is a sharp medicine, but it is a physician for all diseases and miseries'. As the executioner was poised to deliver the blow he called out, 'Strike, man, strike!' He never did have time to finish his *History of the World* which he had begun to compose in 1607 while held in the Tower. He had started at the Creation but at the time of his death had only reached the end of the second Macedonian War in 188 BC.

What is the new news, smoking hot from London? In November 1617, the king issued a declaration to the people of Lancashire on the matter of Sunday sports and recreations; in the following year the *Book of Sports* was directed to the whole country. Archery and dancing were to be permitted, together with 'leaping, vaulting or any other such harmless recreation'; the king also graciously allowed 'May-games, Whitsun-ales and Morris-dances, and the setting up of May poles'. Bear baiting, bull baiting and bowls, however, were forbidden. Clergy of the stricter sort were not favourably impressed by the pronouncement, which soon became known as 'The Dancing Book'. It came close to ungodliness and idolatry. One clergyman, William Clough of Bramham, told his congregation that 'the king of heaven doth bid you to keep his Sabbath and reverence his sanctuary. Now the king of England is a mortal man and he bids you break it. Choose whether [which] of them you will follow.' Soon enough those of a puritan persuasion would become the principal opponents of royal policy.

Ben Jonson's masque *Pleasure Reconciled to Virtue* was performed before the court at the beginning of 1618. It did not please everyone, and it was suggested that the playwright might like to return to his old trade of bricklaying. At the close of the performance, in the scene of dancing, the players began to lag. 'Why don't they dance?' the king called out. 'What did they make me come here for? Devil take you all, dance!' Whereupon Buckingham sprang up and, in the words of the chaplain of the Venetian embassy, 'danced a number of high and very tiny capers with such grace and lightness that he made everyone love him'. James himself demonstrated 'extraordinary signs of affection, touching his face'.

Yet Buckingham's enemies, most notably the Howard family, were determined to supplant him. They introduced another handsome youth to court by the name of Monson. They groomed him for the role, dressed him up and washed his face every day with curdled milk to improve its smoothness. But the king did not take to this new suitor. The lord chamberlain took Monson to one side and informed him that James was not pleased with his importunacy and continual presence; he ordered him to stay away from the king and, if he knew what was best for him, to avoid the royal court.

Buckingham began to use one of the first sedan chairs ever to be seen in the country; the people were indignant, complaining that he was employing men to take the place of beasts. Yet he was still in the ascendant, at which high point he would remain for the rest of the reign.

8

A Bohemian tragedy

In April 1618 a little book, bearing the royal arms, was published. It was entitled *The Peacemaker*, and it extolled the virtues of James as a pacifier of all troubles and contentions. The 'happy sanctuary' of England had enjoyed fifteen years of peace since the time of the king's accession, and so now 'let it be celebrated with all joy and cheerfulness, and all sing – *Beati Pacifici*'.

Contention, however, was about to manifest itself in the distant land of Bohemia (now roughly equivalent to the Czech Republic) which was ruled by the Holy Roman Emperor Matthias. In the month after the book's publication certain Protestant nobles of Bohemia stormed the imperial palace in Prague and threw the emperor's deputies out of the windows; Matthias had tried to impose upon them the rule of Archduke Ferdinand, a fierce Catholic and a member of the Habsburg family. The Bohemian rebels were soon in charge of their country, posing a challenge to the Catholic dynasty of the Habsburgs, which included Philip III of Spain.

The German Calvinists of course took up their cause, thus posing a problem for the king of England. The head of the Calvinist interest was none other than James's son-in-law, Frederick of the Palatinate. Yet James was also seeking the daughter of Philip III for his son. What was to be done? Was James to side with the Spanish Habsburgs against the Protestant party? Or was he to encourage his son-in-law to maintain the Bohemian cause? He prevaricated by sending an arbiter, but none of the combatants was really willing to entertain his envoy. Gondomar, the Spanish ambassador, remarked that 'the vanity of the present king of England is so great that he will always think it of great importance that peace should be made by his means, so that his authority will be increased'. It did not quite work out like that.

In March 1619 Matthias died, and Archduke Ferdinand was elected as the new Holy Roman Emperor. The Bohemians took the opportunity of formally deposing him as their sovereign and invited Frederick to take his place. Frederick hesitated only for a moment. James complained that 'he wrote to me, to know my mind if he should take that crown; but within three days after, and before I could return answer, he put it on'.

After Frederick had accepted their offer, he travelled to Prague in October in order to assume the throne. The Protestants of England were delighted. Here at last was the European champion they had needed. A great comet passed across the skies of Europe in the late autumn of 1618; its reddish hue and long tail were visible for seven weeks, and it became known as 'the angry star'. It was of course considered to be providential, a token or warning of great change. Could it portend the final defeat of the Habsburgs and even the Antichrist of Rome?

James's opinion was not entirely in keeping with that of his Protestant subjects. He was angered by what he considered to be Frederick's rashness in accepting the crown of Bohemia; his son-in-law was in that sense an aggressor flouting the divine right of kings. 'You are come in good time to England,' he told Frederick's envoy, 'to spread these principles among my people, that my subjects may drive me away, and place another in my room.' More significantly, he did not wish to drop the Spanish connection he had so carefully fashioned. And yet his daughter was now queen of Bohemia. Surely there was glory in that? It was the greatest dilemma of his reign, combining in deadly fashion his amity with Spain and his relationship with his fellow Protestants in Europe; he had tried to conciliate both forces, but now they threatened to tear him apart. So he prevaricated. The French ambassador reported that 'his mind uses its powers only for a short time, but in the long run he is cowardly'.

Relations with the Spanish were in a difficult and delicate balance. The business of the marriage of Prince Charles to the infanta was infinitely protracted, and popular opinion in England was one of dismay at a possible liaison with a Catholic power. In the event of marriage, therefore, the king was likely to be estranged from his subjects; but James was too eager for a vast Spanish dowry to heed any warnings. The Spanish in turn required that English Catholics be allowed to practise their religion freely, but the change in law would need the consent of parliament. Parliament would never concede any such request. All was in suspense. When a gentleman from the Spanish embassy rode down a child in Chancery Lane, a crowd developed and tried to seize him; he spurred his horse but the crowd of citizens, now swelled to the number of 4,000 or 5,000, followed him to the ambassador's house. They besieged it, breaking the windows and threatening to force the doors, until the lord chief justice arrived and took away the offender.

It was possible, to put it no higher, that Spain was planning to invade the Palatinate. James was in an agony of indecision, at one moment promising to send a large army to help his son-in-law and at another claiming that he was in no position to aid anyone. He did not wish to meddle in the matter. He could not afford a war, and the country was not ready for military action. Was the election of Frederick, in any case, legally valid? If not, any war on Frederick's behalf might then be unjust as well as unnecessary.

Politics, and diplomacy, could not be separated from the issues of religion; all were intimately related in a continent where the division between Catholic and Protestant was the single most important fact of the age. There were of course divisions within the ranks of Protestants themselves. At the end of 1618 a national synod of the Dutch Reformed Church was held in the city of Dordrecht, known colloquially as Dort, to which came six representatives from England. The debate was of vital interest to the king. It was concerned with the Calvinist doctrine of predestination which was denied by a Dutch theologian, Jacobus Arminius, and his followers. Arminius also condemned religious zealotry of the kind practised by his opponents. He declared that religion was about to suffer the same fate as the young lady mentioned by Plutarch; she was pursued by several lovers who, unable to agree among themselves, became violent and cut the woman to pieces so that each could have a portion of her. The Calvinists, holding the dominant faith of Holland, called Arminius and his supporters to account. The arguments, impassioned and even bitter, lasted for seven months.

An English puritan, Thomas Goodwin, noted that the reports of the synod 'began to be every man's talk and enquiry' and another English theologian, Peter Heylyn, stated that the debates 'wakened Englishmen out of "a dead sleep"'. Theologians were then of the utmost consequence in political as well as spiritual affairs; religion was, in this century, the principal issue by which all other matters were judged and interpreted. At the conclusion of the synod the Calvinists emerged triumphant and their opponents were either imprisoned or deprived of their ministry; 700 families of Arminians were driven into exile. For James it seemed to be a victory for the purity of religion, and one English divine, Francis Rous, excoriated Arminianism as 'the spawn of the papists'. The battle lines of Protestantism were set ever more firmly in stone. Arminianism would emerge in England at a slightly later date, with fatal consequences for the next king.

James was growing sick with the strain and tensions induced by Spain and the Palatinate. He was suffering from an unhappy combination of arthritis and gout together with what was called 'a shrewd fit of the stone'. The death of his wife, Anne of Denmark, in the early spring of 1619 caused a further decline in his health. The king's doctor noted 'continued fever, bilious diarrhoea . . . ulceration of his lips and chin. Fainting, sighing, dread, incredible sadness, intermittent pulse.' The king voided three stones and the pain was so great that he vomited. He seemed likely to die. Charles, Buckingham and the leading councillors were summoned from London to Royston, where he was staying, and he delivered what was considered to be a deathbed speech. Yet this was premature. Within a few days he began to recover, although he was still too weak to attend his wife's funeral in the middle of May. He had been informed that the best remedy for weak legs was the blood of a newly slaughtered deer; so for some weeks he was to be found, after the hunt, with his feet buried in the body of an animal that had just been brought down.

He returned to London at the beginning of June, dressed so

luxuriously that he was said to resemble a suitor rather than a mourner. He had some cause for celebration. The new Banqueting House was about to be completed, one of the few physical memorials of his reign that survive intact. It had been designed by Inigo Jones in the novel and controversial neoclassical style, conceived in the spirit of Palladio and of the Italian Renaissance; it was devised to represent the twin concepts of 'magnificence' and 'decorum', with the king presiding in its ornate and mathematically correct interior as both judge and peacemaker. The Banqueting House was the seat of majesty. It was also considered to be a suitable setting for the eventual reception of Charles and the infanta. Sixteen years later Rubens completed the canvases for the great ceiling; James here is depicted as a British Solomon, uniting the kingdoms of England and Scotland, while on the oval canvas that acts as centrepiece he is raised into heaven by the figures of Justice, Faith and Religion.

The cost was very high, approximately £15,000, at a time when the royal treasury was almost bare. The country itself was also suffering a financial crisis. The growing preference on the continent for cheaper local cloth, as opposed to the more expensive English woollens, and the competitive power of Dutch traders meant that there was a significant fall in economic activity. 'All grievances in the kingdom are trifles,' Sir Edwin Sandys told the Commons, 'compared with the decay in trade.' Lionel Cranfield, who became lord high treasurer in 1621, explained that 'trade is as great as ever, but not so good. It increases inwards and decreases outwards.' The balance of trade, in other words, was not in England's favour. This was one of those spasms of economic distress that have always hit the English economy, but in the early seventeenth century no one really understood what was happening.

Cranfield added that 'the want of money is because trade is sick, and as long as trade is sick, we shall be in want of money'. Too many manufactured goods were entering the country, among them the import of what were widely regarded as vain and unnecessary items such as wine and tobacco. The luxurious world was one of velvets and satins, of pearls and cloth of gold. Yet elsewhere economic failure had become endemic. The export of London broadcloths, in 1622, had fallen by 40 per cent from the figures of 1618; the hardship was compounded by the failure of the harvest in 1623. 'There

are many thousands in these parts,' one Lincolnshire gentleman, Sir
William Pelham, wrote, 'who have sold all they have even to their
bed-straw, and cannot get work to earn any money. Dog's flesh is
a dainty dish, and found upon search in many houses.' This is the
context for the unrest and disturbance of the last years of James's
reign.

It is also one of the principal causes for the number of English
colonists seeking a new life in America. In the autumn of 1620 the
Mayflower set sail from Plymouth; some of its passengers were
religious separatists who had come from Leiden, in Holland, but
the majority were English families looking for land and for material
improvement. It has been estimated that over the next two or three
decades some 60,000 left English shores, one third of them bound
for New England. When they cross the Atlantic, they are lost from
the purview of this history.

It was becoming increasingly likely that the Spanish would invade
the Palatinate in revenge for Frederick's assumption of the Bohemian
throne. A successful attack would have serious consequences for
Protestantism in Europe and might well lead once more to Habsburg
domination; an ambassador was sent to England, therefore, from
the princes and free cities of the Protestant Union in Germany. The
envoy did not receive a warm welcome from the king. James, divided
in his loyalties, decided to do nothing. The archbishop of Canterbury,
horrified at this desertion of the Protestant cause, pleaded with him
to allow voluntary contributions from the clergy for the sake of their
co-religionists. To this the king reluctantly assented.

He was of course still pursuing Spain for the hand of the infanta.
He called the Spanish ambassador, Gondomar, to him. 'I give you
my word,' he said, 'as a king, as a gentleman, as a Christian, and as
an honest man, I have no wish to marry my son to anyone except
your master's daughter, and I desire no alliance but that of Spain.'
He took off his hat and wiped the sweat from his forehead. He had
made an implicit admission, to the effect that he desired no alliance
with Frederick or the German princes. What did Bohemia mean
to him? It was a distant land of which he knew nothing, remarkable
only for the scene of shipwreck in Shakespeare's *The Winter's Tale*,

performed nine years before, in which it was miraculously granted a sea coast.

Gondomar quickly sent a message to Philip III that he could invade Frederick's territories without risk of a war with England. Thus began the struggle which eventually became known as the Thirty Years War, one of the most destructive conflicts in early modern European history that ravaged much of the Holy Roman Empire and spread to Italy, France, the Netherlands and Spain.

At the end of July 1620, the king set out on a progress. The Venetian ambassador reported that he seemed glad to leave London behind. He added that 'the king seems utterly weary of the affairs that are taking place all over the world at this time, and he hates being obliged every day to spend time over unpleasant matters and listen to nothing but requests and incitements to move in every direction and to meddle with everything'. James had remarked, 'I am not God Almighty.'

A few days later news reached him that a Spanish army of 24,000 soldiers was moving against the Palatinate; at the same time the Holy Roman Emperor Ferdinand, whose throne had been usurped, was marching upon Prague. 'What do you know,' James asked an adviser who had questioned him on the perilous situation. 'You are ignorant. I know quite well what I am about. All these troubles will settle themselves, you will see that very soon. I know what I am talking about.'

Yet he was troubled by what he now realized was Spanish duplicity. Gondomar had talked of conciliation while all the time Philip III had been planning for war. James summoned the ambassador to Hampton Court, where he raved about his double-dealing. Gondomar politely replied that he had never said that Spain would *not* invade the Palatinate, whereupon the king burst into tears. Could he not be allowed to defend his own children? His policy of compromise, bred out of vacillation and indecision, was in ruins.

The Spanish were victorious in November 1620, at the battle of White Mountain just outside Prague. The Protestant army was devastated, and Frederick was removed from his temporary kingdom of Bohemia. On the following day he fled for his life into the neighbouring region of Silesia; he could not even return to his homeland, since in the following summer the Spanish occupied half of the Palatinate. He and his wife, Elizabeth, were effectively exiles. In turn the Bohemian leaders of the Protestant rebellion were led to the scaffold and a new imperial aristocracy rose in triumph. The news alarmed and enraged the English public in equal measure, and it was not long before all the blame was being laid upon James.

The Venetian ambassador reported that 'tears, sighs and loud expressions of wrath are seen and heard in every direction'. Letters against the king were scattered in the streets threatening that if he did not do what was expected of him, the people would soon display their anger. All sympathies lay with his daughter Elizabeth, who had been forced to flee without the assistance or protection of her father. Prince Charles, in agony over the unhappy situation of his sister, shut himself in his chambers for two days. The king himself was said to be in great distress but, having recovered from the initial shock, was heard to murmur that 'I have long expected this'.

He very soon took on his favourite role as arbitrator or peace-maker. He devised a plan that might prove acceptable to all sides. Frederick would submit to the emperor and renounce any claim to Bohemia on condition that his Palatinate was returned to him untouched. There ensued a process of elaborate diplomatic nego-tiations that achieved nothing. A parody of the time noted that James would present his son-in-law with an army of 100,000 ambassadors.

It was time to call a parliament; it assembled in the middle of January 1621. It did not augur well that the king had to be carried to its opening in a chair. His legs and his feet were so weak that it was believed he would soon lose the use of them. He did not in any case desire to consult with the Commons on matters of policy. He was there to deliver his demands. He ordered them not to 'meddle with complaints against the king, the church or state matters'. He himself would ensure that the proposed Spanish match between his son and the infanta did not endanger the Protestant religion of England; he also stated that he would not allow his son-in-law's Palatinate to be broken up. And for that he needed money. It was the only reason he had summoned them. He had once said that he was obliged 'to live like a shell-fish upon his own moisture, without any public supply'. It was one of James's arresting similes.

A committee of enquiry had already estimated that a force for the protection of the Palatinate would cost approximately £900,000 each year; James, sensing the outrage such a sum would cause, asked for £500,000; parliament granted him £160,000 before turning its attention to such domestic grievances as the abuse of patents and monopolies by unscrupulous agents. It was the first meeting of parliament for almost seven years and, as such, became a clearing house for all the complaints and problems that had accrued in the interim. In the course of this first session some fifty-two bills were given a second reading.

The weather outside the chamber was bitter. John Chamberlain wrote at the beginning of February that 'the Thames is now quite frozen over, so that people have passed over, to and fro, these four or five days . . . the winds and high tides have so driven the ice in heaps in some places, that it lies like rocks and mountains, and hath a strange and hideous aspect'.

The depression of trade was the single most important theme for the assembly beside the frozen river. The gathering of members of parliament at Westminster gave the opportunity for the exporters, landlords and graziers among them to vent their complaints about falling prices and unsold wool. It was declared that poverty and want were rife. One member told his colleagues that 'I had rather be a ploughman than a merchant'. Disorderly interventions did not quell the embittered speeches. No parties had as yet emerged, in the modern sense, only individuals expressing vested interests or local grievances. It was becoming clear, however, that the political initiative was being grasped by parliament rather than by the king and council.

In the same session parliament drew up a petition against 'Jesuits, papists and recusants'. It was the only way they knew of unravelling the Spanish connection that the king favoured. The member for Bath, Sir Robert Phelips, raised the temperature by saying that if the papists were not checked they would soon comprise half of the king's subjects. So parliament acted. All recusants to be banished from London. All recusants to be disarmed by the justices of the peace. No subject of the king should hear Mass. James was in a quandary, suspended between his parliament and the king of Spain; it was reported that he would accept the principal recommendations but would reserve the particulars for further consideration. This was widely believed to be an evasion.

The feeling of the people against the Spaniards was now palpable. A caricature had been circulated at the beginning of 1621 that depicted the king of Spain, the pope and the devil as conspirators in another 'powder-plot'. The Spanish ambassador, Gondomar, was proceeding down Fenchurch Street when an apprentice called out, 'There goes the devil in a dung-cart.'

One of Gondomar's servants responded. 'Sir, you shall see Bridewell ere long for your mirth.'

'What! Shall we go to Bridewell for such a dog as thou!'

Eventually the apprentice and his companions were whipped through the streets, much to the indignation of the citizens.

Parliament itself was enthusiastic for Frederick's cause. When one member made a speech advocating war against the imperial forces the Commons responded with a unanimous vote, lifting their hats high in acclamation, and vowed to recover the Palatinate. James seemed for the moment to share their enthusiasm, but he was too shrewd or too wary to commit himself to a European war against the Catholic powers. He had in any case grown impatient with parliament. It had sat for four months, and spent most of its time in delivering to him requests and grievances. It had not addressed the necessities of the king, or his request for a further grant of money. So at the beginning of June 1621, he adjourned it.

At a later date a notable parliamentarian, Sir John Eliot, reflected upon the failure of this assembly. The king believed that the liberties of parliament encroached upon his prerogative, while in turn parliament feared he 'sought to retrench and block up the ancient privileges and liberties of the house'. So both sides became more intransigent, the king maintaining his royal power and the parliament standing upon its privileges. Eliot believed that there was a middle ground, but at the time it was overlooked.

This was the rock upon which the constitution would founder. An eminent nineteenth-century jurist, John, Baron Campbell, wrote that 'the meeting of parliament on 30 January, 1621, may be considered the commencement of that great movement, which, exactly twenty eight years afterwards, led to the decapitation of an English sovereign, under a judicial sentence pronounced by his subjects'. A portrait of the king, completed in this year by Daniel Mytens, shows James in his robes of state; he has a preoccupied, or perhaps a perplexed, expression.

When parliament met once more on 20 November, it was clear that its zeal and anger had not noticeably diminished. Its members were in a sense liberated by the absence of the sovereign; James had decided to leave London and, with Buckingham, travelled to Royston and Newmarket. The chamber was united in its horror of recent policies. Sir Robert Phelips was once again on the attack. The Catholic states of Europe were England's enemies, while in England the Catholics had grown so bold that they dared to talk of the Protestants as a 'faction'. Let no supply be granted to the king until the dangers, home and abroad, had been resolved. Edward Coke, now a leader of the malcontents, then rose to remind his colleagues that Spain had sent the Armada, that the sheep scab which destroyed many flocks came from the same country, and that the most disgusting disease to strike humankind – namely, syphilis – had spread from Naples, a city controlled by Spain. That country was the source and spring of all foulness.

The Spaniards were also attacked in violent terms when John Pym, soon to become the fiercest opponent to the pretensions of the Crown, rose to speak against the Catholic threat in England itself, where 'the seeds of sedition' were buried beneath 'the pretences of religion'. The Venetian ambassador reported that the members 'have complained bitterly because his majesty shows them [the Catholics] so much indulgence' The sovereign was indeed the problem; he had asked for a supply, but had not properly disclosed his policy. What could his supporters say on his behalf? The parliament had also raised the matter of the prince's marriage. If the infanta of Spain eventually became the queen of England, one of her offspring would at a future date assume the throne; this would mean the return to the rule of a Catholic king. The members of the Commons drew up a petition in which they asked James to declare war on the Catholic powers of Europe and to marry his son to a Protestant.

When the king received word of this petition he is supposed to have cried out, 'God give me patience!' He wrote to the Speaker of the Commons complaining that 'some fiery and popular spirits' were considering issues that were beyond their competence to resolve; he demanded that no member should in the future dare to touch upon issues 'concerning our government or matters of state'. The

Spanish match was not open for discussion. He then issued a threat that he felt himself 'very free and able to punish any man's misdemeanours in parliament as well during their sitting as after'. He had effectively denied them any rights at all. Phelips described it as 'a soul-killing letter'.

The Commons then drew up a petition in which they asked the king not to believe ill-founded reports on their conduct; they also requested him to guarantee their privileges. When they came with the document to Newmarket, he called out, 'Stools for the ambassadors!' He realized now that they did indeed represent a separate power in the land. In response to the petition, however, he warned them not to touch his sovereign power. One member, Sir Nathaniel Rich, objected to these commands. He took offence at such royal demands as 'Meddle not with this business' or 'Go to this business first'. 'When I speak of freedom of speech,' he declared, 'I mean not licentiousness and exorbitancy, but speech without servile fear or, as it were, under the rod.'

On 18 December 1621, by candlelight in the evening, the Commons issued a 'protestation' in which they asserted that their privileges, and indeed their lives, 'are the ancient and undoubted birthright and inheritance of the subjects of England'. They had every right to discuss foreign affairs. Any matter that concerned the defence of the realm, or the state of religion, came within the scope of their counsel and debate. They demanded freedom of speech and freedom from arrest. James, now thoroughly exasperated, adjourned and then dissolved parliament. He called for the journal of the Commons and with his own hand ripped out the 'protestation'; it now had no status. 'I will govern', he said, 'according to the commonweal, but not according to the common will.' The 'commonweal' was the term for the general interests of the nation. He then consigned Coke and Phelips to prison and confined Pym to his house. 'It is certain,' Gondomar wrote, 'that the king will never summon another parliament as long as he lives.'

The dissolution marked the beginning of the end of James's authority in England. His policy had been a dead failure, and he had alienated all the citizens and gentry who took the side of the Commons. He had no money to fight any war on behalf of the Palatinate, and he was obliged to continue negotiations with Spain. It was also widely believed that Buckingham's advice lay behind the king's intransigence; the favourite was even more distrusted than before. The times were dangerous and uncertain.

The reputation of the king was now constantly under attack. He was accused of being lazy and improvident; his will was weaker than water. He was no more than the king of Spain's viceroy. In January 1622, a man was put upon the rack 'for saying that there would be a rebellion'. A manuscript libel by 'Tom-Tell-Truth' passed among the people, saying that James may be 'defender of the faith', according to his title, but the faith was that of the Catholics; he was head of the Church dormant, not the Church militant or triumphant. 'Tom' added that Gondomar had the golden key to the king's cabinet of secrets and that James himself had committed the most hideous depravities of which a human being was capable. This was a reference to the king's relationship with Buckingham. A preacher at Oxford, a young man named Knight, declared that it was 'lawful for subjects when harassed on the score of religion to take arms against their Prince in their own defence'. Soon enough James issued 'directions concerning preaching' in which the clergy were forbidden to make 'bitter invectives and indecent railing speeches' against the Catholics and were told to avoid 'all matters of state'. 'No man can now mutter a word in the pulpit', Buckingham boasted to the Spanish ambassador, 'but he is presently catched and set in straight prison.'

With the same wish to silence dissent the king proclaimed that 'noblemen, knights and gentlemen of quality' should return to their rural estates. It was claimed that this was a measure to promote hospitality in the countryside but it was widely believed that it was aimed at the gentry who, while residing in London, compounded their discontent by sharing their grievances.

The lawyers of Gray's Inn had decided to take some small cannon from the Tower in order to celebrate Twelfth Night. They shot them off in the dead of night, but the report was so loud that it awoke the king at Whitehall. He started out of his bed crying, 'Treason! Treason!' The whole court was in alarm, and the earl of Arundel ran to the royal bedchamber with his drawn sword in his hand. The false alarm had arisen from the king's own fears. He seemed to lack both moral and physical courage. The Venetian ambassador reported that he was 'too agitated by constant mistrust of everyone, tyrannized over by perpetual fear for his life, tenacious of his authority as against the parliament and jealous of his son's obedience, all accidents and causes of his fatal and almost desperate infirmity of mind, so harmful to the general welfare'.

On the day on which the dissolution of parliament was announced James was riding in the park at his palace of Theobalds when his horse stumbled and threw him into the New River that flowed through the grounds; the ice of January broke beneath him and he sank into the water until only his boots could be seen. He was rescued, and was none the worse after the incident, but it is an apt image of a hapless sovereign.

9

The Spanish travellers

Prince Charles was becoming impatient with the slow progress of the negotiations concerning his betrothal to the Infanta Maria Anna of Spain. The marriage itself had been contemplated twelve years before. Yet there had been endless wrangles about the status of Catholics in England, a sensitive affair that became embroiled with the disputes over the Palatinate and the general state of religious warfare in Europe. There was still some doubt whether the Spanish were in earnest about the match, and disputes arose over the size of the dowry; these doubts were not assuaged by the accession of Philip IV in 1621. It was not at all clear, to put it no higher, that parliament or people would support their sovereign's wishes in the matter. When in 1622 the king ordered that Catholic recusants should be released from prison, after they had given security for any subsequent appearance in court, the fear and anger of the Protestant majority were evident.

It was proposed that Buckingham, now lord high admiral, would himself sail to Madrid; it was also whispered that 'he intended to take his friend with him in secret, to bring back that beautiful angel'. The friend in question was Charles himself. The plan was dropped only to be replaced by another.

In February 1623, Charles and Buckingham approached the king with a scheme of their own devising. It would take too long for a fleet to be prepared for the voyage to Madrid. The effort of obtaining travel warrants for France would be immense. Their plan was to travel to Spain in disguise, with the intention of wooing and winning the most eligible woman in the world. For them it was a great adventure, a grand European romance. The king, sick and weary, seems to have assented; he rarely withstood the blandishments of his favourite or the urgent entreaties of his son.

On the morning after this interview, however, the king was not so sure. Cautious and wary as he was, he anticipated the perils with which the two young men would be surrounded. The heir to the throne would be in foreign hands. Animated by Charles's presence among them, the Spanish ministers might make further demands. An attempt might even be made to convert him. So he remonstrated with them both, and outlined the dangers that they might incur. In response Buckingham merely said that, if he broke his promise of the day before, no one would ever believe him again.

Whereupon James called for one of his principal foreign advisers, Sir Francis Cottington, who was himself a supporter of Spain and the Spanish marriage. 'Here are Baby Charles and Steenie,' the king told him, 'who have a great mind to go by post into Spain to fetch home the Infanta, who will have but two more in their company, and have chosen you for one, what think you of the journey?' Cottington replied that such an expedition was dangerous and unwise; the Spanish were certain to impose new conditions upon the marriage. At this James threw himself upon the bed. 'I told you this before,' he shouted. 'I am undone. I shall lose Baby Charles!'

Buckingham remonstrated angrily with Cottington until he was interrupted by the king. 'Nay, by God, Steenie, you are much to blame to use him so. He answered me directly to the question I asked him, and very honestly and wisely: and yet he says no more than I told you before he was called in.' Reluctantly, however, he renewed his assent to the perilous journey. It was also agreed that the three travellers should be joined by Endymion Porter, a courtier who had been brought up in Spain and might act as translator.

On the morning of 18 February, Charles and Buckingham set off from Buckingham's mansion in Essex; they were wearing false beards and travelled under the names of Tom and John Smith. It was all wildly improbable. They gave a boatman at Gravesend a gold piece and rode away without asking for change; the man convinced himself that they were duellists about to fight each other on a foreign field, and advised the magistrates of the town. An officer was dispatched to intercept them, but he failed to find them. As suspected assassins they were stopped at Canterbury. Buckingham had to take off his false beard in order to assure the mayor that he was the lord high admiral going secretly to inspect the fleet. Eventually they reached Dover, where Porter and Cottington had secured a boat. Soon after their departure the sighing king wrote to them. 'My sweet boys and dear venturous knights, worthy to be put in a new romance, I thank you for your comfortable letters, but think it not possible that you can be many hours undiscovered, for your parting was so blown abroad.' In Buckingham's absence the king had made him a duke, so that he was now pre-eminent even among the eminent.

The two *incogniti* sailed from Dover to Boulogne and, after two days in the saddle, they reached Paris. Two weeks later, after hard and weary riding, they eventually arrived in Madrid and knocked on the door of the English ambassador to Spain. John Digby, newly created earl of Bristol, was described by Edward Hyde, earl of Clarendon, as a man 'of a grave aspect, of a presence which drew respect . . .' He kept his countenance at the unexpected arrival of these two great men, and treated them with all deference and courtesy. But the news of Charles's arrival soon reached the ears of Gondomar, the erstwhile Spanish ambassador who had returned home the year before. He went to the Spanish prime minister, Olivares, with a brilliant smile. Olivares told him that 'one might think you had the king of England in Madrid'.

'If I have not got the king, at least I have got the prince.'

Olivares and Gondomar now approached Philip IV with the astounding news that the prince of Wales had come in person to claim the hand of his sister. But what did Charles mean by travelling all this way to Spain? The grandees came to the conclusion that he was now ready to change his religion. Philip and Charles then agreed that they should meet in the open air, thus avoiding all the pomp and circumstance of a formal audience. The prince did not have a large enough retinue to appear with dignity. So he was invited into the king's carriage, and a few days later he was conducted to the apartments reserved for him in the royal palace.

It was now widely believed that Charles was ready to convert, and indeed he gave no sign to the contrary. He continued to temporize on the matter, eager at all costs not to offend the Spaniards before he had obtained his wife. 'We think it not amiss', he and Buckingham wrote to James, 'to assure you that, neither in spiritual nor in temporal things, there is anything pressed upon us more than is already agreed upon.' They could not have been more wrong. The infanta herself declared that she would never agree to marry a Protestant. She had been told that she would be sleeping with a heretic who would one day burn in the fires of hell.

The foreign policy of England was now also entangled with Dutch affairs. On 27 February 1623, the principal merchant of the East India Company was tortured and then beheaded in Amboyna, now the Maluku islands of Indonesia; he was executed by order of the local Dutch governor, on the grounds that he was planning to attack the Dutch garrison. Nine other English merchants suffered the same fate, and the report of the incident provoked outrage in the nation on an unprecedented scale. It was the subject of plays and ballads, chapbooks and woodcuts, inflaming public opinion against the country across the North Sea.

In the following month some Dutch men-of-war chased privateers into the harbour of Leith and began firing at the town itself; this was considered by James to be an unwarrantable infringement of sovereign territory. A second incident of a similar kind occurred at Cowes, on the Isle of Wight. For the king the actions of the Dutch were intolerable. In retaliation he sent a letter to his son in Madrid, asking him to open negotiations with the Spanish for a joint attack upon the Netherlands which the two countries would then partition. On few occasions has so small a pretext been used for so great a war. Yet it came to nothing. James's anger cooled, and a compromise with the Netherlands was reached. His initial proposals, however, demonstrate how implicitly he still relied upon Spanish support; the whole episode also displays his impulsiveness and unpredictability.

Charles had not yet been given any opportunity of greeting his proposed bride, and so at the beginning of April he was invited to an audience with the queen of Spain and the infanta. The conversation was supposed to be limited to a few formal words of address, but the prince went so far as to speak of his affection for her. This was a grave breach of protocol in a court that maintained the strictest rules of behaviour. Charles realized that he had offended, and fell silent. The infanta herself was not impressed. The prince, however, had been profoundly affected by the sight of her; he wrote to England that she was even more beautiful than he had expected.

It was urged by his hosts that Charles might at least receive some instruction in the precepts of Catholicism. So he agreed to participate in a religious discussion with four Carmelite friars. Their meeting began in silence and, when one of the friars asked if he had any matter to propose for debate, he replied, 'Nothing at all. I have no doubts whatsoever.' Charles even went so far as to ask that the reformed English service might be conducted for him in the palace, whereupon Olivares sent for Cottington and told him that the entry of English chaplains would be resisted by force. This did not bode well for any settlement.

By May it had become clear to Buckingham and the prince that they had made a grave error in travelling to Madrid. If they had remained in England, all the conditions and qualifications could have been discussed by experienced diplomats; they themselves were simply confused and angered by all the demands now being made upon them.

Towards the end of that month a Spanish 'junta of theologians' decreed that the infanta must remain in her native land for twelve months after the marriage had been solemnized. In that period the king of England must prove his good intentions by allowing his Catholic subjects the free exercise of their religion; all penal laws against them were to be suspended. It was further suggested that the prince might also prefer to spend the following year in Spain. He would then enjoy to the utmost the fruits of the marriage.

Sir Francis Cottington returned to England with the news. 'My sweet boys,' James wrote, 'your letter by Cottington hath stricken me dead. I fear it shall very much shorten my days; and I am the more perplexed that I know not how to satisfy the people's expectation here, neither know I what to say in the council . . . Alas I now repent me sore, that ever I suffered you to go away.' He was in fact more concerned about his son than the changes of policy that the 'junta' had demanded. One observer noted that 'the king is now quite stupefied'. 'Do you think', he asked a courtier, 'that I shall ever see the prince again?' He burst into tears.

The prince himself was mired in indecision. He was told that the delay between the marriage and the infanta's departure for England could be shortened by six months. In an audience with Philip IV on 7 July, Charles assented to the terms. 'I have resolved', he said, 'to accept with my whole heart what has been proposed to me, both as to the articles touching religion, and as to the security required.' A few days before, he had made statements of precisely the opposite intent.

James knew well enough that parliament would never allow English Catholics permanent immunity from prosecution; and yet he feared that, if he did not sign the agreement demanded by the 'junta', his son would never be permitted to leave Madrid. He summoned the members of his privy council and pleaded with them to take an oath to uphold the Spanish terms. Faced with the importance of maintaining the king's authority, and alarmed by the prospect of the heir apparent being detained in the Spanish capital, the council reluctantly agreed to take the oath.

The decision of the king, taken in confusion and anxiety, was perhaps not a wise one. It taught the English Catholics that they must rely for their safety on a foreign power, and it told the English people that James was willing to make a bargain with Spain against the obvious wishes of parliament. The Roman Catholic Church, for many years after, was identified with contempt for the rule of law. It was believed by many that, while the prince was detained in Spain, Philip could extort any terms he wished. John Chamberlain wrote that 'alas our hands are bound by the absence of our most precious jewel'. It was widely noted that the crucifix, once the symbol of papistry, had been reinstalled in the royal chapel. Another chapel was even then being erected in St James's Palace for the imminent coming of the infanta. Buckingham's mother converted to Rome. When the archbishop of Canterbury told the king that the toleration of Catholics could not be permitted 'by the laws and privileges of the kingdom', it was related that the king 'swore bitterly and asked how he should get his son home again'.

Two weeks after this reported conversation, on 25 July 1623, Charles and Philip signed the marriage contract. James dispatched jewels of great price to his son as gifts for the expected bride. When the prince asked for horses to be also sent to him, the king answered that his coffers were now empty.

Yet, after all this intrigue and resentment, the marriage never took place. The prince had changed his mind once more. His affection for the infanta had been gradually displaced by his resentment at his treatment in Spain; the king and his courtiers were endlessly prevaricating on the departure of Maria Anna. His companion, Buckingham, had been regarded with ill-concealed distaste. On 28 August he took an oath committing himself to the marriage, but he had already decided to leave Madrid without her. Three weeks later he and Buckingham set sail from Santander to England. The news of their landing at Portsmouth, on 5 October, was the cause of general rejoicing; the blessed prince had been rescued from the jaws of the dragon. He had escaped the wiles of the harlot of Rome. Spain would no longer be able to command the councils of the king. When Charles crossed the Thames he was greeted with carillons of bells; the wealthy laid out tables of food and wine in the streets; debtors were released from prison and felons rescued from death. It was a day of rain and storm yet one contemporary counted 335 bonfires between Whitehall and Temple Bar; 108 bonfires were lit between St Paul's and London Bridge alone. A contemporary ballad set the tone:

> The Catholic king hath a little young thing
> Called Donna Maria his sister,
> Our prince went to Spain her love to obtain,
> But yet by good luck he hath missed her.

A shorter rhyme was also carried from street to street:

> On the fifth day of October,
> It will be treason to be sober.

The two men rode straight from London to the royal hunting lodge at Royston where king, son and favourite all wept. Yet not all was well with the happy family. Buckingham, an erstwhile supporter

of Spain, fell into a fury at all things Spanish; the contempt for
him in Madrid was now common knowledge. One Spanish courtier,
speaking of Buckingham, had said that 'we would rather put the
infanta headlong into a well than into his hands'. Charles was equally
dissatisfied with his treatment at the hands of the Spanish court;
they had denied him his bride and treated him like a fool. 'I am
ready', he told his father, 'to conquer Spain, if you will allow me to
do it.' At a stroke James's well-considered, if not always well-
executed, policy of twenty years would be destroyed.

Yet Charles had learned some useful lessons in Madrid. He had
been impressed by Spanish formality and protocol that emphasized
the divinity hedged about a king; he had also become an admirer
of the art collected by the Spanish royal family and took back with
him, to England, a Titian and a Correggio among other notable
paintings. In his own reign the taste of the court would be generally
elevated even if some of these 'gay gazings', as the paintings were
called, smacked of the old religion.

The popular prejudice against the Catholic cause was strikingly
demonstrated when a garret attached to the French embassy in
Blackfriars collapsed on 26 October 1623. A Catholic priest was
preaching to a congregation of some 400 people when the floor
gave way, pitching the people into the 'confession room' beneath.
Over ninety were killed, among them eight priests and fifteen 'of
note and rank'. It was widely believed that the accident was the
direct result of God's particular judgement against the papists, and
the bishop of London refused to allow any of the dead to be buried
in the city's churchyards. A mob had also gathered outside the
residence of the French ambassador, shrieking execrations against
the old faith. Some of the survivors were assailed with insults or
assaulted with mud and stones.

The press for war against Spain was growing ever stronger. The
situation of the Protestants in Europe was worse than it had been
for many decades. The imperial troops were undertaking the forced
conversion of the people of Bohemia, while Frederick's erstwhile
subjects in the Palatinate were suffering from religious persecution.
The defeat of the forces of Christian of Brunswick, one of the last
Protestant leaders still standing, heralded the supremacy of the Holy

Roman Emperor, Ferdinand II, and his fellow Habsburg Philip IV of Spain. Thomas Gataker, an English Protestant theologian, declared that 'the last hour is now running. And we are those on whom the end of the world is fallen.'

The king himself was growing weaker. A memoir on the king's health drawn up at the end of 1623 reported that he was 'easily affected by cold and suffers in cold and damp weather'; he used to enjoy hunting but 'now he is quieter and lies or sits more, but that is due to the weakness of his knee-joints . . . His mind is easily moved suddenly. He is very wrathful, but the fit soon passes off.' He was now opposed by his son and by his favourite; Charles and Buckingham, as impetuous in their hatred of Spain as they had once been recklessly in favour of a Spanish match, were now directing the pressure for war.

For Buckingham the chance of fighting a pious crusade against the heretic promised great rewards for his domestic reputation as well as for his private fortune; his post as lord high admiral guaranteed him a tenth of all prizes won upon the seas. The policy of 'the sharp edge', as it became known, might also allow the young prince to acquire some sort of military glory without which, as the example of his father showed, kingship lost half of its lustre. It was Charles, therefore, who began to assume command of state affairs. He took the chair of the privy council while his father preferred to remain in the country, where Buckingham was able to insulate the king from any Spanish overtures. The Venetian ambassador told his doge and senate that 'the balance of affairs leans to the side of the prince, while Buckingham remains at Newmarket to prevent any harm . . .'

A parliament assembled in February 1624, when the king's opening speech was tentative and hesitant. He could neither disown his son-in-law and the freedom of the Palatinate nor press for war against Spain and the imperialists. He did not know where to turn. In private he had ranted and sworn, pretending illness to avoid difficult decisions, demanding repose and even death to end his sufferings. In his public speech to parliament, he asked for help. He said that as a result of his son's fruitless journey to Madrid 'I awaked as a man out of a dream . . . the business is nothing advanced neither of the match nor of the palatinate, for all the long treaties and great promises'. In the past James had earnestly upheld his sole responsibility for the conduct of foreign affairs as part of his royal prerogative. But now 'I shall entreat your good and sound advice for the glory of God, the peace of the kingdom, and weal of my children'. Five days later Buckingham met the Lords and Commons in the Banqueting House where he whipped up their anger against the duplicitous Spaniards.

A peace party still existed at the court and council. The lord treasurer, the earl of Middlesex, was adamantly opposed to any war with Spain. There was no money left. It would be folly to embark on a foreign enterprise when there was not coin enough to pay the servants of the Crown in England. Charles and Buckingham, therefore, found it necessary to destroy him. At the beginning of April the earl was charged with various counts of financial corruption; he had no chance. 'Remove this strange and prodigious comet,' Sir John Eliot declared of him, 'which so fatally hangs over us.' He was impeached by the Commons and judged to be guilty by the Lords. James himself was much more aware of the dangers of such a proceeding than his son. He declared that Charles had set a dangerous precedent that would in time weaken the power of the throne. The prince, in other words, had invited parliament to collaborate with him in the destruction of one of the king's own ministers. Would it not be tempted to exploit some of its newfound power? James's prophecy would soon enough have the ring of truth.

For the time being, however, Charles and Buckingham could effectively lead the common cause described by one of their supporters as that of the 'patriots'; it was defined by its anti-Catholic and anti-Spanish animus abroad, together with its supposed fight against court corruption at home. For the first, and perhaps the last, time in his life Charles was in broad agreement with the gentlemen of the Commons and the country. At the end of February 1624, the Lords asked that any negotiations with Spain should be broken off. A deputation to the king in the following month requested the fitting of a fleet and the repair of maritime fortifications; the occupation of the Palatinate by Spanish and Bavarian troops should be ended.

For these measures James needed money and, at his urgent request, he was granted £300,000. But how was any war to be

fought, and against whom was it to be directed? Against the Holy
Roman Emperor or against the king of Spain? Or against Max-
imilian I, duke of Bavaria, who now controlled the Palatinate?
The king prevaricated in his usual manner. 'But whether I shall
send twenty thousand or ten thousand, whether by sea or land, east
or west, by diversion or otherwise, by invasion upon the Bavarian
[Maximilian I] or the Emperor, you must leave that to the king.'
The parliament might wish for war with Spain, but it might be in
the interests of the English king only to threaten war; the Spaniards
might then agree to restore Frederick to his throne. Many in the
court and council were themselves wary of a direct war against the
Spanish; battles on sea or on land cost money, and money could
only be raised by imposing fresh taxes.

The Spanish envoys had meanwhile found their way to the king
through the connivance of certain courtiers. It soon reached the
king's ear that they accused Buckingham of 'affecting popularity',
and charged him with drawing up a plan that would effectively
imprison James in a convenient country house so that the prince
might rule in his name. They suggested that the favourite believed
the king to be a poor old man unfit to govern. There may or may
not have been truth to these claims but the king took the unexpected
step of interrogating his councillors on the matter. All of them swore
that they had never heard a whisper of treason from Buckingham
The favourite was saved.

James had signalled his willingness to prepare himself for the
possibility of war 'if he could be seconded'. The only possible ally was
Louis XIII of France; the French king, at least, had the power to
stand against the Spanish or the imperialists in Germany. Soon after
parliament had assembled, two envoys were sent from London to
Paris with the instruction to seek the hand of the French king's sister,
Henrietta Maria, for Charles. Their proposals were indeed welcomed;
it was in the interests of France permanently to separate England
from Spain. Louis was a better Frenchman than he was a Catholic,
and had no reason to shrink from conflict with his co-religionists. Yet
the French court insisted, at the beginning of the negotiations, that
English Catholics be given the same liberties as the Spanish had
demanded for them in the previous marriage treaty.

This was of course a perilous matter. It would test once more the king's good faith. By marrying a Catholic princess, also, Charles might alienate the very 'patriots' whom he had previously courted. The king therefore decided to prorogue parliament before news of the French demands became known. It had not been an unproductive assembly; it had passed thirty-five public Acts and thirty-eight private. The private Acts alone are evidence that the members were representing local demands and grievances on a significantly increased scale. But parliament had achieved more than that. With its impeachment of the lord treasurer, and its active collaboration with Charles and Buckingham, it had proved itself to be an indispensable limb of the body politic.

Preparations for war with Spain were begun. The Spanish ambassador noted 'the great joy and exultation of all the cobblers and zealous bigots of the town'. Cobblers were well known for their radical Protestant sympathies. The English 'mice', as they were called, were ready to take on the Habsburg 'cats'. On the departure of the Spanish legation from London the citizens cried out: 'All the devils in hell go with you, and for those that stay behind let Tyburn take them!' London and the suburbs were now the venue for newly recruited soldiers, all of them waiting for the happy beat of the drums.

A defensive league was formed with the seven United Provinces; envoys were sent to the kings of Sweden and Denmark with proposals for a holy crusade against the Catholic powers. This served further to excite the martial enthusiasm of the populace. The more realistic of the king's councillors doubted that the Palatinate could be fully recovered, or Spain defeated, but they hoped at least to assert English power and subdue Spanish pretensions. In the summer of 1624 a play by Thomas Middleton, *A Game at Chess*, was staged at the Globe where its satire of Gondomar and the Spanish clique at the English court was an unprecedented success; crowds besieged the theatre for nine days, while the laughter and general hubbub could be heard on the other side of the Thames. 'Sir, your plot's discovered!' one of Gondomar's aides bursts in to tell him. The ambassador asks him which of the 20,958 plots he means. He explains his methods.

With pleasant subtlety and bewitching courtship . . .
To many a soul I have let in mortal poison
Whose cheeks have cracked with laughter to receive it;
I could so roll my pills in sugared syllables
And strew such kindly mirth o'er all my mischiefs,
They took their bane in way of recreation.

Thus spoke the erstwhile Spanish ambassador on the stage.

An Anglo-French league was now likely but by no means certain. The French still insisted in principle that penal measures against English Catholics be lifted, and that they should be allowed to practise their religion in peace. Both the king and his son, however, had promised the last parliament that no articles in favour of the Catholics would ever be entertained. It was considered that, in the last resort, it would be better to go to war without the aid of the French than to force a crisis between Crown and parliament.

All the flexible skills of diplomacy had now to be deployed. An English envoy at the court of Louis XIII suggested to James that the French demands were made for 'their own honour' only, and that 'it will always be in your majesty's power to put the same in execution according to your own pleasure'. It was a policy of hypocrisy and prevarication but none the worse for that. Buckingham was equally sanguine. He was so intent upon martial glory in any Protestant crusade that he urged the king to accept the French terms. James was not willing to concede so much, but he was prepared to write a private letter to Louis in which he promised that his Catholic subjects 'shall enjoy all the liberty and freedom which concerns the secret exercise of their religion which was granted by the treaty of marriage made with Spain'. It was not quite enough. The French insisted upon their original demands, with the enthusiastic support of Buckingham. The king finally yielded, with the proviso that he should sign a letter and not a contractual engagement. It was vital now that parliament should not intervene; a promised summons in the late autumn was therefore postponed until the following year.

On 12 December 1624, the marriage articles were signed; the king's hands were so crippled with gout that he was obliged to apply a stamp rather than a signature. To this document Charles appended a secret engagement to the effect that 'I will promise to all the Roman Catholic subjects of the Crown of Great Britain the utmost of liberty and franchise in everything regarding their religion . . .' Twelve days later the courts were forbidden to prosecute recusants under the penal laws; all Catholics in confinement for their faith were then released from the prisons of England.

In this month the king wrote a plaintive letter to Buckingham.

> I cannot content myself without sending you this billet, praying God that I may have a joyful and comfortable meeting with you, and that we may make at this Christmas a new marriage, ever to be kept hereafter; for, God so love me, as I desire only to live in this world for your sake, and that I had rather live banished in any part of the earth with you, than live a sorrowful widow life without you, and so God bless you, my sweet child and wife, and grant that you may ever be a comfort to your dad and husband
>
> James R.

It was the last letter that Buckingham would ever receive from the king.

The time of war was approaching. Ernest, count of Mansfeld, the principal German ally of Frederick, came to England in search of troops; the soldiers of the previous summer, in their gay feathers and buff jerkins, had been volunteers. Now the county officials had to conscript local men for service and, naturally enough, they preferred to choose those for whom they had the least use. Some of the conscripts preferred radical action to avoid being pressed for service. One hanged himself for fear, while another ran into the Thames and drowned; one cut off all the fingers of his right hand, while another put out one of his eyes with salt. An observer wrote that 'such a rabble of raw and poor rascals have not lightly been seen, and they go so unwillingly that they must rather be driven than led'.

It had been said that an Englishman could not fight without his 'three Bs', namely bed, beef and beer. All three were, on this occasion, in pitifully short supply. Dover had no such commodities in large quantity, and only a few vessels had arrived to transport the men. Their eventual destination was, in any event, not at all clear. James had wished the men to land in France, thus implicating Louis XIII in the war against Spain and the empire; Louis refused them the possibility. So Mansfeld, at the end of January, was obliged to sail for Flushing and begin a march through Holland; his men were to go to the aid of the Dutch fortress city of Breda, then under siege by the Spanish.

Yet the English troops were ill-trained and ill-equipped; they had few provisions, and soon enough a hard frost descended on them, provoking contagious sickness. 'All day long,' one of their commanders, Lord Cromwell, wrote, 'we go about for victuals and bury our dead.' By the end of March a force of 12,000 was reduced to 3,000 armed men. Yet the folly was not blamed so much upon Mansfeld as upon Buckingham, whose military enthusiasm did not include attention to the details of policy or planning. The disaster did not bode well for the conduct of a more general war that the king would not live to see.

James had recovered from the gout that had afflicted him at the beginning of the year. Yet on 5 March 1625 he was attacked by what was known as a tertian ague, of which the symptoms were chills, fever and profuse sweating. He feared the worst but refused to accept the advice of his physicians. Instead he relied upon a posset drink recommended by Buckingham's mother, which seemed to do no good. It was whispered that, at the urging of her son, she had in fact poisoned him; she fell on her knees at the king's bedside and asked for justice against these accusations. 'Poisoned me?' the king asked fearfully. At which point, he swooned.

The end was now very near. On 25 March he suffered a stroke that affected his face and jaw. It was reported that his tongue had become so enlarged that he could not make himself understood. He was also beset by bouts of dysentery that left him drenched in his own filth. Two days later he left this life. With the great lords and prelates of the realm about him, according to a later memorial, 'without pangs or convulsions at all, *dormivit Salomon*, Solomon slept'. Unlike his mother and his son, James I died lying in his bed rather than kneeling on the scaffold. The surgeons, on opening the body, found no evidence of poison. In a letter of the time, by the Reverend Joseph Meade, it was reported that all of his vital organs were sound 'as also his head which was very full of brains; but his blood was wonderfully tainted with melancholy'.

His death was not greeted with much dismay or sorrow among the people. His foreign policy had been an utter failure, and his relations with parliament were at best acrimonious. His finances were in disrepair, and the sexual scandals of his reign were common knowledge. The day of his funeral was marred by foul weather so that any bystanders were greeted with muffled coaches and flaming torches. His passing was greeted, perhaps, with relief. The new king might prosecute the Protestant cause with more vigour and determination. Sir John Eliot wrote that 'a new spirit of life possessed all men'.

There was an alternative vision of the late king's rule. At his funeral service in Westminster Abbey, on 7 May, the bishop of Lincoln, John Williams, preached a sermon in which he praised James's direction of religion. The King James Bible is lasting evidence of his achievement. The bishop also remarked upon the fact that 'manufactures at home are daily invented, trading abroad exceedingly multiplied, the borders of Scotland peaceably governed . . .' In the reign of James, too, the English people had reached out to Virginia and New England; the merchants had visited the ports of Africa, Asia and America. Certainly, the central achievement had been that of peace, the one condition that the king sedulously strove to maintain. A courtier, Sir Anthony Weldon, left a less than flattering account of the king as indecisive, hesitant and cowardly; it was he who reported the opinion that James was 'the wisest fool in Christendom'. Yet he appended to his description the more favourable comment that 'he lived in peace, died in peace, and left all his kingdoms in a peaceable condition'. This would not be the epitaph of his son.

10

An interlude

At the beginning of 1625, while his father was still incapacitated by gout, Charles had organized what the Venetian ambassador called 'a splendid masque, with much machinery, and most beautiful scenery'; the prince and his companions danced for four hours after midnight, perhaps in anticipation of the regal splendours to come.

The masque was the great ceremonial occasion of the court, performed once or twice each year, that came to define Stuart kingship. A group of the nobility advanced upon an especially designed stage, their ornate and artificial dress perfectly consonant with the elaborate scenery all around them. Gold was a token of perfection, white was the colour of faith and blue represented the infinite heavens; shame was crimson while lust was scarlet. The colours which took most wonderfully to candlelight were white, carnation and sea-water green. Oil lamps and candles of white wax were used to impart brilliance to the scene. The old Banqueting House had in fact been destroyed by fire in 1619 when 'oiled paper' and other combustibles used in the entertainment were ignited.

Inigo Jones was the sole deviser and designer of the court masques, and he brought to his practice all the refinements of his art. The discipline and formality of his architecture prevailed in his stagecraft; he was particularly adept at contriving the mechanical devices or 'machines' that were the wonder of the age.

'If mathematicians had lost proportion,' it was said of one of his productions, 'there they might have found it.' He wished to create harmonies in spectacle just as in his architecture he evoked the harmonies of stone.

The texts of the masques were generally composed by Ben Jonson who chose to deploy moral statements and sentiments within euphonious and carefully crafted verse. The two men were not natural collaborators, however, and Jonson soon wearied of a form in which visual display took precedence over sense. He wrote in one poem, 'An Expostulation with Inigo Jones':

> O shows! Shows! Mighty shows!
> The eloquence of masques! What need of prose
> Or verse, or sense t'express immortal you?
> You are the spectacles of State!

Inigo Jones himself admitted that the masques were 'nothing else but pictures with light and motion'.

The stage itself was designed to create the illusion of an infinite perspective, moving from the reality of the king and assembled court into an idealized world where everything had its place and proportion. These perspective stages were a wholly new thing in England, introducing novel principles of symmetry and order. The power of art represented the art of power. The masque was conducted in a formal space in which the laws of nature could be chastened and subdued by the king himself, who sat on the line of perspective from which everything could be perfectly seen. Only in his presence could the seasons miraculously change, or trees walk, or flowers be transformed into human beings.

It was the perfect complement to the doctrine of the divine right of kings that James had professed early in his reign. He sat in the centre of the especially constructed auditorium so that the eyes of the audience were as much upon his regality as upon the performance itself. James had already written in his instruction manual to his elder son, *Basilikon Doron*, that a king 'is as one set on a stage, whose smallest actions and gestures all the people do gazingly behold'. Inigo Jones himself wrote that 'in heroic virtue is figured the king's majesty, who therein transcends as far common men as they are above beasts'.

The stage had three habitations. At the highest level was a metaphysical world populated by divine or allegorical figures; below this was the world of the court, in which the monarch was the emblem of order and authority; beneath these two worlds lay ordinary reality which, with its emblems of Vice and Disorder as well as various 'low' figures, provided the material for the 'anti-masque'. The anti-masques represented mutability and inconstancy; they embodied the threat of chaos that was wonderfully removed from the world of the idealized court. The king defeated all those who threatened or abused him. As Sir William Davenant wrote in his masque *Salmacida Spolia*:

> All that are harsh, all that are rude,
> Are by your harmony subdu'd;
> Yet so into obedience wrought,
> As if not forc'd to it, but taught.

The scene might suddenly change. A palace might become a bower, where fairy spirits tread upon trolls and other wicked things; Oberon may appear in a chariot, drawn by two white bears, before ascending into the air; a statue might breathe and walk; a feather of silk may become a cloud of smoke, surrounded by several circles of light in continual motion. A scene might be set in a courtyard or in a dungeon, in a bedchamber or in a desert. All was framed by a proscenium arch, the direct forebear of the modern theatrical space. That is why the English drama favoured interiors.

A courtier and diplomat, Dudley Carleton, noted of an early production in 1605 that 'there was a great engine at the lower end of the room, which had motion, and in it were the images of sea-horses with other terrible fishes, which were ridden by Moors . . . at the further end was a great shell in the form of a scallop, wherein were four seats; on the lowest sat the queen with my lady Bedford; on the rest were placed the ladies . . . their apparel was rich, but too light and courtesan-like for such great ones'. James never took part in the masques, but his wife and children delighted in them; they rehearsed their parts for as long as two months, emphasizing the importance that they placed upon them.

The speaking roles were performed by professional players while the music and song were provided by court musicians; the dancers and masquers, among them members of the royal family itself, remained mute. At the end of the proceedings they advanced into the dancing space, before the king, and invited members of the especially invited audience to dance with them. The concord of music therefore concluded a display in which the virtues of reason, order and good governance are all conjoined.

The dancers of the masque thus celebrate the restoration of an ideal order, a magical ritual designed to emphasize the Stuart vision of kingship and continuity. The masques therefore became known as 'court hieroglyphics'. It is not unimportant that foreign ambassadors were an integral part of the audience, since the masque was also a form of mystical diplomacy. It was meant to convey, by the expense of the production, the wealth and liberality of the sovereign; the more money spent, the more the glory and the more the praise. In 1618 James spent the unparalleled sum of £4,000 on one production. The fourteen ladies of another masque needed, for their costumes, 780 yards of silk. Yet the masques appealed to appetites other than sight. A lavish banquet, complete with orchestra, often preceded or accompanied the performance.

It was an age of music. In the years between 1587 and 1630 over ninety collections of madrigals, airs and songs were published. Madrigals were compositions for several voices without music, and airs were solo songs accompanied by instruments; the madrigal was the most artificial, and therefore considered the most delightful. Catches were sung by gentlemen in their taverns, by weavers at their looms and by tinkers in their workshops. A man who could not take part in a madrigal, or play the lute, was considered to be unfinished. Lutes and citherns were available in barbers' shops for the diversion of waiting customers. Music books were customarily brought to the table after supper was ended.

No epoch in the history of English music can excel the diversity of genius that flourished in this period. It was the age of Dowland and of Morley, of Campion and of Byrd, of Bull and of Gibbons. It was also the age of songs such as 'Lady, Lie Near Me', 'If All The World Were Paper', 'New, New Nothing' and 'Punk's Delight'. In the time of James, the island was filled with sounds and sweet airs.

In the closing months of 1611, the private theatre at Blackfriars echoed to such harmonies. Shakespeare's *The Tempest* was a work of musical theatre with professional singers and a consort of instruments. The stage directions tell their own story, requesting 'solemn and strange music', 'soft music', 'a strange hollow and confused noise'. 'Enter Ferdinand, and Ariel, invisible, playing and singing.' Ferdinand asks, 'Where should this music be? I' th' air, or th' earth?' It was everywhere, being 'dispersed' music that came from various parts of the stage. In this play Stephano sings sea shanties, while Caliban croons drunken catches. Music was played in the intervals between the acts, and at the close a ritual dance was performed by all of the actors. Music was also played as an accompaniment to scenes of wonder and of pathos, on Prospero's grounds that 'a solemn air' is 'the best comforter to an unsettled fancy'.

The music of the instruments was diverse. The soft and mournful notes of the recorder were accompanied by a consort of strings including viols, lutes and citherns. An organ was suitable for the solemn music of supernatural change and awakening. Ariel often enters with pipe and tabor. Thus Caliban reveals that

> Sometimes a thousand twangling instruments
> Will hum about mine ears; and sometimes voices . . .

The last song of the play is sung by Ariel. The words are those of Shakespeare and at a slightly later date they were given a setting by Robert Johnson, a musician attached to the court of the king. It is clear, however, that the melodic inspiration came to Shakespeare from folk tunes or ballads that were in the air at the time.

> Where the bee sucks, there suck I,
> In a cowslip's bell I lie;
> There I couch when owls do cry.

This is a song of freedom, chanted just before Prospero releases Ariel from his service; perhaps the spirit danced at the close. The part was performed by a boy, or a light-voiced singer, and the role may have been taken by the seventeen-year-old 'Jackie Wilson' who later handed down the settings for the song. Blackfriars was known as a 'private' theatre because it was enclosed by roof and walls; in such a setting, the music would have a more powerful and intimate effect.

The Tempest was also performed before the king at Whitehall on 1 November 1611, and owes some of its ritual and sweet melody to the masques of the court; actors from Shakespeare's company also took part in those masques. There was a marked cultural or courtly style in the early years of the seventeenth century.

The great plays of Shakespeare's maturity were written during the reign of James, *Othello* and *King Lear*, *Measure for Measure*, *Antony and Cleopatra* and *The Winter's Tale* among them. The witches of *Macbeth* were in part inspired by James's own interest in the phenomenon. The king was a more enthusiastic patron of the drama than Elizabeth had ever been. Six days after his arrival in London, from Scotland, he called together Shakespeare and the other members of the Lord Chamberlain's Company and issued to them letters patent that allowed them to perform as the King's Men. The actors were appointed to be grooms of the chamber a few months later.

The era of James I also encouraged other forms of drama. A cardinal, dressed in crimson silk, with a tippet or shoulder cape of sable, comes upon the stage. He is meditating upon a book.

> *Cardinal:* I am puzzled in a question about hell:
> He says, in hell there's one material fire,
> And yet it shall not burn all men alike.
> Lay him by. How tedious is a guilty conscience!
> When I look into the fish-ponds in my garden
> Methinks I see a thing armed with a rake
> That seems to strike at me.

It does not occur to the cardinal that it may be his own reflection.

The Duchess of Malfi, by John Webster, is a defining drama of the period, and is one of a number of plays that subsequently have been brought together under the collective title of 'Jacobean tragedy'. Since it is the only literary genre that carries the name of the age, it may be of some importance for any understanding of it. It signifies melancholy, morbidity, restlessness, brooding anger, impatience, disdain and resentment; it represents the horror of life. The exuberance and optimistic inventiveness of the Elizabethan years have disappeared. The joy has gone. The vitality has become extremity and the rhetoric has turned rancid.

The duchess herself asks, 'Who am I?' To which comes the reply: 'Thou art a box of worm-seed, at best but a salvatory of green mummy. What's this flesh? A little curded milk, fantastical puff paste: our bodies are weaker than those paper prisons boys use to keep flies in – more contemptible, since ours is to preserve earth worms. Didst thou ever see a lark in a cage?' This is perhaps the quintessence of Jacobean dramatic style and can be compared to John Donne's contemporaneous verse on:

> This curdled milk, this poor unlitter'd whelp,
> My body . . .

The Duchess of Malfi was written for Shakespeare's company and was first performed towards the close of 1614 at the theatre in Blackfriars before a fashionable audience that would catch most of the allusions to the plays and poems of the day. In a theatrical world of death and murder, of graves and shrines, music was once again an essential element for conveying suspense and intensity.

The plot itself is a poor thing. The duchess, a widow, wishes to marry the steward of her household in a union which might be perceived to dishonour her. Her two brothers – Ferdinand, duke of Calabria, and one known only as the cardinal – conspire to be revenged upon her. By means of a spy and secret agent, Bosola, the duchess is captured and subjected to a range of mental tortures designed to induce insanity; she is presented with the severed hand of her husband, and a gaggle of mad people is brought into her presence. A curtain is drawn to show a tableau comprising the dead bodies of her husband and children. It is revealed in an aside to the audience that they are waxworks, but not until the *frisson* of their discovery has subsided. The duchess is in the end strangled, but not before being shown the cord that will dispatch her.

> *Duchess*: What would it pleasure me to have my throat cut
>   With diamonds, or to be smothered
>   With cassia, or to be shot to death with pearls?

On sight of her body Ferdinand utters what are the most famous words of the play:

> Cover her face; mine eyes dazzle; she died young.

Out of guilt and despair he then descends into murderous madness.

> One met the Duke 'bout midnight in a lane
> Behind St Mark's church, with the leg of a man
> Upon his shoulder; and he howled fearfully;
> Said he was a wolf . . .

The final scene concludes with a bloody conflict in which both Bosola and the cardinal are killed, bringing the sum total of fatalities in the play to ten. Enough has been quoted, perhaps, to convey the sensibility of the time as well as the taste of the Jacobean audience.

It is a world of secrecy and madness, where characters hide and wait. The duchess sees a trespasser in the mirror and trembles. The broken phrases are forced out. 'What is it?' 'What's that?' 'Oh fearful!' 'Why do you do this?' 'What's he?' A common exclamation is 'Ha!' Some of Webster's favourite words are 'foul', 'mist' and 'dunghill'. The dialogue, when not fabulously ornamental, is direct and rapid, almost a whisper. 'Can you guess?' 'No.' 'Do not ask then.'

The play might be described as morbid or as grotesque, the English version of *Grand Guignol*, were it not for the fact that it is possessed by a wild and almost frantic energy. That energy is part of the characters' desperation, their vitality and misery mingling in frightful images of fever and of death. They seem to be possessed by will and desire rather than belief; they are united only in the quest for survival in an unstable world. They run towards darkness. This is in fact a most significant image of the age and one to which, as we shall see, Hobbes's *Leviathan* is addressed. Indeed, this is a world from which God seems to have departed, leaving it in 'a mist'. There seems to be no meaning in the abyss of darkness that opens beneath their feet. It was also a time when, in the work of Francis Bacon, the natural world was being stripped of its association with the divine presence.

Where some like Bacon were possessed by the possibilities of progress in the natural sciences, others believed that the world was in the process of fatal decline. When in 1612 Galileo discovered the presence of spots upon the face of the sun, it was considered to be proof that even the heavens were in a state of dissolution.

Yet proof of decay also lay closer to home, and much of the atmosphere of *The Duchess of Malfi* is conveyed by the image of a corrupt court.

> A Prince's court
> Is like a common fountain, whence should flow
> Pure silver-drops in general. But if't chance
> Some cursed example poison't near the head
> Death and diseases through the whole land spread.

This is likely to be an indirect allusion to the court of James I, already rendered suspect by whispers of corruption and malfeasance. The loss or abdication of authority is a context for the disorientation and instability that afflict all of the characters. That is why it is a play of scepticism, disillusion and disgust united in an overwhelming pessimism.

> Pleasure of life, what is't? Only the good hours
> Of an ague . . .

The figure of melancholy, therefore, might be used as the frontispiece to the play. Melancholy was the time's delight, its presiding deity. It had its own dark dress and its own music in the compositions of John Dowland such as 'In darkness let me dwell' and 'Flow my tears'. That pensive, fearful and tearful mood also had its greatest celebration and exposition in the reign of James with the publication of Robert Burton's *The Anatomy of Melancholy*. Burton was the master of melancholy in all its moods and phases. His great volume – more than 1,200 pages in its modern form – was first published in 1621 and went through six editions in his own lifetime.

Burton professed that 'all the world is melancholy, or mad, dotes, and every member of it'. We sense here the curiosity of his prose, at once precise and unsettled; it is a characteristically Jacobean touch. Melancholy is a disease both grievous and common, which he describes as 'a kind of dotage without a fever, having for his ordinary companions, fear and sadness, without any apparent occasion'.

So Burton follows it through all its declensions and divisions, its intervals and digressions; he creates three 'partitions' with a variety of sections and subsections into which the various types and forms of melancholy are arranged. There are sections entitled

'Miseries of Scholars', 'The Force of Imagination', 'Poverty and Want', 'Unfortunate Marriage' and 'Old Age'. He devotes a passage to 'Symptoms of Maids', Nuns' and Widows' Melancholy'. Hundreds of pages are consumed by 'Love Melancholy' and 'Religious Melancholy'. The madness, if such it is, can be caused by stars or spirits, by the quality of meat or wine, by catarrh or constipation, by bad air or immoderate exercise, by idleness or solitariness, by anger or discontent, by poverty or servitude or shame.

All was grist to his capacious mill, and he striates his narrative with stories, anecdotes, digressions, quotations, aphorisms and the most colourful detail. 'A young merchant going to Nordeling Fair in Germany, for ten days' space never went to stool; at his return he was grievously melancholy, thinking that he was robbed, and would not be persuaded but that all his money was gone . . . a Jew in France (saith Lodovicus Vives) came by chance over a dangerous passage or plank that lay over a brook, in the dark, without harm; the next day, perceiving what danger he was in, he fell down dead.'

He describes the inner working of obsessive temperaments who are 'to your thinking very intent and busy, still that toy runs in their minds, that fear, that suspicion, that abuse, that jealousy, that agony, that vexation, that cross, that castle in the air, that crotchet, that whimsy, that fiction, that pleasant waking dream, whatsoever it is'. He piles up heaps of words and throws himself into them; he has different voices, and different tones; he elaborates, and then qualifies his elaborations; he can be inconsistent and even contradictory. No opinion is stable, no judgement is certain. On eventually finishing the volume, you may feel that you know everything or that you know nothing.

He anatomized himself. He professed that 'I write of melancholy, by being busy to avoid melancholy'. He was a student of Christ Church, Oxford, until the time of his death, and he confessed that 'I have lived a silent, sedentary, solitary, private life, *mihi et musis* [for myself and the muses] in the university, as long almost as Xenocrates in Athens . . .' He was a cormorant of books whose library of 1,700 volumes of forgotten lore was both his refuge and his inspiration. Burton was the magpie scholar, curator of the world's learning, a lord of books who hoped that by quilting together references and allusions and quotations he could stitch so strong a cloth that he would be able to cover himself with it. He makes reference to more than 1,250 authors. His is a book in praise of books and a literary fancy in praise of reading. He wished to fashion an incantation to exorcize melancholy. The book concludes with an aphorism, 'Be not solitary, be not idle', and an epigraph:

SPERATE MISERI

CAVETE FELICES

You that are unhappy, hope. You that are happy, fear.

We are close, perhaps, to the religious spirit of the age. Lancelot Andrewes, bishop of Winchester, had on many occasions preached before James in the royal chapel and was well known to the court as he mounted the pulpit at Whitehall. He was tall and slim, with a long narrow face and expressive hands; he had a neatly trimmed beard and high forehead. In the winter of 1622 he had preached from the words of the text taken from St Matthew, '*vidimus enim stellam Ejus*', 'For we have seen his star':

> *Vidimus stellam.* We can well conceive that: any that will but look up, may see a star. But how could they see the *Ejus* of it, that it was His? Either that it belonged to any, or that He it was it belonged to. This passeth all perspective: no astronomy could show them this. What by course of nature the stars can produce, that they by course of art or observation may discover. But this birth was above nature. No trigon, triplicity, exaltation could bring it forth. They are but idle that set figures for it. The star should not have been His, but He the star's, if it had gone that way. Some other light, then, they saw this *Ejus* by.

The style is hard and elliptical, almost tortuous in its slow unwinding of the sense. It relies upon repetition and alliteration, parallel and antithesis. It is knotty and difficult, almost impossible for the hearers fully to understand. Yet it is the devotional style of the Jacobean period, fully mastered by a king who prided himself on his scholarship and erudition. Andrewes hovers over a word, even a syllable, eliciting its meaning by minute degrees; he is constantly questioning, refining and rephrasing. He does not express a thought but, rather, the process of thought itself; he dramatizes the act, or art, of creative reasoning. This is the luxuriant etymology of Jacobean scholarship, similar in its strenuous tone to the prose of Francis Bacon.

'Last we consider the time of their coming, the season of the year. It was no summer progress. A cold coming they had of it at this time of the year, just the worst time of the year to take a journey, and especially a long journey. The ways deep, the weather sharp, the days short, the sun farthest off, in *solsitio brumali*, O the very dead of winter.' The prose is disciplined and pure, evincing clarity of thought and expression as well as a great power of ordered analysis. It may not possess the inspired eloquence or impassioned fervour of the great Elizabethan preachers, but it is marked by what T. S. Eliot described as 'ordonnance, precision, and relevant intensity'. Andrewes moves forward in pulses of light; he stops and repeats a phrase for more lucidity; he is always reaching out for the full revelation of the interior sense. An association of words can lead him further forward, caressing or coaxing their intention; he professed that such meanings can 'strike any man into an ecstacy'.

The soaring cadence and expressive emotionalism evident in the sermons of John Donne may seem a world away from the concerted pressure of Andrewes's words; the articulations of any one culture, however, will not be very far apart. On 13 November 1622, the month before the bishop of Winchester gave his sermon to the king on the journey of the Magi, John Donne, the dean of St Paul's, entered the pulpit of the cathedral.

> The first word of the text is the cardinal word, the word, the hinge, upon which the whole text turns. The first word, *But*, is the *But*, that all the rest shoots at. First it is an exclusive word: something the Apostles had required, which might not be had; not that; and it is an inclusive word; something Christ was pleased to afford to the apostles, which they thought not of; not that, not that which you beat upon, *But*, but yet, something else, something better than that, you shall have.

The rapid associations are like a sudden peal of bells.

For Donne the sermon was a species of erudite oratory, a performance that like the plays of the Jacobean tragic stage would surprise and delight the audience. He must remind his auditors of the damnation of being 'secluded eternally, eternally, eternally, from the sight of God'. He must move and direct their emotions or else he had failed. That is why he exerts all the power of the macabre that John Webster had employed. So in one sermon Donne reminds his hearers that 'between that excremental jelly that thy body is made of at first, and that jelly which thy body dissolves to at last; there is not so noisome, so putrid a thing in nature'.

The settled truths of the old medieval faith had utterly gone. It was now necessary to argue and to convince. In this endeavour Lancelot Andrewes and John Donne were united. Yet this meant that they were sometimes engaged in tortuous and self-involved trials of the spirit; this was in many respects a sceptical, ambiguous and ambivalent age, at least in direct comparison with its predecessors, and against that unstable background both preachers protested and declaimed.

The syntactic parallels and paradoxes of both churchmen are attempts to riddle out individual truths and certainties from ambiguous matter. They needed to convince as much as to inspire their hearers. Yet the sermons are characterized by the caustic rhetoric that is so much part of the period. Donne preached that 'sects are not bodies, they are but rotten boughs, gangrened limbs, fragmentary chips, blown off by their own spirit of turbulency, fallen off by the weight of their own pride . . .' The immediacy and urgency of the language, with its rough cadence, are also part of Donne's secular poetry. We may note the pessimism and melancholy, anatomized in an earlier part of this chapter, that also underlie his being in the world. In one of his meditations he enquires about the source of his disease. 'They tell me that it is my melancholy. Did I infuse, did I drink in melancholy into my self? It is my thoughtfulness; was I not made to think? It is my study; doth not my calling call for that?' This is the true music of the Jacobean period, now come to a close.

11

Vivat rex

Charles Stuart had become king of England at the age of twenty-four. He was proclaimed on the same day as his father's death, 27 March 1625, and a contemporary at Cambridge wrote that 'we had thunder the same day, presently on the proclamation, and 'twas a cold season, but all fears and sorrows are swallowed up in joy of so hopeful a successor'. Had the new king not put himself at the head of the anti-Spanish alliance in England?

He was more severe and reserved than his father, with a strong sense of formality and order, and the change of tone at court was soon evident. Charles announced that during the reign of his 'most dear and royal father' idle and unnecessary people had thronged the court, bringing 'much dishonour to our house'. There were to be no more bawds or catamites. The new king had been impressed by the decorum of the Spanish court, where he had spent many months; he appreciated the privacy by which the royal family was protected, and the gravitas with which courtly affairs were conducted. The moral tone appealed to a young man who had become dismayed by the laxness and libertinism of his father's court. He began to dress in black. In the preface to his orders for the royal household he remarked that his purpose was 'to establish government and order in our court which from thence may spread with more order through all parts of our kingdom'. This art of control, however, might be more congenial in theory than in practice.

The Venetian ambassador noted that within days of his accession 'the king observes a rule of great decorum. The nobles do not enter his apartments in confusion as heretofore, but each rank has its appointed place.' The ambassador also reported that the king had drawn up rules and regulations that divided his day, from first rising, into separate compartments; there was a time for praying and a time for exercising, a time for business and a time for audiences, a time for eating and a time for sleeping. He did not wish his subjects to be introduced to him without warning; they were only to be sent for. Servants proffered meals to him on their bended knees, and such was the protocol around royal dining that he seldom if ever ate a hot meal; food took too long to serve. Whenever he washed his hands, those parts of the towel he touched were raised above the head of the gentleman usher who removed it from the royal presence.

Charles set to work in earnest at the beginning of April when he asked Buckingham and other grandees to review all aspects of foreign policy; the fraught relationship with Spain, and a possible alliance with France, were to be considered in the light of Charles's desire to recover the Palatinate for his brother-in-law. A committee was established, a few days later, in order to supervise the nation's defences in case of war. The new king then set up two further commissions to investigate financial fraud by the collectors of the customs and to examine the trade of the East India Company with Russia. It was a business-like start but, as is generally the case with the work of committees and commissions, it achieved very little.

Buckingham was still the principal councillor, as he had been in the reign of James; he stayed in the company of the king all day, and slept in a room next to the royal bedchamber. He possessed the golden key that allowed him entrance to all the apartments of the palace. It seemed that nothing could be done without him. He had an almost vice-regal status and was in part able to compensate for the king's unskilfulness in persuasion and management.

Charles had a stutter which, together with his want of natural fluency in conversation, led him to confess once that 'I know I am not good to speak much'. When he was a child his doctors had tried to cure the problem by putting small stones in his mouth, but this had provided no benefit. He tried to form complete sentences in his mind before uttering them, but the impediment remained. He was always shy and hesitant in speech. So he communicated with his household servants by means of gestures as much as words.

One of his principal advisers at a later date, the earl of Clarendon, noted that his insecurity led him to adopt the suggestions, or yield to the influence, of men who were in fact less capable than himself. He never really discerned the true merits or vices of those around him; he tended to confide in those who were merely boasters and adventurers while ignoring those of real, if silent, merit. The council about him consisted of professional courtiers, many of whom had been close to his father, while the others were friends or trusted servants. The principal decisions, however, were diverted from the full council to selective small groups or committees; suspicion and jealousy were therefore rife.

His first public appearance, in April, was at the port of Blackwall, on the north bank of the Thames, where he visited the royal fleet. He was small, just a little over 5 feet in height, and might be described as rather delicate than otherwise. Yet he had disciplined and trained himself in healthy exercise, so that his slight exterior was deceptive. He was of a pale complexion, set off in his youth by curly chestnut hair; he had a long face with grey eyes and full lips. He was of temperate habits, preferring plain beer to spiced wines, and of an apparently cool and dispassionate nature. He always blushed if he overheard indecent talk. If he could command his own passions, however, he might be able to control those of his kingdom. He collected aphorisms from the Stoics and neo-Stoics on the importance of cultivating detachment from the pressing issues of the moment. 'We have learnt to own ourself by retiring into ourself,' he once said. Yet acute observers, among them portrait painters, were able to sense that he concealed secret or hidden tension. His pace was rapid and hurried.

The potentially dangerous matter of his marriage to the French Catholic princess, Henrietta Maria, soon became the principal topic of London gossip. Many in the court, and in the country, deplored the alliance with a devotee of Rome and conjured up old fears of papal domination. Yet Charles was not inclined to heed any warnings. He had a Scottish father, a Danish mother, and a half-French grandmother in the person of Mary Queen of Scots; he was the perfect representative of the fact that the royal families of Europe were not necessarily nationalist or religious partisans.

The marriage was celebrated by proxy, on 1 May 1625, in front of the west door of Notre Dame; on the same day the king issued a declaration that 'all manner of prosecution' against Roman Catholics should 'be stayed and forborne, provided always that they behave themselves modestly therein'. This had been one of the stumbling blocks in the Spanish negotiations of previous years and a contemporary, John Chamberlain, now complained that 'we are out of the frying-pan into the fire'. In the middle of the month Buckingham himself travelled to Paris in order to accompany Henrietta Maria across the Channel and to expedite the proposed alliance between England and France; he hoped to persuade the French king to treat his Protestant subjects, the Huguenots, with the same tact as Charles was now displaying to the Catholics. He also wished to draw the French into open warfare against the Spanish. In both respects he was unsuccessful, and in any case his flair or arrogance was not to the taste of Louis XIII. He is reported to have worn a white satin suit sewn all over with diamonds, and to have flirted with the wife of the French king; he also danced a saraband in front of her dressed as a Pantaloon.

Henrietta Maria eventually arrived at Dover on 12 June and was taken to the castle where Charles rode to meet her. She seemed to be taller than he anticipated, and she noticed him glancing at her feet in case she were wearing shoes like stepladders. 'Sir,' she said, 'I stand upon mine own feet; I have no helps by art. Thus high I am, and am neither higher nor lower.' She had spirit, therefore, and was described by an English observer, Joseph Mead, as 'nimble and quick . . . in a word, a brave lady'. She was fifteen years old. Soon after her arrival she was discomfited by too much company in an overheated room. Mead reported that 'with one frown . . . she drove us all out of the chamber. I suppose none but a queen could have cast such a scowl.'

A new parliament for the new reign was of paramount importance. Charles would have been happy to recall the old one, since it had favoured his anti-Spanish cause, but he was informed that the death of James had brought it to an end. He should have known this element of constitutional practice. A parliament had been called for May, but the onset of the plague in thirteen parishes of the city led to its postponement for a month. Charles opened the assembly with a speech in which he pressed for money to finance the recovery of the Palatinate. It is not at all clear, however, that the members wished to be drawn into a continental war and instead they seemed intent on domestic matters. After they had observed a day of fasting, they delivered to the king a 'pious petition' in which was demanded the immediate execution of 'all the existing laws against Catholic recusants and missionaries'. The king had married a Catholic princess and, against the opinion of the country, had granted toleration to her co-religionists. The wrath of the Commons was then turned against one of the king's chaplains, Richard Montagu, who in a theological tract effectively denied the Calvinist notion of predestination; the book was declared to be in contempt of the house, and the unfortunate divine was taken into custody.

Only now were the king's finances given consideration. His plea for wartime expenditure was not taken very seriously, on the good grounds that no proper plans or policies had been brought forward. The incompetence of Buckingham, in the ill-timed and ill-executed march towards Breda at the end of the previous reign, was also borne in mind; why give money to inept commanders? 'We know yet of no war,' Sir Robert Phelips said, 'nor of any enemy.' Parliament proposed to give to the king only one tenth of the sum which he had anticipated and, to compound the offence, the customs duties of tonnage and poundage were granted for only one year. All of his predecessors, ever since the time of Henry VI (1421–71), had been awarded them for the duration of their reigns. It is likely that the duties of one year were in fact only a temporary measure, until parliament had the opportunity to debate a permanent settlement. Yet this session had set a precedent. The resistance to increased taxation, and opposition to the king's religious policy, would be the prime movers of later discontent.

Charles was indignant at his lack of success, but he had no

strategy to deal with any parliamentary opposition; he had simply expected that his orders would be followed. Before any remonstrance could be entertained, in any case, the plague intervened. One courtier told his son that 'I . . . in earnest do marvel that anyone who may be called reasonable would be now in London'. The tolling of the neighbourhood bells could clearly be heard in the chamber of the Commons. Joseph Mead wrote, on 2 July, to one of his correspondents that 'my Lord Russell being to go to parliament, had his shoemaker to pull on his boots, who fell down dead of the plague in his presence'. On 11 July parliament was adjourned, to be convened once more in Oxford at the beginning of August.

The change of location did nothing to curb the rising hostility of the members to king and court. On a motion of Sir Edward Coke at the beginning of the session, the subsidies to the king were set to be thoroughly investigated, thus implying that parliament had the power to regulate the king's income at will. Another member rose brandishing a pardon the king had issued to a Jesuit, just the day after he had promised to uphold the 'pious petition' against Roman Catholics. A general silence followed. This affected the integrity and honour of the sovereign. It was agreed that they should wait to hear Charles's response. Charles had made contradictory promises to the French king and to parliament. Which would be the first to be broken?

Charles arrived from Woodstock three days later, and summoned the members to meet him in the hall of Christ Church. His mind was on matters of finance rather than of religion. He needed money for the fleet that Buckingham had collected, but the exchequer was bare. He found that his 'credit' was as yet too slim 'to set forth that navy now preparing'. He was, as usual, spare of words. He said that he would answer the religious petitions in two days' time.

It was still not at all clear how much money was required and to what purpose it would be put. Was a naval war against Spain contemplated? Or would an army be transported to aid the Palatinate? No one in the administration spoke with a certain voice. Why should the members of the Commons support a policy that they did not understand and upon which they had not been consulted? One declared that it would be better if parliament concentrated upon domestic and financial affairs, of which it did have cognizance, rather than concern itself with foreign imbroglios.

Buckingham now came under attack. It could be inferred from the speeches against him that he was incapable of controlling the government or of organizing any credible war effort. So now he bent with the wind. The information was conveyed that he and his master had never really believed in religious toleration for its own sake; it was merely a device to woo the Spanish and then the French. Buckingham was supposed to believe that the religious treaty drawn up with Louis XIII was merely for the sake of form, a piece of paper to appease the pope. The king, with his connivance, was ready to cultivate the Commons by turning on the Catholics.

'If you mean to put the laws into execution,' an envoy from the French court, Father Berulle, told him, 'I neither can nor will endure it, whatever sauce you may be pleased to add.'

'Begone,' Buckingham is supposed to have replied. 'I know that you are only at home in your breviary and your Mass.'

But the duke's evident lack of principle or consistency did not necessarily endear him to parliament. He had gathered together a fleet to boost his standing in the popular cause of war against Spain, but there was no money fully to prepare it. He was deemed to be too young, too rash and too inexperienced. In the ensuing debate, Sir Francis Seymour called out, 'Let us lay the fault where it is.' He then named the duke of Buckingham. Sir Edward Coke, sensing misgovernment and self-serving administrators, declared that 'the ship hath a great leak'. This was coming too close to the king. On 11 August he and his council decided that it was not fit for this parliament to continue. The excuse of the plague, steadily encroaching upon Oxford, was used to save Buckingham from possible impeachment. Where Charles believed that he was defending an honest and faithful minister, the parliamentarians were of the opinion that they were protecting the nation against a selfish and incapable favourite. The Oxford parliament had lasted eleven days. Charles blamed a few troublemakers and 'seditious men' for the turmoil, a miscalculation he would also make in later years.

It is already possible to gauge something of the king's character. He truly believed that his regal authority was paramount and that parliament was merely a compliant instrument to finance his requirements in war and peace. The simple declaration of his wishes was sufficient to command obedience. On state papers he would scrawl, 'Let it be done. C.R.' He had certain firm convictions that could not be altered by arguments or by events; if you agreed with him, you were a friend, but any who questioned his judgement were enemies from that moment forward. Once he had formulated a policy, he maintained it to the end. He could never see the point of view of anyone but himself, and this lack of imagination would one day cost him the throne.

He was so convinced of the rightness of his cause that he never acquired the easiness and bonhomie of either his father or his son. He remained to most of his subjects cold and reserved. The Venetian ambassador wrote that 'this king is so constituted by nature that he never obliges anyone, either by word or deed'. In succeeding years he would become enmeshed in the problems caused by his inability to use tact or craft in the affairs of the world. He once told a churchman that he could never have become a lawyer because 'I cannot defend a bad, nor yield in a good, cause'. He was in other words too righteous for his own good, or for the good of his kingdom.

The official war against Spain was declared in the early autumn of 1625, and in the same period a treaty was established between England and the Dutch republic. Yet the perennial problem of finance had not been solved and, as a desperate remedy, it was proposed that the crown jewels should be sold. The soldiers had been pressed into service but they remained unpaid; they roamed about Plymouth, where the people of south Devon would not or could not supply them with food. So the hungry men killed the available sheep and oxen in front of them. Three of their captains were named Bag, Cook and Love; the joke soon spread that they were Bag without money, Cook without Meat and Love without charity. This was a period when rumours spread throughout the country that the king had been touched by the plague; the report was untrue, but it represented the uncertain atmosphere of the time.

The English fleet under the command of Sir Edward Cecil, who had first seen service in the reign of Elizabeth, finally left harbour on 8 October after much abortive sailing through wind and rain. Its principal purpose was as yet undecided, except that it should in some way strike a blow against the Spanish coast. A council of war was called while the ships were at sea, when it was decided that an assault should be attempted upon Cadiz. The spirits of the men were raised when, at the advance of the English, the Spanish vessels fled the scene. The fort of Puntal, guarding the entrance to Cadiz harbour, was taken; but the attack had alerted the Spanish authorities to the dangers faced by the town.

While a blockade of Cadiz was attempted, news reached Cecil and his commanders that a large Spanish force was on its way to save the town; the English soldiers were disembarked and hurried to meet the threat, but the report was false. No enemy was in sight. Their forced march under a hot Spanish sun, however, had left them without provisions. Casks of wine were taken from neighbouring villages and dwellings; the men gorged themselves on the drink until they were senseless. It was said that every man became his own vintner. The Spanish defenders of Cadiz fell upon them and engaged in a general frenzy of slaughter. The siege of Cadiz, and the occupation of Puntal, were therefore abandoned in embarrassing failure.

The English vessels had also been charged to intercept the Spanish silver sailing from Mexico, but they were in no condition to confront anything. Their hulks were rotten, and their tackle frail. Whether through corruption or neglect, their supplies had been insufficient from the beginning. The drink, possibly a medley of wine and water, was foul; the food was evil-smelling 'so as no dog in Paris Garden would eat it'. Paris Garden was part of the noisome suburb of Southwark. In the middle of November Cecil ordered his ships to return to England. It was a complete, and humiliating, fiasco. An enquiry was held, but such was the conflicting evidence and prejudiced testimony that it was considered best to bury the matter in a public silence.

An attempt was then made to avert the wrath of the country. At the beginning of November the execution of the penal laws against the Catholics was instituted once more; the fines and confiscations were to be used for the defence of the realm. It was reported that at Whitehall 'they look strange on a papist'. Yet there was no stronger papist than the queen. Charles's disillusion with Louis XIII for failing to assist him now seems to have extended to his sister, and especially to her entourage of Capuchin friars. Their rituals and orisons were not welcome at the English court, in which Buckingham was still hoping to lead a Protestant league against Spanish and imperial pretensions.

The king and queen were dining together when her Catholic confessor tried to anticipate the grace being said by a Protestant cleric. He began praying in Latin, in a loud voice, according to Joseph Mead, 'with such a confusion, that the king, in a great passion, instantly rose from the table, and, taking the queen by the hand, retired into the bedchamber. Was this not a priestly discretion?' Charles was heard to state that a man must be master in his own house. But he had also to prove himself master of his own kingdom.

12

A fall from grace

The day of Charles's formal coronation came on Candlemas, 2 February 1626, a little under a year since his accession to the throne. Henrietta Maria refused to accompany her husband to what she considered to be an heretical service, and so he proceeded alone; the queen watched some of the events from an apartment in the gatehouse of the palace yard. Charles did not go on the customary procession through the streets of London, however, and there was neither banquet nor masque after the ceremony; the plague was still leaving its mark. There was little rejoicing at the service itself. When the newly crowned king was presented to the people, they remained largely silent. The earl of Arundel, the lord marshal, then ordered them to cry out 'God save King Charles' at which juncture a few shouts of homage were heard.

Charles wore a cloak of white rather than a robe of regal scarlet; this was considered by many to be an unfortunate innovation in an ancient ceremony. The coronation oath was also carefully changed by William Laud, the bishop of St David's, with a prayer that the king might have 'Peter's key of discipline, Paul's doctrine'. This was not at the time considered to be ominous but, at a later date, Laud was accused of conferring absolute power upon the king to the injury of the people. Any ill will or resentment was at this time, however, largely directed against Buckingham rather than his sovereign.

Parliament met four days later in a state of seething discontent at Buckingham's mismanagement of the expedition to Cadiz. He may have tried to waive blame by pleading that he had been conducting diplomatic negotiations at the time in The Hague, but this did not satisfy the angry members. Sir John Eliot, member for St Germans in Cornwall, had witnessed the return of the fleet to Plymouth after the debacle; he had seen the men, diseased and half-starved, staggering off their ships. He had also seen some of them die in the streets, mortally infecting the people of the town. He did not forget these scenes of suffering, and he placed all the blame for them on the folly and pride of the king's favourite.

The king opened proceedings with a customary short and blunt speech. 'I mean to show what I should speak', he said, 'in actions.' He offered no apologies or explanations for what had transpired; he simply asked for more money. When Eliot rose to speak he demanded that no further supply should be granted until an account had been given of previous sums. He called for the inspection of the admiralty ledgers which, as vice-admiral of Devon, he was uniquely well placed to examine.

But he made a wider plea to the king. 'Sir, I beseech you cast your eyes about! View the state we are in! Consider the loss we have received! Weigh the wrecked and ruined honour of our nation!' Eliot might be described as one of the first great parliamentarians in English history, ready to curb the abuses of the royal prerogative. He went on to say that 'our honour is ruined, our ships are sunk, our men perished; not by the sword, not by the enemy, not by chance, but, as the strongest predictions had discerned and made it apparent beforehand, by those we trust'. The aspects of international affairs were not promising. The Catholic forces of the Holy Roman Emperor were advancing through Bohemia and Germany; the Protestants of France were being threatened, and even destroyed, by the French king.

A committee was established in order to enquire into the problems of the state finances, but it came to no settled conclusions. On 10 March, therefore, Charles let it be known that he wished for an immediate supply for the necessities of the state without any further questions of his past or future conduct being raised. The statement raised the temperature of the debates. The member for Boroughbridge,

Sir Ferdinando Fairfax, wrote to his father that 'if we give nothing, we not only incense the king, who is in his own nature extremely stiff, but endanger a ruin of the commonweal, as things now stand; and if we do give, it may perhaps not be employed in the right way, and the more we part with, the more we shall want another time to bestow'.

It was now generally believed that the cause of all grievances was the duke of Buckingham. He had appointed incompetent officers and was responsible for the calamity at Cadiz. He had taken Crown lands for his friends and family. He had sold many of the offices of state and acquired others for his own aggrandizement. His mother and his father-in-law were both recusants, and might be considered enemies of the state. He was the man to be named.

The king replied to the parliamentarians at Whitehall five days later in a speech in which he declared that 'I would not have the House to question my servants, much less one that is so near me'. He added that 'I would you would hasten for my supply, or else it will be worse for yourselves, for if any ill happen, I think I shall be the last that shall feel it'. Sir John Eliot, addressing his colleagues two days later, counselled steadfastness. 'We have had a representation of great fear,' he said, 'but I hope that shall not darken our understandings.' The king once more ordered them to desist. 'Remember', Charles told them, 'that parliaments are altogether in my power for their calling, sitting, and dissolution; therefore, as I find their fruits good or evil, they are to continue, or not to be.'

The Commons, in no mood now for retreat, still pursued the duke; they were hounds slipped off the leash, all the more confident because they knew that the Lords were supporting them; the nobility, too, had had enough of the overweening favourite. The old peerage were incensed by his control of patronage and by his domination of the king. The earl of Bristol, who as ambassador at the court of Spain had witnessed the conduct of Buckingham in Madrid, brought his own testimony against the favourite. He charged him with the attempt to change the prince's religion; he accused him of kneeling to the sacrament 'to give the Spaniards a hope of the prince's conversion'. He was in effect denouncing Buckingham for treason.

The king was irate at what he considered to be the vainglory of the houses. Yet they were not to be diverted. On 10 May a deputation was drawn up to prepare the articles of impeachment against Buckingham; one of its members, Sir Dudley Digges, stated in perhaps unprecedented terms that 'the laws of England have taught us that kings cannot command ill or unlawful things. And whatsoever ill events succeed, the executioners of such designs must answer for them.' Digges also compared Buckingham to a comet, exhaled 'out of base and putrid matter'. When the members of the deputation presented themselves to Buckingham, however, it was reported that he laughed in their faces. The duke knew the loyalty, or rigidity, of the king. Charles would never abandon him.

The day of the impeachment debate was an occasion for passion and theatrical confrontation. When one member, John Glanville, delivered an exordium in favour of parliament Buckingham 'jeered and fleered' him. 'My lord,' Glanville replied, 'do you jeer me? Are these things to be jeered at? My lord, I can show you a man of greater blood than your lordship, as high in place and power, and as deep in the favour of the king as you, who hath been hanged for as small a crime as the least of these articles contain.'

Sir John Eliot rose to launch a general invective against the favourite. 'What vast treasures he has gotten! What infinite sums of money, and what a mass of lands!' The banquets, the buildings, the costumes, the gold and the silver were the visible tokens of his greed; his wealth was keeping the sovereign, and the nation, poor. Eliot then hinted at the prevailing rumour that Buckingham and his mother had poisoned James I. He compared the duke to a legendary beast, known to the ancients as Stellionatus, that was 'so blurred, so spotted' that it was filled with foulness. By this extraordinary speech, the king was of course much offended.

On the following day, 11 May, the king visited the Lords where he tried to exonerate Buckingham from all the charges attached to him by the Commons. 'I can bear witness,' he said, 'to clear him in every one of them.' On the same day the lower house broke up in turmoil when it was discovered that Sir John Eliot and Sir Dudley Digges had been taken to the Tower. When the Speaker rose on 12 May to commence business he was told to 'sit down'. There was to be 'no business until we are righted in our liberties'. The French ambassador warned the king that if his power did not prevail, he would be as impotent as the doge of Venice, who could do nothing without the approval of his senate.

Parliament stood firm and finally prevailed. Within a week both Digges and Eliot were set at liberty. It was not a good precedent for the king, who appeared to be resolute but in truth prevaricated. He then compounded the offence by appointing Buckingham to be chancellor of the university at Cambridge; such was the displeasure of the Commons that they drew up a general remonstrance for Buckingham's dismissal from public life.

The war of words now intensified. Charles responded with the demand that parliament should proceed immediately to pass a Subsidy Bill, furnishing him with more funds, or he would be obliged 'to use other resolutions'. The Commons debated the matter and decided that the remonstrance should come before any bill for subsidies. They had not in fact proved the charges of venality and corruption laid against Buckingham, but they now pressed for his forced resignation on the sole grounds that the Commons did not trust him. If they succeeded in their purpose, their authority would then outweigh that of the sovereign himself.

If parliament on the other hand were forced to yield, and to grant Charles supply without the redress of grievances, it would set an unfortunate precedent in which the king might be the permanent victor; the members did not, in a current phrase, wish to give posterity a cause to curse them. Court and parliament, at cross-purposes one with another, had reached an impasse. A conversation between the king and Buckingham was overheard and widely reported. 'I have in a manner lost the love of my subjects,' Charles is supposed to have told him. 'What wouldst thou have me do?' On 14 June the king determined to dissolve parliament. The Lords begged for two days more to resolve the situation. The king replied quickly enough. 'Not a minute.'

The day before the dissolution of what was called 'this great, warm, ruffling parliament' a storm of thunder, lightning and hail fell upon the Thames at Westminster and created the phenomenon of a 'whirlwater' or 'water-pillar'. The water was dissolved into a mist and formed a great revolving funnel some 30 yards across and 10 feet in height; the interior was hollow and white with froth. This prodigy of nature crossed the Thames and then began to beat against the walls of the garden of York House, the residence of the duke of Buckingham; as it struck against the bricks it broke into a thick smoke, as if it came from a chimney, and rose high into the air. It then vanished out of sight with two or three peals of thunder. It was considered to be an omen, and perhaps a warning to the duke himself.

Handbills were printed on clandestine presses and distributed through the streets of London.

> Who rules the kingdom? *The king.*
> Who rules the king? *The duke.*
> Who rules the duke? *The devil.*

Three days after the dissolution the king ordered that all copies of the parliamentary remonstrance against Buckingham should be destroyed. By continuing to favour the duke, Charles had provoked a determined and vocal opposition in parliament; the antagonism did not as yet directly touch the person of the king himself, but there were some who looked ahead to possible changes in public affairs. A great constitutional historian, Leopold von Ranke, once suggested that the coming conflict between king and parliament was the product of 'historical necessity'; whether we accept the phrase or not, it is at least evident that there were forces at work that could not easily be contained or averted.

In the course of this parliament, amid the turmoil of domestic affairs, the bishops had also been considering the issues of religion. In particular they had debated the controversy between the puritan members of the Church and those who were already known as 'Arminians'. These latter were the clergy who believed in the primacy of order and ritual in the customary ceremonies; they preached against predestination and in favour of the sacraments, and had already earned the condemnation of the Calvinists at the Synod of Dort seven years earlier. Some of them were dismissed as mere papists under another name, but in fact they were as much estranged from the Catholic communion as they were from the puritan congregation; they wished for a purified national Church, and their most significant supporter was already William Laud, a prominent bishop now in royal favour. The English Arminians in turn became known as 'Laudians', with one of their central precepts concerning 'the beauty of holiness' by which they meant genuflections and bowings as well as painted images. There was even room to be made for an incense pot.

The Arminians had been in an equivocal position during the previous reign because of James's residual Calvinist sympathies and his unwillingness to countenance doctrinal controversy. His son was made of sterner, or more unbending, material. In the weeks after James's death, Bishop Laud prepared for the new king a list of senior churchmen, with the letters 'O' or 'P' appended to their names; 'O' meant orthodox and 'P' signalled a puritan. So the lines were drawn.

The powerful bias towards 'adoration', with all the ritual and formality it implied, was deeply congenial to the young king who had already brought order and ceremony to his court; just as he delighted in masques, so he wished for a religion of splendour and mystery. Charles had in any case a deep aversion to puritanism in all of its forms, which he associated with disobedience and the dreadful notion of 'popularity'; he thought of cobblers and tailors and sharp-tongued dogmatists. Above all else he wanted a well-ordered and disciplined Church, maintaining undeviating policies as well as uniform customs, with the bishops as its principal representatives. It was to be a bulwark in his defence of national stability. Laud himself used to quote the phrase *'stare super antiquas vias'* – it was important to stand upon ancient roads.

With a sermon delivered in the summer of 1626, Laud aimed a direct hit against the puritans by claiming that the Calvinists were essentially anti-authoritarian and therefore anti-monarchical. In the following year George Abbot was deprived of his powers as archbishop of Canterbury and replaced by a commission of anti-Calvinist bishops. When one Calvinist bishop, Davenant of Salisbury, delivered a sermon in which he defended the doctrine of predestination, he was summoned before the privy council; after the prelate had kissed the king's hand, Charles informed him that 'he would not have this high point meddled withal or debated, either the one way or the other, because it was too high for the people's understanding'. After 1628 no Calvinist preachers were allowed to stand at Paul's

Cross, the centre for London sermons. A joke soon followed, asking a question about the Arminians' beliefs.

'What do the Arminians hold?'
'All the best livings in England.'

Yet the Calvinists, and the puritans, did not go gently into the dark. The victory of the Laudian cause in the king's counsels, more than anything else, stirred the enmity between opposing religious camps that defined the last years of his reign. It should be added, however, that these doctrinal discontents wafted over the heads of most parish clergy and their congregations who attended church as a matter of habit and took a simple attitude towards the gospels and the commandments.

Within a few weeks of the dissolution of parliament Charles finally determined to banish his wife's priests and ladies-in-waiting from his court. While parliament had still been in session the queen's religious counsellors advised her to go on a pilgrimage to Tyburn, in bare feet, in order to pray for the souls of those Catholics who had been executed there. It was soon murmured she had offered up her prayers for the cause of dead traitors rather than of martyrs.

Resentment, and even anger, had already risen between husband and wife. She was merry enough with her French followers but in the presence of the king she was sullen and morose; she apparently took no delight in his company. They quarrelled over her wish to distribute some of her lands and houses among her entourage. 'Take your lands to yourself,' Charles himself reports her as saying. 'If I have no power to put whom I will into these places, I will have neither lands nor houses of you. Give me what you think fit by way of pension.'

'Remember to whom you speak,' the king replied. 'You ought not to use me so.'

They continued to argue and, in the king's own recollection of the scene, 'then I made her both hear me and end that discourse'. The court, too, had ears.

At the beginning of August, after a meeting of the privy council, Charles called for the queen. She declined the invitation on the grounds that she had a toothache. So with his council in attendance he proceeded to the queen's private chambers where he found her

French attendants, according to a contemporary letter-writer, Mr Pory, 'unreverently dancing and curvetting in her presence'. He summarily brought the party to a close, and took Henrietta Maria to his own chambers where he told her that he was sending the French attendants back to Paris 'for the good of herself and the nation'. The queen was momentarily bewildered but then, in a fit of temper or frustration, broke the windows in the chamber with her bare hands in order to speak to her people in the courtyard below. Whereupon the women 'howled and lamented as if they were going to an execution'.

The loudest protests could not prevail against the king's angry will. For some days the French refused to leave the queen's court. At that point Charles lost all patience. He commanded Buckingham 'to send all the French away tomorrow out of the town; if you can, by fair means – but stick not long in disputing – otherwise force them away, driving them away like so many wild beasts until you have shipped them, and so the devil go with them! Let me hear of no answer but the performance of my command.' He could use a peremptory tone even with his favourite.

Eventually, under the escort of the Yeomen of the Guard, the French boarded the vessels for their return. As they went down to the Thames by the river stairs of Denmark House, a crowd of Londoners hooted and jeered at them; one of them threw a stone that knocked off the hat of Mme de Saint-Georges. The whole episode incensed the French king, who told the English envoy that his sister had been cruelly treated. It was not a propitious moment to alienate Louis XIII.

The dissolution of the parliament, for example, led ineluctably to urgent attempts to raise money for the king's war against Spain. A loan of £100,000 was requested from the merchants of London, with the crown jewels as security. The appeal was denied. In the following month it was proposed that the freeholders of the various counties would provide a 'free gift' to the Crown; the clergy were ordered 'to stir up all sorts of people to express their zeal to God and their duty to the king'. Charles also decided that he must continue to levy the customs revenues of 'tonnage and poundage' even though parliament had not given its consent. When contributions to the 'free gift' were about to be collected in Westminster

Hall, the cry was raised of 'A parliament! A parliament!' Throughout August and September the refusal to contribute to the king's coffers became widespread. It was then decreed that the king's plate should be sold.

In the middle of August 200 pressed soldiers and sailors made their weary way from Portsmouth to London in order to demand the money still owed to them. By chance or design they came upon the duke of Buckingham's coach; they stopped it and pleaded for redress. Buckingham promised to deal with their demands later in the day, but he escaped by way of the Thames and returned to the security of York House. This was in any case a time of deep distress among the general populace. The great nineteenth-century historian of prices, Thorold Rogers, stated that 'I am convinced, from the comparison I have been able to make between wages, rents and prices, that it was a period of excessive misery among the mass of the people and the tenants, a time in which a few might have become rich, while the many were crushed down into hopeless and almost permanent indigence'. The condition of England now looked to some to be beyond repair. One contemporary asked, 'Is it not time to pray?'

13

Take that slime away

The king's war against Spain and the imperial forces was not going well. Christian of Denmark had depended upon subsidies from his nephew, Charles, but of course no money was forthcoming; on 27 August 1626, his demoralized forces were defeated by the armies of the Catholic League at Lutter in Lower Saxony. As a result the Protestants of north-west Europe could become the prey of the imperialist armies. On hearing the news of the battle Charles abandoned his summer progress and returned to London where he told the Danish ambassador that he would defend King Christian 'even at the risk of his own crown and hazarding his life'. The king's council wished to send four regiments, each comprising 1,000 men, to Denmark, but how were they to be paid?

After the failure of the 'free gift' proposed for the king, and the small sums of money raised by the sale of his plate, the time had come for more severe and aggressive measures. In the autumn of 1626 the king imposed what was essentially a forced loan, and demanded from the counties the equivalent of five parliamentary subsidies. His decision was in part prompted by his deep reluctance to call another parliament. He would manage his finances without the meddling of certain malicious members. He wrote to the various lords-lieutenant of the counties ordering them to put forward the names of their local dignitaries, with details of the amounts they could afford; he also wrote to the peers, asking them to be generous in their financial support. He condemned those who cried out against the loans as 'certain evil-disposed persons'; he declared that he must have the money to subsidize himself and his armed forces and that the duty of all true subjects, in the absence of parliamentary agreement, was 'to be a law unto themselves'. He might have added, in a phrase of the period, that 'need knows no law'.

The general response of the country seems for once to have been favourable. The exigencies of the country, and the possible defeat of the Protestant cause, prompted most communities into payment. It was granted that, in an emergency, the king had the right to call upon special aid. The people of Thetford in Norfolk, for example, 'were all very willing to yield'. By November the forced tax had raised something close to £250,000, sufficient for the king's immediate requirements. Charles himself admitted that the money had been 'more readily furnished than I could have expected in these needy times'.

The judiciary was uncertain about the legality of any forced loan, however, and refused to sign a paper of consent to its imposition. The king called in the chief justice and dismissed him from his office as a warning and encouragement to others. He threatened to sweep all recalcitrant magistrates from their benches, but in so doing he damaged the authority of the judges as well as his own. It was reported that from this time forward they were no longer considered to be impartial or disinterested, and it was long remembered that the king had demanded the resignations of those who refused to accede to his requests. If they possessed opinions of their own, they were to be treated with contempt.

Some were still unwilling to pay the forced loan. The wealthier of these recalcitrants were summoned before the privy council, where they were either dispatched to prison or confined in private houses away from their homes and families; the poorer of them were pressed into the army or navy, where their bodies might serve instead of their money. Among those who refused payment were five knights, who decided to challenge the legality of the loan in the courts and were subsequently placed in their county prisons. They would become the cause of much discontent against the king.

Another opponent acquired great popularity in later years. John

Hampden, a Buckinghamshire squire and former member of parliament, was summoned at the end of January 1627 to explain his refusal to pay the forced loan. 'I could be content to lend,' he replied, 'but fear to draw on myself that curse in Magna Carta which should be read twice a year against those who infringe it.' He was claiming, in other words, that the king had challenged the fundamental rights and liberties of the people. He was consigned to the Gatehouse prison at Westminster for a year and was so strictly held that, according to a contemporary account, 'he never did afterwards look like the same man he was before'. Fifteen years later, in the same prison, Richard Lovelace wrote that:

> Stone walls do not a prison make,
> Nor iron bars a cage . . .

Hampden's mind remained at liberty. He became a celebrated parliamentary commander in the eventual civil war.

Charles's angry will may have begun to cloud his judgement. On the urgent submissions of the duke of Buckingham, it was now proposed to send a naval expedition against France in order to help the rebellion of the Huguenots against Louis XIII. For some months an unofficial maritime war had been taking place between the two countries, leading to the seizure of goods and ships in mutually escalating fashion. At the beginning of December 1626, an order was issued for the capture of all French vessels found in English waters. Three weeks later it was discovered that six or eight ships purchased by Louis from the Low Countries were now at Le Havre ready to sail against England; they had to be either taken or destroyed.

The king was at this time contemplating a war against both France and Spain. To fight against one power was serious enough, but to fight against two at the same time might have been considered akin to folly. In the spring of 1627 new levies of men were dispatched to Portsmouth. It was the old story. Many of them were described as 'base rogues'; there was no clothing for them, and the surgeons had not been paid. Their lordships in the council were happy to issue general orders without caring to follow them up; they were incapable of estimating military costs, and were often ignorant of local geography. They sent regiments to be billeted without informing the relevant county authorities. They were preparing to send wheat to the proposed army in France, but provided no means to grind it. The absence of any working bureaucracy proved fatal. The confusion could have been prevented only if local self-government had been somehow rendered compatible with national conscription. How could a war in Europe be maintained by the men and administrative machinery of the parishes and counties? A national army raised to fight overseas could be managed only by some form of central administration. The conditions of Stuart England made that impossible. So chaos ensued. The pressed men appeared at Portsmouth:

> With an old motley coat and a malmsey nose,
> With an old jerkin that's out at the elbows,
> And with an old pair of boots drawn on without hose,
> Stuffed with rags instead of toes.

The talk of a further expedition against France meant that London, according to Edward Hyde, earl of Clarendon, 'was full of soldiers, and of young gentlemen who intended to be soldiers, or as like them as they could; great licence used of all kinds, in clothes, in diet, in gaming'. It was a city of dice and whores.

On 11 June the king himself reviewed the fleet at Portsmouth and dined aboard the admiral's vessel, where all were merry. The jokes and antics of the king's fool, Archie, were said to have been memorable. The notion of English superiority at sea, despite the failure at Cadiz, persisted. The fleet sailed on 27 June 1627, with two principal purposes. The first was to contest the ambition of Richelieu, the pre-eminent minister of Louis XIII, to make his sovereign the master of the sea. That role was reserved for England. The second aim of the enterprise was to transport certain regiments to the port of La Rochelle, on the Atlantic coast of France; the Huguenots of that town had taken over its administration and were engaged in a struggle for their religious liberty with the French king. The neighbouring island of Rhé was already under royal control. Buckingham's strategy was to occupy that part of it which managed the approaches to La Rochelle.

So on the afternoon of 12 July the men leapt into the landing craft, covered by the fire from their ships. Buckingham was everywhere among them, encouraging them and urging them on. Yet his bravado was not enough. The men themselves were ill-disciplined, and not all of them were inclined to fight; some lingered on board and others did not take up the positions assigned to them. Those who reached the shore were in no hurry to move against the enemy. Buckingham went among them with his cudgel to drive them forward. All this was to no avail.

The French seized the opportunity and rode down upon the English bands, threatening to drive them into the sea. Yet somehow a line of defence was established and the French forces, in difficult and swampy terrain, decided to retreat to the safe fortifications of the citadel of St Martin. Buckingham then ordered that the fort should be placed under siege.

The siege turned into a blockade, but the suffering multiplied on both sides. The women and children within the fort cried out for mercy and for pity, where none were available, while Buckingham's men were worn down by disease and lack of rations. He sent urgent messages to London for more troops and more supplies but the exchequer was, as always, empty. As winter came closer, the English forces grew weaker; they were now practically without food, money, or ammunition. It was reported in the middle of October that the English officers on Rhé were 'looking themselves blind' by scanning the seas with their telescopes for the sight of English ships.

A last desperate assault was made upon the fort, but it was discovered that the scaling ladders were too short. There was nothing for it but to retreat. Yet even this was bungled. On 30 October the English were about to cross by wooden bridge to a smaller island from which they hoped to embark upon their ships; but it was not properly defended. Under prolonged fire the infantry and cavalry were lost in confusion. Many of them were shot down, while others drowned. It was estimated that 4,000 Englishmen had been killed, while the rest eventually made their weary way back to Portsmouth or to Plymouth. La Rochelle had not been relieved. A contemporary, Denzil Holles, observed that 'every man knows that, since England was England, it received not so dishonourable a blow'. It was written of Buckingham himself:

> And now, just God, I humbly pray
> That thou wilt take that slime away.

It was the second signal disaster, in the space of two years, under the duke's command. His flags were now hanging in the cathedral of Notre Dame as a token of the nation's shame. The people were soon calling him 'the duke of Fuckingham'. Yet the king greeted his favourite with a cheerful face and effectively placed all the blame upon his own shoulders. 'In this action you have had honour,' Charles told him, 'all the shame must light upon us here remaining at home.' In truth Buckingham was not entirely culpable. He was a brave man but he was no strategist, a failure compounded by his scant attention to detail. Much of the fault, however, must lie with the administration at home that signally failed to provide the requisite money and supplies to its army overseas.

The king called a council of war in which he pressed for money to finance another expedition to La Rochelle which he had bound himself in honour to defend. His advisers counselled him once more to call parliament. It was the only way to raise money without a thousand complaints and legal challenges. Despite the fact that he expected only remonstrance and debate and petition from its members, he suffered himself to be persuaded.

The atmosphere of parliament in 1628 was not promising. At the beginning of February, a month before the members met, letters had been sent out by the king explaining the necessity for 'ship-money' to furnish another fleet. 'Ship-money' had been a medieval device by which at times of crisis the navy was supplied with boats from the maritime towns; Charles now wished to extend ship-money over the entire country, and to raise it in terms of coin rather than craft. He ordered that the relevant county officials should 'proceed according to the true worth of men's lands and estates'. The fresh attempt to levy taxes, on a dubious legal principle, provoked furious discontent. Many of the towns and counties refused to pay. Lincolnshire rejected 'the unusual and unexpected charge'; Somerset excused itself on the grounds that it 'will be a precedent of a charge which neither they nor their predecessors did ever bear'. Charles, realizing that his will would be openly flouted and his orders disobeyed, conceded the matter a few days later. He had decided 'wholly to rely on the love of our people in parliament'.

He was deluding himself. Love was in short supply at Westminster. The king and favourite had not prepared the ground adequately for further demands upon the nation's resources, and the court had made little effort to pack the Commons with its natural supporters at a time of crisis. A large number of those who met on 17 March 1628 were local men with local grievances; those who had refused to support the forced loan, for example, were almost sure of seats. A dependant of the duke of Buckingham, Sir Robert Pye, was named for one of the constituencies. The rallying cry went up for 'A Pye! A Pye! A Pye!' To which his adversaries called out 'A pudding! A pudding! A pudding!' and others joined in with 'A lie! A lie! A lie!' It was believed that the 'patriots' might trump the 'court party', and that parliament would not last eight days. It was even suspected by some that Charles and Buckingham had engineered such a result. If the parliament did not vote funds to the king, he would dismiss it and blame it for weakness and incapacity at a time of national danger.

When the king opened proceedings he declared that 'these are times for action'; he wanted money, and was not interested in 'tedious consultations'. He then piled insult upon insult by claiming that he did not intend to threaten them 'for I scorn to threaten any but my equals'. It was becoming clear that the major confrontation would not be with Buckingham, the object of the previous parliament, but with the king himself.

The mood of the Commons was not helped by the captivity of the five knights who, in the previous year, had been imprisoned for declining to pay the forced loan to the king. It was pleaded on their behalf that to refuse an illegal loan was no crime; if there was no crime, they could not remain in prison. The knights brought forward writs of habeas corpus to free themselves from illegal detention and declared that, according to Magna Carta, 'no man should be imprisoned except by the legal judgement of his peers or by the law of the land'.

The king's defenders stated in return that the knights were imprisoned at the especial command of their sovereign, and that no other cause was necessary. There followed suitable obfuscation from the judges of the case. They decreed that they would not give the prisoners bail, but that the crown prosecution should at some stage show cause for their further detention. It was an ambiguous judgment but contemporary observers interpreted it as a victory for the king. He would now be able to commit his subjects to prison without due cause. No redress against his sovereign will was permitted.

Sir Edward Coke therefore brought in a bill that prohibited anyone from being detained in prison without trial for more than two months; but this was not enough to avert the growing anger of the Commons. If the king could imprison his subjects for not providing him with money, as he had done in the case of the dissenting knights, where would his dominion end? 'Upon this dispute,' Eliot declared, 'not alone our lands and goods are engaged, but all that we call ours. These rights, these privileges, which made our fathers free men, are in question.' Thomas Wentworth, soon to become one of the most prominent men of the age, stood up to argue that there should be no more illegal imprisonment, no more pressing of men for foreign service, no forced loans and no billeting of soldiers on unwilling households.

At the beginning of April a committee of the Commons agreed three resolutions to be put to the king. No free man might be consigned to prison without cause; everyone had the right to a writ of habeas corpus; every prisoner was to be freed or bailed if no cause could be shown for his detention. The king was growing impatient. He wished the members to vote him financial supply without any delay. He did not understand why they were so insistent upon their so-called liberties. 'For God's sake,' he said, 'why should any hinder them of their liberties?' Parliament was not to be moved. The members decided to draw up a bill on the liberty of persons and property before even considering any matters of money.

Charles seemed to believe that this was no longer a simple matter of grievances to be redressed in the ancient fashion, but an attempt to limit royal sovereignty. A message came to the Commons that the king had taken note that 'this House pressed not upon the abuses of power but upon power itself'. 'Power' was a grand word, but what was its meaning? The debate continued, with the king suggesting that all would be well if only the monetary supply was granted. It was a question of relying upon 'his royal word and promise'. On 5 May a parliamentary remonstrance was presented to him on the matters under dispute. The king, in reply, was willing to pledge that he would not act in the manner he had done in the past; but he refused to allow that any of his future actions could be determined by parliament. The uses of 'power' could be curtailed, in other words, but 'power' itself remained his to wield as he saw fit.

This was not a satisfactory conclusion. The royal promises were too vague. No fundamental principles had been agreed. It was still not clear whether the king was above the law or the law above the king. A committee was drawn up to prepare a 'petition of right' which itself became an important statement of constitutional principle; the notable historian, Thomas Babington Macaulay described it as 'the second great charter of the liberties of England'. It cited the statutes passed in the reigns of Edward I and Edward III; it deplored the fact that 'your people have been in diverse places assembled and required to lend certain sums of money unto your majesty', and demanded that 'no freeman be taken or imprisoned' without due process of law. It also complained that 'great companies of soldiers and mariners have been dispersed into diverse counties of the realm'. The petition really contained nothing novel or radical, despite the king's autocratic sensitivities, and can most profitably be interpreted as a conservative document essentially restating what many considered to be the ancient constitution of the country. It can be concluded, however, that the king was not trusted in the same way as some of his predecessors.

By the end of May, after much debate, the petition had been adopted by both the Commons and the Lords; to sweeten what might be for Charles a bitter pill it was also agreed to offer the king five subsidies. In other circumstances he would no doubt have rejected the petition as a sheer abrogation of his rights and duties, but his foreign policy was in disarray. La Rochelle had still received no aid from England, despite the promises the king had made, and the fall of key German towns to the imperialist forces meant that English intervention in north-western Europe had for all practical purposes come to an inglorious end.

So the king was in urgent need of the money from parliament if he was to retain any shred of honour in foreign policy. Yet he prevaricated. He asked the judges certain leading questions concerning the petition, to which they gave cautious replies. 'Gentlemen,' he told the assembled parliamentarians before granting them his answer, 'I am come here to perform my duty. I think no man can think it long, since I have not taken so many days in answering the petition as you spent weeks in framing it . . .' His impatience was clear. With his finances in parlous state, and his foreign devices wrecked, all these men could do was debate and debate about the 'rights' of the people. The king then announced his reply to the petition. He declared merely that 'right should be done according to the laws and customs of the realm'. His words gave no comfort at all, since it was still the privilege of the king to judge what those 'laws' and 'customs' actually were.

The men of parliament were neither impressed nor reassured. When they met to consider their answer they remained seated for a while in a profound and melancholy silence; when certain members did eventually rise to their feet, their speeches were often interrupted by their tears. Sir John Eliot summoned up their spirits with the stern declaration that at home and abroad all was confused and uncertain. Our friends overseas had been defeated, and our enemies had prospered. The cause of Protestantism in Germany, and the recapture of the Palatinate, had been sacrificed as a result of the king's obsessions with a war against the French king. One member, Humphrey May, was about to interrupt him; but the rest of the house called out to Eliot, 'Go on! Go on!'

'If he goes on,' May said, 'I hope that I may myself go out.'

'Begone! Begone!'

But May stayed to listen to Eliot's oratory. 'Witness [the journey] to Cadiz! Witness the next! Witness that to Rhé! Witness the last! And I pray to God we shall never have more such witnesses! . . . Witness all! What losses we have sustained! How we are impaired in munition, in ships, in men!' At the close of his impassioned peroration he demanded a statement of grievances, or 'remonstrance', to be addressed to the king.

It seems that he was about to name Buckingham as the source of all regal problems, but he was stopped from doing so by the Speaker. The king then sent a message, absolutely forbidding the members further to discuss matters of state on pain of instant dismissal. In the face of this command, touching the liberties of parliament, one member after another rose to speak; others sat on the benches and wept. Joseph Mead, the contemporary writer of newsletters, reported that 'there appeared such a spectacle of passions as the like had seldom been seen in such an assembly, some weeping, some expostulating, some prophesying of the fatal ruin of our kingdom . . . I have been told by a Parliament man that there were above an hundred weeping eyes; many who offered to speak being interrupted and silenced by their own passions.' It was a sensitive and tearful age, in which political and religious controversy were not to be distinguished from personal passion. Eventually Sir Edward Coke rose to ask, 'Why may we not name those that are the cause of all our evils? The duke of Buckingham – that *man* is *the grievance of grievances.*' At that remark the Commons erupted in acclamations. It was said that, when one good hound recovers the scent, the rest come in with a full cry.

On 7 June Charles, now aware of the danger to his favourite and acutely conscious that his financial needs must be satisfied, took his seat upon the throne in the Lords. In front of the peers, and the members of the Commons who crowded to the bar, he ordered that his previous inconclusive answer to the 'petition of right' should be removed and that new words take its place. '*Soit droit fait comme il est désiré.*' This was the usual formula of assent that conferred legality on parliamentary measures: 'Let right be done as is desired.' He then added that 'now I have performed my part. If this parliament have not a happy conclusion, the sin is yours. I am free from it.' The result was delight in parliament itself, and celebration in the streets beyond; the bells were rung and the bonfires were kindled.

Yet the general satisfaction did not prevent parliament from pressing still further against the king. The remonstrance against Buckingham was presented to Charles on 17 June, to which he responded with a few words. He would consider their grievances 'as they should deserve'. Buckingham himself was not disturbed by the charges against him and is reported to have said that 'it makes no matter what the Commons or parliament do, for without my leave and authority they shall not be able to touch the hair of a dog'.

The Commons, not happy with the royal reception of their remonstrance, then went into committee on the question of the king's finances. The king ordained that the parliament should end in the next week. Whereupon a second remonstrance was prepared declaring that the king's collection of customs duties and other taxes without parliamentary assent was 'a breach of the fundamental liberties of this kingdom'. Before the debate could commence the king prorogued the assembly.

So ended the parliamentary session. It has sometimes been seen as one of the most significant in the history of that institution. The members had reminded the king that he was not permitted to violate the liberties of his subjects, and they had obtained from him the recognition of those rights they believed to be most important. Yet the celebrations on the street were perhaps premature. Three days after the conclusion of the proceedings, the king ordered a recall of the second answer he had given 'to be made waste paper'. He also ordered the reprinting of his first unsatisfactory answer, together with a series of qualifications to his second answer. In his closing speech to parliament, he had said that 'my meaning . . . was not to grant any new privileges but to re-edify your old', which could mean anything or nothing.

He prevaricated in his usual fashion, therefore, and as a result diminished the respect in which he was held. It was difficult to believe now in his good faith. One contemporary diarist, John Rous, noted that 'our king's proceedings have caused men's minds to be incensed, to rave and project [scheme]'. It could of course be claimed, on his behalf, that he was merely protecting the power and authority of the sovereign. It is worth noting that the young Oliver Cromwell, member for the town of Huntingdon, was also part of this parliament.

On the evening of 13 June, thirteen days before the prorogation, Buckingham's physician and astrologer was noticed leaving the Fortune Theatre in the northern suburbs of the city; his name was Doctor Lambe. A crowd of apprentices recognized him and began to cry out, 'The duke's devil! The duke's devil!'; they pursued him towards a cookhouse in Moorgate Street where he paid a group of sailors to guard him. By the time he left the cookhouse the mob had grown in size; he told them that he 'would make them dance naked', no doubt at the end of a rope. Still the people followed him, but at Old Jewry his guard beat them off. The crowd was now intent upon violence and, forcing him towards the Windmill Tavern in Lothbury, they beat him senseless with sticks and stones. One of his eyes was kicked out as he lay upon the cobbles. He was taken to a compter or small prison in Poultry where he died on the following morning.

A couplet was soon being repeated everywhere:

> Let Charles and George [Buckingham] do what they can
> Yet George shall die like Dr Lambe.

When the rhyme was discovered among a scrivener's papers he confessed that he had heard it from one Daniel Watkins, who had in turn heard it recited by an illiterate baker's boy. A Suffolk cleric recalled that 'about September 3 I had related to me this foolish and dangerous rhyme, fruit of an after-wit'. So poems and ballads, commonly known as 'libels', circulated throughout the kingdom; they were often left on stairs or nailed to doors or pinned to gates. Some were even put in the open hands of conveniently placed statues. When the attorney general prosecuted a group of minstrels for singing scurrilous ballads about Buckingham, he referred to these 'libels' as 'the epidemical disease of these days'. They are evidence of the political consciousness of the nation and of the 'lower sort', otherwise largely unheard. Even the baker's boy had opinions about the king and 'George'.

The temperature of the nation was also being raised by the publication of printed 'courants' or 'corantos' in ever-increasing quantity; these were regular newsletters or news pamphlets that were circulated in taverns and in marketplaces together with the 'libels' that accompanied any great movement in the affairs of state. While many were printed, others were written by hand. The written varieties were considered more reliable, perhaps because they seemed to be more immediate or perhaps because of the authority of the correspondent. One of the writers of these papers called himself 'your faithful Novellante' or newsmonger; this is of course the derivation of the 'novel'.

In a similar movement of information any great stir in the county towns also reached the capital. The newsletters often deliberately helped to provoke controversy or division, so that, for example, the growing polarization between 'court' and 'country' – between 'courtiers' and 'patriots' – can only have been assisted by their partisan accounts. Ben Jonson's masque, *News from the New World*, portrayed a writer of newsletters declaring that 'I have friends of all ranks and of all religions, for which I keep an answering catalogue of dispatch wherein I have my Puritan news, my Protestant news and my Pontifical news'.

Manuscript copies of the proceedings and debates of parliament of 1628, known as 'separates', were also issued at this time in perhaps the first example of parliamentary reporting. The great speeches of Sir John Eliot and others were thus available to the public, reinforcing the conclusion that parliament had indeed come to represent the will and voice of the people. It is perhaps significant that these papers were often to be found in the libraries of the gentry.

After parliament had been prorogued, the king gave orders that all the gunpowder in London should be taken under royal control. The impression of overweening authority, close to arbitrariness, was further strengthened by the investiture of William Laud as the bishop of London in the following month. His exaltation of the king's authority, and his demand for exact conformity, did not endear him to the 'patriots' of the kingdom who were eager to curb the royal prerogative.

The king also elevated Sir Thomas Wentworth to the peerage. Wentworth had previously taken the part of parliament but, after the publication of the 'petition of right', he came to accept the king's position on matters of sovereign control; he had arrived at the conclusion that the Commons were not fit to manage the affairs of the nation. He was condemned for abandoning his principles but he believed that parliament, not he himself, had changed. He was soon to say in a speech that 'the authority of a king is the keystone which closes up the arch of order and government'. With men such as Laud and Wentworth around him, what might the sovereign not dare to undertake? The atmosphere of the city was uneasy. It was reported that the citizens were filled with alarm, and were taking up arms for their own defence. It was rumoured that the duke and the king were ready to confront their enemies. No one knew what might happen next.

14

I am the man

The plight of La Rochelle, still besieged by the forces of Louis XIII after the forced withdrawal of the English army, was extreme. Its inhabitants were reduced to eating grass and boiled cow-hides. It was reported that they cut off the buttocks of the dead, lying in the churchyard, for sustenance. The honour of the king, and of Buckingham, determined that they must once more come to the aid of the city. So in the spring and summer of 1628 a fleet was fitted out at Plymouth. The normal delays ensued. 'I find nothing', Buckingham wrote, 'of more difficulty and uncertainty than the preparations here for this service of Rochelle.' He was so despised at home that he had been asked to wear protection in order to ward off any attempt at assassination. He replied that 'a shirt of mail would be but a silly defence against any popular fury. As for a single man's assault, I take myself to be in no danger. There are no Roman spirits left.'

On the morning of 23 August, the duke was staying at the house of Captain Mason on Portsmouth High Street; Mason was a naval administrator as well as an officer. Buckingham was at breakfast with his colleagues and some representatives from La Rochelle; after the meal was over, he came down into the hall of the house. He stopped to converse with one of his officers when a man, who had been standing in the passage, stepped forward and plunged a knife into his chest with the words 'God have mercy upon thy soul!' Buckingham staggered back but, crying out 'Villain!' managed to draw the knife from the wound. He tried to pursue his assailant but fell against a table before dropping to the floor.

A great outcry went up among those assembled. The foreigners were suspected, and men cried out, 'A Frenchman! A Frenchman!' Others shouted, 'Where is the villain? Where is the butcher?'

'I am the man. Here I am.' John Felton, with his sword in his hand, came forward. He might have been killed where he stood, but some of Buckingham's officers surrounded him. The wife and sister-in-law of the dead man rushed to the corpse. 'Ah, poor ladies,' Dudley Carleton informed the queen, 'such was their screechings, tears and distractions that I never in my life heard the like before, and hope never to hear the like again.'

The news reached the king while he was at prayer in the royal chapel. When it was whispered in his ear his face betrayed little emotion and he stayed in his place until the service was over. Then he hurried to his private apartments, closed the doors and wept. It was reported that the king used to refer to him as 'my martyr'. Charles believed, in other words, that his favourite had been murdered for carrying out his orders.

Under examination it was revealed that John Felton had served in the disastrous expedition to Rhé, and that Buckingham had denied him promotion. The insult was compounded by the fact that Felton's wages had not arrived. When he asked the duke how he was supposed to live, Buckingham is supposed to have replied that he could hang himself if he had not the means to survive. Felton returned to London, where he brooded on his misfortunes; he read the latest pamphlets, which accused Buckingham of poisoning the former king and of being the source of all the grievances of the realm. Four days before the assassination he purchased a tenpenny knife at a cutler's shop on Tower Hill; he then visited a church in Fleet Street and asked the cleric for prayers as 'a man much discontented in mind'. He made his way to Portsmouth, largely on foot, where he performed the deed. He had sewn certain messages in the crown of his hat, among them one in which he announced himself to be an executioner rather than an assassin: 'He is unworthy of the name of a gentleman or a soldier, in my opinion, that is afraid to sacrifice his life for the honour of God, his king, and country.' He had been the righteous killer of a reprobate who had brought Charles and England into jeopardy.

In that opinion, he was almost universally sustained by the response of the people. The joy at Buckingham's death was widespread and prolonged. Celebratory healths to Felton were drunk in the taverns of London, and congratulatory verses passed from hand to hand. When he was taken through Kingston on his way to the Tower, an old woman cried out, 'God bless thee, little David.' When he arrived at the Tower itself, a large crowd had gathered to greet him, calling, 'The Lord comfort thee! The Lord be merciful to thee!' Charles was much offended by these manifestations of popular sentiment, and he wrapped himself more deeply in the mantle of cold authority.

The day before Felton's arrival at the Tower, Buckingham's funeral had taken place at Westminster Abbey in a hurried and apparently graceless manner with approximately one hundred mourners. But even this ceremony was mere theatre. The body had been privately interred the night before, to avoid any demonstrations against it by the London crowds. The poet and dramatist James Shirley wrote an appropriate epitaph:

> Here lies the best and worst of fate,
> Two kings' delight, the people's hate.

Felton himself, after due trial, was executed at Tyburn; his body was then displayed in chains at Portsmouth dressed in the same clothes he wore when he killed the duke.

The king now took sole charge of the administration. It was reported by his secretaries that he dispatched more business in two weeks than Buckingham had managed in three months. He told his privy council that he would postpone the opening of parliament until the following year. He retained the same ministers as before, but of course he did not trust them as much as he had trusted the duke. There would be no more royal favourites except, perhaps, for Henrietta Maria, who, after the death of Buckingham entered a much more intimate relationship with her husband; it soon became apparent that, after the initial discord, the royal family was at last a happy one. The poet and courtier Thomas Carew claimed that

Charles had 'so wholly made over all his affections to his wife that he dare say that they are out of danger of any other favourite'. Carew's friend, William Davenant, composed some dialogue at the time for a play entitled *The Tragedy of Albovine, King of Lombardy*:

> 'The king is now in love.'
>   'With whom?'
>   'With the queen.'
>   'In love with his own wife! That's held incest in court.'

Six children followed this reconciliation.

Buckingham had not sailed for La Rochelle, after all. Yet in the early autumn of the year a third expedition was sent to the besieged town; it was no more successful than its predecessors. The fleet dared not take the initiative, and its fire-ships were sunk by French ordnance. When the English did eventually land, they were repelled with firmness by the French besiegers. The king's promises of assistance had come to nothing. So in October 1628, the authorities of the town signed a treaty of surrender to the French king; their great walls were demolished. Whereupon Louis XIII announced a policy of toleration to his Protestant subjects, who were to enjoy freedom of worship throughout his kingdom. The fears of the Protestants had been based upon the mistaken belief that their religion was in danger of being extirpated, and it could be said that the foreign policy of Charles I represented a thorough misunderstanding of the policy of Louis XIII.

In the absence of Buckingham the king was more uncertain and irresolute than ever. Should he make a treaty with France against Spain, or a treaty with Spain against France? There was no question of waging outright war against either nation. The king did not have the resources to do so, or any realistic prospect of raising money by other means. In any case the zeal for war was rapidly ebbing in the country. There might be some delay in signing the relevant treaties, but a period of peace had become inevitable.

A day after the assassination of Buckingham a prominent courtier, Sir Francis Nethersole, remarked that 'the stone of offence being removed by the hand of God, it is to be hoped that the king and people will now come to a perfect unity'. Yet the opening of the parliament in January 1629 did not bode well for national harmony. The abiding issue was still that of religion. A royal declaration had been issued in the parliamentary recess that 'the Church has the right to decree ceremonies, and authority to decide controversies of religion'. But what Church? William Laud, now bishop of London, had helped to draw up the proclamation and in the same period a number of his supporters had been promoted to vacant sees. These were the Arminians or 'high churchmen' who rejected the precepts and practices of Calvinism.

For parliament this was a direct challenge to the old and familiar creed of the Church. Sir John Eliot told his parliamentary colleagues that the prelates, with the king's authority, might 'order it which way they please and so, for aught I know, to bring in Popery and Arminianism, to which we are told we must submit'. Another member, Christopher Sherland, said of the Arminians that 'they creep into the ears of his Majesty, and suggest, that those that oppose them, do oppose his Majesty . . .'

It had become a confrontation, therefore, between the Calvinists of the old Church and the Arminian bishops of the new. The recently appointed prelates declared that theirs was the true creed of the Church of England and condemned their opponents as puritan, synonymous with zealotry and nonconformity. It was claimed, for example, that the Calvinists were ready to take up the cause of individual conscience against the precepts of the established faith and the prerogative of the sovereign. The Arminian bishops were in turn accused by their opponents of preaching passive obedience and the divine right of kings. The Calvinists believed in predestination, grace and the gospel; the Arminians put their faith in free will, the sacraments and deference to ceremonial order. It was not conceived by any contemporary that these were controversies that could stir a civil war, but this was the moment when members of parliament and members of the court party began to take sides.

The Commons, animated by the speeches of Eliot and others, affirmed that they alone had the right to determine the religion of the country. John Pym, who had already earned the king's wrath, stated that 'it belongs to the duty of parliament to establish true religion and to punish false'. The members resolved that the faith they espoused was that agreed in the reign of Elizabeth 'and we do reject the sense of the Jesuits and Arminians'. The king, perhaps justifiably, considered this to be a breach of his prerogative in spiritual matters; he was, after all, 'supreme governor' of the Church of England. The Commons had also laid aside matters of 'tonnage and poundage', the customs duties destined for the king's purse, thus depriving him of his traditional revenue. Charles adjourned parliament on 25 February for a week. Both sides were in fact vying for mastery.

This was the point when Eliot decided to appeal to the country in the face of an obvious threat. If the king took the further step of dissolving parliament, its future would be uncertain. If he could obtain his revenues elsewhere, there was no reason at all why he should ever summon it again. He had had, in any case, enough of parliament; he called it 'that noise'. The Arminians were eager to avoid parliaments, also, for the simple reason that they believed they would be persecuted by them; they were of course wholly justified in their suspicion. Eliot had already said of them that 'they go about to break parliaments, lest parliaments should break them'.

So all things were leading to a final quarrel. On 2 March the Speaker, Sir John Finch, announced to the Commons that it was the king's wish that they should adjourn for a further eight days. Such a request had in the past always been accepted. Now the members stood up shouting, 'No! No!' Finch moved to rise from his chair, thus abruptly ending the session, but some of the members barred his way and thrust him back to his seat. 'God's wounds,' Denzil Holles told him, 'you shall sit till we please to rise.' Eliot then announced that the members would have the privilege of adjourning themselves after he had read out a declaration of their intentions.

'What would any of you do,' Finch asked, 'if you were in my place? Let not my desire to serve you faithfully lead to my ruin.' He was in an impossible situation, with incompatible loyalties to parliament and to the king. Some members, realizing the gravity of the approaching confrontation, rose to leave. But the serjeant-at-arms was ordered to close the doors; when he hesitated, another member locked the doors and put away the key.

Eliot once more demanded that the declaration he had prepared should be read. 'I am not less the king's servant for being yours,' the Speaker replied. 'I will not say that I will not put the reading of the paper to the question, but I must say, I dare not.' Eliot then spoke out in a ferocious attack upon the evil councillors that surrounded the king; he also assaulted Arminianism as an open door to popery.

Knocks were heard on the outer door. The king had ordered the serjeant-at-arms to bring away the mace, thus depriving the proceedings of any authority. Sir Peter Heyman then turned upon the Speaker. 'I am sorry', he told him, 'that you must be made an instrument to cut up the liberties of the subject by the roots . . . The Speaker of the House of Commons is our mouth, and if our mouth will be sullen and will not speak when we have it, it should be bitten by the teeth and ought to be made an example; and for my part I think it not fit you should escape without some mark of punishment to be set upon you by the House.' This was one of the first indications of the arbitrary and authoritarian impulses of some parliamentarians.

Talk of punishment was vain, however. It was whispered that the king had sent a guard to force its way into the chamber and end the proceedings. So Denzil Holles swiftly proposed three resolutions. Anyone who tried to introduce popery or Arminianism into the kingdom would be considered a capital enemy. Anyone who should advise the levying of customs duties, without the authority of parliament, would similarly be considered as an enemy. If any merchant should voluntarily agree to pay the duties of 'tonnage and poundage', he would be 'reputed a betrayer of the liberty of England and an enemy to the same'. The resolutions were thereupon adopted. Having delivered his message to the nation, Holles asked that the house now adjourn itself, to which there were immediate calls of 'Ay! Ay!' The doors were thrown open and the triumphant parliamentarians streamed out to announce the news. They would not meet again for another eleven years.

Two days later the king announced the dissolution of parliament, and at the same time nine of its members were arrested. Sir John Eliot was the particular object of the king's wrath; Charles blamed his angry tirades against Buckingham for the favourite's death. In his speech to the Lords Charles did not censure the majority of the Commons, but reserved his anger for 'some few vipers amongst them that did cast this mist of undutifulness over most of their eyes'. It was reported that he was afterwards in very good spirits.

A few days later was published *His majesties declaration of the causes which moved him to dissolve the last parliament*, in which he declared that the men whom he imprisoned had 'more secret designs which were only to cast our affairs into a desperate condition, to abate the powers of our crown and to bring our government into obloquy that in the end all things may be overwhelmed with anarchy and confusion'. He was not alone in this belief. Many considered that the members had gone too far in their opposition to the king. Even a fervently Protestant MP, Simonds D'Ewes, considered that the events of 2 March represented 'the most gloomy, sad and most dismal day for England that happened in five hundred years last past'; he also blamed the turmoil on 'diverse fiery spirits in the House of Commons'.

The immediate aftermath of the dissolution was one of dismay and bewilderment. The majority of the merchants refused to pay the customs duties demanded of them, on the grounds that a future parliament would condemn them as betrayers of the kingdom; so they simply declined to trade. Their recalcitrance lasted for two months until the prospect of financial ruin weakened their resolution.

The nine members of parliament arrested after the scenes in the chamber remained in prison. They could no longer appeal to the Lords or the Commons but they could take their case to the courts; they could appeal to the rule of law in a fundamental attempt to question the powers of the king. They claimed parliamentary privilege, and in particular 'freedom of speech in debate' that had been asserted by the Speaker since the late sixteenth century; four of them, including Eliot, refused to answer questions on anything pertaining to parliamentary business. The king wished them to be tried for conspiracy and treason, but the judges were reluctant to do so. The question of privilege was vexatious, and Charles eventually asked them to cease speaking in riddles.

At the beginning of May the imprisoned men sought to obtain their release on the grounds of habeas corpus, according to the precepts of the 'petition of right'. After much argument and debate the judges decided that the prisoners had indeed the right to bail;

the king then demanded that they reach no verdict until they had consulted their colleagues on the judiciary. This was essentially an appeal for delay, so that the long legal vacation could intervene; the men would therefore languish in gaol for the duration of the summer. At the beginning of October the prisoners were taken from the Tower to Serjeants' Inn, where they were promised their release as long as they signed a bond of good behaviour; most of them refused to do so, on the grounds that this would implicitly justify their arbitrary imprisonment for the last eight months. They were intent upon inflicting the maximum embarrassment on the king and his officers.

The Venetian ambassador wrote that 'affairs grow more bitter every day, and by these disputes the king has made his people see that he can do much more than they may have imagined'. The imprisoned members were testing, piece by piece, the lengths to which Charles would go. When the chief judge of the exchequer made it clear that he was inclined to support parliamentary privilege, the king suspended him from office. It was clear that the guilt of the prisoners was simply to be assumed. The king's action seems to have clarified the opinion of the remaining judges, who declared that the defendants were indeed punishable by law.

The members of parliament had reached the end of the legal process. Three of them, including Eliot, were once more imprisoned at the king's pleasure; the others were detained for shorter periods before being released. It had been a victory for the king, in theory, but it had gravely impaired his authority and reputation. He had revealed himself to be inclined to arbitrary and perhaps illegal measures in order to sustain his sovereignty; he saw treachery and conspiracy in what others considered to be justifiable dissent; he was wilful, and even implacable. Yet those who supported him put a different interpretation upon his actions. Charles had conducted himself in the manner of a true sovereign; he was determined to rule the country without the intervention of enemies or malcontents. He was guided by God. This may be considered to be the tone or principle of the next period of his reign.

15

The crack of doom

After the dissolution of parliament in March 1629, the king entered upon a period of personal government that lasted for eleven years. To all intents and purposes he had begun an experiment in absolute monarchy, with the prospect of an acquiescent nation obeying his commands. He was not ill-equipped for that role. One prominent lawyer, Sir Robert Holborne, observed that 'the king could drive a matter into a head with more sharpness than any of his privy council'. Yet in practice he delegated much of his work to various officials, preferring the pleasures of the hunt to the world of practical affairs.

It was in certain respects a time of silence. There were no debates in parliament, and no elaborate declarations or proclamations from the throne. As in a masque, the king had no need to speak; his presence itself ensured majesty and harmony. As in a masque, also, he could command the workings of the great stage of the world. Charles had a high enough opinion of his supreme office, not unmixed with moral self-righteousness, to believe this.

In the absence of parliament, and with a relatively tame judiciary, the freedoms of the subject were to a certain extent reliant upon the judgement and goodwill of the sovereign. The people of England were simply asked to trust his benevolent intentions. It is true that in many respects he was a gentle monarch, in the course of whose reign no political executions took place. Yet some still considered him to be a tyrant riding over the liberties of the nation and parliament. The continued detention of Sir John Eliot and two colleagues was cited as an example.

Unparliamentary government was not in itself fruitless. It was a time of improvements in transport, with roads repaired and new canals dug; the national postal service was improved, with a regular post on the principal roads taking the place of an irregular system of carriers; in the absence of any national emergency, the administration of local government was strengthened and extended. That domestic peace, however, depended upon external tranquillity. The king could not afford war. And, as long as he could raise sufficient money for his own government by fines and taxation, there was no need to call parliament.

The foreign policy of the nation therefore, in a sense, made itself. Peace was concluded with France in the spring of 1629 and, nineteen months later, a truce was arranged with Spain. By the treaty with France Charles was obliged to abandon the cause of the Protestant Huguenots on the understanding that the principles of his marriage treaty with Louis XIII need not be strictly applied; he need not, for example, grant freedom of worship to Roman Catholics.

The peace with Spain made no mention of the restoration of the Palatinate to Charles's sister and brother-in-law; the fate of the region was now the subject of promises and expressions of goodwill. In another clause of the treaty it was agreed that Spanish silver could be minted in England before being shipped to Antwerp, where the Spanish were engaged in fighting the Protestant Dutch. It was an open question whether these alliances with the Catholic powers would become a cause of dissent in England. Some believed the people to be cheerful and acquiescent; others suggested that the anger or antagonism against the king had simply been driven below the surface.

The public reaction to both pacts, however, was subdued. Little interest was taken in the matter. Charles had no European policy as such, except for the wish that his sister might be returned to the Palatinate with her husband; but with no army or money to enforce his desires he was reduced to inaction. Money was the key. It was said that Henrietta Maria herself had been obliged to close the shutters of her private apartments in case visitors saw the ragged

1. James I of England and James VI of Scotland, in the characteristically regal pose of hand on hip.

2. Anne of Denmark, James's spouse, who became a key artistic patron in the 'Jacobean' age.

3. James in front of his lords, temporal and spiritual.

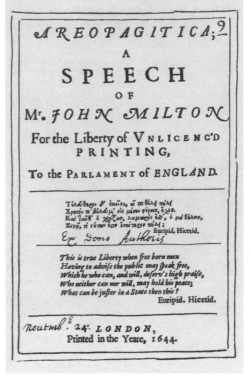

4. The title page of the King James Bible, one of the lasting memorials of his reign.

5. The title page of John Milton's *Areopagitica*, an eloquent plea against censorship.

6. George Villiers, 1st duke of Buckingham, loved by two sovereigns and hated by the people.

7. Henry, prince of Wales, the supposed saviour of Protestant Europe, who did not live long enough to fulfil his destiny.

8. Charles, the future Charles I, as the prince of Wales in armour.

9. Elizabeth, daughter of James I, who was briefly queen of Bohemia, otherwise known as the Winter Queen.

10. A double portrait of the unhappy Charles I and his wife, Henrietta Maria.

11. Three out of seven of Charles I's children, painted by
Anthony Van Dyck.

12. A disapproving illustration of the Rump Parliament, after the purge of the Long Parliament in December 1648.

The Rump and dreggs of the house of Com: remaining after the good members were purged out.

13. What the Cavaliers are supposed to have done with the Puritans.

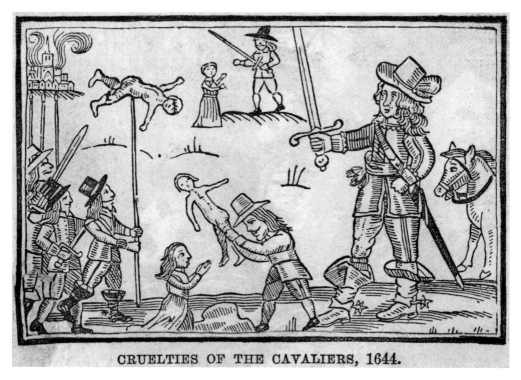

CRUELTIES OF THE CAVALIERS, 1644.

14. Thomas Wentworth, 1st earl of Strafford, the dour supporter of absolute monarchy.

15. A plan of the Battle of Naseby, the outcome of which wrecked the king's chances in the summer of 1645.

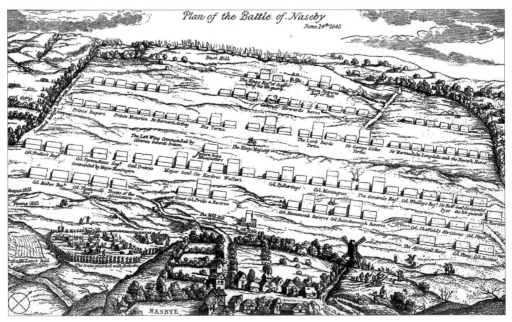

Plan of the Battle of Naseby
June 14th 1645

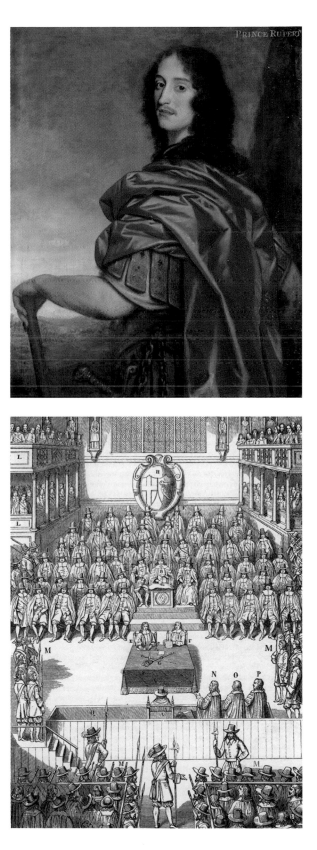

16. Prince Rupert of the Rhine, Charles I's senior commander, brave, but also foolhardy.

17. The trial of Charles I in Westminster Hall.

18. The result of the trial: a death warrant.

19. Cromwell, the chief of men until his death in 1658.

coverlets of her bed. There were times when, roused by Protestant appeals in Europe for assistance, the king asked his council what he might do. He was told that a new parliament would need to be called to raise the money. This was unthinkable. So nothing was done. The French ambassador remarked that lack of revenue made the English government one 'from which its friends can hope for no assistance, and its enemies need fear no harm'.

The king's discomfort was compounded when a new Protestant champion arose in Europe to counter the imperialist triumphs in Poland and Bohemia, Austria and Bavaria, Flanders and the Rhineland. In 1629 the king of Sweden, Gustavus Adolphus, marched into Germany and embarked upon a military conquest as unexpected as it was unprecedented. His chancellor wrote that 'all the harbours of the Baltic, from Kalmar to Danzig, throughout Livonia and Prussia, are in his majesty's hands'. Gustavus Adolphus had created a new Swedish empire and thereby took on the mantle of a Protestant Messiah, the Lion of the North.

How was the English king to treat with such a man? Gustavus Adolphus demanded men and materials from a fellow Protestant king. But if Charles entered into an alliance with the Swedish king, his important friendship with Spain would come to an end; and the trade with Spain was very important. If he refused an alliance with Gustavus Adolphus, he would lose honour and influence if the Swede was eventually victorious.

So Charles prevaricated and tried half-measures to maintain his credit on both sides. He agreed that a private force of 6,000 Scottish soldiers, under the command of the marquis of Hamilton, could join the Swedish army; but the expedition was a disaster, made worse by epidemic disease and insubordination. The king then sent a delegation to the Swedish king 'to enter into a league . . . upon emergent occasions'. This could mean anything or nothing. In practice it meant nothing. At one point Charles banned the news gazettes from reporting on the Swedish victories because they cast such an unhappy light on his own ineffectiveness.

The fortunes of the Swedish king came to an end in a battle outside Leipzig, where his body was found among a heap of naked corpses. The king of England had done nothing to counsel or to assist him. English inaction, or inertia, had created what one anonymous pamphleteer, in 'The Practice of Princes', described as 'a Hispanolized, Frenchified, Romanized or Neutralized' policy. Yet there may have been virtue in that. One week of war can undo a decade of peace. England escaped the devastation that was inflicted upon central Europe.

Funds still had to be raised by one means or another. The fines against the illegal enclosure of common land were more strenuously exacted. The king also raised much money from a great scheme to drain the fens of eastern England. Many articles of ordinary consumption were granted for a fee to monopolists, who could then set their own prices; the articles included iron and salt, pens and playing cards, starch and tobacco, seaweed and spectacles, combs and gunpowder, hats and hops. Patents could also be purchased for such projects as the manufacture of turf or the weighing of hay and straw, for 'the gauging of red herring' and the gathering of rags. In a contemporary anti-masque an actor came on stage with a bunch of carrots on his head, representing a 'projector' or speculator 'who begged a patent of monopoly as the first inventor of the art to feed capons fat with carrots'. The king demanded from the Vintners' Company a payment of £4 on every tun of wine; when they refused to pay the new tax, the Star Chamber forbade them to cook and serve meat for their customers. The loss of trade meant that they came to an 'understanding' with the court, amounting to £30,000 a year.

There was also the curious case of soap. The Company of Soap-makers was in 1631 granted a monopoly to manufacture soap made out of domestic ingredients, such as vegetable oil, rather than out of imported whale oil or fish oil. The company agreed in turn to pay the king an annual tax of £20,000.

The previous soap manufacturers were prosecuted in the Star Chamber for selling the old product; many of them were fined and some of them were imprisoned, while their pans and vats were destroyed. They were of course incensed at their loss of livelihood, but many housewives also complained that the new soap did not wash as well as the old. In seventeenth-century England even the most domestic disputes had a religious dimension. It was believed that the Company of Soapmakers was in fact controlled by the Catholic friends of Henrietta Maria; some of the new monopolists were rumoured to be financed by the Jesuits. Many Protestant households, therefore, objected to the new soap on theological grounds. It became known as the Popish Soap.

So the authorities put on a public demonstration of the efficacy of the new soap. In the Guildhall, under the gaze of the lord mayor, the aldermen and the lieutenant of the Tower, two washerwomen used the rival products in tubs placed beside each other. It was meant to prove that the new soap cleaned and lathered better, but the demonstration does not seem to have persuaded the London public. Eighty great ladies signed a testimonial to the effect that their maids preferred the new soap. This also had no noticeable effect. The old soap was still being sold under the counter. Another demonstration by washerwomen in Bristol was meant to prove that the new product washed 'as white . . . and as sweet, or rather sweeter' than the old. This may be considered a harbinger of modern advertising campaigns. It also made little impression. The old soap was still being manufactured and, as a result of its scarcity, sold at a much higher price.

More personal exactions were made by the king. Individuals were summoned for taxes they had not thought to pay. In 1630, for example, a royal commission was set up to fine those gentlemen who had not taken up knighthoods at the time of the king's coronation. It was a legal requirement that had faded out of memory through disuse. Those who were summoned were aggrieved at this unexpected imposition, and most tried to excuse themselves. Yet they were not successful. By these means the king raised the money he wished for, but at the expense of the affection and loyalty of some of his subjects.

Other expedients were also practised. Royal rights over forest lands were resurrected; those who had encroached upon forest boundaries were charged large sums. Those who had built houses in London 'upon new foundations' were also fined. Mr Moor had erected forty-two new houses in the neighbourhood of St Martin-in-the-Fields, for example, and was fined £1,000 and ordered to demolish the houses; when he refused, the sheriffs took them down and sold the materials to pay the fine.

What, then, was the king's general attitude to the property of his subjects? Could he take it away at will? If he could impose new taxes on his people without recourse to the courts or to parliament, might he not be able to emancipate the Crown from its traditional obligations? Many suggested that the king could indeed tax without consent, and that public good took precedence over private right. Others in turn argued that the Englishman's right to the property of his goods and estates was absolute, and could not be removed from him by any court or sovereign. Domestic peace was also unsettled by the disastrous harvest of 1630, which pushed up the price of grain from 4 shillings to 14 shillings a bushel; the prospect of starvation alarmed many communities, and food riots occurred in Kent, Hampshire and elsewhere.

The fractious atmosphere of the time was also evident in the court's actions against the notable antiquary Robert Cotton. His library had been sealed up, in the belief that it contained ancient tracts and pamphlets that took the side of parliament against the king. History had to be cleansed. One tract was found, according to the archbishop of York, 'containing a project how a prince may make himself an absolute tyrant'. Cotton was taken into custody, and interrogated by the Star Chamber before being released. Yet his life of study was effectively over. He was no longer allowed to enter his library and learned men were advised to cease their visits to him. He told one friend that 'my heart is broken'. He was so worn by anguish and grief that, according to Simonds D'Ewes, 'his face, which had been formerly ruddy and well-coloured, such as the picture I have of him shows, was wholly changed into a grim, blackish paleness near to the resemblance and hue of a dead visage'. He expired soon after, the victim of a nervous and turbulent time.

At the end of 1629 William Laud had, with the assent of the king, composed a 'Declaration on the Articles of Religion'. It was designed to impose order and uniformity upon the English Church by prescribing the forms of worship, the words of the prayers and even the gestures of the clergy. It was ordained that all clerics must accept to the letter the Thirty-Nine Articles, a demand which would in effect prohibit any discussion by Calvinists on such matters as predestination; these were condemned by the bishop of Chichester as 'deep and dark points which of late have so distracted and engarboyled the world'. The declaration was conceived thoroughly in the spirit of the monarch, who believed in order above all things.

Certain observers thereby concluded that Church and nation were to be reduced to uniformity.

Laud was, in the capital, considered to be little more than a papist in love with ritual and with ceremony. A paper was scattered about the streets of London declaring 'Laud, look to thyself, be assured thy life is sought. As thou art the fountain of all wickedness, repent thee of thy monstrous sins, before thou be taken out of the earth.' Laud was not discomfited. 'Lord,' he wrote in his diary, 'I am a grievous sinner; but I beseech thee, deliver my soul from them that hate me without cause.' An opponent of Laud by the name of Alexander Leighton, having written an appeal to parliament entitled 'Sion's Plea against the Prelacy', was condemned to the Fleet Prison for life; he was also to be taken to the pillory at Westminster and whipped before one of his ears was cut off, one side of his nose slit, and his face branded with the mark of 'S.S.' for 'Sower of Sedition'. He was then to be returned to prison for a period of recuperation before being whipped again and his other ear removed. He was afterwards 'to be shut up in close prison, for the remainder of his life'. Part of this sentence was remitted, for the sake of decency, but he was not released from prison until 1641 by which time he could not see, hear, or walk.

His wife was also briefly committed 'for her disordered tongue', according to a news-writer of March 1630, 'and a button maker for putting his mouth to the keyhole of the prison door where he lay, and crying aloud "Stand to it, doctor, and shrink not" and such like words'. In the following month an oatmeal-maker was brought before a religious commission for his unorthodox opinions. He was condemned by the bishop of Winchester, another ally of Laud, as a 'frantic, foolish fellow'. The maker of oatmeal replied, 'Hold thy peace, thou tail of the beast that sittest at the lower end of the table.'

The king expressed his appreciation of Laud's work, however, by appointing him as chancellor of Oxford University in the spring of 1630. Laud worked at once to re-establish order and decorum in the ancient university. The students had previously venerated Bacchus and Venus who were, as Laud wrote, 'the cause of all our ills in church and state'. Discipline was to be restored, thus promoting order and harmony; extravagant dress and long hair were not to be permitted, and alehouses were to be regulated. In the course of Laud's chancellorship, new buildings were erected and new studies were placed upon the curriculum with learned clerics to expound them. The city was refurbished, as it were, in glowing vestments.

The glory of Charles I was also celebrated. In 1630 the lord treasurer, Richard Weston, commissioned a statue of the king on horseback; it was a noble decoration for the garden of his country house in Roehampton. It soon became the abiding image of Charles's rule. In 1633 Van Dyck portrayed the king riding through a triumphal arch in the classical style; the king becomes a Roman conqueror. Two years later the same artist composed *Charles I on Horseback*, in which the king calmly and effortlessly directs the steed on which he rides. Images of chivalry, and of the Christian knight, are conflated with the representation of order.

It is also an image of the sovereign controlling animal nature, bringing the strength and energy of the horse into harness with his own will and desire. The Spanish ambassador, in the same spirit, had once flattered Charles by noting that the horses upon which he was mounted 'laid down all their natural and brutish fierceness in his presence'. The equestrian portraits are thereby a depiction of the manner in which reason must be able to control passion. This is of a piece with Charles's own conception of his rule and of his evident belief that he must control his own nature, by restraint and formality, before he could properly govern the entire kingdom. Art was for the king one of the great emblems of power. Yet it was more than that.

Lucy Hutchinson observed that 'men of learning and ingenuity in all the arts were in esteem and received encouragement from the king, who was a most excellent judge and great lover of paintings, carvings, gravings and many other ingenuities . . .' Charles had seen the artistic wealth of the royal court in Madrid and wished to cultivate a similar state of magnificence. He was in addition an adept and instinctive judge of painting and sculpture; if he had not been a king, he would have been a connoisseur. He was able to recognize the identity of an artist at first glance; this was known as a 'knowledge of hands'. He knew where '*gusto*', passion or taste, was to be found. He commissioned Rubens, Mytens, Inigo Jones and Van Dyck; by the end of his reign he had collected some 500 paintings and tapestries, among them nine Correggios, thirteen Raphaels and forty-five Titians. The Dutch once sent him five paintings to persuade him to resolve a dispute about herring fisheries; the city of Nuremberg gave him two Dürers. He also collected coins and medals; he enjoyed composing music. His love of order was everywhere apparent. When a collection of the busts of senators and emperors of ancient Rome reached Whitehall, he himself took pains to arrange them in chronological order.

A papal emissary to England recalled the occasion when the king, in the company of Inigo Jones, was informed that a consignment of paintings had arrived from the Vatican; he 'rushed to see them, calling to him Jones . . . the very moment Jones saw the pictures he greatly approved of them, and in order to study them better threw off his coat, put on his eyeglasses, took a candle, and together with the king, began to examine them very closely, admiring them very much . . .' The gift included works by Leonardo and Andrea del Sarto. This excitement reveals a sovereign very different from the conventional image of his coldness and reserve. Rubens was to say of Charles's court that it was remarkable 'not only for the splendour of the outward culture' but for 'the incredible quality of excellent pictures, statues and ancient inscriptions which are to be found in this court . . . I confess I have never seen anything in the world more rare.'

The authority of the king's image was amplified by the evidence of his fertility. In the spring of 1630 Henrietta Maria presented him with a son and heir, also to be named Charles. She wrote to a friend in France that her child was 'so serious in all that he does that I cannot help deeming him far wiser than myself'. The baby never clenched his fists, and so it was predicted that he would be a king of great liberality. He was also healthy and strong, looking at four months as if he were already a year old. So the birth augured well. The infant Charles was also the first in English history to be born as heir to the three kingdoms.

Thomas Carew, gentleman of the bedchamber, told the earl of Carlisle that the king and queen were 'at such a degree of kindness as he would imagine him a wooer again and her gladder to receive his caresses than he to make them'. Charles wrote to his mother-in-law, Marie de' Medici, that 'the only dispute that now exists between us is that of conquering each other by affection'. More importantly, perhaps, the birth of a son seemed to indicate that the Stuart dynasty might continue until the crack of doom.

16

The shrimp

All seemed quiet. The appearance of calm may have been deceptive, but it was peaceful enough in comparison with the violent years yet to come. Edward Hyde, 1st earl of Clarendon, claimed in his *History of the Rebellion and Civil Wars in England* that during the personal rule of Charles 'the like peace and plenty and universal tranquillity for ten years was never enjoyed by any nation'. Another historian, Sir Philip Warwick, in his *Memoirs of the Reign of Charles I*, wrote that 'from the year 1628 unto the year 1638, I believe England was never master of a profounder peace, nor enjoyed more wealth, or had the power and form of godliness more visible in it'.

On 9 January 1631, *Love's Triumph*, a masque devised by Inigo Jones and Ben Jonson, introduced Henrietta Maria as the Queen of Love in Callipolis or 'the city of beauty and goodness'. When the scene dissolved the 'prospect of the sea' appeared, into which setting the king himself walked in the guise of Neptune with a train of sea-gods and Cupids. He was then apostrophized as 'the centre of proportion, sweetness, grace!' At the end of the performance 'the throne disappears, in place of which there shooteth up a palm tree with an imperial crown on the top'.

In that same month, by royal command, a 'book of orders' was published. It decreed that two justices of the peace should meet each month in petty sessions to maintain the operations of local government. The overseers of the poor were to ensure that poor children were placed in apprenticeships; the constables and church-wardens of the parish were ordered to discipline offenders and to chase away vagrants. It was also the responsibility of the two justices to make certain that the roads were in a good state of repair and that, in general, law and order were imposed. They were also obliged to submit reports to London concerning 'how they found the counties governed'.

Although the king himself may not have drawn up these provisions, they bear all the marks of his paternal authority and of his predilection for good order. Charles was also determined that the local gentry and nobility should play an active part in the government of their neighbourhoods; a proclamation was issued ordering any of them still dwelling in London to return to the countryside where they belonged. At a later date another royal declaration ordered that urban vintners should stop selling tobacco and that innkeepers should not dress or serve game birds; this was believed to be a device to make the city less attractive to the country gentry.

The servants of the Crown were going about their duties. At the beginning of March William Laud preached at Paul's Cross in celebration of the sixth anniversary of the king's accession. He remarked that 'some are so waspishly set to sting that nothing can please their ears unless it sharpen their edge against authority'; he added, in sententious fashion, that 'I hope I shall offend none by praying for the king'.

The king's other great councillor, Sir Thomas Wentworth, had been dispatched to York as lord president of the north in order to curb disorder. At the beginning of 1632 he was further promoted to become lord deputy of Ireland, where his cause of promoting 'good and quiet government' could be tested. He was a man of strong will and of commanding temper. He believed implicitly in royal authority and in public duty. He told one of his relatives that 'a life of toil and labour' was his effective destiny. The portraits of him by Van Dyck show him to be profoundly animated by zeal or, perhaps, by vision.

Laud and Wentworth shared similar precepts and preoccupations that were embraced by them under the name of 'Thorough', by which they meant a disciplined and energetic response to the problems of the realm. They would not be diverted from their self-imposed task, and held nothing but contempt for those ministers of the state whom they regarded as lax, cowardly, or concerned only with enrichment. The administration of the king and his councillors – parliament was put to one side – should be enabled to push through those policies that were in the public interest. The vital alliance was that between Church and Crown in the cleansing of the kingdom.

The lord treasurer, the earl of Portland, was described by them as 'Lady Mora' or 'Lady Delay'; Laud also described the chancellor of the exchequer, Lord Cottington, as 'Lady Mora's waiting maid' who 'would pace a little faster than her mistress did, but the steps would be as foul'. This represented the difference between complaisant councillors and committed reformers.

Wentworth, like Laud, believed that only royal sovereignty could bring order out of disorder and discipline out of anarchy. As lord deputy of Ireland, therefore, he was inclined to drive himself over any opposition, to consolidate the authority of the king, to lead the people – and in particular the recent English settlers – into the pastures of obedience and docility. He was intent upon recovering the powers of the king, as he said, by 'a little violence and extraordinary means'. By his own light he succeeded, but only at the cost of arousing hostility and even hatred. He brought to his task a less than attractive combination of austerity and obstinacy. It was said, in *A Collection of Anecdotes and Remarkable Characters*, that 'his sour and haughty temper' meant that he expected 'to have more observance paid to him than he was willing to pay to others'.

Laud was more practical than the inspired Wentworth. The bishop wrote to the lord deputy that 'for the State, indeed my Lord, I am for thorough . . . and it is impossible for me to go thorough alone'. 'Thorough' and 'through', spelt in an identical way in the seventeenth century, were for all intents and purposes the same word. Laud added that 'besides, private ends are such blocks in the public way, and lie so thick, that you may promise what you will, and I must perform what I can and no more'. Nevertheless Wentworth was relentless, describing himself at his subsequent trial as 'ever desiring the best things, and never satisfied I had done enough, but did always desire to do better'.

In this period, too, the proclamations of the privy council were given legislative authority; the privy councillors could make laws on those matters which the actual courts of law neglected or avoided. The other governors of the realm maintained the emphasis upon law and order. It was reported in London by a news-writer, John Pory, that 'on Sunday, in the afternoon and after supper, till midnight, my lord mayor visited as many taverns as he could, and gave warning to the vintners not to suffer any drinking in their houses, either that day or night; and the same afternoon also he passed Moorfields and put down the wrestling of the western with the northern men, which was there usual on that afternoon'. The Star Chamber also enjoyed new authority with its enforcement of the proclamations from the council and its pursuit of transgressors.

One of the most prominent of these public offenders, William Prynne, had already aroused controversy with his strongly puritan opinions. He wrote tracts and pamphlets endlessly, his servant bringing him a bread roll and pot of ale every three hours; he was known as a 'paper-worm'. John Aubrey wrote that he 'was of a strange saturnine complexion', and Christopher Wren said that he had the countenance of a witch.

In the late autumn of 1632 Prynne's *Histriomastix: A Scourge of Stage Players* launched a general assault upon the plays and players of London, with a particular attack upon the practice of boys playing female roles and of women themselves appearing on the stage. He wrote that the actresses were 'notorious whores' and asked if 'any Christian woman be so more than whorishly impudent as to act, to speak publicly on a stage (perchance in man's apparel and cut hair), in the presence of sundry men and women'.

Unfortunately for Prynne the queen, Henrietta Maria, took part in a theatrical pastoral entitled *The Shepherds' Paradise* just a few weeks after the publication of his tract. The play itself was in the best possible taste. It was recorded of its audience that 'my lord chamberlain saith that no chambermaid shall enter, unless she will sit cross-legged on the top of a bulk'. It was a serious affair, and was of such complexity that the production lasted for seven or eight hours.

Nevertheless Prynne's attack upon female players was interpreted as an attack upon the queen herself; he had also denounced public dancing as a cause of shame and wickedness, and it was well known that the queen was fond of dancing. Prynne was sent to the Tower, where he faced prosecution by the Star Chamber and by the high commission on religious affairs. He was sentenced to imprisonment for life, fined £5,000 and expelled from Lincoln's Inn where he had practised law. The severity of the judgment was enhanced by the brutal order that both of his ears should be cut off as he stood in a public pillory. The sentence was duly carried out. One of his ears was cut away at Westminster, and the other in Cheapside.

Another opponent of the court, Sir John Eliot, died in confinement at the end of 1632. The king's enmity against him was such that, despite pleas for his health, he had never been allowed to leave the Tower in the course of his imprisonment. He had sent a petition to the king in which he declared that 'by reason of the quality of the air I am fallen into a dangerous disease'; he also stated that 'I am heartily sorry I have displeased your majesty'. The king replied that the petition was not humble enough. Eliot's humiliation was continued after his death. His son petitioned the king to allow his father's body to be carried into Cornwall for burial. Charles scrawled at the bottom of the petition, 'Let Sir John Eliot's body be buried in the church of that parish where he died.' He was in other words to be interred in the Tower.

A sequence of letters between the members of the Barrington family, in the early months of 1632, gives the flavour of the time. Thomas Barrington, writing from Holborn, informs his mother that 'women are cruel this year, Saturn reigns with strong influence: another wife has given her husband a potion of melted lead, but it was because he came home drunk'. His wife, Judith Barrington, wrote to her mother-in-law that 'I find all my friends sick or dying, the air is so bad . . . Here is little news stirring, much expected at the latter end of this week . . . This day was the poor woman burned in Smithfield that poisoned her husband, which is wondered at the cruelty, since there was so much cause of mercy to her.' A week or so later she reported that 'the smallpox is so much here that we wish ourselves with you'. In May Thomas Barrington wrote that 'the current of London runs so contrary and diverse courses as that we know not which way to fasten on certain truths'. London was the city of disease, of cruelty and of false reports.

In the spring of 1633 the king returned to his homeland. He made a leisurely journey northwards, and reached Edinburgh by the middle of June. His relations with Scotland in the past had not been entirely happy; at the beginning of his reign he had asked for the restitution of Church lands in Scotland to the Crown. The measure was not in the end advanced, but it stirred bad blood. When some Scottish lords came to defend the existing landowners, the king made a characteristic remark. 'My lord,' he said to the leader of the deputation, 'it is better the subject suffer a little than all lie out of order.' Charles himself did not seem especially to like the Scots and, in particular, the Highlanders, whom he described as 'that race of people which in former times hath bred so many troubles'. Yet his principal feeling was one of indifference rather than hostility.

He was crowned as king of Scotland in Holyrood Abbey on 18 June, and it was remarked that he had been happy to wait eight years for the privilege. The delay showed no overriding desire to endear himself to his people. The coronation itself was marked of course by ritual and formal ceremony that did not impress the natives; for most Scots, brought up in the Presbyterian faith, it smacked of prelacy and popery.

One of the complaints advanced by the Scots concerned the introduction of English ritual into the service. Yet the chief proponent of that ritual was about to be raised to the highest see. When Bishop Laud came into the king's presence for the first time after the journey to Scotland he was greeted with unfamiliar words. 'My Lord's Grace of Canterbury, you are very welcome.' Charles had just heard of the death of George Abbot, the previous archbishop.

As bishop of London Laud had been the king's principal religious adviser, but his authority had been ill-defined. Now as archbishop he became the source and spring of English religion, with an energy and purpose that the king himself lacked. Yet, at the beginning of his ministry, he was beset by anxiety. He wrote to Thomas Wentworth that 'there is more expected from me than the craziness [infirmity] of these times will give me leave to do'. Nevertheless like Sisyphus he was ready to put his shoulder to the stone.

He was a man of quick temper, small in stature, inclined to

irritability and impatient of contradiction. His harshness and rigour quickly made him enemies, particularly among the puritans whom he excoriated. He was known as 'the shrimp', 'the little urchin' and 'the little meddling hocus-pocus'. The king's fool, Archie, made a pun before a royal dinner. 'Give great praise to God, and little laud to the Devil.' Yet no one could question the new archbishop's sincerity or personal honesty. One English diplomat, Sir Thomas Roe, told the queen of Bohemia that Laud was 'very just, incorrupt . . . a rare counsellor for integrity'.

Thomas Carlyle described him as 'a vehement, shrill voiced character confident in its own rectitude, as the narrowest character may the soonest be. A man not without affections, though bred as a college monk, with little room to develop them: of shrill, tremulous, partly feminine nature, capable of spasms, of most hysterical obstinacy, as female natures are.' He was something between an Oxford don and a bureaucrat. A portrait of him by Van Dyck represents him as austere and quizzical. Not that he would have put much faith in the artist. He described his paintings as 'vanity shadows'.

He was highly superstitious and kept a record of his uneasy dreams. He dreamed that he gave the king a drink in a silver cup; but Charles refused it, and called for a glass. He dreamed that the bishop of Lincoln jumped on a horse and rode away. On one night 'I dreamed that I had the scurvy; and that forthwith all my teeth became loose. There was one in especial in my lower jaw, which I could scarcely keep in with my finger till I had called for help.'

Soon enough his influence was being felt. In October 1633 he and the king caused to be republished King James's *Declaration of Sports*, which had granted a degree of entertainment and recreation on the Sabbath. The king's 'good people' were not to be discouraged from dancing or archery, while the sports of leaping and vaulting were also permitted; 'may-games, whit ale and morris dances, and the setting up of maypoles' were perfectly acceptable to the authorities. It was almost like a return to the more picturesque religion of earlier centuries. For the Calvinists and the stricter sorts of Protestant, the *Declaration of Sports* was a poisoned document set to destroy true religion. Certainly it had unforeseen consequences. A seventeenth-century historian, Thomas Fuller, wrote that many of his contemporaries were 'of opinion that this abuse of the Lord's Day was a principal procurer of God's anger, since poured out on this land, in a long and bloody civil war'. The vicar of Enmore in Somerset declared from the pulpit that 'whatsoever the king is pleased to have done, the king of heaven commands us to keep the Sabbath'.

In the same period it was determined that the plain communion table should be moved from the middle of the church to the eastern end where it was to be railed off; it then more closely resembled the altars of the old faith. The priests now bowed towards it, and some of them employed the sign of the cross to bless it. William Prynne had already satirized the Eucharistic rite when the celebrant . . .

> came near the bread, which was cut and laid in a fine napkin, and then he gently lifted up one of the corners of the said napkin, and peeping into it till he saw the bread (like a boy that peeped after a bird-nest in a bush), and presently clapped it down again, and flew back a step or two, and bowed very low three times towards it . . . then he laid his hand upon the gilt cup . . . so soon as he pulled the cup a little nearer to him he let it go, flew back and bowed again three times towards it.

This was a keen burlesque of the services imposed by Laud.

The archbishop was concerned to augment the beauty and holiness of the rites of the Church, thus inducing respect if not awe. He had previously complained that ''tis superstition nowadays for any man to come with more reverence into a church, than a tinker and his bitch into an alehouse'. It soon became a serious offence for a minister not to bow his head at the name of Jesus. Choirboys came in two by two, and were instructed never to turn their backs upon the altar. Music returned to the cathedrals.

Laudianism, however, was not popery. The archbishop had a distaste for Roman Catholicism that was quite genuine. He was hoping to create a truly national Church devoid of the zealotry and intolerance of the puritans as well as the Mariolatry and superstitions of the papists. He had no appetite or aptitude for theological argument and, on the everlasting debate between free will and predestination, he said only that 'something about these controversies is unmasterable in this life'. He was indifferent towards Geneva and Rome, and looked only towards the king.

Laud was also attempting to fashion religious developments of a structural kind; he appointed only bishops who were of firmly anti-Calvinist persuasion. Charles himself believed that the episcopacy was the fundamental buttress of his sovereignty; no bishop, as his father had said, implied no king. It was believed essential to augment clerical power. The corporations of cathedral towns were called upon to appoint more clerics as justices of the peace, and were further obliged to attend Sunday service in their ceremonial robes. Within a short time Laud was joined by two bishops in the king's council; Bishop Juxon of London, who had been only the king's chaplain two years before, was appointed as lord treasurer of the kingdom. The last cleric to fill the post had been promoted in the reign of Henry VII (1485–1509). England might be considered to have re-entered the world of medieval polity.

A series of 'visitations' to the various parishes followed in order to investigate cases of clerical disobedience and nonconformity. In Manchester, for example, twenty-seven clerics were charged with failing to kneel at the time of communion. Richard Mather of Toxteth, near Liverpool, admitted that he had never worn the surplice. 'What!' exclaimed the Visitor, 'Preach fifteen years and never wear a surplice? It had been better for him that he had gotten seven bastards!'

The old processions and festivals also returned. With the re-publication of *Declaration of Sports* came a general relaxation of social custom. The ritual of 'beating the bounds' was soon followed by the parishes of London; such holy days as All Saints were celebrated once more. The custom of the Lord of Misrule returned with its attendant atmosphere of party games, dancing and drinking of spiced ale. These feasts had never completely died away but, in the new atmosphere of anti-puritanism, they flourished.

The king was further to test the loyalty of the nation. In the autumn of 1634 writs of ship-money were issued once again, for the first time in a period of peace. They had previously been sent out in 1626 and 1627, in the face of a threat of war against both France and Spain; payments had been grudging, but they had been made, and so it was deemed plausible to repeat the exercise. The proximate cause for the reintroduction of the tax was the prospect of new combinations in Europe. The French and Dutch had entered an unlikely alliance to dominate the continent, and a secret treaty between England and Spain was believed to be necessary.

There was no hope, however, that the members of the king's own council would countenance the fact of an English force taking the part of Spain against the Dutch; how could the king ally himself with the pre-eminent Catholic power attacking a Protestant republic? Once again Charles relied upon intrigue with any or every party that seemed likely to favour him. He had to conceal his alliance with Spain and pretend that the ships were being prepared as a defence against attacks from all quarters. It was said that English trade had to be protected from Tunis and Turkey as much as from France or Spain. So the king claimed the right of sovereignty in all of his seas, including the English Channel and the North Sea.

The first writs of ship-money were dispatched only to the ports and to the towns along the coasts; they were ordered to provide a sum sufficient to fit out a certain number of ships as well as to maintain them and their crews for six months. The money was to be given to a collector appointed by the Crown. London alone attempted to oppose the tax, having been required to raise one fifth of the total, but was quickly subdued by threats and talk of treason. The Venetian ambassador commented of ship-money that 'if it does not altogether violate the laws of the realm, as some think it does, it is certainly repugnant to usage and to the forms hitherto observed'.

Yet for what purpose was the fleet being prepared? What was the king to do with his newly fitted ships? Was it enough that they should enforce his sovereignty of the seas by making sure that passing vessels struck their flags and lowered their topsails? In the spring of 1635 the first fleet raised by ship-money finally took sail. The forty-two vessels, nineteen of them over 50 tons, set forth with orders to curb piracy, protect English traders, prevent the Dutch from fishing in English waters and, according to one news-writer, Edward Rossingham, 'to preserve the sovereignty of the narrow seas from the French king who hath a design long to take it from us and therefore he hath provided a very great navy'. They were meant, in other words, to do everything and nothing.

So ship-money had indeed been raised, out of fear or loyalty, and the success of the tax ensured its survival; in the following year it was enlarged to take in the whole country. It was argued that, since the counties and urban corporations were interested in their 'honour, safety and profit', it was appropriate that 'they should all put to their helping hands'. The appeal worked, and the tax of 1635 became the model for the next five years in which 80 per cent of the money demanded was actually paid.

In 1634 the first hackney carriages were allowed to stand for hire in the streets of London, a novelty that generated the usual amount of horror and indignation. It was proposed that no hackney could be hired for a journey of less than 3 miles. The suggestion was accepted on the grounds that too many coaches going on brief expeditions would create a 'lock' or traffic-jam in the streets, damage the pavements and increase the price of hay. Other contemporaries suggested that no unmarried gentleman should be allowed to ride in a hackney carriage without being accompanied by his parents.

17

Sudden flashings

In the summer of 1636 Charles and Henrietta Maria paid a visit to Oxford; it was now, in essence, Laud's university. Yet only the academic officials paid homage to the royal couple. As they rode through the streets there were no calls of 'God save the king'. The scholars and the citizens alike were silent. This did not bode well, and was a salutary reminder that Charles was steadily building up grievances among his people.

Among the aristocracy and the greater gentry, for example, much anger had been aroused by the exactions of the various courts Charles had established to extort money – the court of wards and the court of forest law principal among them. Of the former it was said that even those devoted to the Crown saw that they might be destroyed, rather than protected, by the law. Of the latter, the fines for encroachment upon the royal forests had, according to Clarendon, 'brought more prejudice upon the court, and more discontent upon the king, from the most considerable part of the nobility and gentry in England, than any one action that had its rise from the king's will and pleasure'.

Charles was also in the process of alienating his subjects elsewhere. He had unilaterally published a body of 'canons' to be adopted by the Scottish Church; the people themselves interpreted these requirements as nothing more than new laws imposed upon them by strangers. No one could receive the sacrament except upon his or her knees. No man should cover his head during the divine service. No person should engage in spontaneous prayer. The clergy should not allow private meetings for the expounding of Scripture. These were all novel commandments, and caused much disquiet that soon enough would break out in riot.

The puritan reaction in England to the Laudian orthodoxy was no less strong if, perhaps, more carefully concealed. In London, for example, a secret network of conventicles and discussion groups had been established; they communicated with each other by means of manuscript tracts and sermon notes as well as by conferences and 'conversations' behind closed doors. This was a world of fasts, of prayer meetings and of scriptural discussions in such centres of sectarianism as Coleman Street and Friday Street in the capital.

Lady Eleanor Davies, who had the reputation among the godly of Lichfield as a prophetess, entered Lichfield Cathedral on one communion day at the end of 1636 with a brush and kettle. She announced that she had come to sprinkle her 'holy water' on the hangings and newly decorated communion table; the holy water itself was composed of tar, pitch and puddle-water which she then liberally distributed with her brush. She was deemed to be out of her wits and sent to Bethlehem Hospital. By curious chance Charles and Henrietta Maria had visited that institution just a few months before, according to Edward Rossingham, 'to see the mad folks where they were madly entertained. There was every one in his humour. Two mad women had almost frighted the king and queen, and all their attendants, out of the house, by their foul talk.'

Lady Eleanor Davies was not alone in her disgust at the Laudian innovations. One puritan writer, John Bastwick, complained that 'the Church is now as full of ceremonies as a dog is full of fleas'. Oliver Cromwell, looking back at the end of his life, remarked in a speech to parliament that Laud and his allies had wished 'to innovate upon us in matters of religion, and so to innovate as to eat out the core and power and heart and life of all religion, by bringing on us a company of poisonous popish ceremonies . . .' The conditions were, in a phrase of the day, 'too hot to last'.

In the summer of 1637 three sectarians were led before the Star Chamber on the charge of maligning the bishops of England.

William Prynne was well known to the judges, and four years earlier had lost his ears before being consigned to the Tower; yet somehow he had managed to write pamphlets in his prison cell which were then smuggled away by friendly visitors.

He was joined now in court by Henry Burton and John Bastwick. In *The Litany of John Bastwick* the latter had written, 'From plague, pestilence and famine, from bishops, priests and deacons, good Lord, deliver us!' When the chief justice saw Prynne he asked the officers of the court to hold back his hair so that he might see the scars of the mutilated ears. 'I had thought Mr Prynne had no ears,' he said, 'but methinks he hath ears.' The executioner had not been as savage in his punishment as he might have been, which left open the possibility that a further assault might finally sever them altogether. The sentences were as brutal as they were predictable. Loss of ears, and life imprisonment, were the verdicts upon the three men.

Many contemporaries were still unsympathetic to the condemned. News-writer John Burgh remarked that 'they are desperate mad factious fellows, and covet a kind of puritanical martyrdom or at least a fame of punishment for religion'. In that expectation they were successful. The previous sentence upon Prynne had been carried out with no obvious signs of public displeasure. Now the three men were cheered to the foot of the pillory, their path strewn with herbs and flowers. They stood in the pillory for two hours. They were not attacked with dirt or stones. They talked freely and cheerfully to the crowd around them, and their words were greeted by some with applause and shouts of approval. Burton's wife sent him a message that 'she was more cheerful of that day than of her wedding day'.

After two hours it was time for the more severe punishment. The hangman began to cut away at the ears of Burton, and as each ear was severed there came a roar of pain from the members of the crowd, so deep was their sympathy with the victims. When the blood came streaming down upon the scaffold, some of the crowd dipped their handkerchiefs in it. The stumps of Prynne's ears were further mutilated in a very contemptuous and brutal fashion. Bastwick was similarly treated. The fortitude of the men, in not flinching during their ordeal, aroused much admiration.

The prisoners were then taken out of London to their respective dungeons in the castles of Carnarvon, Launceston and Lancaster.

When Prynne travelled with his gaolers along the Great Northern Road, he was greeted with shouts of sympathy. When Burton left London by the Western Road, calls of 'God bless you!' echoed around him. Bastwick was followed by what seemed very like a triumphal procession. It was not a victory for Archbishop Laud. The rigour of the punishment had not overawed the crowd and Wentworth told the archbishop that 'a prince that loseth the force and example of his punishments loseth withal the greatest part of his domain'. The fate of the three men only served to alienate still further those who believed that Laud and the king were becoming a weight upon the body politic. The archbishop's own chaplain, Peter Heylyn, later wrote that the whole occasion 'was a very great trouble to the spirits of many very moderate and well-meaning men'. A proverb was current: 'To break an egg with an axe'.

The news from Edinburgh was even more disturbing. In the spring of 1637 a new Service Book for Scotland was published by the king. It applied much of the English Book of Common Prayer and abolished most of John Knox's Book of Common Order. It was in effect another English imposition, bearing all the marks of the intervention of Archbishop Laud. It was first read in public at St Giles, recently become the cathedral church of Edinburgh. The dean ascended the pulpit, but when he began to recite the words of the new book, shouts of abuse came from the women of the congregation. 'The Mass is entered among us!' 'Baal is in the church!' The bishop of Edinburgh then stepped forward to calm the angry women and begged them to desist from profaning 'holy ground'. This was not a phrase to be used in front of a puritan assembly, and further abuse was screamed against him; he was denounced as 'fox, wolf, belly god'. One of the women hurled her stool at him which, missing its target, sailed perilously close to the head of the dean.

The magistrates were then called to clear the church but the women, once ejected, surrounded the building; its great doors were pummelled and stones were flung at its windows as the unhappy ceremony proceeded to its end. Cries could be heard of 'a pape, a pape, anti-Christ, stone him, pull him down!' When the bishop came out, the women shouted 'get the thrapple out of him' or cut his windpipe; he barely escaped with his life. This was not a spontaneous combination of irate worshippers, however, but a carefully organized assault on the Service Book; certain nonconformist gentry and clergy had been planning the event for approximately three months, even though the scale of the riot was not perhaps anticipated. The incident became known as 'Stony Sunday'.

On hearing the news of the riots in Edinburgh the king ordered the immediate suppression of the malcontents. In a city where the majority of the populace was on their side, this was not a plausible command. Laud asked the Scottish bishops if they were ready to 'cast down the milk they have given because a few milkmaids have scolded at them. I hope they will be better advised.' Yet the archbishop was the one in need of counsel. The Edinburgh magistrates stated that no member of the clergy would be able to read the new service. Most of the ministers abhorred its contents, and all of them feared further riot.

Petitions were now arriving from all parts of Scotland deploring the papistical intentions of the new prayer book, so far from the old form and worship of the Kirk. The Scottish council wrote to the king that 'the murmur and grudge' at the innovations were unprecedented. Their remonstrances became all the more urgent after a second riot broke out in Edinburgh; the news had spread that the lord provost had tried to prevent a petition against the Service Book from reaching London. The petitioners, as they became known, were now by far the largest element in the city.

A moderate Presbyterian minister, Robert Baillie, confided to his journal that 'what shall be the event, God knows . . . the whole people thinks popery at the doors; the scandalous pamphlets which come daily new from England add oil to this flame; no man may speak anything in public for the king's part, except he would have himself marked for a sacrifice to be killed one day'.

Charles did not know what to do. He had not anticipated such an unwelcome act of defiance and disobedience. It is reported that his first words were 'I mean to be obeyed'. Yet how was he to enforce his will? He had no army, and only unwilling support from his representatives in Scotland. A solution to the immediate impasse was then suggested by members of the Scottish privy council. The petitioners would leave Edinburgh and return to their homes, leaving a group of commissioners to speak and act in their name. It was clear that, in effect, these commissioners would become the voice of Scotland.

It is possible to see the incidents in Edinburgh as a prelude to the more fatal antagonisms that led to civil war in England; yet no one at the time could have conceived such an outcome. One event just followed another in apparently random or at least unconnected fashion, and only at a later date could a pattern be discerned. Some time afterwards, for example, Henrietta Maria called the new order of service for Scotland 'that fatal book'. But who would have believed that a woman throwing a stool would mark the beginning of a great war?

Scotland had set an example of defiance that was regarded with admiration by some in England. Charles ruled over three kingdoms that were as vitally connected as filaments in a web; a disturbance in one part affected the equilibrium of the whole. Another great controversy concerning the king's authority now emerged in London. In the summer of 1637 the king decided to call John Hampden before the court of the exchequer for refusing to pay his portion of ship-money. Hampden had been imprisoned ten years earlier for declining the king's forced loan, but the experience does not seem to have curbed his independence.

At the beginning of the year twelve senior judges had declared that, in the face of danger to the nation, the king had a perfect right to order his subjects to finance the preparation of a fleet; in addition they declared that, in the event of refusal, the king was entitled to use compulsion. Leopold von Ranke believed that 'the judges could not have delivered a more important decision; it is one of the great events of English history'. The royal prerogative had become the foundation and cornerstone of government. Simonds D'Ewes wrote that if indeed it could be exacted lawfully, 'the king, upon the like pretence, might gather the same sum ten, twelve, or a hundred times redoubled, and so to infinite proportions to any one shire, when and as often as he pleased; and so no man was, in conclusion, worth anything'. It was a powerful argument, to be tested in the trial of John Hampden.

The court case lasted from November 1637 until the following summer and was watched with extreme interest by the political nation. It was a test of power between sovereign and subject, and was considered to be one of the most significant cases ever put to judgement. The prosecution essentially rested upon two points. The

Crown contended that all precedents, from the time of the Anglo-Saxons, allowed the king to gather money for his navy; Hampden in turn maintained that previous methods of taxation had in no way resembled the recent writs for ship-money sent to the inland counties. The Crown also defended the reasonableness of its claim for financial assistance in the face of foreign danger; by the time any parliament could be assembled to debate the matter, the country might have been attacked or even invaded. Hampden argued that the writs had been sent out six months before any ships were fitted, and there had been ample time for an assembly at Westminster; the writs were in any case contrary to statutes forbidding any tax without the consent of parliament.

The court was packed with spectators. A squire from Norfolk had come to London simply to attend the trial but when he arrived 'at peep of day', the crowd was already so great that he could get only 2 or 3 yards from the door of the court. Those who did obtain entrance seem largely to have taken Hampden's part. When one of his counsels, Oliver St John, opened the defence he was according to a puritan observer, Robert Woodford, 'much applauded and hummed by the bystanders, though my lord Finch [the chief justice] signified his displeasure for it'; at the close of St John's argument, 'they adventured to hum him again'. The argument continued beyond the walls of the court, where debates between the opposing sides could become very fierce. The vicar of Kilsby, in Northamptonshire, had exhorted his congregation 'to pay his majesty's dues'; whereupon the parish constable told him that the king's taxes were worse than the pharaoh's impositions upon the Israelites. Conversations of a similar kind took place all over the realm.

The judges deliberated and eventually gave a decision in favour of the court, seven against five. It was the smallest of all possible majorities for the king. Nevertheless the words of the chief justice in his support were repeated throughout the country. Finch declared that 'acts of parliament to take away his royal power in the defence of the kingdom are void'. Or, as another judge had put it, '*rex est lex*' – the king *is* the law. The ancient rights of Englishmen were of no importance, and the declarations of Magna Carta or the 'petition of right' were inconsequential. Neither law nor the parliament could bind the king's power. Clarendon, in his *History of the Rebellion*, states that 'undoubtedly my Lord Finch's speech made ship-money much more abhorred and formidable than all the commandments by the council table and all the distresses taken by the sheriffs of England'.

When a judge at the Maidstone assizes read out the judgment of the court in London the people, according to a contemporary, Sir Roger Twysden, 'did listen with great diligence and after the declaration made I did, in my conceit, see a kind of dejection in their very looks . . .' A justice of the peace in Kent wrote in a memorandum that 'this was the greatest cause according to the general opinion of the world was ever heard out of parliament in England. And the common sort of people are sensible of no loss of liberty so much as that hath joined with it a parting from money.' The opposition to ship-money became much more fierce than before; some refusing to pay now cited the arguments made by those judges who had favoured John Hampden.

In the middle of the trial, on 9 February 1638, the king issued a proclamation to Scotland in which he stated that 'we find our royal authority much impaired' and declared that all protests against the new prayer book would be deemed treasonable. The king's response was characteristic. Any attempt to curb his power was of course treachery and he believed that, if he made any compromise or accommodation, he would be fatally weakened; he did not want to become as powerless as the doge of Venice and he informed his representative in Scotland, the marquis of Hamilton, that he was 'resolved to hazard my life rather than suffer authority to be condemned'. He was not simply referring to his authority but to the concept of 'authority' itself. Yet he could be wily and secretive at the same time, and told Hamilton that 'I give you leave to flatter them with what hopes you please'. Since the leaders of the prayer book rebellion were essentially traitors, they could be deceived and betrayed with impunity.

In response the commissioners in Edinburgh, representing the petitioners, drew up a national covenant in which the precepts of the Kirk were re-established. Among its declarations was one that the innovations of the new prayer book 'do sensibly tend to the re-establishing of the popish religion and tyranny, and to the subversion and ruin of the true reformed religion and of our liberties, laws and estates'. The people were in truth not rebelling against their king per se, but at the alliance of secular and religious authority that he had come to represent. The elect were now bound to God in solemn contract, as the Israelites once had been, with a clear moral obligation to fulfil His commands. 'If thou walk before me, and serve me, and be perfect . . . I am willing to enter into covenant with thee' (Genesis, 17: 1–2). The national covenant was carried in triumph through the streets, accompanied by crowds of women and children who alternately cheered and wept.

The people of Scotland took their lead from the inhabitants of Edinburgh and signed the covenant in their hundreds of thousands, declaring that they would rather die than accept the new liturgy. They raised their right hands to heaven before they took up the pen. Many of the orthodox Scottish bishops fled to England, with the archbishop of St Andrews, John Spottiswoode, lamenting that 'all we have been doing these thirty years past is now thrown down at once'. This came from the king's attempt to master his subjects in the same way as he mastered his horse.

The responses of others were mixed. The great minister of France, Richelieu, was inclined to support and even to aid the Scottish rebels on the grounds that trouble for the English king was always welcome. In turn Charles did not wish the world to believe that his authority had been spurned by some of his subjects; all his life he feared to appear weak. The English dissenters, already excited and agitated by the trial of John Hampden, welcomed the defiant actions of the Scots; many of them hoped that the Scottish example might be followed closer to home. The most impassioned denunciations of the king's policy could be read in the verses and broadsides distributed in the streets of London.

Laud wrote to Wentworth that 'my misgiving soul is deeply apprehensive of no small evils coming on'. Wentworth himself was urging the king to stricter measures. He believed that, if the arrogance and bravado of the Scots were not 'thoroughly corrected', it would be impossible to know how far the evil of dissension might spread. Some people were already wary of the coming conflict. When in 1638 one of the godly in the Wiltshire village of Holt found a beggar at his door he refused to give him alms on the grounds that 'shortly you will be pressed for war, and then you will fight against us'.

When the general assembly of the Church of Scotland met in Glasgow Cathedral towards the end of November, the bishops were charged with violating the boundaries of their proper authority. The marquis of Hamilton attended in the name of the king, and he reported to his master that 'my soul was never sadder than to see such a sight; not one gown amongst the whole company, many swords but many more daggers – most of them having left their guns and pistols in their lodgings'. The voting of course went against the orders and wishes of the king. Hamilton thereupon declared the assembly dissolved but, after he had left the church, the delegates voted to continue their debate. They also passed a resolution declaring that the Kirk was independent of the civil power, in effect stripping Charles of any religious supremacy he had previously claimed.

For the next three weeks the delegates revised the whole form of the Scottish faith that had recently been imposed upon them. The new liturgy was abolished. The bishops were excommunicated. The king's writ no longer ran in Scotland.

The preparations for war were now intensified. The king ordered a convoy of military supplies to be sent from the Tower to Hull while the marquis of Hamilton advised him to take in hand the further fortification of Berwick, Carlisle and Newcastle. The lords-lieutenant of the counties were ordered to organize and exercise their local militias for readiness in combat. The leaders of the Scots, in turn, divided their country into seven military regions from which recruits would be taken; the commissioners also requested that the Scots mercenaries, fighting for the cause of Protestantism in Germany, should come home for a more significant war. Their lord general, Alexander Leslie, knew that they would bring with them new forms of military training and expertise taught by Dutch and Swedish commanders. It was believed that they would be a far more professional force than their English adversaries.

Omens were noticed and reported. A Yorkshire gentleman, Sir Henry Slingsby, confided to his diary an old prophecy that, after the victories of the Saxons and Normans, England would next be mastered by the Scots. Freak winds and lightning were seen. Henry Hastings reported to his father that, at eight o'clock one evening, the clouds dispersed to reveal apparitions 'like men with pikes and muskets, but suddenly the scene being changed they appeared in two bodies of armed men set in battalion, and then a noise was heard and sudden flashings of light seen and streaks like smoke issuing out of these clouds'. The forces of war were gathering.

18

Venture all

At the beginning of 1639 Charles sent out a summons for the soldiers of his kingdom to meet him at York. The peers of the realm were ordered to appear in person, together with the retinues that befitted their status. The trained bands – the local militia made up of citizens – of the north were required to attend under the command of the lords-lieutenant of their counties. The rest of the men were conscripted, mainly from the midlands; they were formerly ploughmen or carters or thatchers, and had no stomach for a fight. Neither trained nor organized, they were being sent to unknown regions of the country for a cause about which they knew very little or nothing.

The men raised from Herefordshire attacked and wounded their officers before returning to their towns and villages. Other conscripts proceeded to pillage the hamlets through which they passed. They tore down the hated enclosures that parcelled up previously common land; they fired the gaols and freed the prisoners, many of whom had been detained for refusing to pay royal taxes; they attacked the undergraduates of Oxford; the more precise of them attacked the altars and communion rails of the churches. They were, as one royalist commander, Lord Conway, put it, 'more fit for Bedlam or Bridewell' than the king's service.

The peers and nobles, gathered about the king by old feudal bonds, were equally reluctant to risk their lives in the royal cause. Many of them pleaded sickness, and the majority of them travelled to York against their will. If the king lost, their lands and even their lives might not be spared by the Scottish covenanters; if he won, and became supreme, their liberties would be further at risk. The prospect of another parliament, for example, would recede even further into the distance. The puritan party, in particular, had no reason or desire to fight against their co-religionists in Scotland. It would be an act of faithlessness on an unparalleled scale. Many of them believed that the war was being fought on behalf of the episcopate, and that its principal aim was to restore the bishops to their authority in Scotland. So the war became known as *bellum episcopale* or the Bishops' War. It was all the more hated by some because of it.

Yet it was abhorred principally because it was an unfamiliar and unwelcome intrusion into the affairs of the nation. England had avoided foreign wars, and enjoyed domestic peace, for many years; no shots had been fired, and no drums heard, in the land. Yet that quiet was about to be shattered. Sir Henry Slingsby wrote that it was 'a thing most horrible that we should engage ourself in a war one with another, and with our own venom gnaw and consume ourself'. The long period of peace also meant that the instruments of war had been degraded; the swords and muskets and pikes, laid aside, were now tarnished or broken. Horses were in short supply.

At the end of March 1639, the king rode into York to meet his army. Charles and his principal officers were lodged at the King's House, the residence of the lord president of the north, while other officers and gentry found room in the various inns of the city such as the Talbot and the Dragon. The king was also graciously pleased to watch his 'cavaliers' exercising on their horses in the meadows known as the 'ings'. The 'cavaliers' were now a recognizable body of officers attached to the king's cause; some of them were already professional soldiers who had seen service in the European wars, while others were the sons of gentlemen in search of martial glory. Many of them, however, earned a reputation as braggarts and as anti-puritan bullies given to drink and gaming. According to a pamphlet of the time, 'Old News Newly Revived', anyone with 'a tilting feather, a flaunting periwig, buff doublet, scarlet hose, and a sword as big as a lath' could be mistaken for one. They were now ready to fight what one of the king's men, Sir Francis Windebank, in turn castigated as 'those scurvy, filthy, dirty, nasty, lousy, itchy, scabby, shitten, stinking, slovenly, snotty-nosed, logger-headed, foolish, insolent, proud, beggarly, impertinent, absurd, grout-headed, villainous, barbarous, bestial, false, lying, roguish, devilish . . . damnable, atheistical, puritanical crew of the Scottish Covenant'.

The king seems to have presumed, as Clarendon put it in his *History of the Rebellion*, that his calling together the peers of the realm with their retinues meant that 'the glory of such a visible appearance of the whole nobility would at once terrify and reduce the Scots'. In that presumption he was quite wrong. He could not even rely upon the nobility itself. Alarmed by talk of collusion with the covenanters, the king demanded that the lords and gentry at York should take an oath of allegiance. Two of them declined, Lord Brooke and Viscount Saye refusing to do so on the grounds that it was unconstitutional to demand any such oath that had not been approved by parliament. Saye added that, since the crowns of England and of Scotland were now unified, he could not take it upon himself to kill a Scot. Charles remonstrated with him angrily: 'My lord, there be as good men as you that will not refuse to take it, but I find you averse to all my proceedings.' He ordered that both men be arrested.

It was the talk of the city, and it seems to have been generally agreed that the peers had become martyrs to the king's will. Charles was soon advised that they had done nothing illegal in refusing the oath; much to his chagrin he was obliged to release them. His authority had suffered another grave blow. It transpired soon enough that Viscount Saye had indeed been in secret discussion with the leaders of the covenant cause. They held the puritan creed in common, and their clandestine collaboration would be significant in the events of later months.

On 1 May Charles advanced to Durham. His envoy to Scotland and now commander of his ships, the marquis of Hamilton, wrote to him that 'your majesty's affairs are in desperate condition. The enraged people here run to the height of rebellion, and walk with a blind obedience as by their traitorous leaders they are commanded . . . You will find it a work of great difficulty and of vast expense to curb them by force, their power being greater, their combination stronger than can be imagined.' Hamilton, himself a Scot, declared that 'next to hell I hate this land'. His discomfort was also heightened by his mother's threat that, if he returned in arms to his native country, she would shoot him.

Charles could not afford 'expense' of any kind. By the best estimate he had enough money to support his army to the end of the summer, but no longer. By the end of May, however, the lord treasurer announced that the revenue was exhausted. The knight marshal, Sir Edmund Verney, wrote to his son that 'our men are very raw, our arms of all sorts naught, our victual scarce, and provision for horses worse'.

The Scots were soon on the move. The drums were beaten, morning and evening, to summon the soldiers for divine service; they listened to two sermons each day in support of their cause. When the men were not engaged in martial exercise, they studied the Scriptures or sang hymns or prayed aloud. It was a formidable force. At the beginning of June they set up an armed camp at Kelso on the Scottish borders. The king ordered the earl of Holland to march 3,000 men to the north and drive them out. So the earl led his cavalry forward to test the purposes of the Scots. The English forces climbed an incline from which they could see the enemy below them. Holland was about to order a charge when a cloud of dust could be seen approaching very quickly; this was taken to be the token of a larger Scottish army. The English retreated in order but in haste; discretion, as on many other occasions, surmounted valour. It was said that they were spared a slaughter by the elders of the covenant who only wished for the strangers to leave their country.

The fiasco was a double blow to the English forces. They had not only been humiliated by the Scots but the Scottish lord general, Alexander Leslie, seemed to know in advance the movement of Holland's men. It looked very much as if there was a spy or traitor in the camp. Sir Edmund Verney wrote once more to his son that 'I think the king dares not stir out of his trenches. What counsels he will take, or what he will do, I cannot divine.' It had become clear to everyone that the enterprise was a huge mistake.

On 5 June Alexander Leslie arrived with an army of 12,000 men, and encamped on a hill about 11 miles from the king's position. Charles was devoid of fear, or indeed of any other emotion except perhaps curiosity; he took a view of the Scottish forces through his telescope. 'Come let us go to supper,' he said, 'the number is not considerable.' Yet he could not afford to fight them. The Scots were well-disciplined and ready to fight for 'Christ's Crown and Covenant'; he had only an ill-organized and largely apathetic army already painfully aware of its lack of provisions.

The king had to gain time to prepare himself more fully for armed warfare. The Scots, in turn, were reluctant to invade England; the temper of an aroused nation would then be such that victory was by no means certain. Parliament might be called, and all the material wants of the king resolved. It could become a hard fight. So the conditions were right to obtain a truce and agree to a treaty. On 11 June six commissioners from the Scots and six commissioners from the king sat down together at Berwick in the tent of the earl of Arundel; Charles himself then joined them.

The covenanters were described by one Scottish historian as 'men a little too low for heaven, and much too high for earth'. But on this occasion they were willing at least to treat with the king. In the event the negotiations at Berwick meant nothing. Ambiguities, confusions and caveats were the sum of all talk so that in the end, according to Clarendon, 'there were not two present who did agree in the same relation of what was said and done . . .' Nobody meant what he said, or said what he meant. The treaty was merely a paper peace and within six months the antagonists were preparing for a later and greater conflict. The first Bishops' War, a war without a set battle, had come to an end.

Charles I had hoped to lead a glittering army to victory but had instead been forced to come to terms with a people that had, to all intents and purposes, become a separate nation beyond his power to command. The Scots gained the reputation that he himself had forfeited. It was more painful for him to lose authority than to part with his lifeblood. He had come to realize the reluctance of many of the peers and gentry to join him in his quarrel. So he disbanded the army without thanking any of its commanders, who had undergone the sacrifice of bringing up their men, and without giving honours to his faithful followers. The earl of Essex, one of the great nobles whom the king distrusted, was dismissed without a word. Soon enough he would become a principal opponent of the king.

Charles was anxious and dissatisfied. When the Scots published a document that purported to contain the matter of the treaty it was burned in London by the common hangman. The covenanters proclaimed, however, that in maintaining their own rights they were also fighting for English liberties; they insinuated that the proscription or exclusion of their religion would infallibly lead to the destruction of the cause of puritanism in England.

There were many of that nation who agreed with them, Pym and Hampden among them; for these Englishmen, the Scottish defiance of a stubborn and authoritarian king was an inspiration. Letters passed between the 'malcontents' or 'malignants' of both nations, as the king called them, in the hope of planning a common strategy to preserve their religion. The earl of Northumberland wrote that 'the north is now the scene of all our news'; the theatre of the three kingdoms was now situated in Edinburgh. English politics now became thoroughly mingled with Scottish affairs.

The king had also lost authority on the high seas. In the autumn of 1639 a Spanish fleet had been discovered in the Channel by a Dutch squadron and, after a hot pursuit, took refuge in the Downs off the coast of east Kent; Charles offered, for a large sum, to take the Spaniards under his protection and convey them to the coast of Flanders. Yet the Dutch were unwilling to lose their prey and, with reinforcements, they attacked the Spanish vessels and sank many of them. The English fleet, under the command of Vice-Admiral Pennington, merely looked on as the security of their home waters was violated. The sea road to Dover was known as 'the king of England's imperial chamber', but that king had failed in his first duty of protecting it.

The paralysis of Charles was part of a much wider problem of foreign policy where, in want of money and preoccupied by the problem of Scotland, he was obliged to play off one party against another in the hope of something 'turning up'. France, Holland and Spain had to be appeased equally.

On 27 July, just before he left Berwick, Charles had summoned an emissary sent by Thomas Wentworth from Ireland; they held a long and secret conversation on matters that the king would not confide to paper. Wentworth had already told the king that he should conclude an armistice, and postpone any attack upon the Scots until he was quite certain that he could defeat them. Charles now merely sent a message to the lord deputy, saying, 'Come when you will, you shall be welcome.' The king was already scheming.

Wentworth returned from Dublin in the autumn of the year, and at once became the king's most trusted councillor. He possessed all the self-confidence and energy that the king himself lacked. One courtier, Sir Philip Warwick, recorded that 'his countenance was cloudy, while he moved or sat thinking; but when he spoke, either seriously or facetiously, he had a lightsome and very pleasant air'.

Wentworth urged Charles to take the affairs of Scotland into his own hands, and in addition to call parliament in order to be supplied with funds. The king of course distrusted and even despised the members at Westminster, but Wentworth believed that he could organize a court party which would be able to outmanoeuvre any opposition from such familiar suspected persons as Pym and Hampden. The king would also be absolved of the charge of absolutism, of wishing to rule without parliament, and might once again earn the approval of the nation. If the members of the Commons did not cheerfully grant his demands, in the face of evident danger from the Scots, then the world would know who to blame. Within a few months Wentworth received the earldom of Strafford.

At the end of 1639, therefore, parliament was summoned. The news was greeted with relief by those who had feared the complete abandonment of conventional government. Others were not so sanguine, however, and the Venetian ambassador reported that 'the long rusted gates of parliament cannot be opened without difficulty'. The king's councillors professed to believe that the newly elected parliament, shocked by the insolence of the Scots, would rally around the king.

The general election proceeded apace, with all sides and factions trying to organize support in an informal way. Only sixty-two of the elections were contested, with the other candidates selected by the principal landowners in the country and by the municipal corporations of the towns and cities. Other members of parliament were chosen by individual patrons who owned the right of nomination. A contested election was considered to be a mark of failure by the local elite to resolve matters satisfactorily.

The contested seats were indeed scenes of great division; there had been no such competition for eleven years. The court sent out lists of its favoured candidates as soon as the writs were issued. The local ministers preached to their congregations largely in favour of puritan candidates, while the peers supporting the court often tried to bribe or intimidate the electors of their regions. Newsletters and speeches abounded, as did the more nebulous reports of rumour and gossip. Violence, and threats of violence, were commonplace. A verse was circulated in opposition to the court party:

> Choose no ship sheriff, nor court atheist,
> No fen drainer, nor church papist.

There were no 'parties' in the modern sense, of course, merely individuals with various interests or principles who might or might not form an association with those who largely agreed with them. Some of them described themselves as 'good commonwealthmen' or 'patriots' who played upon the people's fears of taxation and popery. Other candidates tried to rally the electors to the cause of king and country. The tide was against them. It was said by a Kentish gentleman, Sir Roger Twysden, that 'the common people had been so bitten with ship-money that they were very averse from a courtier'; in Leicestershire the freeholders, who made up the constituency, were opposed to one candidate because 'he is a courtier and has been sheriff and collected the ship-money'.

It has been estimated that, of the sixty or so candidates nominated or supported by the court, only fourteen were successful. It would be fair to say, however, that the majority of those elected were not partisan in any obvious sense; they were individuals who came to Westminster with a lively sense of local complaints and who, when congregated together, might find that they had grievances in common.

Preparations for another war against Scotland were even then being made. It was intended to press into service 30,000 foot-soldiers from the counties south of the Humber, the northern counties having given service in the last war. The covenanters were equally active in Scotland, where a call to arms was about to be issued. It did not seem possible that war could be avoided. A group of covenanters came to London, where it was reported that they held secret consultations with their English allies.

The newly elected parliament opened on 13 April 1640, in great excitement. The wife of the earl of Bridgewater was advised to procure a place at a window by six o'clock in the morning, in order to watch the passing scenes at Westminster; after that time the press of the people in the street would make it impossible for her to reach the house. John Finch, newly appointed as lord keeper of the great seal, made an opening speech on behalf of the king in which he dilated upon the threat that the Scots posed to the country; the king had been obliged to raise an army in its defence and, for the payment of that army, he needed funds. Finch revealed that a bill had already been prepared with all the relevant measures in place; it was only necessary for parliament to pass it. Then, and only then, would the grievances of individual members be discussed. He stated that 'the king did not require their advice but an immediate vote of supplies'. It was noted that Finch had at no stage mentioned the primary source of discontent, the ship-money which was once again being exacted.

The members soon made their reply to the lord keeper's speech. On the first day of the session the earl of Northumberland wrote that 'their jealousies and suspicions appear upon every occasion and I fear they will not readily be persuaded to believe the fair and gracious promises that are made to them by the king'. In this opinion he was correct. The member for Colchester, Harbottle Grimstone, delivered a speech in which he stated that the invasion of individual liberties at home was more threatening than the ambitions of any enemy abroad. On the following day petitions from the various counties, complaining about unjust exactions, were presented to the Commons.

On 17 April John Pym rose to speak on the nature of parliamentary authority. He declared that 'the powers of parliament are to the body politic as the rational faculties of the soul to man'. He was asserting more than the usual claims of parliamentary privilege; he was outlining what amounted to a new theory of government without any mention of the divine right of kings. He then turned to the matter of religion, and condemned the innovations introduced by Laud and others; they had managed only to raise 'new occasions of further division' and to dismay 'the faithful professors of the truth'. The grievances of his eleven years' silence now poured forth in an attack upon ship-money, monopolies, forest law and the other measures that the king had imposed. When he sat down he was greeted with cries of 'A good oration!'

There was one group or faction in this parliament that helped to shape the session. The Providence Island Company had first been established to assist the emigration of 'godly' settlers to an island off the coast of what is now Nicaragua; it was hoped that a little republican commonwealth would then emerge that would finance itself with tobacco and cotton. Among the begetters of this scheme were the most prominent puritans in the country, among them Oliver St John, John Pym, John Hampden, Viscount Saye and Lord Brooke; the most eminent of them, however, was the earl of Warwick. All of these men now took their seats in parliament, both in the Commons and in the Lords, where they could plan their strategy in concert. They had familial as well as religious connections, lending them a unity and strength of purpose that were almost without precedent. The court party, in contrast, was riven with conflicts over personality and policy.

On 21 April the king summoned both houses to Whitehall, and demanded that the financial subsidies be granted to him. Two days later the Commons went into committee and requested a conference with the Lords on the grounds that 'until the liberties of the House and kingdom were cleared, they knew not whether they had anything to give or no'. At this act of defiance Charles was extremely angry. On 1 May the Commons decided by a large majority to call before them a cleric who had stated that the king had the authority to make laws without parliament; this was considered by the court to be another act of insubordination. On the following day the king demanded an immediate answer to his request for money; he was met with pre-varication. On 4 May Charles sent another message in which he agreed to give up the collection of ship-money in return for twelve subsidies amounting to approximately £850,000. The committee of the Commons again broke up without reaching any definite con-clusions. One of the royal councillors, Sir Henry Vane, told the king that there was now no hope that they 'would give one penny'.

It had become apparent, at least to the court party, that the Commons had no real desire to support the king's war against Scotland; it might even be supposed that they were leaning towards the Scottish covenanters. The king had asked for supplies five times, and five times he had been rebuffed. He had twice appeared in person, to no palpable effect. He had tried to negotiate but his offers had been rejected with silence. He had pressed for speed in their decisions, with the possibility of an imminent invasion from the north, but parliament had been dilatory and evasive.

Rumours now reached the king that, under the influence of Pym, a petition was even then being drawn up asking him to come to terms with the Scots. He summoned the Speaker and forbade him take his place on the following day, thus avoiding the possibility of any debate. He then hurried to the Lords and on 5 May summarily dissolved the parliament. Since it had endured for only three weeks, it became commonly known as the 'stillborn parliament'; posterity christened it the 'Short Parliament'. It had achieved nothing, but it had changed everything. It had given voice to the frustration and anger of the country at the behaviour of the king; it had become a national forum where none had existed before.

One newly elected MP, Edward Hyde, who would later become better known as Lord Clarendon, was disconsolate. He supported the king but did not know what the future might hold for him. He wrote later that one of the leaders of the parliamentary revolt, Oliver St John, 'observing a cloudiness in me, bade me "be of good comfort; all would go well; for things must be worse before they could be better"'. St John added that 'we must not only sweep the house clean below, but must pull down all the cobwebs which hang in the top and corners'. He was hoping for a crisis or disaster, in other words, that would overturn the familiar order.

Another member may be introduced here. Sir Philip Warwick came into the house later in the same year,

> and perceived a gentleman whom I knew not, very ordinarily apparelled; for it was a plain cloth suit that seemed to have been made by an ill country tailor; his linen was plain and not very clean and I remember a speck or two of blood upon his

little band which was not much larger than his collar; his hat was without a hatband; his stature was of a good size; his sword stuck close to his side; his countenance swollen and reddish; his voice sharp and untunable and his eloquence full of fervour.

Such was the young Oliver Cromwell, who had sat unnoticed in the parliamentary sessions of 1628 and 1629. Now he had found his voice.

On the afternoon of the dissolution the king's council met in which the newly ennobled earl of Strafford, according to notes taken at the time, advised the king to 'go on with a vigorous war as you first designed, loosed and absolved from all rules of government, being reduced to extreme necessities. Everything is to be done that power must admit.' He added that 'you have an army in Ireland you may employ here to reduce this kingdom'. It was, perhaps, not clear which 'kingdom' needed to be reduced; this was an ambiguity that would cost him dear.

The dissolution aroused much discontent. The calling of the first parliament for eleven years had been hailed as a victory and as a deliverance from bondage; yet it had ended in defeat. Clarendon recalled that 'there could not a greater damp have seized upon the spirits of the whole nation'. The king blamed 'the cunning of some few seditiously affected men'; he genuinely believed, for example, that the members of the Providence Island Company were in direct contact with his Scottish enemies in an effort to defeat him.

Many in London and elsewhere, however, were ready to condemn the king and his councillors, principal among them the earl of Strafford and Archbishop Laud. Strafford now became known as 'black Tom Tyrant', the hatred for him compounded by the suspicion that he was indeed planning to bring over an Irish army to subdue English dissent. Yet William Laud was still the principal target. He was, in the judgement of many, the secret power behind the throne.

On 7 May, two days after the dissolution, the lord mayor and his aldermen were summoned before the council and ordered to provide the king with a loan of £200,000. If they refused they were to return three days later with a list of the wealthiest Londoners who could furnish the necessary funds. On 10 May they returned, bearing no list. 'Sir,' Strafford said to the king, 'you will never do good to these citizens of London till you have made examples of some of these aldermen. Unless you hang up some of them, you will do no good upon them.' The king did not execute them, but he did commit four of them to prison. This added more fuel to the fire that was about to break out in the streets.

Placards had been posted at the Royal Exchange, and elsewhere, calling upon the apprentices to meet at St George's Fields in Southwark and 'hunt William the fox, the breaker of the parliament'. A force of 500 attempted, on the night of 11 May, to storm the archbishop's palace at Lambeth; the protestors were driven off by gunfire from the trained bands. Three days later the prisons that held some of the rioters were broken open, and the men released. The trained bands of Essex, Kent and Hertfordshire were summoned to the capital where they successfully restored a semblance of peace. Yet there were still victims. One captured apprentice was, on the orders of the king, tortured on the rack in the vain hope that he would name his accomplices; his crime had been to beat the drum in the vanguard of the rioters. It was the last example of judicial torture in English history. A sailor was convicted of high treason for attempting to open the gates of Lambeth Palace with a crowbar; he was hanged, drawn and quartered as punishment for his mighty offence.

The anger against the archbishop was augmented by the deliberations of the convocation. This body of the higher clergy always met at the time of parliament but, on this occasion, it was not dissolved after the abrupt conclusion of the recent short session. It continued to meet, granted a subsidy to the king, and announced seventeen new canons that exalted the sovereign's power. It was ordered that, four times in each year, the clergy should preach to their congregations on the theme of divine right. It was further decreed that all of the clergy must take an oath to maintain both the doctrine and the discipline of the Church and not to allow any alteration in its government by 'archbishops, bishops, deans and archdeacons etc.'. This became known derisively as 'the etcetera oath'. How could clerics obey a ruling of which the contents were so uncertain? Without the assent of parliament, in any case, the decree was illegal. When the chancellor of the bishop of London entered one church to exact the oath, with a great mace carried before him, the verger stopped him with the words: 'I care nothing for you, nor for your artichoke.' The new canons were similarly derided. A drawing by Wenceslaus Hollar depicted some clergymen standing about a faulty cannon as Laud lights it. A verse beneath it read:

> This cannon's sealed, well forg'd, not made of lead
> Give fire. Oh no, 'twill break and strike us dead.

The Scots were greatly heartened by events in England. A parliament met in Edinburgh at the beginning of June, despite an effort by Charles to prorogue it. Its members now believed that the people of England were no longer inclined to support their king; they passed into law, without royal assent, various Acts that removed the bishops from the Kirk and materially diminished the king's authority. It was a tacit declaration of war.

Yet what could the king do? He had formed no fresh army, and the troops still quartered at Newcastle after the last conflict were untrained and impoverished. Once more the king demanded ship-money from London. The sheriffs went from house to house to exact the tax but only one man, in the entire City of London, agreed to pay it. Schemes for loans from France, and from Genoa, came to nothing.

The labourers and craftsmen of England were again pressed into service, in the king's army, for a cause about which they knew or cared little. News of disorder came from most of the southern counties, and one of the first open mutinies broke out in Warwickshire. Some men of Devon, stopping at Wellington in Somerset, murdered a Roman Catholic lieutenant who refused to accompany them to church. When all of these unlikely and unwilling recruits arrived at Selby, in North Yorkshire, their commander described them as 'the arch-knaves of the country'. Thus began the Second Bishops' War.

19

A great and dangerous treason

In July 1640, the lord general of the Scottish forces, Alexander Leslie, began to create the nucleus of an army to take the fight once more into England. His intention was first to seize Newcastle; with its mineral wealth in his hands, he knew that he could exert pressure upon London that depended upon 'sea-coal' for its fuel. He believed that he would meet no resistance from the northern counties; the dissolution of parliament, and the general belief in a 'popish plot' led by Laud, had put an end to any appetite for a struggle against Scotland. Leslie's contacts in England had in fact assured him that the next parliament, when summoned, would demand peace; otherwise, it would give no financial assistance to the king. There may have been a closer connection. It seems probable that the leaders of the 'godly' cause in England had effectively invited the Scots to invade as a way of curbing or destroying the power of an authoritarian king. Leslie's march would be welcomed by some, therefore, and treated with indifference by the rest.

On the morning of 20 August the king set out from London to meet his forces in the north. On that night a Scottish army of 25,000 men crossed the Tweed. As soon as they entered English territory, their ministers formed the vanguard with Bibles in their hands. A declaration was issued to the effect that they were not marching against the English but against the papists, the Arminians

and the prelates. They would remain in England until their grievances were heard by a new parliament.

They informed the people of Northumberland, too, that they
would not take any food or drink without paying for it; they were
well disciplined and respectful. Thomas Wentworth, the earl of
Strafford, had hoped that the mere sight of an invading army would
enrage all good Englishmen, but that proved not to be the case.
The English commander in the north, Viscount Conway, noted that
'the country doth give them all the assistance they can. Many of
the country gentlemen do come to them, entertain and feast them.'
In London, after the king's departure, all was in confusion. A courtier, Sir Nicholas Byron, wrote that 'we are here, and in every place,
in such distraction as if the day of judgment were hourly expected'.
The constable of the Tower was ordered to prepare his fortress for
a possible siege. Meanwhile the Scots were still marching southward.

Viscount Conway had been ordered to fortify the banks of the
Tyne, and to defend Newcastle; he left two-thirds of his troops to
protect the city, and took the remainder some 4 miles above
Newcastle to a ford in the river at Newburn. The Scots took up a
commanding position on the north bank, from where they fired on
the enemy; the English soldiers, unaccustomed to gunshot, fled after
some of their number were killed. The cavalry also retired in disarray.
It was the first major victory of the Scots over the English for 300
years. Charles I had failed in battle, the single most important
disgrace that stained the honour of a king. The battle of Newburn
might also be considered the first of the civil war, since two rival
parties had fought on English soil.

After their egregious defeat the English army retired to the
borders of Yorkshire, leaving Durham and Northumberland in the
hands of the enemy. The vital city of Newcastle had already surrendered. The earl of Strafford wrote to his friend, Sir George Radcliffe,
from Northallerton in North Yorkshire where he had gone to meet
the fleeing army:

> Pity me, for never came any man to so lost a business.
> The army altogether necessitous and unprovided of all neces-
> saries . . . Our horse all cowardly; the country from Berwick
> to York in the power of the Scots; an universal affright in all;

a general disaffection to the king's service, none sensible of his dishonor. In one word, here alone to fight with all these evils, without anyone to help. God of his goodness deliver me out of this, the greatest evil of my life.

The news of the royal defeat at Newburn was greeted with celebrations in London. Twelve peers of puritan persuasion, among them the earls of Warwick and Bedford, now issued in the traditional manner a 'petition' to the monarch in which they called for a parliament to resolve the grievances and evils of the nation; they stated that 'your whole kingdom [has] become full of fears and discontents'. They were following a carefully prepared strategy. If the king declined to act on their advice, they themselves were prepared to summon parliament, just as the barons of Henry III had threatened almost 400 years before.

The king reacted in a thoroughly medieval way. He received the petition while at York, and summoned a great council of the peers. He may have hoped that they might raise large sums of money, without the assistance of parliament, but in this hope he was destined to be disappointed. Archbishop Laud was more realistic, and believed that the great council would lead inevitably to the calling of another parliament that might bode no good.

So the peers of England met in the hall of the deanery at York on 24 September. They represented a vast social power; they exercised local authority over tenants and dependants but they also wielded political power by means of their influence in county and borough elections. In his opening speech to them the king announced that he would indeed summon parliament to meet at the beginning of November; it was hoped that, on the basis of this undertaking, the City would be ready to lend him money. He said further that an 'army of rebels' was lodged within the kingdom and he wished for the peers' advice so that 'we might justly proceed to the chastisement of these insolencies'.

In the debate that followed it was eventually decided that commissioners should be sent to negotiate with the invaders. The Scots had already demanded money from the northern counties where they were lodged; they now insisted that the payments be maintained by the leading gentry, and that Charles should call parliament, where a peace treaty could be agreed. They trusted parliament, in other words, rather than the king. On these conditions they would remain where they were, and not proceed any further into an unhappy and divided kingdom.

Negotiators from both sides met at Ripon, where it was concluded that the king would pay the Scots £25,000 a month until a peace treaty had been reached. It seemed likely that only parliament could supply such a sum. The peers at York were asked to advise the acceptance or rejection of the agreement. It was of course no contest. The king had no choice but to submit to the claims of the invaders and to call parliament. The experiment of absolute monarchy had come to an end.

In his diary entry for 30 October John Evelyn noted that 'I saw his majesty (coming from his northern expedition) ride in pomp and a kind of ovation, with all the marks of a happy peace, restored to the affections of his people, being conducted through London with a most splendid cavalcade'. Edward Rossingham wrote to Viscount Conway that 'we are all mad with joy here that his majesty does call his parliament, and that he puts his Scotch business into the hands of his peers who, the hope is here, will make peace upon any conditions'. The earl of Northampton considered 'one word of four syllables', namely parliament, was 'like the dew of heaven'.

Others were not so sanguine. A few days before the king's arrival into the city Archbishop Laud had entered his study, in search of certain manuscripts, only to find his portrait by Van Dyck lying face down upon the floor. He was a superstitious man. 'I am almost every day threated with my ruin in Parliament,' he confided to his diary. 'God grant this be no omen.'

The 'godly' parliamentarians were well prepared. They met at the house of John Pym, close to Gray's Inn, where their plans were discussed in detail. They became known as 'the Junto', with Pym their leader in the Commons and the earl of Bedford their representative in the Lords. They knew the disposition of the Scots and in turn the covenanters relied upon the help of their English friends in parliament to engineer the necessary changes in religion. This was the 'Protestant Cause'.

The voting in the parliamentary elections was unusually combative, with eighty-six contests outside the charmed circle of seats where only one uncontested member stood. The king's party was again at a disadvantage, with local as well as religious interests matched against the courtiers and their acolytes. Of twelve lawyers chosen by the king to be selected, for example, only three were appointed. On 3 November the king travelled to the new parliament by water in order to avoid the public gaze. The Venetian ambassador noted that the lack of ceremony 'shows more clearly than ever to his people that he consents to the summons merely from compulsion . . . and not of his own free will to please the people'. Who could have guessed that this parliament would last, with intervals, for almost twenty years?

As soon as they were assembled in debate, the members of the Commons issued a catalogue of grievances against the conduct of the king's councillors, Strafford and Laud chief among them. The dissolution of the 'Short Parliament', before any measures of reform could be agreed, had not improved the temper of the members; 60 per cent of them had sat in the previous assembly and they were now more belligerent than ever. Yet the largest group in the Commons was still that of the landed gentry, who were essentially conservative and not inclined to innovation. They did not want to destroy the king or the orthodox constitution. They wanted government to be restored upon the old model. Yet they, too, had been grievously disappointed. They had watched the king lose a war. They had seen him alienate his natural supporters. They had observed him in the company of the popish courtiers around his wife. They had witnessed the disruption of law and order in their regions.

All of the parliamentarians now understood their strength. They knew that the king relied upon them to salvage him from his distress; if parliament did not supply him with funds, he would not be able to pay the Scottish army as he had agreed to do. Alexander Leslie might then order a march upon Whitehall, with no English army to prevent his progress. As long as the Scots remained in England, therefore, parliament was supreme.

In the debate that followed the opening, one member remarked that it was common knowledge that the judges had overthrown the law and that the bishops had overthrown the gospel. Another intimated that a popish plot was being hatched by some about the king. Yet another rose to complain that the government was the weakest for generations and had produced nothing but national disgrace; it was surmised that those who had most loudly proclaimed the king's authority had also been those who had wasted the king's money.

When John Pym rose to speak the members were already much agitated. Pym began by saying that 'the distempers of the time are well known'. Much of his bitterness was reserved for Strafford himself, whom he believed to be the author of 'a design to alter law and religion'. Many contemporaries and colleagues were taking Pym's side. The Scots believed that Strafford was the cause of the war between the two nations. The puritans hated him. The City, now more powerful than ever, remembered how he had threatened its aldermen with hanging. He had created an absolute rule during his period of government in Ireland, and it was believed that he wished to repeat the experiment in England.

Strafford was aware of the perils of his position. He could have stayed in York, safe from the depredations of parliament, but the king urged him to join him in Whitehall; he assured him that 'he should not suffer in his person, honour or fortune'. The king's promises were, in the event, worth nothing at all. Strafford wrote that 'I am tomorrow in London with more dangers beset, I believe, than ever any man went with out of Yorkshire . . . '.

John Pym in turn had some reason to fear Strafford. When the earl arrived in London on 9 November he advised the king to provide the evidence that would implicate Pym and his colleagues in a treasonable association with the Scots. That evidence, perhaps of intercepted letters, has never since emerged. News reached Westminster that Strafford was ready to 'prefer an accusation of high treason against diverse members of both houses of parliament'; they would no doubt include Warwick, Saye and Brooke from the Lords with Pym, Hampden and others from the Commons.

It was agreed by the king and his councillors that the defences of the Tower should immediately be strengthened; the fortification was meant as a warning to the City. The Tower was also the likely destination for those about to be arrested. Strafford was quoted as saying that 'he hoped the City would be subdued in a short time'.

On 11 November the king was expected to travel to the Tower and inspect its garrison.

On that day rumours of an attempted coup reached Westminster. The Commons ordered that all strangers should be cleared from the lobby. Strafford took his seat in the House of Lords, but said nothing; he was biding his time. Yet Pym knew of the accusations against himself and his colleagues. He had to remove Strafford before Strafford could destroy him. In a phrase of the time, 'my head or thy head'.

In a speech delivered to the Commons Pym attacked one of Strafford's most notable allies, Sir Francis Windebank, for concealing a popish plot. It might or might not be interpreted as an attack upon Strafford himself, but it was a method by which Pym could test the readiness of his colleagues to take action against his enemies. Another member, John Clotworthy, now suggested or insinuated that Strafford planned to use the Irish army 'ready to march where I know not' in order to curb dissent in England.

It was moved that a committee be established to consult with the Lords on the accusations; this committee was packed with Strafford's enemies, and a 'charge' against the earl was swiftly pre pared and presented to the Commons. Some members urged caution and delay in the assault upon Strafford, but Pym replied that any procrastination 'might probably blast all their hopes'.

With a throng of members around him Pym then went to the Lords in order to accuse Strafford of high treason, and to recommend that he be 'sequestered from Parliament'. If the Lords wished to know the grounds of this serious charge, 'particular articles and accusations' against him would be delivered to them shortly. Strafford had been told of the events then unfolding. 'I will go,' he said, 'and look my accusers in the face.' It must be said that the Lords themselves had many grievances against the king's arrogant and difficult adviser and, on his entry, he was commanded by them to withdraw. An order was then passed committing Strafford to the custody of the gentleman usher. He was directed to enter the chamber and to kneel while the order was read to him. He asked permission to speak, but was refused; his sword was taken from him before he was led away.

In his *History of the Rebellion* Clarendon wrote that the crowd looked upon the earl without pity, 'no man capping to him, before whom that morning the greatest in England would have stood discovered'. No man had taken off his hat in respect.

'What is the matter?' someone asked him.

'A small matter, I warrant you,' he replied.

Another called out, 'Yes indeed, high treason is a small matter.'

Strafford was effectively removed from public life. Charles had lost his principal councillor. It was widely assumed that a great work had been accomplished. The king was obliged to disperse the garrison he had established within the Tower and to dismantle the guns that had recently been mounted. His attempt to coerce or overawe his opponents had failed, in another of those humiliating reversals that had become associated with his rule.

With the threat of dissolution or a coup now removed, parliament could begin its work on what it believed to be wholesale renovation. A public fast was observed on 17 November as a way of enlisting divine assistance in this task. Some sixty-five committees were established to investigate all cases of abuse and corruption. One of them was devoted to seeking out and removing 'persecuting, innovating or scandalous' ministers, justices of the peace and other royal officers; when its members requested 'informations from all parties' to assist them, hundreds of individuals descended upon Westminster with their own particular grievances.

A committee for petitions was then established to deal with their complaints. Warwick, Brooke, Essex, Bedford and Saye and their colleagues were in command of its actions. It sat in the Painted Chamber at Westminster and became an alternative court of law, investigating all aspects of the government's work. Parliament had in the past been summoned simply to transact the king's business; now it busied itself about national affairs without any reference to the king.

The evidence against Strafford was presented on 24 November 1640, and was formulated in the first article of the indictment against him. The Commons was asked to declare that 'Thomas, earl of Strafford hath traitorously endeavoured to subvert the fundamental laws and government of the realms of England and Ireland, and instead thereof to introduce an arbitrary and tyrannical government against law'. In his speech to the Commons Pym argued that the accusations amounted to a great and dangerous treason, animated by malice and guided by evil mischief. He accused the earl of attempting to spread discord between the king and the people. It had become clear that Strafford could not be allowed to survive; if he evaded the charge of treason he might become the focus of royalist hopes, and might even herald the resumption of non-parliamentary government.

At the end of November the three dissenters who had been mutilated and imprisoned at the behest of Archbishop Laud – Prynne, Burton and Bastwick – returned in triumph to the capital; they wore rosemary and bay in their hats, and flowers were strewn before them. Rosemary was the herb of remembrance and bay of victory. It was for Henry Burton, a puritan divine, 'a sweet and glorious day, or time, which the sun of righteousness, arising over *England*, was now about to procure for us'. That bright dawn still depended on the presence of the covenanters in the north, and in the early days of December parliament voted subsidies for the Scottish army.

Arguments over religion were the soul of this first session of what became known as the 'Long Parliament', outweighing any concerns over secular misgovernment. Already the devout were in full pursuit of the Arminians. A London crowd had burst into St Paul's Cathedral where it destroyed the altar and tore up the book of the new liturgy. At Stourbridge Fair a preacher stirred up a crowd by calling out 'Pardon! Pardon! Pardon!' for the superstition and idolatry imposed by those in authority. In Brislington, Somerset, a dissenting minister who had been suspended from office preached to his flock beneath the shade of a tree in the street, whereupon the congregation led him back to the church and gave him the key.

On 11 December the citizens of London presented a petition to parliament for 'reformation in church government'. It declared that 'the government of archbishops and lord bishops, deacons and archdeacons etc. . . . has proved prejudicial and very dangerous both to the church and commonwealth'; it urged that this ecclesiastical government should be destroyed 'with all its dependencies, roots and branches'. Fifteen hundred supporters gathered in Westminster Yard, well-dressed, well-organized and good-tempered, and after delivering their petition they returned quietly to their homes. The

'root and branch' petition, as it came to be known, was passed by
Pym to a committee where it remained for some months.

More immediate remedies were at hand. On 16 December the
canons passed by convocation in the spring of the year, among them
'the etcetera oath', were voted by parliament to be illegal. It was
now time to attack the archbishop himself. On 18 December Laud
was impeached and taken into custody. He was accused of fostering
doctrines that lent support to the king's arbitrary measures, and of
using the courts both to impose innovations in worship and to
silence the true professors of religion. One member of parliament,
Harbottle Grimstone, described him as 'the root and ground of all
our miseries and calamities'. Other bishops soon joined him in the
Tower. The bishop of Ely, Matthew Wren, was to spend seventeen
years in confinement. Parliament could be as vindictive and as
authoritarian as the king, perhaps because both parties believed that
they were fulfilling the divine will.

Someone had scribbled, on the door of St Stephen's Chapel at
Westminster, an appeal to 'remember the judges'. Their time was
not long in coming. All those who had supported the king in their
judgments were questioned or arrested. Many of the king's courtiers
now fled the approaching storm. Sir Francis Windebank, whom
Pym had accused of concealing a Catholic conspiracy, was rowed
at night across the Channel. Lord Keeper Finch fled the country
for Holland on the day he was impeached.

The members of parliament now determined to consolidate their
strength. On 24 December it was recommended that 'the English
lord commissioners', which in effect meant the puritan lords who
had launched the petition for parliament in the summer, should be
responsible for the disbursement of money to the Scots. Five days
later Pym advised that the customs officials, who were the king's
principal financial agents, should 'forbear to pay anything' to the
exchequer until authorization was 'settled by Parliament'; his
proposal was carried without any division. The king now lacked the
resources even to pay his own household expenses.

In this last week of December it was further agreed that parliament should meet at fixed times with or without the co-operation
of the king. The 'Triennial Act' was passed to compel parliaments
to meet every three years. The Venetian ambassador reported that

'if this innovation is introduced, it will hand over the reins of government completely to Parliament, and nothing will be left to the king but mere show and a simulacrum of reality, stripped of credit and destitute of all authority'. It remained to be seen whether Charles would willingly relinquish his powers. The contest had only just begun.

20

Madness and fury

The new year, 1641, was for the godly a time of jubilation. It was the year in which, according to cant phrases of the time, a period of 'great affliction' was succeeded by an age of 'seasonable mercies'. Some writers were dating their letters '*annus mirabilis*' or '*anno renovationis*'. It was a golden year in which God's goodness and mercy to the nation were vouchsafed. A pamphleteer, John Bond, exulted in 'England's Rejoicing for the Parliament's Return' that 'papists tremble . . . Arminians tumble . . . the priests of Baal lament their fortunes'. For those of a royalist persuasion, however, the year marked the culmination of all their woes that had begun at the battle of Newburn.

The king was in desperate straits with his authority and revenue threatened, and with his principal counsellors languishing in the Tower. Henrietta Maria was enraged at the situation of the royal household, and continued to argue for more determined measures against her husband's opponents. She even wrote to the Vatican asking for a large loan, perhaps with the intention of raising troops.

Charles himself did not surrender to the calamity that faced him. His health was good, and he was not inclined to anxiety; he maintained a daily regimen of prayer and exercise; he enjoyed an excellent appetite. He believed implicitly that the enemies of the Lord's anointed would of necessity fail, and that all traitors would eventually be brought to the bar of justice.

On 23 January Charles summoned both houses of parliament
to the Banqueting House at Whitehall, and delivered a speech in
which he complained about the obstructions placed in his path by
men who 'put no difference betwixt reformation and alteration of
government'. Yet he seemed willing to compromise, and promised
to return the laws of religious polity to the 'purest times of Queen
Elizabeth's days'. He stated further that 'whatsoever part of my
revenue shall be found illegal, or heavy to my subjects, I shall be
willing to lay it down'. He had in effect cancelled the exaction of
ship-money, and curbed all other questionable ways of raising
revenue.

The status of his most faithful servant was still in doubt. It was
already whispered at court that Strafford must rely upon his own
protestations of innocence and, if they should fail, upon the mercy
of parliament. Charles was unwilling to fight for his quondam
counsellor; he seems to have realized that only Strafford's death
could preface the reconciliation he desired with his people. At the
end of the month the charges were drawn up against the earl;
twenty-eight separate articles, covering the last fourteen years of his
career, were outlined over two hundred sheets of paper.

At the beginning of February the Commons voted £300,000 to
the Scots under the name of 'brotherly assistance'; the two nations
were not to be divided. They needed one another, for the moment,
in their confrontation with the king. They also needed the 'Triennial
Bill' that guaranteed the meeting of parliament on a regular basis.
The bill was a grievous blow to the royal prerogative, and Charles
had been most reluctant to give his assent; his power would be
limited, and his authority compromised. Yet on 16 February he was
persuaded to concede the issue, partly from advice that he would
receive no money after any refusal. So he declared in the old Norman
fashion that '*le roi le veut*', 'the king wishes it'. In private the king
raged. In effect the Act made him reliant upon parliament and gave
that assembly the permanent existence that it had never known
before. The bells of London rang out. The earl of Leicester wrote
in his commonplace book that now 'the parliament which is a
corporation never dies, nor ceases at the death of the king, that is,
the death of the king is no determination of it, and it is not likely
that they will be weary of their immortality'.

It had already been rumoured that a new privy council was about to emerge that would reflect the wishes of the Commons as well as of the king. The earl of Bedford was to become lord treasurer while his lieutenant in the Commons, John Pym, would be chancellor of the exchequer; the earl of Bristol would be made lord privy seal. On 19 February seven other members of the puritan Junto were nominated to be privy councillors, among them Viscount Saye and the earls of Essex and Bedford. Clarendon wrote in his *History* that they were 'all persons at that time very gracious to the people or the Scots . . . had all been in some umbrage at court and most in visible disfavour'.

The king had declared himself indirectly to be a moderate, therefore, equally ready to forgive his erstwhile enemies and to trim or turn his policies in the light of complaints directed against them. Yet at the same time he had also managed to divide the opposition against him. Many in parliament did not share the religious enthusiasm of the Scottish covenanters and had no wish to see the English Church remodelled to satisfy their demands; others were already beginning to resent the amount of money being spent for the maintenance of the Scottish army in the north. If Charles could gain the support of such men, parliamentary assistance would be at hand in his fight against the Junto.

The compromise with the puritans of parliament did not in the end succeed. The king had insisted that, in order to take up the offices of state he had promised to them, they must agree to retain the bishops in the Lords and to save Strafford's life. They in turn demanded to be granted the offices before doing anything at all. No grand reconciliation was possible.

On 24 February Strafford was brought from the Tower to the chamber of the House of Lords in order to answer the charges laid against him. It was noticed with surprise that the king had taken his place upon the throne, by which he indicated his support for the earl. When the king eventually departed, however, it was resolved that the proceedings would have to begin all over again. Strafford defended himself with eloquence and wit, throwing into serious doubt the result of any trial. Within days it was reported that the parliamentary leaders were unsure how to proceed with their case. It was easy to proclaim Strafford to be a traitor, but a more difficult matter to prove it in open court.

His trial opened on 22 March, when he was taken by barge from the Tower to Westminster Hall. He was dressed entirely in black, as a dramatic token of sorrow, and the hall itself became known to the participants as 'the theatre'. This was the spectacle that might determine the fate of the nation, as the prisoner fought for his life and for the cause of the king. Negotiations of course continued behind the scene. The puritan grandees were ready to spare Strafford's life, for example, if the king agreed to grant them the great offices of state.

On the first day the peers of the realm filed into their places on both sides of the hall; tiers of seats had been placed, on either side of the peers, for the Commons. A committee of the Lords had already decided that it was not proper for the king himself to be present; so an empty throne stood at the northern end of the improvised courtroom while the king and queen were in fact sitting in seats behind, like a box in a theatre. Strafford himself was to stand on a dais at the southern end, facing both houses of parliament. The visual impression, in fact devised by Inigo Jones, was of one man against all the representatives of the nation. The hall was packed with spectators who made much clamour and 'clattering'; it was remarked by one observer, Robert Baillie, that there was 'much public eating, not only of confections but of flesh and bread, bottles of beer and wine going thick from mouth to mouth without cups'.

When the twenty-eight articles of impeachment were read out to him, Strafford was seen to smile; he could already see the legal difficulties that beset his accusers. They were attempting to prove treason on the basis of an accumulation of several separate charges. A remark passed around at the time was: you know at first sight whether a man is short or tall, you do not need to measure the inches. With Strafford's supposed treachery, you would need to count the inches carefully. At one point Strafford said that 'opinions may make a heretic, but that they make a traitor I never heard till now'. The days passed, with witnesses and questions and arguments, in the course of which Strafford seemed to delight in outwitting the counsels for the prosecution; they in turn were considered to be bombastic and hectoring.

It soon became clear to the members of the Junto that their cause could be lost, and they began to suspect that a majority of the peers was in fact secretly or openly supporting the cause of Strafford. When on 10 April the Lords allowed an adjournment for the prisoner to consult his notes before making a closing speech, the Commons protested in fury. They rose in consternation. Some of them, according to the parliamentary notes of Simonds D'Ewes, called out, 'Withdraw! Withdraw!', which was misheard by others as 'Draw! Draw!'; their hands went to the hilts of their swords in anticipation of battle. The confusion delighted Strafford to the extent that 'he could not hide his joy'; the king, in his box behind the throne, was seen to laugh. The two houses of parliament were in dispute.

The members of the Commons returned to their chamber in the afternoon, and at this opportune moment certain notes taken at a previous meeting of the privy council were conveniently revealed. This was the council during which Strafford had told the king that 'you have an army in Ireland you may employ here to reduce this kingdom'. The earl's accusers interpreted this 'kingdom' to be England rather than Scotland. This of course was treason. The Commons readily agreed. A Bill of Attainder was drawn up, a medieval device whereby both houses of parliament could try and condemn an enemy of the kingdom without the formality of a trial. It was also a way of persuading the Lords to vote for Strafford's death without the burden of legal proof.

On 19 April the king ordered all military officers immediately to return to their regiments. When a negotiator from Scotland had an audience with the king two days later, he reported that 'his mind seems to be on some project here shortly to break out'. It was also rumoured that the French, exhorted by the queen, were about to invade. What the leaders of the Junto most feared was a dissolution of parliament, a device that would result in the immediate cancellation of both the trial and the proposed attainder. They called out their supporters, and a crowd of many thousands gathered at Westminster in the belief that dangerous measures were about to be introduced. On 19 April, too, the Commons passed the Bill of Attainder against the earl of Strafford. Those of the Commons who had not supported the decision were derided as 'Straffordians or enemies to their country'; their names were listed and placed on posts and other visible locations in the city. The members of the godly party were not above intimidation and violation of parliamentary privilege.

When the Commons passed the attainder the king wrote to Strafford to reassure him once again he had his word that his life, honour, or fortune would not be touched. On the last day of the proceedings in Westminster Hall, 29 April, Strafford seemed merry. Oliver St John then rose to deliver a three-hour tirade against the prisoner which was of such eloquence that it profoundly influenced the intentions of the peers; when he finished, the spectators in the hall broke into applause. Two days later the king addressed both houses of parliament from the throne. In his speech he emphasized that he would never act against his conscience; this was taken to mean that he would veto any attainder against his counsellor. Let them find Strafford guilty only of a misdemeanour, and he would act. The king also refused to disband his Irish army, which in turn raised fears of military action.

He stayed for a while after his oration, looking for supporters, but Simonds D'Ewes reported 'there was not one man gave him the least hum or colour of plaudit to his speech, which made him, after some time of expectation, depart suddenly'. It was widely believed that he had intruded in a matter still under parliamentary debate, which was considered by the Commons to be 'the most unparalleled breach of privilege that had ever happened'. It seemed that a confrontation between king and parliament was inevitable.

Rumours of plots and counter-plots were soon everywhere. For some weeks a vessel, chartered by Strafford's secretary, had been moored in the Thames. The boat could easily take an escaped prisoner to France. Some of the reports proved to be true. On Sunday 2 May, Sir John Suckling, courtier and army commander, poet and gambler, called sixty men to the White Horse Tavern in Bread Street; they wore battledress of buff cloth and carried swords as well as pistols. They were supposed to gain entrance to the Tower of London, in the guise of reinforcements, where they would at once overwhelm the guard and secure Strafford's liberty. It was a wild scheme, made all the more improbable by the sight of sixty armed men milling about in the middle of London. Their presence was quickly known and interpreted, the news passed immediately to the leaders of parliament. A tumultuous crowd of Londoners gathered about the Tower to defend it against any invasion.

The rumours of a military rebellion, and plans for the flight of

Strafford, had thoroughly alarmed the people of London. A fresh crowd gathered on Monday outside the doors of the Lords, bellowing for the execution of Strafford; some of them cried that if they could not have his life, they would take that of the king. The parliamentary journal for that day wrote of the members of the Junto that 'they caused a multitude of tumultuous persons to come down to Westminster armed with swords and staves, to fill both the palace-yards and all the approaches to both houses with fury and clamour and to require justice, speedy justice, against the earl'. It was clear that Strafford would die. Oliver St John, one of the parliamentary leaders, had said that it was right and proper to knock wolves and foxes on the head. It was also remarked that 'stone dead hath no fellow'.

When the Commons assembled, Sir John Pennington spoke of Suckling's unsuccessful gathering. Thomas Tomkins added that 'many Papists were newly come to London'. The king had been misled by false counsellors and, as John Pym put it, 'he that hath been most abused doth not yet perceive it'. The parliament must open the eyes of the king.

It was now proposed that a religious manifesto should be published. The 'Grand Remonstrance' devised by the Commons was in a sense an English version of the Scottish covenant, binding those who signed it to an oath that they would remain loyal to 'the true reformed Protestant religion' against 'popery and popish inno-vation'. The remonstrance claimed that during the present session of the parliament its members had 'wrestled with great dangers and fears, the pressing miseries and calamities, the various distempers and disorders which had not only assaulted, but even overwhelmed and extinguished the liberty, peace and prosperity of this kingdom'. It was printed and circulated throughout the country, addressing and inspiring what might now be called a parliamentary party.

On 5 May the Commons, fearful of a papist uprising, ordered the towns, cities and counties of England to ensure that their arms and ammunition were well prepared. A papist plot amounted, in this context, to a royal plot. On that day a new bill was passed allowing parliament to remain in session until it voted for its own dissolution. It has been said that this was the moment that reform turned into revolution; it deprived the monarch of his right to govern.

The Lords themselves had directed that an armed force should take command of the Tower, thus divesting the king of responsibility for military affairs. It was another blow to his authority. The earl of Stamford proposed a motion 'to give God thanks for our great deliverance, which is greater than that from the Gunpowder Treason [of 5 November 1605]. For by this time, had not this plot been discovered, the powder had been about our ears here in the parliament house, and we had all been made slaves.' The threat of military force had alarmed the Lords as much as the Commons; on 8 May, the Bill of Attainder against Strafford was passed by the upper house.

A delegation from both houses of parliament now carried the document of attainder to the Banqueting House for the king's signature; the members were accompanied by a crowd of approximately 12,000 calling out, 'Justice! Justice!' The king, understandably cast down and demoralized, said that he would give his response on Monday morning; this delay did not please the crowd, who had promptly gathered again outside Palace Gate. If the king refused to sign the attainder it was predicted that the palace would be attacked, and that the king and queen would be captured.

Charles conferred with his bishops and his privy councillors, most of whom urged him to sign the bill condemning Strafford to death. The archbishop of York told him that 'there was a private and a public conscience; that his public conscience as a king might not only dispense with, but oblige him to do, that which was against his private conscience as a man'. Slowly and reluctantly he assented; he had promised to protect the earl's life and fortune, but now for reasons of state he was obliged to break his word. In the process he had been humiliated and weakened almost beyond repair. Pym, on hearing the news of the king's capitulation, raised his hands in exaltation and declared, 'Has he given us the head of Strafford? Then he will refuse us nothing!'

On 12 May Strafford went to his death on Tower Hill in front of what was said to be the largest multitude ever gathered in England. Crowds of 200,000 people watched his progress in an atmosphere of carnival and rejoicing. The lieutenant of the Tower asked him to make the short journey from the prison to the scaffold by coach, thus avoiding public fury; Strafford is supposed to have replied that

'I dare look death in the face and, I hope, the people too. Have you a care that I do not escape, and I care not how I die, whether by the hand of the executioner or the madness and fury of the people.' As he walked to his death he looked up at the window of the chamber in which Laud was confined, and saw the archbishop waiting for him there. He asked for 'your prayers and your blessings', but the cleric fell into a dead faint.

In his speech from the scaffold the earl declared that 'I wish that every man would lay his hand on his heart, and consider seriously whether the beginning of the people's happiness should be written in letters of blood'. He knelt in prayer for half an hour, and then laid himself down on the block. It took one stroke. The spectators rushed through the streets of London waving their hats and shouting, 'His head is off! His head is off!' In his prison Archbishop Laud observed, a few days later, that Strafford had served 'a mild and gracious prince who knew not how to be, or to be made, great'.

21

A world of change

While the trial of Strafford continued, the Commons seemed uncertain about the direction of other public business. Parliament did nothing but, in the phrase of the time, beat the air. On one occasion, after prayers had been said, the members of the Commons lapsed into silence and simply looked at one other; they did not know where to begin. On another occasion, according to a contemporary account, the Speaker stood up and asked what question he should put to them; answer came there none. A loss of initiative in the cause of reform was one of the reasons for a public fast in April.

Yet the death of the earl seems finally to have lent stimulus to the proceedings. The sight of blood quickened the appetite, and in July a series of fresh initiatives was debated and agreed. It seemed that the king himself had become almost an irrelevance in the business of renovating the kingdom. The familiar grant of tonnage and poundage was made to him but on the understanding that his previous exactions had been illegal; no new money was to be given to the royal household without permission of parliament. Of course parliament itself needed revenues both for work at home and for payment to the Scots. A new subsidy was imposed upon the counties and a poll tax introduced to raise additional income. This did not endear parliament to many of the people.

The old centres of royal authority were abolished. The council

of the north, the religious court of high commission and the Star
Chamber were all swept away. Ship-money was condemned as
contrary to the law. The limits of the royal forests were declared to
be those that had obtained in the twentieth year of James I. The
dissolution of the Star Chamber, in particular, lifted the final impediment to public expression. That body had decreed, four years before,
that no book could be published without a licence; the order was
now dead. Even before the chamber had been dissolved the appetite
for news was fed by pamphlets and tracts eagerly passed from hand
to hand, most of them predicting great innovations in Church and
state. There were 900 of these publications issued in 1640, 2,000
in 1641 and 4,000 in 1642.

The number of print shops doubled in this decade, but they
were joined by what were described in one satirical pamphlet as
'upstart booksellers, trotting mercuries and bawling hawkers'.
Wandering stationers and balladmongers would call out, 'Come buy
a new book, a new book, newly come forth'. Pamphlets with titles
such as 'Appeal to Parliament', 'A Dream, or News from Hell' and
'Downfall of Temporising Poets' abounded. It was no longer necessary to go to the bookstalls about St Paul's or the Exchange to find
newssheets. They were sold on the streets of London. Broadsheets
cost a penny, eight-page pamphlets a penny or twopence. One
commentator derided Pym's 'twopenny speeches'. A member of
the congregation in Radwinter, Essex, threw a religious pamphlet
to his curate, saying, 'There is reading work for you, read that.' The
mixture of information and opinion was compounded by plays,
processions, ballads, playing cards, graffiti, petitions and prints.

The leading members of the Commons published their speeches
which, according to the puritan Richard Baxter in his autobiog-
raphy, were 'greedily brought up throughout the land, which greatly
increased the people's apprehension of their danger'. The king
himself was moved to write against these 'poisoners of the minds
of his weak subjects; amazed by what eyes these things are seen,
and by what ears they are heard'. Yet pamphleteering was not
confined to the godly men of the parliament. The sermons of the
principal preachers were also distributed. From the pulpit came a
multitude of declarations and denunciations; but the pulpit also
acted as a distributor of news. The cleric might explain the events

of the day, or the week, and comment upon them to his excited congregation. The Presbyterian minister Robert Baillie said that 'many a sore thrust got both men and women thronging into our sermons'. The words from the church were then taken up in discussions at the taverns and the shops, the streets and the markets.

Yet the pamphlets were not simply directed against one or other of the factions then gaining ground. They were part of a vigorous debate on the ideas and ideals of political and religious life. What were the grounds of a just monarchy? Was there in truth an ancient constitution? Were king, parliament and people uniquely joined? The publication and dissemination of these concepts materially helped to extend and to inform the political nation. The radicals used the printing presses to disseminate their own opinions of Church and state, leading John Milton to proclaim that London had become 'the mansion house of liberty' with its citizens 'sitting by their studious lamps, musing, searching, revolving new notions and ideas wherewith to present, as with their homage and their fealty the approaching reformation'.

Yet the royalists fought back with their own pamphlets. Richard Carter, in 'The Schismatic Stigmatised', attacked the dissenting preachers who were even then crowding Westminster and its environs. 'And instead of orthodox divines, they set up all kinds of mechanics, as shoe-makers, cobblers, tailors and glovers . . . these predicant mechanics and lawless lads do affect an odd kind of gesture in their pulpits, vapouring and throwing heads, hands and shoulders this way, and that way, puffing and blowing, grinning and gurning.' A doggerel verse circulated through the streets:

> When women preach, and cobblers pray,
> The fiends in hell make holiday.

The parishes of London were indeed filled with dissenters of any and every kind. A separatist congregation met at a house in Goat Alley, off Whitecross Street; they arrived in twos or threes, and one man stood at the door to warn of any approaching strangers. The man appointed to preach stood in the middle of the room while the others gathered in a circle about him. Among these lay preachers were, according to a political satire sold in the streets, 'Greene the feltmaker, Spencer the horse-rubber, Quartermine the brewer's clerk, with some few others, that are mighty sticklers in this new kind of talking trade, which many ignorant coxcombs call preaching'.

The conventional clergy of the Church were derided in the streets and sometimes their surplices were stripped from their backs. The cry went up, 'There goes a Jesuit, a Baal-priest, an Abbey-lubber, one of Canterbury's whelps . . .' When a bishop went up to the pulpit in St Olave's, in Old Jewry, some hundred 'rude rascals' called out, 'A Pope! A Pope! A Pope!'

In this fevered atmosphere rumours of every kind circulated like hurricanes. It was said that a papist cavalry was concealed in caves in Surrey; it was reported that a plot had been hatched to blow up the Thames with gunpowder and thus drown the city. One of Pym's colleagues, Sir Walter Earle, told the Commons that a conspiracy had been discovered to demolish parliament; in their excitement the members leaned forward in their seats better to hear him, and part of the floor of the gallery gave way. One member exclaimed that he smelled gunpowder and another, leaving his seat, shouted that 'there was hot work and a great fire within'. The news soon spread, and a mob flew to Westminster. It was of course a false alarm, but the sudden panic testifies to the agitated state of the capital.

It was a world of change; as the king had said to parliament earlier in the year, 'You have taken the government all in pieces.' 'The Brothers of the Blade', a dialogue issued in 1641, considered 'the vicissitudes and revolutions of the states and conditions of men in these last days of the world'. 'Revolution' meant in conventional terms recurrence or periodic return; in these years it became associated with more earthly disorder. It was widely believed that the times were awry; anxiety and even despair were experienced by many. Brilliana Harley, a royalist letter-writer, expressed her belief that 'things are now in such a condition that if the Lord does not put forth his helping hand his poor children will be brought low'.

In the weeks after Strafford's death the king seems to have become resigned to his loss of power. He signed the bill for abolishing tonnage and poundage, telling both houses of parliament that 'I never had other design but to win the affections of my people'. He made a leading puritan, the earl of Essex, his lord chamberlain. Yet he was in fact playing for time.

There were already the makings of a king's party from those outraged at the pretensions of parliament in assuming executive powers; others were displeased at the idea of a puritan state Church controlled by parliamentary lay commissioners in place of bishops. The 'root and branch' party, which favoured such a change, was still in a minority. In this year many petitions reached Westminster from those who wished to preserve the Church and protect the Book of Common Prayer from more change. Some supported the mainten-ance of the episcopacy on the basis that the office was good even if the man was indifferent. From Oliver Cromwell's own county of Huntingdon, for example, it was pleaded that 'the form of divine service expressed and contained in the book of common prayer' was the best. These petitioners wished to extirpate those immoderate and bitter reformers who fomented nothing but trouble and disorder in the churches of the country.

It is hardly surprising, therefore, that those who were moderate or orthodox in their religion were beginning to take the side of the king and to believe that the political settlement imposed by parlia-ment had gone far enough. Instead of relief and liberty, it had brought anxiety and division. The imposition of taxes had not im-proved the temper of the nation. One gentlewoman from Yorkshire, Margaret Eure, wrote: 'I am in such a great rage with parliament as nothing will pacify me, for they promised us all should be well, if my lord Strafford's head were off, and since then there is nothing better, but I think we shall be undone with taxes.' It was agreed by many that the king should take wise counsel but few accepted that parliament had the power to choose who those counsellors should be. It was also possible that the king could still divide the Lords from the Commons; in June 1641, the peers threw out a bill ex-cluding the bishops from their number. They were not prepared to consider any 'further reformation'.

In the same month of June John Pym introduced what were known as the 'ten propositions', measures that were designed to increase parliamentary control of the king's court and council. All priests and Jesuits were to be banished from the court and, in particular, from the queen's entourage. Henrietta was defiant; she would obey her husband, she said, but not 400 of his subjects. Another proposition demanded that the king remove his 'evil' counsellors, and insisted that none in future were to be appointed unless they were such 'as his people and Parliament may have just cause to confide in'. The armies of Scotland and of England were to be disbanded as quickly as possible. There was no reference to the king. This might be seen as a step towards a republican government, however carefully obscured by the rhetoric of loyalty.

The 'ten propositions' had been in part prompted by the king's recent and carefully resolved decision to travel to Scotland. It was feared that in fact his destination would be York, rather than Edinburgh, where he might take control of his English army garrisoned there; hence the call that the English and Scottish armies should stand down. But if he did indeed journey to Edinburgh, what then? He might, for example, enlist his native subjects in some attack upon Westminster. If he agreed to grant the Scots the 'pure' religion they demanded, and allowed them to resume their just liberties, they might return to their old allegiance to the Stuarts; Charles had already written to the earl of Argyll, chief of Clan Campbell, with the pledge to 'establish the affections of my people fully to me'. If the Scottish and English armies were joined together, under the command of the king, they would represent an almost irresistible force.

John Pym and his supporters were now seized with anxiety and alarm. They even convened parliament on Sunday morning, at the beginning of August, to debate the nature of the threat. They begged for a delay to the king's journey, and he consented to a pause of one day. He had in the interim been engaged in talks with the Scottish commissioners and, according to the Venetian ambassador, the Scots were boasting that 'they would do all in their power to place the king in his authority once again. When he appeared in Scotland, all political differences would be at an end, and they would serve their natural prince as one man in such a cause.'

As the king prepared to go on his journey a crowd gathered in Westminster entreating him not to leave. It may be that his presence in London acted as a form of reassurance, at a time of great disorder, or it may be that some in the crowd suspected his intentions. He went to parliament on the morning of his departure in a mood of ill-concealed hostility and impatience. He named a commission of twenty-two men who would administer affairs in his absence; among them was the earl of Newcastle, a notable enemy to the parliamentary cause.

The Commons immediately retired to their chamber and debated the means 'of putting the kingdom into a posture of defence'. An 'ordinance' was passed, the first of its kind, appointing several key parliamentarians to attend the king in Scotland; they were of course to be spies rather than companions, hoping to supervise his actions. An ordinance had in the medieval period been a device by means of which the king could make a declaration without the consent of parliament; now the two houses were issuing ordinances without the consent of the king. Another confrontation seemed to be inevitable.

Charles was greeted in Edinburgh with every sign of acclamation. He at once proceeded to gain the approval of the Scots. He attended the services of the Scottish Church with an outward display of piety, and agreed to the demand of the covenanters that bishops be excluded from the reformed Church. He attended the sessions of the Scottish parliament, and agreed to the terms of an Anglo-Scottish union whereby his powers over parliament and the army were severely circumscribed. Some at Westminster believed that they might obtain similar benefits, but it occurred to others that Charles had simply managed to neutralize the Scots in any future conflict.

In these months parliament had begun to govern; it paid the army, and it issued orders to royal officials such as the lieutenant of the Tower. It had made decrees about the liturgy and the forms of religious worship. Laud had been impeached and imprisoned, while Strafford had been executed; various of the supposed 'evil counsellors', among them Lord Keeper Finch, had fled. The judges and sheriffs who had supported the king's exactions had been summoned to parliament and asked to explain their conduct. The Star Chamber, the northern council and the high commission, the seats of Charles's rule, had been abolished. Laud's judicial victims, such as Prynne and Bastwick, had been liberated and brought back to London in triumph. Most importantly, perhaps, it had been decreed that the present parliament could not be prorogued without its own consent.

It is possible, however, to see these developments in another light. Parliament had acted in an arbitrary and imperious manner.

It had misinterpreted the polity or unwritten constitution of the country, and arrogated powers to itself that it had never before possessed. It had illegally hounded Strafford to death. It had colluded with the king's enemies and an alien army. It had organized mobs to intimidate its opponents. It had proposed a new system of religion to be enforced upon an unwilling people. It had passed a bill ensuring its permanence. In the process the king had been stripped of his royal prerogative and had suffered a severe defeat in all the matters that touched him most closely. He had always said that his enemies wished to relegate him to the status of the doge of Venice. He was not mistaken.

22

Worse and worse news

Parliament reassembled on 20 October 1641, determined to wring from the king the same concessions that the Scottish parliament had already obtained from him. This was the period when the title of 'King Pym' came into general use. John Pym had started his career, perhaps surprisingly, as a receiver of Crown lands, and he was in general a good man of business. He was the great orchestrator of parliamentary affairs and had the ability to direct various men and factions towards one end; he was an effective, if not eloquent, debater but his real energy and power lay in his handling of parliamentary committees. By his use of such committees, in fact, he proved that parliament could govern as ably as the king. He sat close to the Speaker in the Commons, together with the other parliamentary leaders, and it was reported that 'the Speaker diligently watches the Eye of Pym'.

He was shrewd, and tireless, with a fierce hatred of popery and a genuine commitment to what he considered to be the true religion; his maiden speech was an attack upon one of his colleagues who had branded a Sabbath bill as a 'puritan' bill, and in another speech he declared that 'no impositions are so grievous as those that are laid upon the soul'. He possessed a round face, full lips and heavy jowls; he also sported a curling moustache and short pointed beard.

Yet he was not necessarily of a severe disposition; he was known for his cheerfulness and conviviality.

At the beginning of this session a letter was delivered to him as he sat in his place in the Commons. A gentleman had hired a messenger on Fish Street Hill, and given him a shilling to deliver the missive. When Pym opened it a rag dropped out that was, in the words of Clarendon, 'foul with the foulness of a plague sore'; it was a rag that had covered a plague wound. It was accompanied by a letter that denounced Pym for treason and threatened that, if the plague did not kill him, a dagger surely would. It ended with 'repent, traitor'.

Pym and his colleagues were now intent upon stripping Charles of his prerogative power, namely his ability to appoint his officers and councillors without reference to parliament. Yet they had first to deprive the upper house of its majority in favour of the king, and so they moved to expel the thirteen bishops who sat there. A bill was passed by the Commons to disqualify any cleric from accepting secular office, but naturally enough it was delayed by the Lords themselves.

Pym tried to raise the temperature of the debate with news of fresh army plots and of a furore in Edinburgh, where three covenanter lords had fled the king's court in fear of their lives; this became known as 'the incident'. The king then fervently declared before the Scottish parliament that he had played no part in any such plot to assassinate them and asked for 'fair play'. The fact that the principal conspirator had been Will Murray, the groom of the king's bedchamber, served to throw doubt upon the king's protestations of innocence. Whether true or not, the rumours only deepened parliamentary alarm about the king's intentions; it simply confirmed the fact, known by all, that he could not be trusted. Yet, in turn, why should he trust those who conspired against his throne? It still seemed very likely, in the early days of the parliament, that any attempt at more radical reform would come to nothing. Many members were now of the opinion that the changes in religion, in particular, were coming on too fast. Here were the makings of the king's party.

Just at that moment, at the very beginning of November, news reached parliament that a rebellion had broken out in Ireland. The

information was brought to the Commons by seventeen privy councillors, and Clarendon reported that 'there was a deep silence . . .
and a kind of consternation'. It aroused all the fears of the Protestants
of England, and one courtier who had been asked to remain at
Westminster and report on parliament, Edward Nicholas, wrote to
the king in Edinburgh that 'the alarm of popish plots amaze and
fright the people here more than anything'. It was reported that
papists were storing weapons and stocking gunpowder. A pamphlet
circulated with the question 'Oh ye blood-thirsty papists, what are
your intents?' The rebellion came as a cataclysmic shock, but the
conditions for it had been slowly gathering.

There were three defined elements in Irish society. The New
English were the Protestant settlers who had established themselves
after the Reformation; they controlled the Dublin parliament and
were intent upon imposing English 'standards' upon the natives.
The Old English had arrived before the Reformation, some as early
as the twelfth century, and had become so acclimatized that they
identified themselves with Ireland rather than with England; many
of them were Catholic while some merely conformed in public to
the Protestant Church of Ireland. They owned about one third of
the best land. The third group, known by their masters as the 'mere
Irish' or 'natives', made up the largest part of the population but,
like most of the downtrodden of the earth, have left little record of
their loyalties or beliefs.

But the Irish and the Old English had much cause for grievance. The Crown had in previous years confiscated one quarter of
the land that had been held by the Anglo-Irish gentry and by the
native Irish; it had already been decided, in the reign of James I,
that no landowner could have the title to his land unless he could
prove that he held proper feudal tenure. If he could not provide
these credentials, his lands might be confiscated and planted with
new English or Scottish settlers. Thus James had presented the
citizens of London with 40,000 acres in County Derry, the territory
therefore becoming known as Londonderry. The six counties of
Ulster had also largely fallen into the hands of Scottish Presbyterians.
The dismal state of the Church of Ireland, and the zealous work
of Jesuit missionaries, had in any case emboldened the Catholic
cause. The Catholics had good reason for resentment; they were

unable to educate their children, and their priests, given no benefices, were forced to rely upon the charity of their parishioners. Fines could also be imposed upon those who did not attend Protestant services.

Many forces were therefore at work in the revolt. The Irish Catholic leaders, who included the Old English, drew up a remonstrance in which they claimed to be rising up for the safety of their religion and for the defence of their lives and estates. They were aware of the proceedings of the English parliament, and of the concessions made by the king to the Scottish Presbyterians, and so felt all the more keenly the injustice to their native religion; they feared also that the reformers or 'puritan faction of England' had so deep a detestation of Catholicism that they would impose more restraints upon, and exact new duties from, them. They might even go further and in a statement of Irish grievances it was suggested that the Scots and English, combined, might 'come into Ireland, with the Bible in one hand and the sword in the other, for to plant their puritan, anarchical religion among us, otherwise utterly to destroy us'. Why should Irishmen not rise up in their own defence before it was too late? This was a grand irony of the period. The negotiations between England and Scotland had the result of forcing Ireland into revolt. Charles had found it impossible in practice to administer three kingdoms, when each one had pledged its loyalty to a separate religion.

On 23 October 1641, they rose up against their English masters. A rebellion in Dublin on the previous day had been partly discovered and quelled, but insurrection spread through the land. Parties of armed men would ravage an English-owned plantation, and then retire to their own territory; others would actively supplant the English owners and replace them with the former proprietors. The English fugitives sought refuge in the nearest army garrison, where they remained in fear and consternation.

The more radical members of the Commons were already preparing a remonstrance to the king with the purpose of appealing for renewed public support, when news of what was called an Irish 'massacre' invested their efforts with fresh urgency. The most frightful reports had reached them. It was stated that many thousands of Protestants had been killed, that women had been raped and mutilated, that babies had been burned. A pamphlet, 'Worse and Worse News from Ireland', revealed the list of war crimes. A letter read out to the House of Commons alleged that the Irish rebels in Munster were engaged in

> exercising all manner of cruelties, and striving who can be most barbarously exquisite in tormenting the poor Protestants, wheresoever they come, cutting off the privy members, ears, fingers and hands, plucking out their eyes, boiling the heads of little children before their mothers' faces, and then ripping out their mothers' bowels, stripping women naked, and standing by them being naked, whilst they are in travail [labour], killing the children as soon as they are born, ripping up their mothers' bellies as they are delivered . . .

The more sober truth was that approximately 5,000 English Protestants had been killed, and that an equal number of Irish Catholics had fallen in the course of the English counter-attack.

On 5 November Pym rose from his seat to pledge his life and estate to the cause of suppressing the rebellion but added that 'unless the king would remove his evil counsellors, and take such counsellors as might be approved by Parliament, we should account ourselves absolved from this engagement'. A bill was then passed that 'supplicated' the king to employ only men acceptable to parliament. On 8 November Pym told the Lords that, if the king rejected their supplication, he and his fellows would have to 'resolve some such way of defending Ireland from the rebels as may concur to the securing of ourselves'. Parliament, in other words, would be in charge of organizing and directing its own Protestant army that might in turn be employed to defend its own cause. The king would become merely a figurehead or talisman.

This was the occasion for the debate on a document that later became known as the 'Grand Remonstrance', a lengthy tract of some 204 clauses that anatomized the history of abuses perpetrated by the 'malignant party' close to the king. These evil counsellors had set out 'a malignant and pernicious design of subverting the fundamental laws and principles of government, upon which the religion and justice of this kingdom are firmly established'. It was a catalogue of errors and abuses that was designed to inflame the temper of

the nation, and thus to check the resurgence of loyalty towards the
king.

Violent objections were raised to what amounted to a manifesto;
some believed that it was an act of treachery against the king, while
others believed that the Commons had no right to produce such a
remonstrance without the agreement of the Lords. Sir Edward
Dering, the royalist member for Kent, said that 'when I first heard
of a remonstrance I presently imagine that like faithful councillors
we should hold up a glass to his majesty . . . I did not dream that
we should remonstrate downward, tell stories to the people and talk
of the king as a third person'.

Pym sensed that a royalist party was acquiring more support. He
agreed that certain clauses of the remonstrance might be amended or
deleted but 'it is time to speak plain English, lest posterity shall say
that England was lost and no man durst speak the truth'. The final
debate took place on 22 November and went on through that winter
afternoon; it continued in candlelight until one o'clock in the morning.
When the house finally divided Pym had gained the victory by eleven
votes. It was said that the decision was like that of a 'starved jury',
alluding to the custom of depriving jurors of meat and drink until
they had reached a verdict. But the narrowness of the result meant
that the king had created a sizeable party.

As soon as the division was announced some of the royalists
entered their protestations. One member, Sir Geoffrey Palmer, accused
the majority of being 'a rabble of inconsiderable persons, set on by a
juggling Junto'. When a motion was introduced that the remonstrance
should be published at once, the tempers of the opposing sides erupted.
Some waved their hats in the air while others, according to Simonds
D'Ewes, 'took their swords in their scabbards out of their belts and
held them by their pommels in their hands, setting the lower part on
the ground'. Sir Philip Warwick wrote that 'I thought we had all sat
in the valley of the shadow of death; for we, like Joab's and Abner's
young men, had catched at each other's locks and sheathed our swords
in each other's bowels'. The significance of the occasion is marked
by Oliver Cromwell, who said on leaving the chamber that 'if the
remonstrance had been rejected, I would have sold all I had the next
morning, and never have seen England more'.

*

Edward Nicholas wrote to the king on the first day of the debate on 8 November, that 'it relates all the misgovernment and unpleasing things that have been done by ill counsels (as they call it) . . . if your majesty come not instantly away [from Edinburgh to London] I trouble to think what will be the issue of it'. So Charles returned to London from Edinburgh seventeen days later and, on his entrance into the City, he was met by a cavalcade. He told those assembled to greet him that he would maintain the good old laws and the Protestant religion. He would do this 'if need be, to the hazard of my life and all that is dear unto me'.

It is likely that the welcome from the City was a genuine one. The 'former tumults and disorders', as Charles called them, were no better for commerce than the new taxes that were being imposed by parliament upon the merchants and men of business. A fund of loyalty for the king also existed among the prosperous sort who were averse to the radicalism of his opponents; they disliked the spectacle of apprentices and minor tradesmen quoting Scripture at them, and they feared any uprising of the multitude. The Venetian ambassador had already reported that anonymous placards had been posted in the streets of the city, naming the lords of the puritan Junto as traitors and the authors of sedition.

Charles knighted the lord mayor amid cries of 'God bless and long live King Charles and Queen Mary', the name by which Henrietta Maria was often known, after which he rode in procession, accompanied by 1,000 armed men, to the Guildhall for a great banquet. The conduits at Cornhill and Cheapside ran with claret as the bells rang and the bonfires blazed. It was a ceremony of ancient provenance and it emphasized the virtues of the traditional order. No guests from the Commons were invited to the feast at the Guildhall.

The king was encouraged, however, by his greeting in the City and by the fact that the remonstrance had been strongly resisted by so many members of the Commons. Determined to surrender nothing more, the king was resolved to extirpate his enemies under the forms of law. The parliament had destroyed Strafford by ingenious means of attainder, and it was open to him to use the same or similar methods.

Just before the king had left Scotland he, too, had received the news that his Irish subjects had erupted in rebellion. He had appeased one of his kingdoms only to find another in arms. His first reaction was simply the hope that the revolt 'may hinder some of these follies in England', by which he may have meant that the desperate news might bring parliament to its senses. Yet it could be lent a more sinister meaning. Could the Irish not be treated as a threat to the puritans?

Pym and his colleagues were inclined to blame Charles for the rebellion in a more direct sense. Some of the Irish rebels claimed that they had a commission from the king under the great seal 'to arrest and seize the goods, estates and persons of all the English Protestants'. It was a false claim, but at the time it persuaded Pym that the king had deliberately fomented the revolt in order to raise a force against the parliament; that Charles was willing to tolerate Catholicism in Ireland in return for the support of the 'Old English' in his fight against parliament. It was said of the Irish rebels that England 'is that fine sweet bit which they so long for and their cruel teeth so much water at'.

There was bitter controversy over the size and direction of the military campaign in Ireland. The king said that one man, rather than 400 men, was best able to direct a campaign; the Junto naturally disagreed, claiming that Charles could not raise an army without the express approval of parliament. In the last two months of the year the earl of Warwick set about creating what was essentially a parliamentary force. Charles wanted a wholly volunteer force composed of his supporters, while the Junto insisted upon pressing men into service. At every stage in the process the Commons, with a small majority against the king, was opposed by the Lords.

In the event only one regiment was sent to Ireland, at the end of the year, and a further force of 5,000 men arrived five months later. The English garrisons in Ireland were essentially left to fight their own battles. It might be fair to assume that Pym and his fellows wished to muster their resources for a conflict closer to home.

23

A world of mischief

At the end of 1641 a royalist member of parliament, Sir Henry Slingsby, wrote that 'I cannot say we have had a merry Christmas, but the maddest one that ever I saw'. He added that 'I never saw the court so full of gentlemen, every one comes thither with his sword . . . Both factions talk very big and it is a wonder there is no more blood yet spilt, seeing how earnest both sides are.' The citizens had come to Westminster, their swords by their sides, ready to protect the puritan members. John Venn, one of the London members of parliament, said in a shop off Cheapside that 'you must go to the parliament with your swords, for that party which is best for the commonwealth is like to be over-voted'. The parliament itself had been warned many times of threats against its activities and even its life.

On 21 December elections were held in London for the common council and the results favoured the puritan cause. On that day the king dismissed the lieutenant of the Tower, Sir William Balfour, and appointed Thomas Lunsford in his place; Lunsford was known to be a zealous and sometimes violent partisan of the king, and was therefore deeply distrusted. If any of the parliamentary or civic leaders were arrested, he would be sure to hold them fast. Simonds D'Ewes wrote that 'all things hastened apace to confusion and calamity, from which I scarce saw any possibility in human reason for this poor Church and kingdom to be delivered'.

The lightning flash was reserved for the thirteen bishops who sat in the Lords; they provided the majority for the king which was able to override all the bills and declarations of the Commons. When the Lords gathered in Westminster at the end of December a crowd of apprentices and others began to call out, 'No bishops! No popish lords!' The archbishop of York lunged at one of the noisiest of the participants, but he himself was hustled and his gown torn. The Lords then asked the Commons to join with them in a declaration against riotous assemblies, to which Pym answered, 'God forbid the House of Commons should proceed in any way to dishearten people to obtain their just desires in such a way.' He was on the side of the mob who had threatened the bishops.

An opposing force, made up of military volunteers and soldiers of fortune, had also gathered in the city; they had come to serve the king in Ireland and elsewhere, but they could also be guaranteed to turn upon the crowds who supported parliament. They might prove useful if the king should ever attempt to mount a *coup d'état*. One London news-writer, John Dillingham, reported that these soldiers 'offered their majesties to untie the knot' before adding 'what was meant you may judge'.

This was the period in which the terms of 'roundhead' and 'cavalier' became common currency, deriving from the short hair of the citizens and the long locks of the royalist soldiers. The latter term, deriving from *caballeros* or Spanish troops, was meant to be one of abuse but it soon became associated with honour and gallantry. It should be remembered that the leaders of the parliamentary cause, in the Commons and in the Lords, also wore their hair long as befitted the members of their social rank.

With the steady formation of two antagonistic powers, there was already talk of a civil war. Argument and dissension sprang up everywhere. Two days after Christmas the crowds once more gathered around Westminster to demand a response from the Lords to another petition against the bishops; a group of soldiers fell upon them but the citizens fought back with ferocity inspired by fear. They attacked the troops with sticks and stones and cudgels; some sailors joined them with truncheons until the soldiers were beaten down or had run away. A number of apprentices had been arrested and detained in the Mermaid Tavern; a group of their fellows stormed the tavern and released them. On the following morning soldiers charged out of Westminster Abbey and fell upon the citizens with their swords and pistols; that afternoon, they hacked at a group of apprentices. In retaliation the citizens threatened to shut up their shops and refrain from trade.

In the Lords the bishops sat huddled in the torchlight, listening to the rage and menace of the crowds. They were forced to leave the chamber by means of subterfuge, some of them under the protection of the great lords and others directed to secret passages out of the building. The earl of Huntingdon reported that 'ten thousand prentices were betwixt York House and Charing Cross with halberds, staves and some with swords. They stood so thick that we had much ado to pass with our coaches, and though it were a dark night their innumerable number of links [lights] made it as light as day. They cried "no bishops, no papist lords", looked in our coaches whether there were any bishops therein, that we went in great danger.'

On the following morning the citizens and apprentices returned to Westminster with the stated intention of murdering any bishops who dared to venture forth. Whenever they spied a bishop's boat coming across the Thames they called out, 'A bishop! A bishop!' and prevented him from landing. It is likely, but not proven, that these angry assemblies were in fact planned and organized by the parliamentary party to bring additional pressure upon the king.

On 29 December a group of twelve bishops laid the complaint that they had been 'violently menaced, affronted, and assaulted, by multitudes of people' and that in their enforced absence the proceedings of the Lords were void. This was tantamount to asserting that, without the bishops, any parliament was illegal. The members of the Commons were incensed at what they considered to be the arrogance of the claim, and on the following day the bishops were impeached for high treason and sent to the Tower on a bitter night of snow and frost. The senior dignitaries of the Church, including both archbishops, were now behind locked doors. It was possible that, in their absence, the puritan Junto would at last be able to pass its radical measures through the Lords. The king was by no means alone in his policy of coercion and conspiracy.

On the following day a large number of the king's old military officers, described by Simonds D'Ewes as 'desperate and loose persons', were seen milling about the court and the environs of Westminster. John Pym ordered that the doors of the chamber be locked. He then declared that he had discovered a plot to destroy the Commons before nightfall. It was yet another rumour thrown upon the fire.

On the first day of the new year, 1642, matters came to a head. Committees from the Commons and the remaining Lords met at the Guildhall to consider their strategy. It was agreed that the trained bands should be summoned on the authority of parliament; at this meeting plans may also have been drawn up to impeach the queen for communing with the Catholic rebels in Ireland. The threat was, perhaps, designed to provoke the king into violent action. The trained bands were indeed raised for the cause of parliament, effectively placing London under its control; to summon armed troops without the king's permission was an act of treason, but nobody seemed to care any more.

Charles was in any case already drawing up plans to impeach certain members of parliament; he had said previously that their correspondence with the Scots, at time of war, 'shall not be forgotten'. On 3 January the charges against Lord Mandeville, John Pym, John Hampden, Arthur Haselrig, Denzil Holles and William Strode were read to the Lords. On the following day Pym sent a delegation to the common council of London, newly elected in the puritan interest, to plead for help; on that day the council elected a 'committee of safety' for the city.

It was not a moment too soon, since the king was ready to strike later that day. Pym had been alerted to the assault, perhaps by spies at the court, and prepared for a notable act of theatre. The accused men took their seats in the Commons early in the afternoon, knowing full well that the king would be informed of their presence. At three o'clock Charles left Whitehall with an armed guard of 300 men and made his way to Westminster. The news reached the Commons and the indicted members slipped from their seats and hid in the court of the king's bench before being rowed into the City; even as they made their departure the king's party could be heard clattering on the stairs into the lobby. The king entered the chamber of the Commons alone but the doors were left open so that the members could see the armed force waiting outside.

'Gentlemen,' Charles said, 'I am sorry to have this occasion of coming unto you.' He asked for the accused members to be surrendered to him. He then realized that his bluff had been called. He looked about him, and saw that they were gone. 'I do not see any of them,' he muttered, 'I think I should know them.' He added that 'I am come to tell you that I must have them, wheresoever I find them. Is Mr Pym here?' There came no answer. 'Well, well! 'Tis no matter. I think my eyes are as good as another's.' He then asked the Speaker to help him find the offending members.

'May it please your majesty,' Speaker Lenthall replied, 'I have neither eyes to see nor tongue to speak in this place, but as this House is pleased to direct me, whose servant I am here; and I humbly beg your majesty's pardon that I cannot give any other answer than this to what your majesty is pleased to demand of me.'

There followed what contemporaries described as a 'long pause' or a 'dreadful silence'. 'Well,' the king eventually said, 'since I see all the birds are flown, I do expect from you that you will send them unto me as soon as they return hither. If not, I will seek them myself, for their treason is foul, and such a one as you will thank me to discover. But I assure you, on the word of a king, I never did intend any force, but shall proceed against them in a legal and fair way, for I never meant any other.' He left much discomfited as the cries of 'Privilege! Privilege' were raised all around him.

The members of the king's party in the Commons realized at once that he had committed a major, and perhaps fatal, blunder; his authority was for the moment lost, and in a mood of understandable dismay they meekly submitted to the decision of parliament to adjourn itself to the hall of one of the London guilds as a place of greater safety. On the evening of the failed attempt the city had all the air of an armed camp. Barricades were set up and chains drawn across the principal thoroughfares; the people of the suburbs, as well as the city itself, offered their support to parliament in case Charles's army should march against them. The women boiled water ready to throw upon any encroaching cavaliers. The members who had absconded were now safely concealed in a house on Coleman Street, a notable centre for radical sectarians. The call went up among some that the king was unworthy to live. Charles had effectively lost the capital.

Yet London was not the only place of disaffection. In the days immediately following, thousands of men from Kent and Buckinghamshire, Northamptonshire and Leicestershire, Essex and Sussex, rode or marched to Westminster with petitions for parliament. They complained in general about the decay of trade provoked by the divisions and distempers in the state. The country was, as a result of the crisis, confronted by sudden economic decline; the loss of confidence restricted trade, and the tradesmen and merchants of London hoarded their money in the hope of better times. The majority of the people yearned for peace. It is important to note, however, that the petitioners from Kent and elsewhere had addressed parliament as the centre of authority in the nation.

On 10 January the king left London for Hampton Court, arriving so quickly and unexpectedly that the beds had not been prepared for him and his family. He told the Dutch ambassador that he had feared for the safety of his wife in the capital; he would not see London again until he returned nine years later as a prisoner. On the following day the members of parliament who had been charged by Charles with high treason came back by water to Westminster where they were greeted by triumphant crowds.

The military arsenal of the nation was placed at Hull, where 20,000 weapons and 7,000 barrels of gunpowder were secured. The king appointed the earl of Newcastle to be the governor of the port and arsenal but he was circumvented by the swift action of a young parliamentarian, John Hotham, who persuaded the mayor of Hull to admit his men. His father, Sir John Hotham, was then appointed as the town's governor.

The Commons drew up a declaration to the officials of all the counties urging them 'to put themselves in a position of defence', and a day or two later asked them to nominate their own lieutenant-generals in the place of those loyal only to the king. The king then sent a letter to Westminster in which he proposed that he would preserve the privileges of its members and protect the interests of true religion in exchange for a commitment to preserve his authority and his revenues. The Lords wished to send a simple reply of thanks but the Commons responded with the demand that the fortresses and militia of the country should be placed in the hands of their supporters.

At the end of January Charles summoned all of his faithful lords to Windsor, to which castle he had now retired; fourteen of the peers joined him there, thus tipping the majority of those remaining in Westminster to the side of the puritan Junto. The lords of the puritan coalition could now rely on a majority in their own house to pass all the necessary legislation. Thus on 5 February the Commons sent up to the Lords a bill concerning the exclusion of the bishops from parliament. The pace quickened. By the middle of that month Charles and Henrietta Maria were at Canterbury, on their way to Dover where the queen would embark for Holland. She was travelling ostensibly to escort her daughter to an arranged marriage with the prince of Orange, but she also had more covert aims; she was attempting to buy men and *matériel* since, as she told the Venetian ambassador, 'to settle affairs it was necessary to unsettle them first'.

The bill for the exclusion of the bishops now reached the king. He was advised that, if he did not give royal assent to the document, the queen's journey might be prevented by parliamentary supporters; the queen herself then added her voice urging him to assent. As far as she was concerned, the bishops were dispensable. So Charles consented, even though he had promised in his coronation oath to maintain the ecclesiastics in all their privileges. He may have calculated, however, that he could rescind his decision at a later time and in more favourable circumstances.

When Charles travelled back to his palace at Greenwich, he sent for his eldest son. He was determined to keep the prince of Wales with him as a guarantee for the preservation of the royal family; father and son would remain together for the next three years through all the vicissitudes of warfare. The members of parliament now asked him to stay in the vicinity of Westminster; his presence elsewhere might provoke conflict and danger. He replied that 'for my residence near you, I wish it might be so safe and honourable that I had no cause to absent myself from Whitehall; ask yourself whether I have not'. He did not, in other words, feel safe in proximity to parliament and the citizens of London.

On the following day he set out for royalist York rather than the capital. While en route, at Newmarket a parliamentary delegation came to him in order to present their case; they read out a declaration in which all the king's actions, including his recent attempt to arrest the five members of the Commons, were detailed. The king was very uneasy. 'That's false,' he said at one point. 'That's a lie!' He gave his answer to them the next day. 'What would you have? Have I violated your laws? Have I denied to pass any bill for the ease and security of my subjects?' He then added, 'I do not ask what you have done for me.'

The earl of Pembroke, a member of the puritan Junto, urged the king to return and set out his demands or wishes. 'I would whip a boy in Westminster School', Charles replied, 'that could not tell that by my answer.' Pembroke then asked him to grant power over the army to parliament. 'By God,' the king said, 'not for an hour!' He added that 'you have asked that of me in this, which was never asked of a king'. A king would not surrender his troops to what was effectively the enemy.

On 16 March the members of the Commons issued a proclamation claiming supreme power for parliament within the nation. When Lords and Commons 'shall declare what the law of the land is, to have this not only questioned and controverted, but contradicted, and a command that it should not be obeyed, is a high breach of the privilege of Parliament'. At the same time the members issued an ordinance requiring the leaders of the local militias to be appointed by them; these men would in turn raise forces on behalf of parliament. An Act was then passed to levy new taxes for that cause, much to the horror of the regional communities.

The members of parliament were becoming unpopular. Clarendon wrote that 'their carriage was so notorious and terrible that spies were set upon, and inquiries were made upon, all private, light, casual discourses which fell from those that were not gracious to them'. It seemed to many that they had become despots rather than representatives, inquisitors rather than champions. As a supporter of the Crown Clarendon may have been a biased witness, but he mentioned the case of one member of the Commons who was expelled from the house and sent to prison for having said that parliament could not provide a guard for itself without the king's consent.

There was as yet no necessity for war. The local communities of the realm were at peace; the borough sessions, the leet courts and the quarter sessions still met. Bread was weighed and the quality of ale was measured. In the wider world it still seemed possible that a political solution could be reached. Neither side appeared to have the power, or resources, to raise and command an army. No one wanted to be found guilty of having started a civil war. Nobles on both sides were eager for some form of compromise.

The king, in the company of his son, made a slow journey to York. Charles heard an oration at Cambridge as the cry of '*Vivat rex!*' came from the scholars; the sheriff, however, did not appear to greet him. The prince of Wales reported to his sister that their father was 'disconsolate and troubled'. The king's reception in Yorkshire was not designed to reassure him. He had arrived at York with only thirty-nine gentlemen and seventeen guards, but the gentry did not flock to his side; the recorder of York, in his address of welcome, urged him 'to hearken unto and condescend unto' his parliamentary opponents. Margaret Eure, the Yorkshire gentlewoman mentioned before, expressed the wish: 'Oh that the sweet parliament would come with the olive branch in its mouth. We are so many frighted people; for my part if I hear but a door creak I take it to be a drum. Things stand in so ill a condition here as we can make no money of our coal-pits.' This may be said to summarize the mood of the nation, a compound of fear and dismay. No one could quite believe what was happening. Surely a solution could be found? The participants seemed to be sleep-walking towards disaster.

The king himself still professed a measure of optimism, saying that he could easily assemble an army of 16,000 men. He declared that he would raise a force in Cheshire and descend upon the rebels in Ireland. He wrote to parliament explaining that he had 'firmly resolved to go with all convenient speed into Ireland, to chastise those wicked and detestable rebels'; he added that, for this purpose, he intended to raise a force of 2,000 foot and 200 horse which should be armed 'from my magazine at Hull'. He may of course have had a different enemy in mind.

Here lay the problem. Hull was in the hands of parliament represented by its governor, Sir John Hotham. Hotham knew, as well as anyone, that the king may have required arms for 'wicked and detestable rebels' closer to home than Ireland. He also knew that the king would soon ride out and demand obedience. The members of parliament had already anticipated this action, and had told him not to open the town gates except by their authority. The members stated later that 'the king's supreme and royal pleasure is exercised and declared in this high court of law and counsel [themselves], after a more eminent and obligatory manner than it can be by personal act or resolution of his own'. They could not have declared in a clearer or more unambiguous manner that they were the masters now.

In the last week of April Charles approached Hull with a company of 300 horsemen, preceded by a message that he had come to dine with the governor. Sir John Hotham resolved with the municipal leaders to curtail any triumphant entry; when the king arrived he found the gates shut and the drawbridge raised with a guard upon the ramparts. He demanded entrance as their lawful sovereign, but was told by Hotham that 'I dare not open the gates, being intrusted by the Parliament with the safety of the town'. Charles replied that 'I believe you have no order from the Parliament to shut the gates against me or to keep me out of the town'. To which Hotham answered that the king's force was so great that 'if it were admitted I should not be able to give a good account of the town'. It seems that Hotham then told him that he might enter with a company of twelve men. He refused the condition as an affront to his person and, to the sound of a trumpet, proclaimed Hotham to be a traitor. His dignity, and his self-respect, had been deeply injured.

When he returned to York he sent a message to parliament acquainting the members with the insult given to him by Hotham 'who had the impudence to aver that Parliament had directed him to deny His Majesty entrance'. The two houses stated in reply that 'Sir John Hotham had done nothing but in obedience to the commands of both Houses of Parliament' and that 'the declaring of him a traitor, being a member of the House of Commons, was a high breach of the privilege of Parliament'. They also ordered the sheriff of Yorkshire to 'suppress' any further forces raised by the king. All parties prophesied a world of woe.

24

Neither hot nor cold

In the spring of 1642 the two houses resolved that 'the king, seduced by wicked counsels, intends to make a war against the Parliament'. So they began to prepare men and arms. In May a levy of 16,000 soldiers was ordered. The trained bands of London were secured for service, and were mustered in Finsbury Fields; the weapons at Hull were transferred to the Tower. A forced loan, to be repaid at an interest of 8 per cent, helped to fill the coffers of the parliamentary treasury with coin or with plate. In the course of this spring parliament nominated the earl of Warwick to be lord high admiral of the English fleet. He worked quickly to gain the loyalty of his men, and ships that supported the cause of the king were promptly boarded and overpowered. Clarendon later observed that 'this loss of the whole navy was of unspeakable ill consequence to the king's affairs'. A king of England without sovereignty of the sea could scarcely be considered a king at all.

Men and money were also arriving for the king at York. Members of the nobility and the clergy, together with the gentry and the scholars of both universities, sent him jewellery and plate as well as ready money. Some ventures were less successful. The queen dispatched a vessel from Holland containing ammunition and sixteen pieces of cannon, but it was captured off Yarmouth. Just as parliament had sent out a 'militia ordinance' to recruit troops, so the king now sent out 'commissions of array' to raise a volunteer army. These commissions were formal documents, written in Latin and impressed with the great seal, sent to every city and county in the nation; they named certain leading men who would secure their territory for the king and at the same time gather men and money for the royal cause. Yet the soldiers on either side had not yet necessarily been raised to fight; they might be used to deter the other side from violence or to provide support in any subsequent negotiations.

The contradictory commands of the militia ordinance and the commissions of array caused much disquiet. While walking in Westminster on a May morning a notable moderate and former soldier, Sir Thomas Knyvett, was approached by two men of parliament who brought with them an order 'to take upon me, by virtue of ordinance of Parliament, my company and command again'. He told his wife that 'I was surprised what to do, whether to take or refuse'; he accepted it, however, since this 'was no place to dispute'. Then a few hours later 'I met with a declaration point blank against it by the king'. He consulted with others in the same predicament, and they agreed that they would be obliged to follow their consciences in the matter. Meanwhile, Knyvett wrote, 'I hold it good wisdom and security to keep my company as close to me as I can in these dangerous times, and stay out of the way of my new masters till these first musterings be over.' These are the words of a modest and relatively impartial man caught between the two factions. His voice, like that of many others, would soon be muffled by the increasingly rebarbative tones of those urging stronger and stronger action against their opponents. One Londoner who refused to follow the lead of parliament was advised 'to leave the town lest his brains were beaten out by the boys in the streets'.

Events now had a momentum of their own, each move prompting a counter-move and each rumour producing a further reaction. Bulstrode Whitelocke, a parliamentary supporter, remarked later that 'it is strange to note how we have insensibly slid into this beginning of a civil war, by one unexpected accident after another, as waves of the sea, which have brought us thus far'. Many volumes have been written on the social or religious 'cause' or 'causes' of the civil war, but one principal motive may simply have been that of fear. Pym and his colleagues knew that, if the king were to prevail, they could all suffer a traitor's death.

One parliamentarian, Lord Wharton, wrote in June 1642 to the chief justice who was with the king at York. He asked him how it was that the kingdom did not contain one person of prudence and skill 'to prevent the ruin coming upon us'? His colleagues at Westminster were not disloyal, and he knew that those about the king 'wish and drive at an accommodation'. So why could not an agreement be reached by both sides? Thomas Knyvett believed, two years later, that 'the best excuse that can be made for us, must be a fit of lunacy'.

At the beginning of June parliament, guided by Pym's opportune and careful management, delivered 'nineteen propositions' to the king; among them was the wish, or command, that the king dismiss his forces and accept the validity of the militia ordinance. He was to accept the religious reforms outlined by the members of parliament and to exclude popish peers from the Lords. His principal officers should be appointed only with the approval of parliament, and all important matters of state must be debated there. The document became in the words of one parliamentarian, Edmund Ludlow, 'the principal foundation of the ensuing war'. Ludlow said that the question came to this: 'whether the king should govern as a god by his will and the nation be governed by force like beasts; or whether the people should be governed by laws made by themselves, and live under a government derived from their own consent'.

The king of course rejected the demands out of hand with the words *nolumus leges Angliae mutari* – we do not wish the laws of England to be changed. He said that acceptance of parliamentary demands would ensure that he became 'but the outside, but the picture, but the sign, of a king'. The propositions were 'a mockery' and 'a scorn'. Yet some still held back from confrontation. A parliamentarian, Sir Gilbert Pickering, wrote to a friend that 'there are now some overtures of accommodation . . . and most men think they smell the air of peace. Yet provide for war.' Seventeen counties sent forth petitions for such an 'accommodation' between the two sides.

At the beginning of July it was reported that the royalists had mustered in Herefordshire, Worcestershire and Warwickshire; it was soon known that the king had placed himself at the head of a force of cavalry. On 11 July parliament declared that the king had already begun the war, thus diverting any blame for beginning the conflict. On the following day the earl of Essex was placed in charge of a parliamentary army, and the king promptly declared him to be a traitor. The first blood was shed three days later, when a townsman of Manchester died from wounds inflicted by a group of royalist troopers. The two sides now competed to seize control of the munitions of the local militias.

A 'committee of safety' was set up by parliament which, through the summer and autumn, began to organize soldiers, weaponry and supplies; it was a high command in another sense, since it oversaw military strategy and communicated between parliament and the commanders in the fields.

The two sides were now beginning to acquire a definite shape. The early supporters of the king were prompted by loyalty and by the doctrine of obedience. Sir Edmund Verney expressed it best by saying of the king that 'I have eaten his bread and served him near thirty years, and will not do so base a thing as to forsake him'. Verney lost his life, shortly after writing this, in the first great battle of the conflict. His sense of honour overrode all other considerations. It was a question of what was known as 'the old service' or 'the good old cause'.

A majority of the peers and the greater landowners supported the king, since his privileges guaranteed their own. Twice as many families of the gentry also took the king's part. The puritan gentry, of course, were parliamentarians. A puritan divine, Richard Baxter, anatomized the situation very well. He claimed that 'on the parliament's side were the smaller part, as some thought, of the gentry in most of the counties, and the greatest part of the tradesmen and freeholders, and the middle sort of men, especially in those corporations [towns] and counties which depend on clothing and such manufactures'. An element of popular or lower-class royalism, still to be recognized today, was evident in the zeal of porters and watermen, butchers and labourers, for the king's cause in the larger towns and cities; the language of the street often condemned 'parliament dogs' and 'parliament whores'. They wore red ribbons in their hats as a sign of their allegiance.

Religious dissenters overwhelmingly took the side of parliament, of course, while the Roman Catholics and those of orthodox faith supported the king or, for fear of reprisals, remained neutral. The universities and cathedral cities were largely for the king, although the clergy were often opposed by the aldermen, while the dockyards and chief ports were for parliament. A great number of towns, however, wished to stay out of the conflict altogether.

In the most general terms the north and west were sympathetic towards the king while the south-east, and London in particular, supported the parliamentary cause. Yet all of the counties were divided. The north of Lincolnshire was largely royalist, for example, while the south remained generally for parliament. It has been recorded of Derbyshire that the belt of iron and coal in the eastern stretch of the county was royalist while the lead areas of the north supported parliament. This may be an aspect of human society rather than of geology; the lead areas contained many independent small masters, while the areas of coal and iron depended upon larger enterprises controlled by a single master or landlord. In other counties the wooded areas containing isolated and self-sufficient parishes harboured the puritan cause, while the communal villages exploiting 'mixed' farming took the royalist side.

More subtle calculations have also been made. It has been estimated that the royalists were slightly younger than the parliamentarians, this statistic boosted by the fact that many young men joined the king in a spirit of bravado as well as patriotism; in parliament itself the royalist members had been on average eleven years younger than their puritan colleagues. It is clear that the judges of the land were divided in their allegiance, some of them worried by the constitutional pretensions of the king, while the staff of the various offices of the state were more likely to be active parliamentarians. The lawyers, too, had a long history of hostility towards the courtiers.

The majority of the population were neither hot nor cold; they may have been indifferent to the opinions of either side, but they were alarmed and intimidated by the change that had come over the kingdom. The partisans on both sides had provoked the conflict, and it was they who would end it. The rest stood by and waited. They did not care about the form of government, according to one member of parliament, Arthur Haselrig, as long 'as they may plough and go to market'. Some said that the affair should be decided by a throw of the dice.

Sir William Waller, the parliamentary general in the west, wrote to his royalist counterpart, Sir Ralph Hopton, that 'my affections to you are so unchangeable that hostility itself cannot violate my friendship to your person; but I must be true to the cause wherein I serve'. He declared that he hated a war without a true enemy but 'I look upon it as *opus domini* [the work of the Lord] . . . We are both on the stage and we must act those parts that are assigned to us in this tragedy. Let us do it in a way of honour, and without personal animosities.' This is one of the noblest sentiments uttered in the period.

There was not a town or county that remained undivided by opinion and argument; factional conflict was everywhere apparent from the largest town to the humblest parish. Some sportsmen named their packs of hunting dogs 'roundheads' or 'cavaliers', and the children in the streets would engage in mock battles under those names.

Many families were also split in their allegiances, although it was sometimes believed that this was a convenient ploy to save family property if one or the other party finally prevailed. First sons were likely to be royalist, while younger sons remained 'neutral' or 'doubtful'. Yet not all family differences were settled amicably. Sir John Oglander, who took no part in the conflict, wrote in his commonplace book that 'thou wouldest think it strange if I should tell thee there was a time in England when brothers killed brothers, cousins cousins, and friends their friends'.

On the afternoon of 22 August Charles rode into Nottingham, where the royal standard was taken from the castle and fixed in the ground beside him. It was a silk flag with the royal arms and a motto, 'Give Caesar his due'; it was suspended from a long pole that was dyed red at the upper part, and was said to resemble a maypole. The king quickly scanned the proclamation of war, and corrected certain words. The declaration was then read in an uncertain voice by the herald, after the trumpets had sounded, but all threw their hats into the air and called out: 'God save King Charles and hang up the roundheads.' The standard was blown down that night in the middle of a storm. Clarendon reported that 'a general sadness covered the whole town, and the king himself appeared more melancholic than he used to be'. The civil war had begun.

25

The gates of hell

By the late summer of 1642 the king had managed to gather an army, partly comprised of the trained bands of the counties who remained loyal to him and partly of the ready supply of volunteers animated by loyalty or by the desire for pay and plunder. By the time he left Nottingham he was leading seven or eight regiments of infantry, and on his subsequent march he was joined by several regiments of cavalry; altogether he had the command of some 14,000 men.

Others might soon be inclined to join them since, at the beginning of September, parliament declared that those who opposed its intentions were 'delinquents' or 'malignant and disaffected persons' whose property could be confiscated. Those who had favoured the king without taking any action for him, or those who had remained neutral, now believed themselves to be threatened. The declaration further divided the nation into two parties. Many landowners and grandees who had taken no part in the struggle now decided to raise forces for their king so that their own lives and estates might be defended. Simonds D'Ewes, the parliamentarian diarist, confessed that the declaration 'made not only particular persons of the nobility and others but some whole counties quite desperate'. The king was greatly hearted by his opponents' error, and confidently expected many more recruits to his cause. In that hope, he was not mistaken.

On 9 September the earl of Essex rode out to his army at

Northampton. He took with him a coffin and a winding sheet as a token of his fidelity to the end. He commanded an army of 20,000 men and it was widely believed that he would defeat the king with ease. Clarendon wrote of him that 'his pride supplied his want of ambition, and he was angry to see any other man respected more than himself, because he thought he deserved it more, and did better requite it'. He was a man of great wealth and power. He liked to be known as 'his excellence', and was considered to have no equal but the king. He had the habits, and the manners, of a great lord like those of the Wars of the Roses. But it was not yet clear that he was a great commander. His reserve and his aloof manner were perhaps mistaken for wisdom. He was not a natural rebel, in any case, and his position at the head of the parliamentary forces rendered him deeply uneasy. It seems that his ultimate purpose was to detach the king from his 'evil councillors' and bring him back to London in the role of a constitutional monarch working alongside parliament. That is not what his parliamentary allies required.

In the course of this autumn some 40,000 men were gathered, and by the summer of 1643 the number had risen to 100,000. The armies were in many respects equally matched. They contained many men who believed that the war would be a short one, and that they would return to their fields in time for the next harvest; it was widely considered that one great battle would decide the issue. Many of them were poor and had been pressed into service by their landlords or employers.

From one Shropshire village, in the army of the king, were a farmer in debt, the son of a man who had been hanged for horse-stealing, a decayed weaver, a vagrant tailor and a family of father and three sons who lived in a cave. The soldiers on both sides were sometimes scorned as 'the off-scourings of the nation'. Men were released from prison and pressed into service. It was said that some of the best trainees were butchers, because they were used to the sight of blood. For some the war came as a welcome relief from more mundane suffering, and such men eagerly sought the opportunity to seize money or goods. One veteran, Colonel Birch, recalled that 'when I was in the army some said, "Let us not go this way, lest the war be ended too soon"'. They were also given provisions that were more plentiful than their food at home; the normal ration was supposed to be 2 pounds of bread or biscuit and 1 pound of meat or cheese each day. They were allowed one bottle of wine or two bottles of beer.

The royalist troops in particular were accused of drunkenness and lechery, and in the early months of the war it was reported that a group of them had murdered an eight-months pregnant woman in Leicestershire. Nehemiah Wallington, a puritan artisan from Eastcheap, wrote that 'they swagger, roar, swear, and domineer, plundering, pillaging or doing any other kind of wrong'.

Yet the abuses were not reserved to one side. The royalists may have wrecked the taverns, but the parliamentarians desecrated the churches. The climate of war turns men into animals. It was said that, when troops were quartered in a church or hall, the smell they left behind was frightful. They pissed and defecated in corners. They often brought with them contagious diseases that became known as 'camp fever'.

Many of the soldiers had of course volunteered out of genuine conviction. The parliamentary soldiers often chanted psalms as they marched, and the ministers preached to them upon such texts as the sixty-eighth psalm, 'Let God arise, let his enemies be scattered . . .' More secular rivalries also animated them; it was reported that the men of Herefordshire fought against the men of Gloucestershire, the Lancastrians against the Northumbrians.

The men carried pikes or muskets, but some were still armed with bows and arrows in the old fashion. The pike itself was supposed to be 18 feet long, with a steel head, but many of the soldiers cut it down as too cumbersome; the pikemen were also armed with a short sword. The muskets were charged with weak gunpowder and the men were advised to shoot only when the weapon was close up against the body of the enemy; since there were no cartridges, the musketeer held two or three bullets in his mouth or in his belt. They had to load and then fire with a lighted cord known as a 'match'. Others preferred to shoot arrows from their guns. They wore leather doublets and helmets that looked like iron pots.

Not all of the troops, however, were untrained or ill-prepared. There were professional soldiers among them who had fought in France, Spain and the Low Countries. Mercenaries were also used on both sides. Many of the commanders had seen service on the

European mainland. These were men who had perused such manuals as *Warlike Directions* or *Instructions for Musters and Arms*; they were the leaders who would have to give basic training to their troops. 'Turn the butt ends of your muskets to the right . . . Lay your muskets properly on your shoulders . . . Take forth your match. Blow off your coal. Cock your match . . . Present. Give fire.'

A first skirmish or encounter took place near Worcester. Essex had moved his army towards the town and, on hearing the news, the king sent Prince Rupert to support the royalist stronghold. Rupert of the Rhine was the king's nephew and, at the age of twenty-three, had already enjoyed great success as a military commander. His expertise, and his experience, were considered to be invaluable. He was high-spirited and fearless; he was also rash and impatient. Yet on this occasion, in a limited engagement, he routed the parliamentary cavalry and killed most of its officers.

Clarendon wrote that the incident 'gave his troops great courage and rendered the name of Prince Rupert very terrible, and exceedingly appalled the adversary'; he added that 'from this time the Parliament began to be apprehensive that the business would not be as easily ended as it was begun'. Oliver Cromwell himself had grave reservations about the conduct of the parliamentary army. He told his cousin, John Hampden, that 'your troopers are most of them decayed serving men and tapsters, and such kind of fellows, and their [royalist] troopers are gentlemen's sons, younger sons, and persons of quality'. Cromwell believed that if parliament were to prevail, a new and more glorious force should be formed.

There was perhaps still one way to avert the conflict. The parliamentarian grandee of Worcestershire, Lord Brooke, declared that he wished 'to avoid the profusion of blood'. So he offered his royalist counterpart in the county, the earl of Northampton, to 'try the quarrel by sword in single combat'. A duel might therefore have decided the course of the civil war. It was a medieval expedient but it emphasizes the extent to which this war was essentially still seen as a baronial combat. Yet the political and social world had changed since the fifteenth century.

The king moved with his army to Shrewsbury, only 50 miles away from the parliamentary forces. For three weeks both sides remained close to one another, but neither made any move. No one was eager for battle. Charles decided to press the issue and advance towards London. Essex was obliged to prevent him. The earl also wished to present a petition to the king, but Charles refused to see him. Why should he parley with a traitor?

The king moved forward slowly towards London, but Essex remained on his trail. The first battle of the civil war took place at Edgehill, in southern Warwickshire, where the royalist forces had rested on the evening of 22 October; the parliamentary army was only a short distance away and Charles had decided to attack from the summit of a range of hills that gave him the advantage. It was an uncertain struggle, with Rupert's cavalry for a while in the ascendant but the parliamentary infantry holding its own. Both sides claimed the victory, when in truth neither prevailed. The number of the dead amounted to a little over 1,000. A trooper wrote to his mother that 'there was a great deal of fear and misery about that field that night'.

It was the first experience of battle for most of the participants, and it came as a salutary shock. The soldiers had been badly organized and Rupert's cavalry, in particular, had run out of control. Many of the men and some of the commanders, weary and disgusted at the slaughter, fled for their homes. The king, never before in a war, was himself horrified by the death of some of his most loyal commanders. He seems also to have been alarmed by the extent of the enemy, and murmured before the battle that he did not expect to see so many arrayed against him. The earl of Essex was equally dismayed. He had hoped that one great battle would resolve the issue, but the result had been bloody and uncertain. Might this be a harbinger of the whole war? He had raised his standard against his sovereign, however, and there was no easy way forward.

The king was urged by Rupert immediately to march upon London, but instead Charles rode with his men 20 miles south to Oxford, where he had determined to establish his headquarters. It was from here, at the beginning of November, that he once more set out for the capital. On the news of his approach the terrified citizens took up whatever weapons they possessed; parliament sent a delegation to the royal camp to open negotiations but the king, while giving gracious words, still pressed forward. Prince Rupert attacked a parliamentary force at Brentford, 8 miles out of London, and then proceeded to fire some of the houses in the town; the word 'plunder' now entered the English vocabulary. It was to be the prince's method throughout the war.

The citizens of London decided, under the direction of their parliamentary masters, to make a stand. The apprentices and trained bands, to the number of 6,000, were assembled in Chelsea Field near the village of Turnham Green in Chiswick. The earl of Essex went into the city and pleaded for more men, until eventually a ragged army of 24,000 Londoners advanced to Turnham Green close to the royalist army. On Sunday 13 November, the two forces stood face to face without giving way. The king, fearing any grievous loss of life, withdrew to Hounslow. Even his most ardent supporters would have hesitated before launching a general assault upon the city itself. Yet he had lost his best, and last, chance to defeat his enemies. He was not given the credit for his mercy, however, and his withdrawal at the last minute was considered to be a public humiliation. Thus it was presented, at least, in the printing presses controlled by parliament.

A pause in hostilities prompted calls from some quarters for peace and accommodation. Parliament raised four proposals for the attention of the king; it already knew that he would reject them. A crowd of Londoners approached the common council calling for 'Peace and truth!' whereupon someone shouted out, 'Hang truth! We want peace at any price!' Demands for an end to hostilities were frequent throughout the course of the war but, at each stage of the process, the activists won their cause over their more diffident colleagues. The more combative members of parliament, for example, believed that a peace with the king would amount to capitulation. Instead they began to make approaches to Scotland in an attempt to gain military aid.

It was also important that more money should be raised. On 25 November it was agreed that an assessment should be levied upon London, but that was only the beginning. In the next few weeks and months John Pym worked to pass legislation concerning land taxes, general assessments, confiscations, property taxes and rises in excise duty. All men of property were obliged to make contributions to the public funds, on the understanding that the money would eventually be repaid by 'public faith', an obscure and possibly meaningless phrase. The levies were excused on the familiar grounds of necessity and imminent danger. In the following year an order went out that those who had not voluntarily contributed would be fined one fifth of their income from land and one twentieth of the value of their personal property.

The king now established his household and himself in Christ Church, Oxford, while Prince Rupert moved into St John's College. All Souls became an arsenal while the king's council assembled at Oriel. A strange change came over the face of the university. The main quadrangle of Christ Church was turned into a cattle-pen. It became a substitute court, also, with satires and love poems circulating from hand to hand.

Both sides now considered their strategies for the conflict to come. The royalist plan was slowly to descend on London from the north and the west, with Prince Rupert and his cavalry offering assistance from Oxford. The ports of Plymouth and Bristol in the west, and Hull in the north-east, were to be seized from parliament so that they could not become a menace to the flanks of any advancing armies. Parliament in turn already held London as well as the counties of the south-east and the midlands; it had determined to form them into 'associations' so that they could more easily combine and co-operate in the face of the enemy.

Oliver Cromwell held true to his intention, expressed to his cousin, John Hampden, of creating a regiment that would be a match for 'the gentlemen' of the other side; he picked industrious and active men from a range of occupations whom Richard Baxter, a leader of the puritans, considered to be 'of greater understanding than common soldiers'. If any of them swore he was fined a shilling; if he became drunk, he was set in the stocks. They became known, sometimes in praise and sometimes in irony, as 'godly' or 'precious' men.

The first news was kind to Charles and his forces. One of his commanders, the earl of Newcastle, took York and seemed firmly in command of the northern counties. The king himself stormed Marlborough and seized it from a parliamentary force; he was, according to the French ambassador, 'prodigal of his exertions . . . more frequently on his horse than in his coach, from morning till night marching with his infantry'. Parliamentary prisoners were often sent to Coventry under armed guard; hence the familiar expression.

Many still held to the belief that it would soon be over, their confidence strengthened by the opening of negotiations at Oxford between the two sides at the beginning of February 1643. Parliament had drafted some propositions for peace; in particular the king would be obliged to honour the bills already approved by parliament and allow the trial of certain 'delinquents'. Although these terms were not to the king's liking he maintained that 'I shall do my part and take as much honey out of the gall as I can'. In a private communication, however, he wrote that God himself could not 'draw peace out of these articles'. He replied with a list of conditions, the first of which was the return to him of his forts, revenues and ships. A few days later parliament voted that his answer was no answer at all. The hopes for peace were short-lived.

The pace of the war was quickened with the return of the queen, Henrietta Maria, together with money and fresh arms from her brief exile. A severe and prolonged tempest kept her at sea. 'Comfort yourselves, my dears,' she told her attendants, 'queens of England are never drowned.' After she had landed at Bridlington in Yorkshire some ships in the service of parliament bombarded with cannon fire the house in which she lodged, forcing her to take refuge under a bank in a field. Parliament then destroyed her chapel in Somerset House, and a painting by Rubens that had been placed over the high altar was thrown into the Thames. Yet 'Her She Majesty Generalissima', as she styled herself, was not cowed. She travelled from York to her husband in Oxford with 3,000 infantry, thirty companies of horse and six cannon. In the early spring of 1643 John Evelyn recorded in his diary that the whole of southern England saw an apparition in the air; it was a shining cloud, in the shape of a sword with its point reaching towards the north 'as bright as the moon'.

The balance of the fighting in subsequent months seemed to be tilting towards the side of the royalists, but nothing was decided. The battles were small and often indecisive, but local victories were won on both sides. The best troops were those who fought for their own territories, naturally enough, but no large-scale engagement changed the fortunes of war.

It was fought, piece by piece, across the nation without much central planning or control. Leeds had to be taken by the royalists, for example, to relieve the earl of Newcastle who might then go on to assist the earl of Derby who was hard-pressed in Lancashire. The king's forces were besieging Gloucester but an army of Londoners under the command of Essex relieved it. The royalists were making gains in the north, but they lost the key town of Reading. Taunton fell to them, but Plymouth was saved by the parliamentary fleet. Small wars erupted in almost all of the counties. The citizens of one town might furnish a force for parliament while the adjacent manor houses collected troops for the king. Very little of the action was co-ordinated properly. Opposing armies would come upon one another by chance. No one knew what was really happening.

London was harassed by fears and rumours, its population swollen by refugees from the fighting elsewhere. In the spring of 1643 a great defensive earthwork began to rise around the city, and many houses in the suburbs were demolished to provide clean lines of fire from twenty-eight 'works' or forts that were ranged along it. Ramparts were constructed behind a ditch 3 yards wide, and the total height of the fortifications in some places reached 18 feet; the 'wall' surrounded the city in a circuit of 11 miles. Much of it was built within three months by the citizens themselves. The Venetian ambassador estimated that 20,000 men, women and children were engaged in the work; the 'furious and zealous people', as John Evelyn described them, were so enthusiastic that they even worked on Sundays. No trace of this great wall of London survives.

The city also had to be defended from the enemy within. It was believed that one third of the population still supported the king, and that many royalists had infiltrated the trained bands. At the beginning of June a royalist plot was discovered to take over the city and to arrest the leading parliamentarians; loose talk by some of the conspirators led to their arrest and interrogation. There was another enemy inside the city. It was ordered that the Cheapside Cross should be removed from the site where it had stood for 350 years; all other 'popish monuments' were also to be destroyed.

In May 1643 a small skirmish acquired, in retrospect, much significance. Oliver Cromwell was 2 miles outside Grantham with a small force of horsemen when he came across a division of royalists; they were twice the size of his company but at once he gave the signal to charge. Speed and surprise were always his favourite methods of warfare. The royalists broke ranks and fled from the scene or, as Cromwell himself put it, 'with this handful it pleased God to cast the scale'. A number of 'godly' men, inspired by their commander, had defeated an apparently stronger enemy.

At the beginning of July the spiritual world was to be set in order. An assembly of divines met at Westminster to administer a thorough purging of faith and worship, religious discipline and religious government. They were to draw up a 'directory' to take the place of the Book of Common Prayer, and to compile a 'confession of faith' to which all men must subscribe. This was the true heart and inspiration for the civil struggle that had so lately begun. The commissioners first met in Henry VII's chapel but, as the weather grew bleaker, they withdrew into the relative comfort of the Jerusalem Chamber. They sat for five years, and engaged in more than 1,000 meetings from nine in the morning until one or two in the afternoon.

They wept, and fasted, and prayed. Robert Baillie, one of the new Scottish commissioners, described that

> after Dr Twisse had begun with a brief prayer, Mr Marshal prayed large two hours most divinely. After, Mr Arrowsmith preached one hour, then a psalm, thereafter Mr Vines prayed near two hours, and Mr Palmer preached one hour, and Mr Seaman prayed near two hours, then a psalm. After Mr Henderson brought them to a short, sweet conference of the heart confessed in the assembly, and other seen faults to be remedied, and the convenience to preach against all sects, especially Baptists and antinomians.

The syntax might be faulty, but the fervour is evident.

When they were not at prayer they debated predestination, election, justification and reprobation. They also discussed more political affairs. Ought the state to impose one form of religion, or should the free will of the individual decide the matter? Ought the state to punish those of a faith different from that of the majority? For a month they considered the role of individual congregations within the broad unity of a Presbyterian regime. What did it say in Scripture about these topics? How had the Church of Antioch been related to the Church of Jerusalem? Thus solemnly they debated with one another. The Scottish Presbyterian divines argued with their English puritan counterparts; the English were all in favour of a 'civil league' that would keep 'a door open in England to independency' while the Scots favoured a 'religious covenant'. It was never likely, however, that the English would accept the full rigour of the Scottish religion or that parliament would concede predominance to any national Church. Oliver Cromwell himself was a notable Independent who favoured toleration and plurality; many of the leaders of the parliamentary army shared his convictions.

A few days after the formal opening of the Westminster assembly Essex made a startling proposal. He suggested that the terms of truce given to Charles at Oxford should be offered to him again. If the king refused them once more, he should withdraw from the field so that the two armies could settle the matter in one pitched battle. It was a form of duel. This proposition could not be construed as a serious one, but it does emphasize the attachment of Essex to an old chivalric code. This was not, however, an age of chivalry. Pym declared the notion to be 'full of hazard and full of danger'. It was the first serious indication from Essex of weakness or doubt about the progress of the war, and it was the cause of much apprehension. He was now, according to a newsletter, the *Parliament Scout*, 'abused in pictures, censored in pulpits, dishonoured in the table talk of the common people'.

A number of reversals dismayed the parliament. At Roundway Down, in Wiltshire, a parliamentary army was vanquished and those who survived were taken prisoner; among them were the members of a regiment completely clad in armour, known as 'the Lobsters'. At Chalgrove, in Oxfordshire, the royalists were the victors again and John Hampden died of his wounds. Prince Rupert stormed and overcame Bristol, the second city of the kingdom; this victory was followed by the surrender of Poole and Dorchester, Portland and Weymouth. Gainsborough and Lincoln would soon be lost.

A 'peace party' had now grown up in the Lords, thoroughly shaken by news of the defeats, but Pym and his cohorts faced them down with the help of intimidation by the London mobs. But the *mobile vulgus* could be fickle. In the second week of August 2,000 or 3,000 women descended on Westminster with white ribbons in their hats. Simonds D'Ewes recorded that they 'came down in great confusion and came to the very door of the House of Commons, and there cried as in diverse other places, Peace, Peace'. He added that they 'fell upon all that have short hair' and cried out, 'A round-head! A roundhead!'

Parliament was rendered even more unpopular by the imposition of a new tax called 'excise', a flat rate charged upon commodities such as meat, salt and beer. The king in turn raised money through voluntary donations and a tax raised on the royalist counties known as 'the contribution'; nevertheless his funds were very much lower than those of parliament.

Charles had again taken the offensive and was marching towards Gloucester. Cromwell wrote to parliament that 'you must act lively! Do it without distraction! Neglect no means!' On 10 August the royalist army had reached the city; Charles invited the officers of Gloucester to submit and, on their refusal, he encircled it and laid siege for three weeks without gaining entry. On 5 September a parliamentary force under the command of the earl of Essex arrived on the scene and, in the face of failure and exhaustion, Charles's forces withdrew.

It was the first major success of parliament for many months, and was greeted by jubilation in London and Westminster. In his history of the war Clarendon wrote that 'the Parliament had time to recover their broken forces and more broken spirits, and may acknowledge to this rise the greatness to which they afterwards aspired'. He also wrote that on the royalist side there was 'nothing but dejection of mind, discontent and secret mutiny'. On the withdrawal from Gloucester the prince of Wales asked his father if they were going home. Charles replied that 'we have no home'.

The forces of the earl of Essex could not remain in Gloucester indefinitely, since they were needed elsewhere. The royalist army waited in the neighbourhood for their eventual withdrawal, with the purpose of cutting them off from London. For a few days the troops turned and manoeuvred, marched and counter-marched, both sides making for London. The king's men spent one unhappy night of wind and rain before pursuing the enemy as far as the town of Newbury in west Berkshire. On 20 September a battle ensued that lasted all day with the parliamentary forces pushing slowly against the royalists through winding lanes and hedges; the soldiers of the king held on to their position, keeping the enemy from the road to London, but they eventually withdrew that night. They were thoroughly exhausted, and it seems likely that they had run out of ammunition. It had not been a battle notable for tactics or for strategy but rather a grim and bloodstained stalemate; all had depended, in the phrase of the period, on 'push of pike'. Both sides of course claimed the victory.

It is easy to recite the names and dates of battles but less simple to describe their nature. In truth they were composed of a hundred desperate struggles between individuals who had no notion of what was going on around them; there would have been waves of panic fear when a group of men was consumed with the horror of dying and fled; it would have been impossible for the commanders to direct the action except by impetuous chance and sudden instinct. It was a flailing, wavering, shuddering mass of men and horses. Victory, or defeat, was largely a matter of chance.

The terror and confusion were such that both sides believed that they had advanced upon the burning gates of hell. A royalist captain, Richard Atkyns, recalled of one conflict that

> the air was so darkened by the smoke of the powder that for a quarter of an hour together (I dare say), there was no light seen, but what the fire of volleys shot gave: and 'twas the greatest storm that I ever saw, in which thought I knew not whither to go, nor what to do, my horse had two or three musket bullets in him immediately which made him tremble under me at a rate, and I could hardly with spurs keep him from lying down, but he did me the service to carry me off to a led horse, and then died.

A more prominent royalist commander, William Cavendish, described how 'the two main bodies joining made such a noise with shot and clamour of shouting, that we lost our ears, and the smoke of powder was so thick that we saw no light, but what proceeded from the mouth of guns'. Chaos descended. The savage shouts, and the screams of the wounded or the dying, resounded through the darkened air.

26

The women of war

The reader may grow tired of the deeds of arms and men. If women were not exactly invisible in the period of civil war, they were still at a notable disadvantage in the affairs of the world. Yet exceptions can be found. In the summer of 1638 Lucy Apsley married John Hutchinson, who at the opening of the war enlisted in the parliamentary army. He was an Independent, like Cromwell, and was therefore acceptable to the army command; in 1643 he was appointed to be governor of Nottingham Castle. He was one of those who eventually signed the king's death warrant. Some years after the war was over Lucy Hutchinson wrote for her eldest son an account of this unhappy time. It was eventually published under the title of *Memoirs of the Life of Colonel Hutchinson*.

The book is not a history of the war in the style of Clarendon, but rather a vivid and intimate account of its proceedings from the point of view of a committed participant. Although Lucy Hutchinson is ostensibly writing an encomium on the life and career of her husband, her own character and beliefs continually break through. She even provides a brief sketch of her early years that emphasizes how unusual she was among her contemporaries. She disliked plying the obligatory needle and thread, and had a horror of playing with other children. When she was forced to mingle with her young contemporaries she delivered lectures to them and made it quite plain that she detested their company. She abhorred their 'babies', better known now as dolls. She infinitely preferred the 'serious discourses' of the adults which she memorized and repeated. In the time allowed for play she preferred to apply herself to her books.

So the account of the war itself springs from the pen of a spirited and remarkable character. It is not a record of battles and sieges, but in large part a collection of character portraits and of first-hand accounts of life in the field of conflict. She describes these portraits as 'digressions' but in fact they convey the human face of the war, with all its threats and suspicions, hypocrisies and lies. She rejects the name of 'roundhead' for her husband, for example, on the grounds that he had a full head of hair. Since it was not cropped short, however, his puritan comrades distrusted him.

Lucy Hutchinson's memoir is in fact most revealing for its account of the internecine suspicion and conflict between the members of the puritan party; John Hutchinson was at odds with his army council in Nottingham, for example, while the members of parliament and the army were always in conflict. Even the leaders of the various parliamentary contingents were themselves 'so emulous of one another, and so refractory to commands, and so peeking in all punctilios of superiority' that it was surprising they could ride together on the same field.

A command came from Westminster for John Hutchinson to gather together all the horse he could spare for the relief of Montgomery Castle; as a consequence, he proceeded to consult with the political committee of the local members of parliament that had oversight of Nottingham. Lucy Hutchinson reports that her husband asked that a number of soldiers be requisitioned, to which request they replied '*None*'. Hutchinson, falling into a rage, reminded the committee that a direct order from parliament had to be obeyed. She describes the members as 'factious little people' who fomented squabbles, divisions, delays and scandals. Their behaviour only added to the chaos of war.

She herself was courageous at times of crisis. A few months before her husband took charge of Nottingham he was run to ground in Leicester, where a royal warrant was issued for his arrest. A sudden trumpet alerted her family to the presence of the king's troops but Hutchinson 'stayed not to see them, but went out at the other end as they came in'; he may have escaped through one of the city gates, or perhaps through a 'geat' or opening. Lucy Hutchinson, then heavily pregnant, remained to confront the officers.

> *Captain*: 'It is a pity you should have a husband so unworthy
> of you that he has entered some faction and dare not be
> seen with you.'
> *Lucy Hutchinson*: 'You are mistaken sir. My husband would
> not hide himself from you, or not dare to show his face.'

Then Lucy told a lie. She called down her brother-in-law, George Hutchinson, and announced to the captain that this man was in truth her husband. The subterfuge worked; John Hutchinson got clean away while George eventually obtained his liberty. It was a close-run thing, however, and is testimony to the dreadful risks that Lucy Hutchinson was willing to run.

She recounts in some detail the siege of Nottingham by the king's army, marked by no great strategic initiative but by endless bickering and argument among those who were besieged. 'What is the cause to me,' one doctor asked John Hutchinson, 'if my goods be lost?'

'You might prevent that hazard by securing them in the castle.'

'It pities me to spoil them. I had rather have the enemy have them than that they should be spoiled in the removal.' The doctor then rebuked Hutchinson 'for countenancing the godly townsmen' to whom he referred as 'puritanical prick-eared rascals'. He infinitely preferred the 'malignants' or royalists.

When John Hutchinson was eventually charged with colluding in the execution of the king, after the war was over, Lucy Hutchinson forged a letter in his name to the Speaker of the House of Commons with the request that he should not be taken into custody but called to account when he was needed. Her forgery was accepted. She was a formidable woman. Her husband, however, eventually died in prison for complicity in another plot. He gives the impression of being an impulsive and contentious man who was supported by a strong-minded and strong-principled woman; it is impossible to estimate how many other such relationships flourished in the Civil War. The evidence suggests, however, from the exploits of Lucy Hutchinson to the female crowds who often assembled at

Westminster, that there was a tradition of adventurous women who helped to fuel the conflict. In the ballad literature of the time it is suggested that some women dressed as men in order to join the armies of either side.

It should be noted of course that Lucy Hutchinson came from a relatively privileged family and was not in that sense necessarily representative of her sex; but older and deeper traditions of female liberty persisted still. Puritanism itself was uniquely susceptible to the authority of women, and actively promoted a partnership of the sexes in religious duties and devotions; many puritan women became part of an informal network of communication, for example, exchanging manuscripts and treatises between neighbouring families. Some of them also took part in forming congregations and nominating ministers. Letters, manuscripts and commonplace books testify to a distinct religious and intellectual female community.

The wives of certain Baptist, and 'leveller', leaders shared their husbands' faith to the extent that they inhabited the same prison cells. Other women were intent upon defending their homes when they were placed under siege. Lady Elizabeth Dowdall defended Kilfenny Castle, in Limerick, on her own initiative even though her husband was himself on the premises. She wrote that on 'the ninth of January, the High Sheriff of the county, and all the power of the county, came with three thousand men to besiege me. They brought two sows [cannon] and thirty scaling-ladders against me. They wrote many attempting letters to me to yield to them which I answered with contempt and scorn.'

Other royalist women played their own part in the civil struggle. Ann, Lady Fanshawe, was the daughter of Sir John Harrison, a child of superior birth who was educated in the usual fashion with needle, thread, virginals and lute; but above all else she enjoyed riding and 'was I wild to that degree . . . I was that which we graver people call a hoyting girl'. All the clichés and stereotypes of childhood tend to fall apart in the face of direct testimony. Were girls and women really as servile or as domesticated as the courtesy books suggest? Could all the domestic novels, the family portraits and the sentimental poetry have got it wrong? Perhaps only the plays, with their rampant and mischievous women, got it right.

Fanshawe came from a fiercely royalist family and, at the opening of hostilities, her brother joined the king at Nottingham; her father was threatened with transportation to 'the plantations' while all of his goods were sequestrated by parliament. He was put under house arrest, but managed to escape and to join the king at Oxford. She fled with him, as she put it, 'from as good houses as any gentlemen of England . . . to a baker's house in an obscure street'. But she coped with the overcrowding, the sickness, the plague, the lack of supplies and the general fear of catastrophe. This was wartime Oxford.

In 1644 she married her second cousin, Sir Richard Fanshawe, who was even then a member of the council attached to the prince of Wales with the title of secretary of war. As such he and his family moved in tandem with the prince's court. Ann Fanshawe rarely writes of the war itself but reserves her comments for the peripatetic life she was obliged to endure. She was not without resource. She procured a pass for her husband through the good offices of 'a great Parliament man whose wife had formerly been obliged to our family'. She carried £300 of money from London to Paris without being searched. The household travelled to Cork, perhaps to gain money or support, but at the beginning of October 1649, 'by a fall of a stumbling horse (being with child), broke my left wrist'.

While she lay in bed that night, her wrist bound, she was roused by the news that the Irish were firing the town after it had been taken by Cromwell. Her husband had gone to Kinsale on business; pregnant and in pain she gathered together her husband's manuscripts for fear of seizure and managed to pack in wooden crates all of their portable belongings, including clothes and linen; she also managed to conceal £1,000 in gold or silver which, to their puritan assailants, would have been a treasure worth killing for. At three o'clock in the morning, attended only by a man and a maid, she walked by the light of a taper into the crowded marketplace where she was confronted by 'an unruly tumult with their swords in their hands'.

Bravely enough, she demanded to see the commander-in-chief of the Protestant forces. By great good fortune he had once served with Sir Richard Fanshawe, in different circumstances, and under the weight of her entreaties and in light of her evident plight he granted her a safe conduct. Bearing the pass she walked unmolested 'through thousands of naked swords' until she reached Red Abbey, a fourteenth-century Augustinian establishment that acted as a meeting place. Here she took out some loose coin and hired a neighbour's cart, into which she piled all of her belongings, before making her way to her husband in Kinsale. It is a story of bravery to match any told by the soldiers of either side.

On another stage of her adventure she was aboard a Dutch ship with her husband when a Turkish galley, well manned, advanced towards them. She was ordered by the captain to go below, on the grounds that if the Turks saw a woman they would know the ship to be part of a merchant fleet and therefore attack it. If they spied only men, they might believe it to be a man-of-war. Once she had gone below she called for the cabin boy and, giving him half a crown, purchased his cap and coat. Suitably concealed she returned to her husband's side on deck.

She seems to have been an expert at disguise. On another occasion she dressed herself as a 'plain' or 'lowly' woman in order to obtain a pass for a journey to Paris. She made her way to the parliamentary military headquarters at Wallingford House in Whitehall.

'Woman, what is your husband and your name?'

'Sir, he is a young merchant, and my name is Anne Harrison.'

'Well, it will cost you a crown.'

'That is a great sum for me but, pray, put in a man, my maid, and three children.'

'A malignant would give me five pounds for such a pass.'

Once she had received it she managed by careful penwork to change the name from 'Harrison' to 'Fanshawe'; there was no need for further concealment because she was already known to the 'searchers' at Dover, having passed that way before.

'Madame,' one of the 'searchers' told her, 'I little thought that they would give pass to so great a malignant, especially in such a troublesome time as this.'

Even in times of war certain known opponents could still come and go as they pleased.

Ann Fanshawe wrote her memoirs in the 1670s, after the death of her husband, for the benefit and education of her family. They are a notable addition to the literature of the civil conflict, but they also throw an indirect but welcome light upon the otherwise generally hidden women of the war.

27

The face of God

In the middle of November 1643, parliament announced itself to be the supreme power in the land by authorizing the use of a 'great seal' to replace that of the king; on one side were the arms of England and Ireland while on the other was engraved an image of the Commons sitting in their chamber. One of their most important members, however, was no longer present. John Pym had been the key strategist of the parliamentary cause; he had been the quiet revolutionary, playing his cards largely behind the scenes, exploiting temporary setbacks or victories, and in some part controlling the mobs of London. Cautiously and slowly he had maintained the direction and impetus of the movement against the king.

His death from cancer of the lower bowel only reinforced the divisions and factions at Westminster, where some wished for an honourable settlement with the king and others demanded total victory. Disagreements were also evident in the royal court at Oxford, where questions of immediate tactics and general strategy were furiously debated; some wanted an attack upon London, for example, while others favoured the capture of the south-west. One of the king's courtiers, Endymion Porter, remarked that God would have to intervene in order to cure all the divisions between the royal supporters; as is so often the case, the most bitter fights were between those on the same side.

At the end of January 1644, Charles summoned a parliament of his supporters at Oxford to which came the great majority of the Lords and approximately one third of the Commons. There were now two parliaments in the country striving for mastery. The ceremony for the opening of the Oxford parliament took place in Christ Church Hall, and in his customary address the king said that 'he desired to receive any advice from them which they thought would be suitable to the miserable and distracted condition of the kingdom'. He had also taken the precaution of bringing over from Ireland some of the regiments of the army he had dispatched to extirpate the rebels.

In the following month the Westminster parliament established a 'committee of both kingdoms'. In one of the most important circumstances of the war 20,000 Scots had already, in the middle of January, crossed the border to support the parliamentary cause; after prolonged negotiations with their English allies, they had come to defend the common Protestant faith in the form of a 'solemn league and covenant' between the two nations. It had been voted by parliament at the beginning of February that this covenant should be taken and sworn by every Englishman over the age of eighteen; the names of those who refused to take the oath would be sent to Westminster. A new committee, composed of English and Scottish representatives, would manage the direction of the war; among its members were the earl of Essex and Oliver Cromwell.

The advantage lay now for the first time with parliament. In a battle at Cheriton in Hampshire, the royalist forces were overwhelmingly defeated; the parliamentary cavalry was now more than a match for its royalist counterpart. Oliver Cromwell himself had been promoted to become lieutenant-general of the 'eastern association', where he began to form the cavalries of seven counties into a coherent fighting force. With its command of London and many of the significant ports, in any case, the financial resources of parliament were far greater than those of the king. Charles had armies of approximately half the size of those commanded by his enemy. Many people, on both sides, recognized that his cause would suffer the more the war was prolonged.

In the early summer of the year two parliamentary armies, under the command of the earl of Essex and Sir William Waller respectively, advanced upon Oxford in order to hold the king in a vice of their making. The king managed to make his escape with 7,000 men and, on 6 June, fled to Worcester. He had also received news that his forces in York were besieged, and wrote from Worcester to Prince Rupert 'in extreme necessity'. Charles urged his nephew to ride to the relief of York in order to save the cause.

Prince Rupert arrived outside York, in the last days of June, only to find that the forces of the parliamentary besiegers had made a tactical retreat. Animated by bravado or by faith in his strategy he pursued his enemy to Marston Moor, in the north of the country, for what might have been a final confrontation. The parliamentary soldiers, wearing white handkerchiefs or white pieces of paper in their caps, were the stronger force; they were the first to charge, from the advantage of higher ground, and their sudden onslaught scattered the royalists. An eyewitness, Arthur Trevor, wrote that 'the runaways on both sides were so many, so breathless, so speechless, so full of fears, that I should not have taken them for men'.

In what was the largest battle ever fought on English soil, 4,000 of the king's troops had been killed, and his army had disintegrated. In a letter to his brother-in-law, Valentine Walton, Cromwell said of the enemy that 'God made them as stubble to our swords'. Prince Rupert, in a spirit of mockery rather than admiration, dubbed the victorious commanders as 'Ironsides'. The cities of York and New-castle surrendered. It was a notable victory for parliament and, at least in retrospect, it marked a turning point of the civil war.

The victory of Cromwell at Marston Moor lifted him to eminence in parliament no less than on the field of battle. One of his most notable opponents, the earl of Clarendon, admitted that he possessed 'a great spirit, an admirable circumspection and sagacity, and a most magnanimous resolution'. He was resolute and fearless, and thus a fitting adversary for a king.

He had not distinguished himself in early life and seems happy to have farmed the flat land of the south-east midlands. He once declared that 'I was by birth a gentleman living neither in any considerable height nor yet in obscurity'. He was one of what were called the 'middling sort'. Yet even in that enviable condition he was not free from superstitious terror, and in his first years of married life he consulted a London physician who recorded in his case-book that Cromwell was '*valde melancholicus*'; by this he meant that his patient was nervous or depressed to an abnormal degree. Another doctor had suggested that he suffered from hypochondria and indeed, under stress or nervous excitement, he would sometimes fall ill.

His religion was the most important aspect of his character. His depression of spirits may have been the context or the catalyst for the sudden revelation – we do not know when it was vouchsafed – that he was one of 'the elect'. The blinding light of God's grace surrounded him, and he was transformed. He wrote to his cousin, Elizabeth St John, that 'I live (you know where) in Mesheck, which they say signifies Prolonging; in Kedar, which signifies blackness; yet the Lord forsaketh me not'. The reference is to the 120th psalm: 'Woe is me, that I sojourn in Mesech, that I dwell in the tents of Kedar!' This scriptural allusiveness and simple piety are at the heart of Cromwell's faith.

He knew that he had been saved by the grace of God, and the certainty of redemption lay behind all of his judgements; he believed implicitly in the power of divine will to guide the actions of men. He waited on providence. He prayed for a sign. He wrote that 'we follow the Lord that goeth before'. He sought for the divine mean ing of the events occurring around him and saw all things in the context of the eternity of God. Since he had a private sense of what he called 'true knowledge' or 'life eternal', he was impatient of religious debate and doctrinal niceties. What did they matter before the overwhelming power of God? He once said that 'I had rather that Mahometanism were permitted among us than that one of God's children should be persecuted'.

His first years in parliament were not particularly auspicious; he was regarded as a forceful and impetuous, rather than elegant, speaker whose manner was sometimes clumsy or unprepossessing. But together with his family connections at Westminster – the puritan party was in some sense a wide circle of relatives – he fought steadily and assiduously for the parliamentary cause. He was adept at committee work, and was blessed with an acute understanding of human character. Yet he professed not to have been ambitious on his own behalf but rather for the cause he had chosen.

Cromwell was of singular appearance. The London doctor whom he had consulted noted that he had pimples upon his face. These seem to have been supplanted by warts on his chin and forehead. His thick brown hair was always worn long over the collar, and he had a slim moustache; a tuft of hair lay just below his lower lip. He had a prominent nose and one of his officers, Arthur Haselrig, once said to him that 'if you prove false, I will never trust a fellow with a big nose again'; his eyes, in colour somewhere between green and grey, were described by Andrew Marvell as being of 'piercing sweetness'. He was about 5 feet 10 inches in height and, according to his steward, John Maidstone, 'his body was well compact and strong'; he had a 'fiery' temperament but was very quickly settled, and was 'compassionate . . . even to an effeminate measure'. He was often boisterous in company, with a taste for rough country humour; there were times indeed when, according to Richard Baxter, he displayed too much 'vivacity, hilarity, and alacrity, as another man hath when he hath drunken a cup too much'.

Like his opponents he thoroughly enjoyed hawking and the pursuits of the field; he also liked to play bowls. He had a great love of music and one of his colleagues, Bulstrode Whitelocke, recalled that 'he would sometimes be very cheerful with us, and laying aside his greatness he would be exceeding familiar with us, and by way of diversion would make verses with us and everyone must try his fancy. He commonly called for tobacco, pipes and a candle, and would now and then take tobacco himself; then he would fall again to his serious and great business.'

That great business was, at the latter end of 1644, to drive the war forward until the king surrendered; in this purpose, however, he was not supported by other parliamentary commanders. The earl of Essex and the earl of Manchester, in particular, were in favour of some accommodation with Charles; it was suspected by some, therefore, that they were less than zealous in their military offensives. Manchester used to say that it was easy to begin a war, but no one could tell where it would end. He was in command of the eastern association, with Cromwell as his lieutenant-general, and the earl's desire for peace led to a complete breakdown in trust between the two men. Manchester in particular had an impatient dislike of sectarians and what he called 'fanatics', among whom he placed Cromwell himself.

At a council of war the following exchange took place.

Manchester: If we beat the king ninety and nine times yet he
is king still and so will his posterity be after him; but if
the king beat us once we shall all be hanged and our
posterity made slaves.

Cromwell: My lord, if this be so why did we take up arms at
first? This is against fighting ever hereafter. If so, let us
make peace, be it ever so base.

Cromwell had already written to his brother-in-law that 'we
have some among us much slow in action'.

The argument between the two military commanders came to
a head after an inconclusive battle with the king at Newbury, where
it seemed that Manchester had deliberately held back his army. He
is supposed to have said to one of his colleagues, who urged instant
action, that 'thou art a bloody fellow. God send us peace, for God
does never prosper us in our victories to make them clear victories.'
It was now believed, by Cromwell and others, that Manchester had
become a traitor to the cause.

Towards the end of November Cromwell came into the
Commons in order to denounce Manchester; the earl's 'backward-
ness of all action' and his 'averseness to engagement' sprang from
his unwillingness to prosecute the war 'to a full victory'. He was
therefore questioning his loyalty. Three days later Manchester
returned fire, in the Lords, and charged his opponent with insubordination and slander. Cromwell was accused of saying that he
hoped for a day when there would be no peers left in England. The
'peace party' on the parliamentary side now considered a move to
impeach Cromwell for treason, but was persuaded that it was not
wise to do so. A single sheet of print was found in the streets of
the city attacking Essex and Manchester with the words 'Alas poor
parliament, how art thou betrayed!'

On 9 December Cromwell pressed home his advantage. He
told the Commons that 'it is now a time to speak, or forever hold
the tongue. The important occasion now is no less than to save a
nation out of a bleeding, nay almost dying, condition which the
long continuance of war hath already brought it into, so that without a more speedy, effectual and vigorous prosecution of the war
. . . we shall make the kingdom weary of us and hate the name of

Parliament'. He realized that only a clear victory over the king would decide the issue.

The eastern association had already informed the 'committee of both kingdoms' that local contributions were not enough to maintain an army, and the committee therefore decided 'to consider of a frame or model of the whole militia'. This was Cromwell's opportunity. It had become time to reorganize the various armies on a different basis, and for Cromwell the most obvious model was that of his own regiment of 'godly' men. He had said that 'I had rather have a plain russet-coated captain that knows what he fights for, and loves what he knows, than that which you call a gentleman and is nothing else'.

Immediately after Cromwell's speech another member of the Commons, Zouch Tate, rose to suggest a thorough reorganization of the army. It was first necessary to dismiss such fractious and incompetent commanders as Essex and Manchester. So Tate, no doubt in collaboration with Cromwell, proposed what was called 'a self-denying ordinance' by means of which no member of either house could take on a military command or an official place in the state. This removed at a stroke the noble earls. In theory it also removed Cromwell but it was widely and correctly believed that an exception would be made for such a successful military leader. The whole business might therefore be seen as an enterprising bid by Cromwell for sole command.

It may be worth remarking that this session of parliament was the one that abolished Christmas. The traditional festival was deemed by the Commons to encourage 'liberty to carnal and sensual delights' and instead the day was to become one of fast and penance.

Cromwell had told his colleagues that until 'the whole army were new modelled and governed under a stricter discipline' there would be no certain or ultimate victory. So the force became known as the New Model Army, known to its enemies as the 'New Noddle'. It was effectively a standing army from which all aristocratic commanders had been displaced; no English army had ever before been so constituted. It was to be organized on a national basis, and financed by a new national tax; the morale of the soldiers would therefore be maintained by consistent payment. It was to be professional, disciplined and purposeful. Its commander, known as 'Black

Tom' for his muddy complexion, was Sir Thomas Fairfax, who had previously been in charge of parliament's northern army.

It was an amalgamation of older regiments rather than a new army, but it was designed to be a more stable and coherent force drawn up with the sole purpose of defeating the king in battle. That is why Essex and Manchester had been removed from any military command. The commission given to Fairfax made no mention of the old provision that he was bound to preserve the king's safety on the field of battle. New muskets, swords and pistols were manufactured; the coats of the infantry were of red cloth, becoming the standard uniform for the next 200 years.

Some of its officers believed in a religious mission for themselves and their soldiers; Cromwell's regiment, for example, considered itself to be a 'gathered Church'. 'Go now,' one preacher declared, 'and fight the battles of the Lord!' It is unlikely that the rest of the army shared that godly purpose, but they may have been animated by the zeal of their more pious fellows.

But what was now meant by the godly? Cromwell and his colleagues favoured the Independent cause in religion, effectively espousing toleration in England; the earl of Manchester and his supporters had adopted the Presbyterian cause with no room for other sects or groups. In this endeavour they were supported by their Scottish allies. Even while parliament was debating the arrangements of the new army, the Book of Common Prayer was abolished and a puritan Directory of Worship took its place; this new text was to be delivered to the people by means of a national Presbyterian system. That system was not destined to last for very long.

One of the great expositors of the Book of Common Prayer was now led to the scaffold. On 10 January 1645, Archbishop Laud was taken from the Tower to the place of death on Tower Hill. He told the people assembled there that 'this is a very uncomfortable place'. As he knelt for the executioner, he prayed aloud for 'grace of repentance to all bloodthirsty people, but if they will not repent, O Lord, confound all their devices'. Essex lamented the old man's death. 'Is this', he asked, 'the liberty which we promised to maintain with our blood?' The political philosopher Thomas Hobbes wrote that 'it was done for the entertainment of the Scots'. It had been a year of much blood.

There was now very little intention of compromise on either side, but some brief negotiations took place at Uxbridge in February 1645. The two parties divided the town, with the parliamentary team in one inn and the royalist delegation in the other. Nothing was achieved, of course, but the king was still sanguine about his chances. Despite the disaster at Marston Moor he had not yet been decisively defeated, and he believed that the divisions in the opposite party between Independents and Presbyterians would work to his advantage. He was calm and indomitable, sustained by his belief that no one could touch the Lord's anointed. His commanders, and his forces, were still a match for those of parliament.

He had also received welcome news from Scotland where his principal supporter, the earl of Montrose, had already won notable victories over the Scottish covenanters. 'Give me leave', Montrose wrote to him, 'with all humility to assure your majesty that through God's blessing I am in the fairest hopes of reducing this kingdom to your majesty's obedience.' This in turn rendered the covenanting army in the north uneasy, distracted by the argument that they should withdraw from England and return to fight for their home territory. Charles was firmly persuaded that the fortunes of battle might still be with him.

The new campaign opened in the spring of 1645. At the beginning of May the New Model Army, under the command of Sir Thomas Fairfax, was about to begin the siege of Oxford. In the course of this action he received another message from Westminster. Charles had summarily taken his army into the east midlands, where he stormed and sacked the parliamentary town of Leicester. Fairfax now decided to follow him, with Oliver Cromwell as his second-in-command.

The great confrontation could no longer be delayed. On 14 June the two armies were in the fields outside the village of Naseby, in Leicestershire, where the parliamentary army had a large advantage in numbers. When the parliamentary forces made a tactical withdrawal to reach higher ground, Prince Rupert mistook the movement for a retreat; so with his cavalry he made for the enemy. Cromwell managed to beat them back, and then charged the royalist infantry. The king's soldiers resisted for a while but, under the combined assault of Fairfax and Cromwell, they fell apart and fled. They were pursued by the parliamentary troopers for 14 miles before they reached the safety of Leicester.

Naseby was a devastating defeat for the king. His infantry had been destroyed and 5,000 of his men, together with 500 officers, had been captured; his arms and artillery had been taken. The women of the royalist camp were treated with great ferocity; those from Ireland were 'knocked on the head' – killed is another word – while those from England had their faces slashed with daggers. Oliver Cromwell, after the battle, declared that 'this is none other than the hand of God, and to Him alone belongs the glory'. Clarendon concluded that at Naseby 'the king and the kingdom were lost'.

For the king, indignity was heaped upon dismay. Among the wagons captured after the battle was one that contained all of his private correspondence. When the king's cabinet was opened, it revealed the extent of his dealings with the Irish Catholics in search of troops; it also disclosed his plans to use French, or Swedish, soldiers for the sake of his cause. It could now be asserted that the New Model Army was truly a national army ready to defend England, and at Naseby it had decisively proved its worth. It had also demonstrated that the Independent cause was now the strongest. Cromwell himself was the man singled out for future glory and, according to Bulstrode Whitelocke, he began 'to grow great even to the envy of many'. Yet many also believed that God was with him.

Most of the king's supporters and councillors believed that his case was desperate, and that he must yield to necessity by negotiating with parliament. The king himself on occasions feared the worst and, in a secret letter to his son, wrote that 'if I should at any time be taken prisoner by the rebels, I command you . . . never to yield to any conditions that are dishonourable, unsafe to your person, or derogatory to royal authority'. Yet he refused to have 'melancholy men' about him; he chose to entertain himself with sports and pastimes. He wandered about the country between Hereford, Oxford and Newark; these were three of his last remaining fortresses in his kingdom.

Prince Rupert, whose rashness may have cost Charles the battle of Naseby, now hurried on to Bristol; he needed to make that city safe against an enemy army that might descend upon it at any moment. From there he wrote to a colleague that 'his majesty hath now no way left to preserve his posterity, kingdom and nobility, but by a treaty'. When he was shown the letter the king was incensed. In his reply he wrote that in his role as a soldier or statesman 'I must say there is no probability but of my ruin'; yet as a king and a Christian he knew that 'God will not suffer rebels and traitors to prosper'.

This was not necessarily so. At Langport to the south of Bristol, on 10 July 1645, the New Model Army, fresh from its victory at Naseby, decisively defeated the royalist army of the south-west; the cavalry of the king had been destroyed, and his last hope of winning the contest seemed to be over. Cromwell exulted. 'To see this,' he said, 'is it not to see the face of God?'

28

The mansion house of liberty

One parliamentary occasion has gone unnoticed in this account of victories and defeats on the field. An ordinance of 14 June 1643 had been passed 'to prevent and suppress the licence of printing'. It was declared necessary to suppress the 'great late abuses and frequent disorders in printing many false, forged, scandalous, seditious, libellous, and unlicensed papers, pamphlets, and books to the great defamation of religion and government'; a committee of censors, therefore, was appointed to license new publications and to seize any that were unlicensed.

One republican deplored what he considered to be this reversion to the evil practices of the past that had no place in the new world for which he so devoutly wished. The Presbyterian members of parliament, who were largely behind the measure, might as well 'kill a man as kill a good book; who kills a man kills a reasonable creature, God's image: but he who destroys a good book, kills reason itself, kills the image of God, as it were, in the eye. Many a man lives a burden to the earth: but a good book is the precious life blood of a master spirit, imbalmed and treasured up on purpose to a life beyond life.' This is the unmistakable prose of John Milton.

Milton was a Londoner animated by a spirit of enquiry and an awareness of his own genius. From an early age he pored over his books by candlelight in Bread Street, brooding over fables and histories until he had knowledge and time enough to compose the fables and history of his own country. He was a born republican, averse to authority and discipline in any of its forms. There would come a time when he would denounce Charles I in Latin, so that the world might hear. He declared that England was 'the elect nation', a prophecy endorsed by other clerics and divines of the period, thus emphasizing the millennial aspirations of the seventeenth century.

In 1637, in his twenty-ninth year, Milton wrote in a letter that 'my genius is such that no delay, no rest, no care or thought almost of anything, holds me aside until I reach the end I am making for, and round off, as it were, some great period in my studies'. He read as if for life; for him, it *was* life. Yet the storms of the world would soon surround him, obscuring for a time that bright particular star by which he set his course.

He had studied at Cambridge and followed his period at that university with an intensive course of private scholarship that continued for some eight years. Blessed with a fair face, and an even fairer mind, he began a tour among the devoted scholars and learned poets of Europe; his voyage of sweet discovery was curtailed, however, when he was obliged to return to London in 1639 at the time of the Bishops' War.

He had studied with the overriding ambition to become a poet that the world would not willingly ignore. But the desperation of the age turned him from poetry to prose, to the language of men in debate and conflict. He began writing his pamphlets against the bishops in 1641 and indulged his taste for polemic at a time of delusion and disagreement. In *The Reason of Church Government* he denounced those prelates who 'have glutted their ingrateful bodies' with 'corrupt and servile doctrines'; they were fed 'scraggy and thorny lectures . . . a hackney course of literature' and were filled with 'strumpet flatteries . . . corrupt and putrid ointment'. They were scum and harlots and open sepulchres. The language of the streets, which he heard all around him, came naturally to a Cockney visionary.

Milton wrote his treatise *Areopagitica* in Aldersgate Street; but the little pamphlet in due course made its way around the world as the most eloquent and inspiring defence of the freedom of expression. For this founding statement upon the liberty of speech he modelled himself upon the Attic orators who had once spoken to the Athenian people; the Areopagus was the rock upon which the final court of appeal held its sessions. Milton was clearly adverting to the republican and even democratic status of the English parliament which he described as 'that supreme and majestic tribunal'. He wrote copiously and elegantly, constructing sentences that have been described as baroque palaces, but all the time his style was tempered by the urgency and seriousness of the puritan cause.

Areopagitica was ready for the press by the autumn of 1644, two or three months after Cromwell's victory at Marston Moor; hopes for the Independent cause were high, and Milton himself was touched by the optimism of the moment. All was still possible. On the title page was printed:

AREOPAGITICA

A SPEECH OF MR JOHN MILTON

For the Liberty of UNLICENC'D PRINTING,

To the PARLIAMENT OF ENGLAND.

Milton's passion for free speech, for liberty of thought and conscience in the making of a new world, was a powerful corrective to all the obfuscators and doctrinaires of parliament who had partly triumphed with the signing of the solemn league and covenant with the Scots in the previous year. He railed against those with closed minds, of which the Presbyterians were the largest number. Censorship and licensing would be 'the stop of truth'. The people of England would suffer from the change, when 'dull ease and cessation of our knowledge' would inevitably lead to 'obedient uniformity' or to 'rigid external formality'.

He insisted that 'we must not think to make a staple commodity of all the knowledge in the land, to mark and license it like our broad-cloth and wool packs'. He recalled his travels into Italy where he visited Galileo 'grown old, a prisoner to the Inquisition'. If the silence of conformity were to be imposed upon England, too, it would 'soon put it out of controversy that bishops and presbyters are the same to us both name and thing'. What if the Presbyterians were no better than the Laudian Church writ in sterner letters?

What did the censors and opponents of freedom have to fear? 'He that can apprehend and consider vice with all her baits and seeming pleasures, and yet abstain, and yet distinguish, and yet prefer that which is truly better, he is the true warfaring Christian. I cannot praise a fugitive and cloistered virtue, unexercised and unbreathed, that never sallies out and sees her adversary, but slinks out of the race, where that immortal garland is to be run for, not without dust and heat.' Milton's phrases rise like waves before they fall upon the shore, the poetry of his being flooding beneath them. His sentences are grave, sonorous and magniloquent but not untouched by the occasional asperity of irony or wit.

In *Areopagitica* he addresses the political nation with an encomium that proclaims the fervent seriousness of the time. 'Lords and Commons of England, consider what Nation it is whereof ye are, and whereof ye are the governors: a Nation not slow and dull, but of a quick, ingenious and piercing spirit, acute to invent, subtle and sinewy to discourse, not beneath the reach of any point the highest that human capacity can soar to.' It is an excellent tribute to the intellectual resources of the country in this period of conflict and argument. Milton considered England to be particularly blessed by what he called 'the favour and love of heaven'. It was this faith that gave strength and optimism to the puritan cause.

He writes, too, of London as a beacon of that cause. 'Behold now this vast City; a City of refuge, the mansion house of liberty, encompassed and surrounded by His protection . . . Under these fantastic terrors of sect and schism we wrong the earnest and zealous thirst after knowledge and understanding which God hath stirred up in this City.' He is suggesting that there is nothing to fear in the proliferation of sectarians and schismatics; they are all part of the glory of God.

Of all the writers of the period Milton is the one most able to embody the seriousness and the determination of the religious cause. In the loftiness of his mind, in the dignity and grandeur of his most stately utterances, we may glimpse the essential nobility of the age. 'Methinks I see in my mind a noble and puissant Nation rousing herself like a strong man after sleep, and shaking her invincible locks. Methinks I see her as an eagle muing [renewing] her mighty youth, and kindling her undazzled eyes at the full midday beam; purging and unscaling her long abused sight at the fountain itself of heavenly radiance . . .'

In later years Milton served as Latin secretary for Cromwell and the protectorate, in which capacity he served the puritan cause as faithfully as before. Yet disillusion would set in soon enough, followed by bitterness and despair. Like many of his generation he was, by the end of Cromwell's rule and the return of the king, beset by misery and isolation, bewilderment and grief.

29

A game to play

The last twelve months of war were confused and uncertain. No one knew when, or how, it would end. The king no longer had the resources to fight any more major battles; he held on to a few cities such as Bristol and Worcester, but his strength was essentially limited to individual fortresses or garrisons. A campaign of siege warfare had begun, with parliamentary forces coming upon one royalist stronghold after another. The rules of siege were well known to all the participants. After the defence had put up as good a fight as they could, they could then demand a 'parley' and bargain upon the terms of surrender; if they capitulated, they were spared. If they refused to surrender, they were likely to be stormed and massacred.

In this weary and bloody period groups of men and women emerged ready to defy and fight both parties in order to save their neighbourhoods. The 'clubmen' were called after the primitive weapons they often carried. The farmers and yeomen of Wiltshire and Dorset, for example, had already established bands of watchmen to seize any soldiers caught in the act of plunder and to march them back to their respective camps for punishment. They did not know which side was winning or losing. They did not know of Naseby or of Langport. They wished only to preserve their lives and property.

Now some countrymen, armed with sickles or scythes as well

as clubs, took the offensive. They gathered to protect their harvests and their granaries with the message that:

> If you offer to plunder and take our cattle
> You may be sure we'll give you battle.

If the clubmen had any other message, it was simply that the two sides should come together and that the war should be ended. Clubmen risings took place in several counties, from Sussex to South Wales, but particularly in those regions that, as one of their leaders put it, had 'more deeply . . . tasted the misery of this unnatural internecine war'. Money and supplies had been extorted from them; soldiers had been quartered upon them against their will, local authority had often broken down. They wanted a return to order and to the 'known laws'.

The unsettled mood of the localities may perhaps be traced in the large number of witch trials in the period. Three days after the battle of Naseby thirty-six supposed witches were put on trial at the Essex assizes, and all but one of them were executed on the charge of black art and of conjuring up the devil. It has been estimated that, in this summer, one hundred old and young women were executed. This was a world of anxiety.

The king was now reduced to limited forays to lift a siege here or support a town there, but he lived in fear of any parliamentary army bearing down upon him; he was concerned that, if he were captured, he would suffer at the hands of the puritan troops. He received some comfort from the fact that the Scots seemed prepared to negotiate with him. They were ready to break with parliament, now that it was beginning to incline towards Cromwell and the Independent cause. They had been accused of doing little since their first arrival in England, and their payments were in arrears.

Yet this small hope for the royalist cause was almost overwhelmed by the news that Bristol had fallen; Prince Rupert had signed a treaty of surrender. Sir Thomas Fairfax had surrounded the city towards the end of August and laid siege. By the beginning of September Rupert realized that he could hold out no longer. He did not have enough troops to defend the walls of the city, and the citizens were increasingly desperate. Fairfax was growing impatient and directed an assault against some royalist defenders; when they had been cut down he sent the terms of surrender to his combatant. The prince accepted and, on 11 September, evacuated the town.

The loss of the second city of the kingdom was a grievous blow to the king, who at once suspected a plot to suborn him. He even considered the possibility that Rupert was about to launch a military coup and remove him from the throne before negotiating a truce with parliament. 'Nephew!' he wrote in anger, 'though the loss of Bristol be a great blow to me, yet your surrendering it as you did is of so much affliction to me, that it makes me not only forget the consideration of that place, but is likewise the greatest trial of my constancy that hath yet befallen me; for what is to be done, after one that is so near to me as you are, both in blood and friendship, submits himself to so mean an action?' He dismissed him from his service, and advised him to return home. The prince had not been a popular figure and, as he marched out of Bristol, the citizens cried out, 'Give him no quarter! Give him no quarter!'

Two or three days later the cause of the king was shaken further with the news that the forces of Montrose in Scotland had been defeated, and that the earl had fled back to the Highlands. The king's best hope had gone. In this period it was ordered by parliament that 'the boarded masque house at Whitehall' should be pulled down and its materials sold. The days of the cavalier were coming to an end.

In October Prince Rupert made his way to Newark Castle, where the king was lodged. He strode up to his uncle and told him that he had come to give him an account of his conduct at Bristol; the king would not speak to him and sat down to supper, during which he ignored him. Eventually he allowed his nephew to give evidence before a council of war, the members of which decided that the prince had not been guilty of any want of courage or fidelity. He could have done no other but surrender or face the entire destruction of his troops and of the town. The king reluctantly accepted the verdict, with the proviso that he believed his nephew could have held out longer. Charles left Newark a few days later, and quickly made what had now become a dangerous journey back to Oxford.

In his extremity the king began negotiating with various parties in order to preserve himself. He had already told his son to sail for France and remain under the protection of his mother who had sailed from Falmouth in the summer. Now he sought to divide the two principal groups in parliament by dealing separately with the Independents and the Presbyterians; he seemed willing to grant liberty of conscience to the former while inclining towards the latter on the grounds that the army was too democratic. He told his wife that 'I had great reason to hope that one of the factions would so address themselves to me that I might without difficulty obtain my so just ends'. He had opened provisional negotiations with the Scots, also, and was still attempting to treat with the Irish.

The fighting in the last few months of the war became sporadic and desultory. Prince Rupert set out from Oxford on cavalry raids, but achieved little. The royalist troops on the border of Wales and England tried desperately to hold on to Chester and its related ports in the hope of welcoming an Irish army. That army never arrived and, in any case, Chester eventually fell. Sir Thomas Fairfax conducted the parliamentary campaign in the west against a divided and demoralized enemy. A royalist army was raised to confront him but, at Torrington, it fell to pieces.

In the last battle of the great civil war, near Stow-on-the-Wold in Gloucestershire, the royalist forces were soon overpowered and surrendered en masse. The royalist commander, Sir Jacob Astley, told his captors that 'you have now done your work and may go play, unless you fall out among yourselves'. And that is what they proceeded to do.

The king, now facing ruin, tried to buy time with various proposals, secret or otherwise. He offered to come to Westminster, but his overture was rejected; it was considered likely that he would try to detach one faction and place himself at its head. Charles himself wrote that 'nothing will satisfy them but the ruin, not only of us, our posterity and friends, but even monarchy itself'. Eventually he decided that he would go over to the Scots; he was their native king, after all, and they did not share the levelling principles of his principal parliamentary opponents. He would be secure both in conscience and in honour; he would also be under the protection of a large army.

The Scots themselves had to act warily, since they did not wish to antagonize their paymasters at Westminster. They would be obliged to come upon the king, as it were, by accident. On 27 April

1646, the king left Oxford in disguise as a servant, and by a circuitous route made his way to the Scottish army at Newark. The
Scottish commanders told their English allies that this was a 'matter
of much astonishment' to them.

Soon enough Charles realized that he was as much a prisoner
as a guest. When he tried to give the word of command to his
guard he was interrupted by the lord general, Alexander Leslie, who
told him that 'I am the older soldier, sir; your majesty had better
leave that office to me'. It seems likely that the Scots wished to
keep their king as a hostage until parliament paid them the money
they were owed. They took him to Newcastle, where almost at once
he became subject to their demands. He must sign the covenant.
He must impose Presbyterianism on all of his people. He must
abandon the Book of Common Prayer. When one minister told
him that his father, James VI, would welcome such a settlement the
king replied that 'I had the happiness to know him much better
than you'. 'I never knew', he wrote to his wife, 'what it was to be
barbarously treated before.' Yet he pretended to compromise while
playing for time; he hoped that his opponents would become further
divided, and he believed that fresh aid would come from France or
Ireland or the Highlands or anywhere.

At the end of July, parliament sent the king a number of propositions to which he should accede if he wished to retain the throne.
He should embrace Presbyterianism and extirpate the bishops; he
should persecute Independents or Catholics, and give up his army
for twenty years. Privately he swore that he would not surrender
'one jot' but in his public response he agreed to consider the demands
in a mild and obliging spirit. He wrote privately to his wife that he
had to deliver 'a handsome denying answer', an unenthusiastic
response that would not alienate his captors. All of these secret
letters were written in code and smuggled out of his quarters.

The flight of the king to the Scottish army had precipitated the
final split between the forces of his enemies. The Scottish army and
parliament now deeply distrusted one another, and their differences
were reflected in the open divisions between the Presbyterians and
Independents at Westminster. It is of no importance whether we
choose to call them religious sects or political parties; now they
were both. They were known as 'factions' or 'juntoes' or 'cabals'.

The Presbyterian cause, in its ideal state, proposed that its Church should rule by inherent right as the one divinely ordained form of religious government, and that no other churches or sects should be permitted. The Independent cause rested on the belief that a true Church was a voluntary association of believers and that each congregation had the right to self-government; it was Calvinist in tendency but it favoured toleration. Cromwell had said that 'he that ventures his life for the liberty of his country, I wish he trust God for the liberty of his conscience'. A Presbyterian divine stated, however, that 'to let men serve God according to the persuasion of their own consciences, was to cast out one devil that seven worse might enter'. Another Presbyterian divine, Thomas Edwards, published a book entitled *Gangraena* in which he listed the heresies of the radical sectarians, each one to be crushed in its egg 'before it comes to be a flying serpent'. Here, then, was the great divide. In the broadest secular terms the Presbyterians supported parliament, while the Independents favoured the army.

Conflicts and divisions arose frequently in parliamentary debate. On one occasion the Commons spent the day discussing matters of religion until darkness fell upon the assembly; a motion was advanced to bring in candles, but this was disputed. When a division was called it was already too dark to count the members on either side, and it was suggested that candles be introduced to resolve the issue. But could candles be brought in before the house had formally requested them? So the affairs of the nation were determined. This was a new age of political life.

The eventual refusal of the king to take the covenant undermined his value to the Scottish Presbyterians, who now thought it best to make a bargain with parliament. On receipt of the moneys owing to them, they would hand back the sovereign; under these circumstances, perhaps, Charles might negotiate a treaty with their allies at Westminster. So for the sum of £400,000 he was surrendered. The haggling over money damaged their credibility, however, and the earl of Lauderdale predicted that it 'would make them to be hissed at by all nations; yeah, the dogs in the street would piss upon them'. As the army marched out of Newcastle, leaving the king behind, the fishwives of the city cried out, 'Judas! Judas!' The king himself said that they had sold him at too cheap a rate.

Charles set out for parliamentary custody at the beginning of February 1647 almost as a conquering hero, and cheering crowds lined his route. At Ripon he touched for the king's evil, thus asserting his divine power over the disease of scrofula. At Nottingham the lord general of the New Model Army, Sir Thomas Fairfax, dismounted and kissed his hand. The king arrived at Holmby House, in Northamptonshire, in the middle of February. He remained for five months; he spent much time in his private quarters or 'closet', played at bowls or rode in the neighbourhood.

The Presbyterians and their supporters at Westminster now began to plan for the disbandment of the New Model Army and for its replacement by a less sectarian and more reliable force. They also ignored the English army's demands for payment of arrears in wages, and for an indemnity against prosecution for any actions committed in the late war. It was now becoming a dangerous dispute between army and parliament. In this period Oliver Cromwell collapsed, and almost died, from something known as an 'impostume in the head'; it was some kind of swelling or abscess, perhaps in part induced by nervous strain.

The sectarians and supporters of the army, or as they called themselves 'well-affected persons', sent a 'Large Petition' to parliament in which they asserted the supreme authority of the people; they also demanded that the Lords and Commons exempt 'matters of religion and God's worship from the compulsive and restrictive power of any authority upon earth'. Among these passionate sectarians emerged a group that were known as 'the levellers'. Royalist newsletters had given them the name, since 'they intend to set all straight, and raise a parity and community in the kingdom'. We might perhaps describe them as spiritual egalitarians.

They were essentially a London group who issued several hundred tracts, and could muster perhaps a few hundred sympathizers; their colour was sea-green and they wore sea-green scarves or ribbons. One of their unofficial leaders, John Lilburne, wrote to Cromwell in this year that he and his co-religionists 'have looked upon you as the most absolute single-hearted great man in England, untainted or unbiased with ends of your own'.

The army itself was in a state of agitation close to mutiny, and sent a petition of complaint to Sir Thomas Fairfax. In turn parliament passed a declaration denouncing 'enemies of the state and disturbers of the peace'. The army that had saved parliament was therefore branded as an enemy, which in turn was considered to be in effect a declaration of war. 'The Apology of the Soldiers to their Officers', published at the beginning of May, complained that their intentions were 'grossly and foully misconstrued' and asked 'Was there ever such things done by a parliament . . . is it not better to die like men than to be enslaved and hanged like dogs?'

Against this background the people of England suffered. This year, 1646, marked the beginning of six terrible harvests in a period when the price of bread doubled and the cost of meat rose by more than a half. The agriculture of England was its life and staple; its partial collapse therefore shook the already troubled kingdom.

The members of the New Model Army were quartered at Saffron Walden, where some parliamentary commissioners came to recruit soldiers for service in Ireland; they were greeted with complaints and questions. The troops wanted to know when, in particular, their arrears of payment would be met; they received no coherent response. Eight of the ten cavalry regiments then chose representatives who would in time become known as 'adjutators' (or, as their opponents called them, 'agitators') for the army's cause. Cromwell pleaded for a compromise, arguing that if parliamentary authority 'falls to nothing, nothing can follow but confusion'. Yet parliament was in turn determined to crush the army, on the principle that 'they must sink us, or we sink them'. It was now being whispered that the army sought an accommodation with the king, whereby it might contrive to destroy the Presbyterian cause. Fairfax explained that Charles had become 'the golden ball cast between the two parties'. Which way would he roll, or be rolled?

The army leaders believed that parliament was about to establish a new army with the king at its head, so they moved to act first. At six in the morning of 4 June 1647, the king emerged from Holmby House to be confronted by a party of 500 horse, drawn up in neat ranks, under the command of Cornet Joyce. Joyce asked permission to escort Charles to some other place. The king demanded to see his commission, but Joyce prevaricated. 'I pray you, Mr Joyce, deal with me ingenuously and tell me what commission you have.'

'Here is my commission.'

'Where?'

Joyce turned around and gestured towards the assembled horse-men. 'It is behind me.'

'It is as fair a commission,' the king replied, 'and as well written as I have seen a commission written in my life: a company of as handsome, proper gentlemen, as I have seen a great while.'

The New Model Army took him to the village of Childerley outside Cambridge. Charles did not particularly care in whose camp he rested; it was enough for him, as he put it, to set his opponents by the ears. Yet, with the king in its hands, the army had now become a political as well as a military force. The role of Cromwell in the Holmby House plot has never been clear; Joyce visited him five days before the action, however, and it is not likely that they discussed horsemanship. When Cromwell told the king that Joyce had acted entirely on his own initiative Charles retorted that 'I'll not believe you unless you hang him'. In fact Joyce received promotion and a generous pension.

On the day after Charles had been taken to Childerley Hall the regiments met near Newmarket in order to draw up a 'solemn engagement' in which they pledged to stay together until their legitimate demands were met. 'Is that the opinion of you all?' 'It is, of all, of all.' There were also cries of 'Justice, justice, we demand justice!' A new 'general council of the army' was established, with Cromwell among its members. He had ridden to the army head-quarters at Newmarket from London, having heard rumours that the Presbyterians were about to consign him to the Tower. He had endeavoured to hold the peace between the opposing factions, but now he formally took the army's part as its chief representative.

On hearing the news of the king's seizure, parliament convened and hastily granted all arrears of pay to the New Model Army; the city fathers now demanded that a force of cavalry be raised for the defence of the capital. The army itself was on the move and marched to Triploe Heath, 7 miles nearer London, and began to advance ever closer to the city. Cromwell wrote a letter to the civic author-ities, asking for a just settlement of the liberties of the people under the aegis of parliament; he warned, however, that if the army met concerted opposition it would be freed from the blame for 'all that ruin which may befall that great and populous city'.

When the army reached St Albans, a little over 20 miles from London, *The Declaration of the Army* was published in which were proposed shorter and more representative parliaments beyond the reach of oligarchy or regal authority; no force in the nation should have 'unlimited power'. Its author was Sir Henry Ireton, Cromwell's new son-in-law. The *Declaration* was accompanied by charges against eleven named Presbyterian members of parliament; they were accused of treasonable dealings with royalists at home and abroad. Parliament seemed willing and able to defend them but, on 26 June 1647, the eleven men thought it prudent to withdraw from Westminster and eventually to flee abroad. This was the period in which 'purge' entered the English political vocabulary. The great constitutional historian Henry Hallam wrote that on this day 'may be said to have fallen the legislative power and civil government of England'.

Throughout the month of June the leaders of the army were in constant and courteous contact with the king. It is clear enough that they still wished to reach a settlement which would allow him to retain his throne with altered powers; he was the only power that might conceivably unite the nation now dangerously divided between army and parliament. Yet he was still beset by accusations of hypocrisy and double-dealing. At one point the king told Henry Ireton that 'I shall play my game as well as I can'; to which Ireton replied that 'if your majesty have a game to play, you must give us also liberty to play ours'.

The New Model Army had by now worked its way around to Reading, which provided a more convenient route to London. The more radical of the 'agitators' now pressed for a final march upon the city, but Cromwell favoured delay and negotiation. Ireton had drafted a policy document, *Heads of the Proposals*, that effectively repeated the propositions set out in *The Declaration of the Army* including a biennial parliament and a new council of state.

Parliament, noticeably more moderate or more fearful after the expulsion of the eleven members, voted to accept the proposals. They agreed in particular that control of the city militia should be returned to the old committee of militia, which meant effectively that the city force would be under the command of the now dominant army. The Lords and Commons, however, had not calculated the ferocious response of the Presbyterians in London itself who feared for their lives and property if the army came to rule. A crowd of citizens and apprentices accompanied a deputation of Londoners and besieged the Lords, shouting that 'they would never come out' unless they reversed their decision. Another crowd, or mob, burst into the Commons and demanded that they repeal their earlier judgement. 'Vote! Vote!' The members were too terrified to do anything other than comply. Parliament had proved itself to be at the mercy of any powerful group, and was thus unable to legislate for anything; sixty of the Independent members, together with the Speaker, now fled to the army at Reading for safety. They lent added legitimacy to the soldiers' cause.

The *Heads of the Proposals* had been submitted for the king's consideration. Some of the terms were mild enough. The bishops would not be abolished but deprived of the power of coercion; the old liturgy and the new covenant would have equal force in a broad context of religious liberty and toleration. The army and navy would be returned to the king after ten years. Only five royalists would be excluded from pardon. If Charles had accepted these terms, he could have returned to the throne with his honour intact. The king, however, rejected the document without giving it any serious consideration. His stated response was that 'you cannot be without me. You will fall to ruin if I do not sustain you.' One of his advisers, Sir John Berkley, whispered to him, 'Sir, your majesty speaks as if you had some secret strength and power that I do not know of.' The moderates on both sides now began to lose all hope.

The intimidation of parliament by the London mob, and the failure of negotiations with the king, prompted the New Model Army finally to march upon London. A brigade of horse took Southwark on the night of 3 August, and the civic leaders of the city woke up to find their principal avenue across London Bridge in the hands of what must now be called the enemy. The sudden occupation 'struck them dead', according to Clarendon, and 'put an end to all their consultation for defence'. Their only object now was to conciliate those whom they had previously offended and to prevent the army from firing and plundering their mansions.

The whole army of 18,000 men, under the command of Sir Thomas Fairfax, now entered the city; Cromwell rode at the head of the cavalry, while Fairfax sat in a carriage beside Cromwell's wife. Fairfax was met at Hyde Park by the mayor and aldermen, who proffered a formal apology and offered him a gold cup; he refused to accept the gift, and sent them on their way. With the Speaker and the members of the Commons with him, he seemed now to represent the legitimate authority of the nation. One puritan Londoner, Thomas Juxon, wrote after watching the soldiers marching through the streets of London, that "tis remarkable that it never was in the minds of the army to carry it so far; but were brought to it, one thing after another, and that by the designs of their enemies'. The army also made sure that the great defensive wall, erected by Londoners at the beginning of the war, was pulled down. Fairfax did not intend a military occupation of the city, however, and established the army headquarters some 6 miles away at Putney.

Charles, now residing at Hampton Court, was willing graciously to listen to the proposals put forward by Cromwell and the other leaders of the army; but he was resolute in defence of his interests, and refused to compromise. Many Independent members were willing, and indeed eager, to dispense altogether with the king. They even accused Cromwell of pursuing his own self-interest in continuing to negotiate with him; it was whispered that he was about to be honoured as the new earl of Essex.

Yet Cromwell was in truth becoming angry and frustrated at the king's constant prevarications and refusals; he began seriously to doubt his sincerity. At some point, towards the end of October, he refused to travel any more to Hampton Court. Those who attended the monarch now began to notice an alteration in the manners and civility of the soldiers who were stationed about him; the king's guard was doubled.

30

To kill a king

The army now began to take stock of its power and its situation. The levellers made an early contribution to the debate when in October they published a pamphlet, 'The Case of the Armie Truly Stated', in which they demanded a more representative parliament; they maintained the then revolutionary doctrine that all power was 'originally and essentially in the whole body of the people of this nation'. No mention, therefore, was made of king or lords. They had support among the more radicalized soldiers who agreed with their call for national renovation. 'The Case of the Armie' was swiftly followed by the 'Agreement of the People' that argued for a new political order based upon a written constitution. Both sets of proposals seemed to be guiding the army towards the establishment of a republic.

Some of the principal officers, Cromwell among them, did not support the more extreme measures being canvassed; it was proposed, therefore, that the arguments be tested in open debate. The deliberations were held at St Mary's Church, on the southern side of Putney Bridge, at the end of October and lasted for three weeks; gathered here were the several generals, together with four representatives from each of the thirty-two regiments. The importance of the proceedings was not lost upon any of the participants, and indeed the 'Putney debates' of 1647 remain one of the most significant expressions of English political thought.

On the first day Edward Sexby, one of the representatives of the soldiers, complained that 'we have laboured to please a king, and, I think, except we go about to cut all our throats, we shall not please him'. Cromwell then remarked that the radical 'Agreement of the People' was naively formulated in the belief that a new constitution could be created without any consideration of English tradition or precedent. He had been told that faith would make a way through all difficulties but 'we are very apt all of us to call that faith, that perhaps may be but carnal imagination, and carnal reasonings'. He was suggesting that expediency and self-deception may be at the heart of political revolution. He also made more practical criticisms. All of this change was to be achieved in the name of the people but he questioned, 'Were the spirits and temper of the people of this nation prepared to receive and to go along with it?'

A defining moment of the debate arrived when Thomas Rainsborough, one of the representatives of the levelling movement, declared that 'I think that the poorest he that is in England has a life to live as the greatest he' and should therefore be allowed the vote. It was a call that was not to be answered until 1918. Henry Ireton rejected the idea of manhood suffrage, however, and argued that the vote should be given to 'persons in whom all land lies, and those in corporations in whom all trading lies'. Only those with a financial stake in the country, in other words, should be allowed to determine its direction.

At one point in the proceedings Cromwell was moved to declare that 'the foundation and the supremacy is in the people, radically in them', but he also argued that the sovereign authority must be that of a parliament however constituted. In this uncertain time the force of power was absolutely required. He compared himself to a drowning man. 'If it have but the face of authority, if it be but a hare swimming over the Thames, I will take hold of it rather than let it go.' A more ominous note, for the king, emerged when Captain Bishop claimed that the woes of the nation came from 'a compliance to preserve that man of blood' by which he meant Charles. The captain was alluding to a passage from the second Book of Samuel: 'Thou art taken in thy mischief because thou art a bloody man.' The phrase soon became commonplace.

The final set of proposals that emerged from Putney did not

reflect the demands of the levellers or the debate about the future of the king; it was designed only to preserve the unity of the army. It recommended an extended franchise but maintained the ancient framework of king, Commons and Lords with the Commons in effective control. The commanders of the army then brought the debates to a summary close by ordering all of the participants to return to their regiments. A partial mutiny by some of the more radical troops was quickly put down. A restructuring of the army, in the following year, allowed its leaders to remove those soldiers of suspect sympathies.

The king now confounded everyone by escaping from Hampton Court. He had gone down some private stairs and, meeting with two associates, fled south. He seemed to have had no certain destination but eventually decided to make for the Isle of Wight where he had the sea at his back. He left behind some papers, one of which was an anonymous letter warning him of the danger of assassination. He also left a letter to parliament in which he asked to 'be heard with freedom, honour and safety, and I shall instantly break through this cloud of retirement and show myself ready to be *pater patriae*'.

The governor of the Isle of Wight, Robert Hammond, received this father of the nation with no little apprehension; he was under the command of the army, and had no wish to disobey his superiors. But he was violently opposed to the levellers in the ranks and could guarantee the king's safety from their attentions. It may also have suited Cromwell to leave the king on the island; he was far from the reach both of the more sanguinary levellers and of the Scots who might wish to negotiate with him. In the best possible circumstances the king might even take to the sea and journey to exile in France.

The king was now in Carisbrooke Castle under guard. He could set himself up as an object for auction, as it were, with many prospective bidders. Cromwell might still wish to come to an accommodation with him. Despite Robert Hammond's best endeavours, the Scots might somehow be able to find a way of communicating with him. Almost as soon as he was ensconced in the castle he began to practise his subterfuges; he concealed messages in the lining of gloves, he engaged in secret conversations with his servants, he drew up elaborate plans for sending and receiving clandestine letters.

This was the period in which Cromwell openly broke with the king and spoke bitterly against him in the army council. There is a story, never fully substantiated, that Cromwell intercepted a secret letter to the queen in which Charles announced that he would make an arrangement with the Scots rather than with the army. It was soon remarked at Westminster that, in Carisbrooke, Charles had thrown a bone between two spaniels and laughed at their enmity. That alone would have been enough to turn Cromwell against him. He now began to sympathize with the position of the more radical soldiers as resolute anti-monarchists. He observed that 'if we cannot bring the army to our sense, we must go to theirs'.

Cromwell's suspicions were soon confirmed. Towards the end of December the king, after secret negotiations with the Scottish commissioners, signed an agreement known as 'the Engagement'. He promised to introduce Presbyterianism as the state religion for an initial three years; he would confirm the 'solemn league and covenant' in the English parliament, but would not oblige his subjects to take its oath. In return the Scots would support Charles's demand for a personal treaty and the disbandment of all English armies; a Scottish army would then be dispatched to London to expedite 'a full and fair parliament'. The document was sealed in lead and buried in the garden of the castle. He then refused to deal with a parliamentary deputation, at which point Colonel Hammond dismissed the king's servants and doubled his guard.

Charles: Shall I have liberty to go about to take the air?
Hammond: No. I cannot grant it.

On 3 January 1648, the Commons passed the 'Vote of No Addresses' by a majority of fifty. No more communications, or proposals, would be put to the king. Cromwell fully supported the decision on the grounds that the people should not 'any longer expect safety and government from an obstinate man whose heart God has hardened'. The council of the army also pronounced that it would stand by the kingdom and parliament 'without the king and against him'.

Yet at a subsequent dinner the army was still manifestly divided.

The commanders argued amongst themselves about the relative merits of 'monarchical, aristocratical or democratical government', but could come to no conclusion. At the end of the discussion Cromwell, in one of those fits of boisterousness or hysteria that punctuated his career, threw a cushion at one of the protagonists, Edmund Ludlow, before running downstairs; Ludlow pursued him, and in turn pummelled him with a cushion.

Colonel Hammond was soon informed that a treaty with the Scots had been signed while the king was in his safe-keeping, and he determined to find it. He entered the king's chamber without warning; the king rose from his bed in alarm and put on his gown; Hammond proceeded to search its pockets, at which point Charles struck him. It was reported that, against all precedent, the colonel returned the blow.

The king's incarceration incensed those who supported the royalist cause. Riots occurred in Ipswich and in Canterbury. A news-writer in London reported that 'the counties are full of discontent, many insurrections having been lately made, even near this city'. The majority of the newspapers and pamphlets were strongly royalist and on the anniversary of the king's accession, 27 March, celebratory bonfires blazed in the capital. Coach travellers, driven through the streets, were compelled to drink the king's health. The butchers of the city declared that if they could catch Colonel Hammond 'they would chop him as small as ever they chopped any of their meat'.

At the beginning of April the lord mayor sent some trained bands to disperse a crowd of apprentices in Moorfields; the crowd turned on the bands, captured their weapons and marched off shouting on behalf of 'King Charles!' Petitioners, seeking the rule of a king again, flocked to London from Kent, Essex and Surrey. The cavaliers were jubilant, and the Presbyterians once more gained a hold over parliament. In April the Commons passed a motion calling for a treaty with the king.

The signs of civil war were once more apparent. The first acts came from Wales where, in April, a royalist commander occupied Tenby Castle; soon enough the whole of South Wales had declared in the sovereign's favour. The leaders of the army spent a day in tears and prayers. How could it be that blood and battle had returned to the nation? Had the previous war been fought for no purpose? At a meeting of the New Model Army in Windsor it was concluded that 'it was our duty, if ever the Lord brought us back again in peace, to call Charles Stuart, that man of blood, to an account for the blood he had shed'.

The army council then ordered Cromwell to enter South Wales with two regiments of horse and three of foot; it took him six weeks to defeat the rebels. Other anti-parliamentary forces had emerged throughout the country, guided not so much by zeal for the king as dismay at the taxes and county committees imposed by parliament. Berwick and Carlisle were taken by the disaffected; Pontefract was also seized in a surprise attack, and Scarborough declared for the king. The men of Essex marched under a banner raised by a royalist commander, General Goring. A section of the fleet off the Downs also declared themselves for the king, and joined with the men of Kent in their revolt. It had also become clear that the Scottish army was being assembled on the border in order to fight for the king.

This represented a serious challenge to the authority of parliament but this second civil war, as it became known, ended once more in victory for the New Model Army. The Scottish army did not cross the border until July, by which time most of the risings in England and Wales had been put down by the army's superior military force; Cromwell dealt with the north, and Fairfax with the south. It had not been a war, but a series of scattered risings and outbreaks of fighting with no serious attempt to co-ordinate what might have been a successful rebellion. Without a coherent strategy the rebels were no match for the New Model. They had waited vainly for the Scots until it became too late to fashion serious resistance.

The second civil war had a bloody ending on its two principal fronts. The Scottish army, under the command of the duke of Hamilton, had made a slow progress southward through the rain and wind of an unseasonably cold summer; ill-trained, and much smaller than expected, it was sustained by no great cause, and as a consequence its morale was low. The New Model was at least bolstered by the knowledge that it was fighting an invasion force.

The two sides encountered each other at a pitched battle near the walls of Preston, on 17 August, in which the infantry of both armies pressed hard upon each other. The Scots were eventually pushed back, with the loss of 1,000 men. Cromwell pursued the remainder of the Scottish army which, battered and broken, laid down its arms. It was the first battle in which he enjoyed overall command, and it was his most signal victory.

All the remaining royalists from the south-east had fled behind the walls of Colchester where, in the middle of June, Sir Thomas Fairfax prepared for a long siege against them. It was the most distasteful and inglorious event of the entire civil war. Fairfax had decided to starve the city into submission until there came a time when the inhabitants, having exhausted the provisions of cats and dogs, were forced to devour soap and candles; it was reported that the royalist soldiers had told the inhabitants to eat their children. The royalist commander, the earl of Norwich, then sent 500 women and children out of the town; Fairfax refused to receive them and with threats they were driven back behind the walls. By the end of August, reduced, as it was said, 'by Captain *Storm* without and by Captain *Hunger* within', the royalists surrendered; two of their commanders were then put in front of a firing squad. This second phase of the civil war was more harsh and intense than the first; there was no longer time for mercy.

After his victory at Preston Cromwell believed that he had seen once more the hand of God. He trusted that he was doing the work of the Lord; that is why he waited upon divine providence to guide his actions and to direct his way forward. He was a blind mole in search of grace, sometimes surrounded by darkness, yet his faith in providence was his rock and his refuge. He wrote to a friend and colleague, Philip Wharton: 'I can laugh and sing in my heart when I speak of these things.'

The battle at Preston effectively marked the end of the second civil war, and of the turmoil that had mangled the kingdom since the king had first raised his banner six years before. It has been calculated that 100,000 soldiers and civilians died in the course of the conflict, and that a larger portion of the population perished than in the Great War of 1914–18. It has therefore justly been described as the bloodiest war in English history. One hundred and fifty towns, and fifty villages, suffered significant damage; 10,000 houses were destroyed.

In the course of the second civil war Charles made several attempts to escape from Carisbrooke Castle. He had never ceased to conspire, and to devise stratagems against his captors and his enemies; he would, for example, conceal coded messages in the heels of his servants' boots. Some supporters managed to smuggle to him a cutting tool and a supply of nitric acid, then known as *aqua fortis*, to dismantle the iron bars of his window; but the design was forestalled and came to nothing. On another occasion he tried to squeeze through the bars but became trapped, stuck between his chest and shoulders, and could only extricate himself with difficulty.

Yet after the final victory parliament still wished to treat with him, against the wishes of the army whose leaders had denounced him as 'a man of blood' who had effectively instigated the second civil war. The majority of the members of the Lords and Commons, together with the large part of the population, now wished for peace at any price. The king was therefore taken out of confinement in the castle and lodged with his friends and servants in Newport, to which town the parliamentary commissioners came. He sat under a canopy of state with his advisers behind him; the parliamentary delegation sat before him.

He was in a more tractable mood, no doubt because the victory of the New Model Army brought an effective end to his resistance. He wished to come to an agreement with parliament on the very good grounds that he feared the army much more. So within a few days he had conceded thirty-eight of their propositions and in return was granted four of his own. He submitted in large part to the religious demands of the commissioners, and agreed to give up control of the militia for a period of twenty years. The parliamentary negotiators were no doubt aware that he might renege on these promises if ever he returned to full power.

The king himself wrote to an adviser, Sir William Hopkins, that 'the great concession I made this day – the Church, militia and Ireland – was made merely in order to my escape . . . my only hope is that now they believe I dare deny them nothing, and so be less careful of their guards'. Yet at the same time he was ever mindful that a different fate might await him. He might be a king who had emasculated his sovereignty. He might be condemned to perpetual imprisonment. He might die upon the scaffold. He also feared assassination by friends of the army, and while at the castle had lived in terror of being poisoned by Hammond or one of his gaoler's associates.

One of the king's secretaries, Sir Philip Warwick, saw his master standing at a window with the parliamentary legation behind him and noticed that he was crying 'the biggest drops that ever I saw fall from an eye'. From the moment his servants had been withdrawn by order, he had neglected his personal appearance; his beard remained untrimmed while his clothes were worn and faded. His once luxurious hair had turned almost entirely grey, thus imparting a new shade of melancholy to his face.

The army was growing increasingly impatient with the negotiations at Newport and, in November, drew up a 'remonstrance' calling for 'exemplary justice' for the notorious man of blood. The leaders of the army were calling for his death. They had also begun the march back to London after completing their business against the Scots in the north.

On the first day of December the king was removed from the Isle of Wight and taken to Hurst Castle on the coast of Hampshire. Cromwell and his colleagues feared, rightly, that parliament had drawn up plans to invite him back to Westminster. They were also apprehensive of any kind of formal agreement between the two parties. Cromwell declared that any Newport treaty would be only a 'little bit of paper'. He wrote to Hammond that the king was 'an accursed thing' with whom there could be no agreement.

On 5 December parliament resolved to settle with the king on the basis of the terms concluded at Newport. On the following day Colonel Thomas Pride stood outside the chamber of the Commons with a list of names; he checked them off, one by one, as each member tried to enter. Some were allowed to go forward while others were detained or arrested by soldiers who stood behind him. The Presbyterian members, who favoured the Newport treaty, and other of the king's supporters, were summarily removed. It was the first, and last, military *coup d'état* in English history. It seems to have been engineered by Henry Ireton rather than by Oliver Cromwell, but when Cromwell returned to London that night from Yorkshire he declared that 'I was not acquainted with this design, yet, since it is done, I am glad of it'. As far as he was concerned, all the providences of God were coming together without his claiming responsibility for them.

In a dreary castle, on the edge of a stretch of shingle spit, the king was immured for two weeks; it was a place of mist and fog where the air was damp and heavy from the marshes that lay all around it. His room was small and dark, lit with candles even at noon, and from the slit of a window he could look out across the Solent. The soldiers brought in his meals 'uncovered', not wearing their hats. 'Is there anything more contemptible', he is supposed to have asked, 'than a despised prince?'

He must have known, or guessed, that all hope was at an end; the army was the master of the kingdom, and must now surely seek his death. Yet, like Cromwell, he was seized with a sense of destiny and of religious purpose; he believed that he might enjoy the fate of a martyr to a holy cause. He had meditated on all the sufferings and ignominies that were likely to befall him, and had hardened his resolve against the rebuffs of the world. Like Cromwell, too, he valued his own life less than the principles for which he fought. So even in this extremity he remained apparently calm and even cheerful.

After 'Pride's Purge', as it became known, approximately 200 members were left of the previous assembly; yet they now constituted the House of Commons and eventually became known as 'the Rump Parliament' or, as Clarendon interpreted it, 'the fag-end of a carcass long since expired'. Some of them had not stayed necessarily to support the army but to avert the prospect of direct military rule without any parliament at all.

On 19 December the king began the journey from Hurst Castle to Windsor where, by the order of the army officers, he was to be 'secured in order to the bringing of him speedily to justice'. Yet the nature of that 'justice' was unclear. Many in the army did not wish for a sentence of death. Despite his fierce words about the man of blood, Cromwell seems to have been among those who did not favour condign punishment. Charles might now be so chastened and so desperate that he would yield. The army, and perhaps a newly elected parliament, would thereby acquire legitimacy and authority if they held power with the assent of the king. In the event that he was tried and found guilty, he might be deposed rather than executed. Charles's death was as yet by no means a necessity.

Another consideration moved Cromwell. An envoy had been sent to Ireland by the king intent upon raising an army; if Charles could be dissuaded from following the project, another great threat would be lifted. The prospect of a royalist Ireland was enough to persuade Cromwell to make one last attempt at a settlement.

The army leaders then sent an envoy to Windsor in order to discuss the terms of a possible agreement, but the king refused to see him on the grounds that he had already 'conceded too much, and even so had failed to give satisfaction, and he was resolved to die rather than lay any further burden on his conscience'. So the prospect of death came ever nearer. The refusal of the king to make any further compromise seems to have persuaded Cromwell that he must indeed be tried and executed. He told the Commons that 'since the providence of God hath cast this upon us, I cannot but submit to providence'.

On New Year's Day 1649, the Rump Parliament passed without any opposition an ordinance for the king's trial on the grounds that he had contrived 'a wicked design totally to subvert the ancient and fundamental laws and liberties of this nation'; he had wished to make himself a tyrant and had prosecuted a cruel and bloody war for that purpose. The Lords rejected the ordinance, whereupon the Commons passed a resolution that 'the people are, under God, the original of all just power' and that they themselves represented the people. The Commons therefore declared themselves to be the supreme power in the state. They also passed an ordinance to establish a new high court of justice with 135 commissioners. In the event only 52 arrived on the appointed day of the king's trial. The army council was also divided. One of its members asserted that the king of England could be tried by no English court. Cromwell responded: 'I tell you, we will cut off his head with the crown upon it!'

Charles was to be brought from Windsor to St James's Palace on 19 January. When the king was told of the coming journey, he replied that 'God is everywhere'. The trial began on the following day. The soldiers brought him from the palace to Whitehall in a closed sedan chair, and then to Westminster in a curtained barge. The roll of judges was called and, when the name of Sir Thomas Fairfax was announced, a woman cried out that 'he has more wit than to be here'; it was the voice of his wife.

The king was conducted into Westminster Hall and sat down in the place provided without the least sign of unease; all the judges, according to Clarendon, were 'fixing their eyes upon him, without the least show of respect'. The solicitor general, John Cook, then read out the charges against him. 'Hold a little,' the king said. He tapped Cook on the shoulder with a silver-tipped cane but the official paid no attention. He tapped him twice more, when the silver tip came off and rolled across the floor. No one picked it up for him. A few days later he confessed that 'it really made a great impression on me'. It might also be seen as an omen of his beheading. When Cook called him 'a tyrant and a traitor', he laughed aloud. How could a sovereign be accused of treason when the meaning of treason was a crime against the sovereign? He did not understand that the word now denoted a trespass against the sovereign power of people and parliament. The king's state, formerly preserved in all honour and authority, had been turned into 'the state'.

After the recital the president of the court, John Bradshaw, asked him for an answer to the impeachment against him. Bradshaw sat in a crimson velvet chair before the king, with the judges arrayed behind him; the guard was ranged to the left and right of the prisoner as well as behind him. The spectators sat in galleries on either side, or stood at the lower end of the hall.

'I would know', the king asked, 'by what power I am called hither?' This was the supreme question. He added that 'there are many unlawful authorities in the world, there are robbers and highwaymen'. He had managed to overcome his habitual stammer.

He was informed that he had been brought to trial 'in the name of the people of England, of which you are elected king, to answer them'.

'England was never an elective kingdom, but a hereditary kingdom for near these thousand years.'

The dialogue continued a little longer until Bradshaw adjourned the proceedings. As the king passed the great sword of justice on the clerk's table he was heard to say, 'I have no fear of that.'

On the second day of the trial the king once more refused to plead. He did not recognize the authority of the court. Bradshaw ordered him to be taken away.

'I do require that I give in my reasons—'

'Sir, 'tis not for prisoners to require.'

'Prisoners! Sir, I am not an ordinary prisoner.'

On the third day he again refused to plead, declaring that 'it is the liberty of the people of England that I stand for'. He was asked to plead forty-three times, altogether, but he would not accept the authority of parliament over him. On 27 January the judges, sitting in the Painted Chamber at Westminster, declared the king to be 'a tyrant, traitor, murderer and a public enemy' who deserved death 'by the severing his head from his body'. Before sentence was passed upon him in the court Charles argued that the case was so serious that it should be put before a joint session of parliament. Some of the judges, anxious to be relieved of the responsibility of regicide, favoured the idea. 'Art thou mad?' Cromwell hissed at one of them. 'Canst thou not sit still and be quiet?' The king's proposal was not accepted.

After Bradshaw had read out the sentence of death Charles asked permission to speak.

'No, sir, by your favour, sir. Guard, withdraw your prisoner.'

'I may speak after the sentence. By your favour, sir, I may speak after the sentence ever.' He was roughly led away by his guard as he continued to cry out. 'By your favour, hold! The sentence, sir – I say, sir, I do – I am not suffered for to speak. Expect what justice other people will have.' All around him the soldiers and the spectators screamed, 'Justice! Justice! Justice!'

In truth the trial and death of the king were contrived by a small, if committed, minority who in no way represented the wishes of the nation. Two Dutch ambassadors pleaded for his life. Sir Thomas Fairfax made a similar supplication to the council of the army. The prince of Wales sent a blank sheet of paper, signed and sealed, so that parliament might write down any conditions it wished. These pleas were not enough. Cromwell and Ireton, in particular, were obdurate. The king must die. Otherwise there would be no safety for themselves or for the new commonwealth.

The last days of the king were for those around him a sorrowful mystery. On 29 January he burnt his papers and his ciphered correspondence. Two of his young children, Elizabeth and Henry, still in the hands of his enemies, were permitted to visit him. When they caught sight of their father, they both burst into tears. He told his thirteen-year-old daughter that he was about to die a glorious death for the liberty of the land and for the maintenance of the true religion. He told his ten-year-old son that the boy must not permit the army to place a crown on his head while his older brothers were still alive. The boy replied: 'I will sooner be torn in pieces first!' The king's guards wept. This was an age of tears.

On the last night of his life, 29 January 1649, the king slept soundly for approximately four hours. When he awoke he told his personal servant that 'this is my second marriage day'. He asked for two shirts since 'were I to shake through cold, my enemies would attribute it to fear'. When he left St James's Palace several companies of infantry were waiting to escort him to Whitehall Palace; the noise of their drums was so loud that the king could not be heard. He was taken to his bedchamber where he waited until parliament had passed a resolution prohibiting the announcement of any successor to the throne. He refused dinner but instead took a piece of bread and a glass of wine. At the appointed time he was escorted to the great Banqueting House.

It was so cold that the Thames had frozen. When he stepped out, from a window on the first floor, the low scaffold was before him; it was draped in black, and the two executioners were heavily disguised. Their identities have never been discovered. The cavalry were at either end of the street and armed guards kept back the people; spectators were on the rooftops, in the houses and in the street itself. The king tried to speak to them but they were too far off. So he dictated his last words to a shorthand writer and two attendants, among which was his declaration that 'a subject and sovereign are clear different things'. He then claimed that 'I die a martyr to the people' before lying down with his head upon the scaffold. The bishop of London was with him.

> *Bishop:* There is but one stage more; it is turbulent and
>   troublesome, but a short one. It will carry you from
>   earth to heaven, and there you will find joy and comfort.
> *King:* I go from a corruptible to an incorruptible crown.
> *Bishop:* You exchange an earthly for an eternal crown – a
>   good exchange.

One blow dispatched him. The principal executioner then took up the head and announced, in traditional fashion, 'Behold the head of a traitor!' At that moment, according to an eyewitness, Philip Henry, 'there was such a groan by the thousands then present, as I never heard before and desire I may never hear again'.

31

This house to be let

The death of the king had delivered a mortal shock to the body politic but as a pamphleteer, Marchamont Nedham, put it, 'the old allegiance is cancelled and we are bound to admit a new'. There was work to be done. The Rump Parliament passed an Act for the 'sale of the goods and personal estates of the late king'. The image of Charles was removed from all public buildings, and his statue at the Exchange was smashed into pieces; on its now empty pedestal were inscribed the words '*exit tyrannus, regum ultimus*' (the tyrant is gone, the last of the kings).

At the beginning of February the House of Lords, and the office of king, were formally abolished; kingship was declared to be 'unnecessary, burdensome and dangerous to the liberty and safety and public interest of the nation'. In theory the Rump Parliament now had unlimited authority, yet it was hardly representative of the people. It contained approximately ninety members, since the rest of them had been purged or had voluntarily withdrawn. Other members returned to parliament later, when they could not be charged with collaboration in the king's death, but of course all of them were divided in their principles and their allegiances. Under the pressure of immediate events, however, they remained a relatively coherent body; only later would it become clear that no consistent ideology could be expected from them. They were reformers rather than revolutionaries, driven by the force of events and circumstances. The Rump was essentially improvised rather than organized; it was born out of necessity and expediency.

Yet the army was also an indispensable power in the new state; Cromwell was a member of parliament as well as a leading army officer. Where did supremacy really lie? If the sword truly ruled, then the answer was obvious. But the main participants professed to believe that they had engineered a constitutional settlement under the aegis of parliament. The politics of ambiguity prevailed, in a situation where no single or fundamental authority was ever named.

A council of state, comprising some forty-one members with thirty-one of them coming from parliament itself, was established to determine policy. Cromwell was the presiding officer. Standing committees were set up for the army, for the navy, for Ireland and for foreign affairs in general. The most pressing concern was that of money; with an army of 70,000 soldiers to maintain and pay, funds were desperately needed. The councillors resorted to fresh taxation, pleas of loans from the City, and the confiscation of royalist estates. It did not help that this was a year of disastrous harvest, in which many inhabitants of Lancashire and Westmorland perished through starvation. Bulstrode Whitelocke reported that the magistrates of Cumberland certified that 30,000 people 'had neither bread nor seed corn, nor the means of procuring either'. Yet the council had other great tasks; it was expected to unify the three kingdoms, to assert the nation's ascendancy at sea and to protect commerce.

The councillors, faced with these burdens and charges, seem to have been largely enthusiastic and efficient. A French envoy, sent by Cardinal Mazarin to spy out the land, wrote that 'not only are they powerful by sea and land, but they live without ostentation, without pomp and without mutual rivalry. They are economical in their private affairs, and prodigal in their devotion to public affairs, for which each man toils as if for his private interest. They handle large sums of money, which they administer honestly, observing a strict discipline. They reward well and punish severely.' It was reported that in this period Oliver Cromwell and Henry Ireton were 'extremely well pleased' at the pace of affairs. Every revolution has its early heroic days.

In the middle of March Cromwell was chosen by the council

to become commander-in-chief of the army with the central purpose of subduing royalist Ireland. Scotland also posed a problem. Its government, on hearing of the king's execution, immediately proclaimed his eighteen-year-old son Charles II as king. The most serious threat came from Ireland, however, where the royalist lieutenant-general, the duke of Ormonde, was dominant. He had aligned himself with the confederate Catholics, rulers of two-thirds of the country after the rebellion of 1641, in support of the new king. Cromwell would soon go back to war.

In May the Rump passed a final Act that proclaimed England to be a free commonwealth; a kingdom had become a republic. All things must now be directed towards what was called the public good; and of course all things might be justified by invoking it. As Milton put it, 'more just is it, if it come to force, that a less number compel a greater to retain their liberty' than that a greater number compel the rest to be their fellow slaves. From this time, for example, we may date the emergence of the fiscal state with national taxation and public spending as its principal activities.

Yet this was also, according to the inscription on the new great seal, 'the first year of freedom, by God's blessing restored'. The revolution in public affairs now lent additional energy and purpose to religious enthusiasts and radicals of every kind. It was time for a new heaven and a new earth. A woman rose up among the congregation in Whitehall Chapel and stripped naked with the cry 'Welcome the Resurrection!'

The Ranters believed that to the pure all things were pure; Laurence Clarkson, 'the captain of the Rant', professed that 'sin had its conception only in imagination'. They might swear, drink, smoke and have sex with impunity. No earthly magistrate could touch them.

The Fifth Monarchy men and women were actively preparing for the reign of Christ and His saints that was destined to supersede the four monarchies of the ancient world; the reign of Jesus would begin in 1694. They would clap hands and jump around, calling out, 'Appear! Appear! Appear!'; they would be joined by travelling fiddlers and ballad-singers until they were in an emotional heat.

The Muggletonians also had apocalyptic and millenarian tendencies. They believed that the soul died with the body and would be raised with it at the time of judgment, and that God paid no attention to any earthly activities. They also asserted that heaven was 6 miles above the earth and that God was between 5 and 6 feet in height.

On 16 April some Diggers came to St George's Hill, near Weybridge in Surrey, where they proceeded to dig and sow seed in the common land. One of them, William Everard, proclaimed that he had been commanded in a vision to dig and plough the land. They believed in a form of agrarian communism by which the English were exhorted finally to free themselves from 'the Norman yoke' of landlords and owners of estates before 'making the earth a common treasury for all'.

The Quakers believed that no visible Church was necessary and that divine revelation was permitted to every human being; Christ might enter the soul and kindle an inner light. They also called for the abolition of lawyers and universities; they refused to pay tithes or to take off their hats in the presence of their 'superiors'. They were also known to disrupt the orthodox church services. They called each other 'saints' or 'friends of the truth' but, because of their tremblings and quiverings in worship, they became popularly known by the name now attached to them.

At the beginning of May a translation of the Koran was issued from the press. Religious liberty was contagious. Two months before, John Evelyn had attended an Anglican service in Lincoln's Inn Chapel.

Political, as well as religious, radicals were in the ascendant. John Lilburne, one of the levellers who had helped to promote agitation in the New Model Army, had turned against the new administration. In 'England's New Chains Discovered' he lambasted Cromwell and the army grandees for dishonesty and hypocrisy; he accused them of being 'mere politicians' who wished to aggrandize themselves while they pretended 'a waiting upon providence, that under the colour of religion they might deceive the more securely'. A pamphlet, 'The Hunting of the Foxes', complained that 'you shall scarce speak to Cromwell but he will lay his hand on his breast, elevate his eyes, and call God to record. He will weep, howl and repent, even while he does smite you under the fifth rib.'

Cromwell was incensed at the pamphlet and was overheard

saying at a meeting of the council of state, 'I tell you, sir, you have no other way to deal with these men but to break them in pieces . . . if you do not break them, they will break you.' By the end of March Lilburne and his senior colleagues had been placed in the Tower on the charge of treason. The levellers, however, were popular among Londoners for speaking home truths about the condition of the country. When thousands of women flocked to Westminster Hall to protest against Lilburne's imprisonment the soldiers told them to 'go home and wash your dishes'; whereupon they replied that 'we have neither dishes nor meat left'. When in May a group of soldiers rose in mutiny for the cause of Lilburne, Cromwell and Fairfax suppressed them; three of their officers were shot. As Cromwell said on another occasion, 'Be not offended at the manner of God's working; perhaps no other way was left.'

Assaults also came from the opposite side with royalist pamphlets and newsletters mourning 'the bloody murder and heavy loss of our gracious king' and proclaiming that 'the king-choppers are as active in mischief as such thieves and murderers need to be'. The authorities were now awake to the mischief of free speech, and in the summer of the year the Rump Parliament passed a Treason Act that declared it high treason to state that the 'government is tyrannical, usurped or unlawful, or that the Commons in parliament assembled are not the supreme authority of this nation'. There was to be no egalitarian or libertarian revolution. At the same time the council of state prepared 'An Act against Unlicensed and Scandalous Books and Pamphlets' that was designed to prohibit any pamphlets, papers or books issued by 'the malignant party'. A resolution was also passed by the Rump that any preacher who mentioned Charles Stuart or his son would be deemed a 'delinquent'.

On Tuesday 10 July, Cromwell left London and travelled west in a coach drawn by six horses. He was on his way to Ireland. He had hesitated at first, not wishing to leave the country in turmoil and confusion. But once he reached his decision, or professed to believe that providence had directed him, he was very firm. 'It matters not who is our commander-in-chief,' he once said, 'if God be so.' The army leaders had feared a royalist invasion from Ireland, although in truth there was very little chance of one. Nevertheless they could not endure an enemy close to England's shores; it presented a clear and dangerous menace to the new republic.

Cromwell arrived, in the middle of August, at a favourable moment; the royalist navy had been swept from the seas by the ships of the commonwealth, and the duke of Ormonde's army had been all but annihilated outside Dublin after a surprise attack by parliamentary forces. Cromwell wrote from his ship that 'this is an astonishing mercy'. He believed that he was indeed the Lord's chosen servant and, when he landed at the port of Dublin after a stormy crossing, he promised a crusade against 'the barbarous and bloodthirsty Irish'. They were for Cromwell vastly inferior both in race and in religion; he treated them as if they were less than human.

Cromwell wished to do his work rapidly and effectively but, despite his command of 20,000 men, no set battles were fought. Instead he proceeded to conquer the enemy in a series of sieges. He went first to the city of Drogheda, a little over 30 miles north of Dublin, where he summoned the royalist governor to surrender. On the following day, 11 September, having received no formal submission, he attacked; in a series of bloody battles and skirmishes the defenders were overwhelmed. According to Cromwell's express orders all those who were carrying weapons were put to the sword. That was the rule of war: 3,000 of the garrison, as well as all priests and friars, were killed. 'I am persuaded', Cromwell wrote, 'that this is a righteous judgement of God upon these barbarous wretches.' The slaughter has remained in the folk memory of Ireland to this day.

From Drogheda Cromwell and his men marched down to Wexford, a little over 70 miles south of Dublin, where there was yet more killing in the name of God. The city did not need to be stormed since the gate had been opened in the face of imminent attack; yet when the soldiers entered the town they began a fierce onslaught upon the inhabitants, many of whom begged for mercy in vain. It is reported that 200 women were killed beside what is now the Bull Ring; a memorial plaque is on the site of the massacre.

Cromwell stayed in Ireland for another nine months. Any hope that the Irish would capitulate after the spectacle of bloodshed in Drogheda and Wexford was soon dispelled, and he found himself engaged in a series of struggles against stubborn resistance. At the beginning of December he abandoned the siege of Waterford under a storm of rain, 'it being as terrible a day as ever I marched in all my life'. As soon as the army moved inland, away from the coast, the climate and geography of the country reduced them more quickly than did the enemy; fog and rain and mist descended upon them, while dysentery and malarial fever also did their work. Problems of supply were added to those of morale.

The war itself continued for another two years; it had acquired the character of what might be termed guerrilla warfare with the native forces attacking the invading army in a series of raids and skirmishes. Yet by his swift and punitive response Cromwell had achieved the task of destroying any potential for a royalist attack upon England.

The remaining enemy now lay in the north. The Scots had already invited King Charles II to travel to his kingdom, and negotiations between the two sides began in March at Breda, a city in the south of the Netherlands where the young king and his court resided. Parliament and the council of state were thoroughly alarmed at the conjunction, and Cromwell was soon made aware that his presence was needed at home. At the end of May 1650, he sailed for England, leaving behind him Henry Ireton as lord deputy of Ireland; when he landed at Bristol, he was given the welcome for a returning hero.

Charles II needed to find support wherever he could, and the chance of a Scottish army was not one to be missed. So aboard ship on 23 June, just before landing in Scotland, he signed a solemn oath to uphold the national covenant and to ensure that Presbyterianism became the official religion of England as well as of Scotland. He swore this in bad faith, having no regard for the Presbyterian cause or its proponents, but his immediate interests were of more importance. One Scottish negotiator, Alexander Jaffray, later concluded that 'he sinfully complied with what we most sinfully pressed upon him'. The king had learned, like his father, the arts of disguise and dissimulation. Yet his signature meant that war was now certain.

Sir Thomas Fairfax refused to lead the English army into Scotland on the grounds that the invasion would violate the 'solemn league and covenant' that had been signed between the two nations seven years before and never repealed. Cromwell countered with the question 'whether it is better to have this war in the bowels of another country or of our own'; his argument was persuasive and it was he who led the army once more. Fairfax, uncertain about the direction of the commonwealth and unwilling wholly to depose the king, now resigned as lord general. Cromwell was appointed to be his successor.

Cromwell crossed the border on 23 July with 11,000 horse and foot, but the enemy was not to be seen. The commander of the Scottish forces, David Leslie, had determined upon a strategy of harassment rather than open battle in order to cut off Cromwell's communication with England; he was successful in that regard, and Cromwell was forced to draw back to the coastal town of Dunbar 30 miles to the east of Edinburgh. Leslie then swept forward to ensure that Cromwell could have no contact with England. The commanders of both armies believed in divine providence and the sacredness of their cause; both sides fasted and prayed, their respective ministers exhorting them in long sermons. In the phrase of the time, only the harder nail would be able to drive out the other.

At Dunbar Leslie believed that the English were trapped between his army and the sea; he waited on high ground but the Scottish ministers in the camp persuaded him to move down towards the enemy. Cromwell saw the manoeuvre and exclaimed that 'God is delivering them into our hands; they are coming down to us'. And so it proved. The English called out, 'The Lord of Hosts!' while the battle cry of the Scots was 'The Covenant!' The Scots were routed after a brief resistance; 3,000 were killed and 10,000 captured. Very few English casualties were reported. A witness informed John Aubrey that, after the battle, Cromwell 'did laugh so excessively as if he had been drunk; his eyes sparkled with spirits'. The whole of southern Scotland now fell to the English. Other consequences followed. With the apparent judgement of God against them, the Presbyterian ministers lost much prestige and authority; never again would the covenanting movement maintain its previous power over Scotland.

The young king was now in desperate circumstances. After his submission to the presbyters in the early summer of 1650 he was now at Perth in the power of the 'committee of estates', who governed Scotland when parliament was not in session. He hated Scotland and despised the Presbyterian ministers who exhorted him and preached at him; he detested their hypocrisy, as he saw it, and was nostalgic for the simple pieties of the Church of England. After he heard of Leslie's defeat he tried to escape from his oppressors, but some troops from the 'committee of estates' managed to intercept him and to persuade him to return on the promise that he would be granted more powers. On the first day of 1651 Charles was crowned king of Scotland in Scone; the medieval village was the traditional and hallowed site of kingship.

Cromwell remained in Edinburgh for almost a year after his victory at Dunbar, while Leslie strengthened the remains of his army less than 40 miles north-west at Stirling. But there was no possibility of the two armies clashing in the vicinity; the nature of the terrain, and the wild weather of winter, made any campaign unlikely. In any case Cromwell fell dangerously sick in February 1651. He suffered from a 'feverish ague', perhaps contracted in Ireland and exacerbated by the campaign in Scotland; he had told his wife, the day after Dunbar, 'I grow an old man, and feel the infirmities of age marvellously stealing upon me.' He was on the brink of death on three separate occasions and, in alarm, parliament dispatched two physicians to his bedside. He himself was convinced that God had sent him sickness in order to test his faith.

By the early summer, however, he was fully recovered; he believed that he had been saved for a purpose, and almost at once took advantage of the more favourable weather to renew his campaign. In a series of manoeuvres he so arranged matters that the roads south to England remained open to the royalist forces. It might have seemed like an unpardonable blunder, but in fact Cromwell had wanted to remove the Scottish troops from Scotland where they could not otherwise be dislodged. He had set a trap that Charles now entered. Cromwell warned the Speaker of the Rump Parliament that 'I do apprehend that if the enemy goes for England, being some few days march before us, it will trouble some men's thoughts and may occasion some inconveniences'. Yet he believed that all would be well, and all manner of things would be well.

The king, hopeful that the royalists of England would flock to his banner, came across the border by way of Carlisle. Certain 'scares' and conspiracies had been reported in these early days; disaffected royalists met at racecourses or in taverns to plot their schemes but, without any organized direction, they remained inchoate. The government also sent agents provocateurs among them, known as 'decoy ducks'. In the spring of this year a royalist conspiracy was discovered in the City of London that involved several Presbyterian ministers; one of their number, Christopher Love, died on the scaffold. This was considered by some to be an affront to religion while others, such as John Milton, celebrated it as a blow against disobedience and treason.

Yet few supporters joined the king on his journey south, principally because the Scots were not popular among the English people; they could not support an ancient enemy, even if a lawful monarch led them forward. David Leslie himself was doleful and, when the king asked why he was so sad in the presence of such a spirited army, he replied quietly that 'he was melancholic indeed, for he knew that army, how well soever it looked, would not fight'. Nevertheless the king made his way down the north-western counties, through Cumberland and Cheshire and Staffordshire; he could not think of changing course towards London, since the regiments of the enemy were now pursing him. Cromwell's strategy had been entirely successful.

Charles took refuge at last in the perennially royal city of Worcester. 'For me,' the king said, 'it is a crown or a coffin.' Cromwell had not the patience to try a siege on this occasion but decided instead upon an immediate attack, on both sides of the town, by means of the Severn. With the royalist army at half the strength of its antagonist, the result was not really in doubt. Charles, watching the action from the tower of the cathedral, made one last effort to consolidate his forces in a battle that lasted for three hours. When he rallied some of his men for another fresh sally, they threw down their arms. 'Then shoot me dead,' he said, 'rather than let me live to see the sad consequences of this day.' Brave words were not enough, however, and by the early afternoon of 3 September 1651, the royalist army had been scattered to the winds. The young king disappeared into the greenwood, among the birds and foxes, where he could not be found. It was Oliver Cromwell's last battle and it was for him, as he wrote, 'a crowning mercy'.

The wanderings of the young king have become the stuff of legend; he made his secret way through England for forty-two days, and was concealed in eighty-two different hiding places; forty-five people, by the smallest count, knew who he was and where he was. Yet not one of them betrayed him. The image of the king still burned brightly in some loyal hearts. It was noted that many of those who preserved him were Roman Catholic.

In the course of his peregrinations he was disguised as a labourer; he hid in a barn, in a wood and on a farm. He adopted the disguise of the son of a tenant farmer, and was recognized in silence by the butler of the manor where he rested. He stayed in a 'priest hole', devised to protect visiting Jesuits, and lay concealed among the boughs of an oak tree in the grounds of Boscobel House. He dressed as a country man, in a worn leather doublet, and as a servant in a grey cloak. Posters were pasted in villages and market towns asking for the capture of 'a tall, black man, over two yards high'; the 'black' referred to his somewhat swarthy complexion. On one occasion he was surprised by the sound of bells and sight of bonfires, arranged after a false report of his death.

In Bromsgrove, Worcestershire, a blacksmith told him that the king should be hanged for bringing in the Scots. At Bridport, disguised as a servant, he entered a street that was filled with troops searching for him; he dismounted and led his horse as if he were taking it to a stable. At Brighton an innkeeper knelt down and kissed his hand, saying 'that he would not ask him who he was, but bid God bless him whither he was going'. One attempt at escape by sea was abandoned, but on 14 October he sailed from Shoreham to the relative safety of Normandy. On his return to France the young king was asked if he would ever return to Scotland, to which he replied that he would rather be hanged first. When he arrived at the French court he was still ragged and dirty after his adventures.

Cromwell returned in triumph to London bearing with him, like a Roman emperor, the prisoners whom he had taken. He was granted an income of £4,000 per year, and the palace at Hampton Court was bestowed upon him. There could be no doubt that he was the first man of the state.

Yet he came back to a city very different from that which he had left at the beginning of the Irish campaign. The first 'year of freedom', after the heady days of the council of state, had been less than glorious. The Rump Parliament had been almost overwhelmed with the pressure of business; it set up committees for legal or ecclesiastical reform, but then did nothing to carry their conclusions into effect. Accusations of favouritism, and even of corruption, were often heard. It was widely believed that its principal concern was for its own survival.

Parliament did pass a few bills, however, designed for the supposed good of the commonwealth; one of them was an Act making adultery a capital offence. It was not a great success. Four women, and no men, were executed. In many other respects the members of parliament seemed to have lapsed into a state close to inertia. It was reported that the present government was reduced to a 'languishing condition' in the provinces.

Yet Cromwell's triumphs were evident. Scotland was seized and strengthened by one of Cromwell's key generals, George Monck, and was governed by a military regime for the next eleven years; Cromwell remarked that 'I do think truly they are a very ruined nation'. No king of England had ever conquered Scotland. Ireland was in no better case; after Cromwell's withdrawal another general, Edmund Ludlow, practically completed the conquest of that country. The Act of Settlement, passed in the summer of 1652, condemned Catholic landowners to the wholesale or partial forfeiture of their estates while those who had actively supported the Irish rebellion were in theory condemned to death. Cromwell had achieved the unparalleled feat of ascendancy over the three kingdoms.

When he returned from his victory at Worcester he was told that great things were expected of him in peace no less than in war; it was his task, according to a letter sent to him, to 'ease the oppressed of their burdens, to release the prisoners out of bonds, and to relieve poor families with bread'. Yet he could only achieve these laudable aims through the agency of the Rump Parliament that seemed in no way inclined to obey his orders with the same promptness as the soldiers of the New Model Army. Those parliamentarians who were members of the council of state were in most respects still conscientious and diligent, yet others were not so easily inspired by Cromwell's zeal or vision.

Cromwell had argued for an immediate dissolution of parliament, making way for a fresh legislature that might deal with the problems attendant upon victory. Yet the members prevaricated and debated, finally agreeing to dissolve their assembly at a date not later than November 1654. They gave themselves another three years of procrastination. The army was by now thoroughly disillusioned with those members who seemed intent upon thwarting or delaying necessary legislation. The more committed soldiers believed them to be time-servers or worse, uninterested in the cause of 'the people of God'.

In truth the Rump was essentially a conservative body, while the army inherently favoured radical solutions; there was bound to be conflict between them. Yet Cromwell himself was not so certain of his course; he wished for godly reformation of the commonwealth but he also felt obliged, at this stage, to proceed by constitutional methods. He did not want to impose what was known as a 'sword government'. Another possibility was also full of peril. In the current state of opinion it was possible that, unless fresh elections were carefully managed, a royalist majority might be returned; this could not be permitted.

The condition of England was enough to cause dismay. The late wars had badly injured trade, with a consequent steep increase in unemployment; bands of beggars roamed the land in numbers not seen since the last century. The country gentry and other land-lords were devastated by the various taxes imposed upon them; those who favoured the royalist cause found their lands in danger of confiscation or sale. The prisons were filled with debtors. The Church was in confusion, with radical sectaries and orthodox believers still engaged in recrimination and complaint. Episcopacy had been abolished but no other form of national Church government had taken its place; it was said that the mass of the people could not find ministers to serve them. Many called, without success, for legislation to abolish burdensome taxes, to simplify and improve the judicial process, to ease the public debt and to lower the cost of living.

One evening in the autumn of 1652, Cromwell was walking in St James's Park with a member of the council of state, Bulstrode Whitelocke. Cromwell asked his companion for his counsel on the present condition of affairs, remarking of the Rump Parliament that 'there is little hope of a good settlement to be made by them, really there is not'. Whitelocke then replied that 'we ourselves have acknowledged them the supreme power'.

Cromwell: What if a man should take upon him to be king?
Whitelocke: I think that remedy would be worse than the disease.
Cromwell: Why do you think so?
Whitelocke: As to your own person the title of king would be of no advantage, because you have the full kingly power in you already, concerning the militia, and you are general.

Cromwell went on to reflect, at least according to Whitelocke's diary, that 'the power of a king is so great and so high', that 'the title of it might indemnify in a great measure those that act under it'; it would in particular be useful in curbing 'the insolences and extravagances of those whom the present powers cannot control'. It is possible that the conversation sprang from hindsight on the part of Whitelocke but its purport is confirmed by Cromwell's remark in an earlier meeting of officers and parliamentarians that 'somewhat of a monarchical government would be most effectual, if it could be established with safety to the liberties of the people'. Certainly he believed that his military victories had been delivered to him by God. Why should his destiny now be in the hands of a Rump? He could have waited patiently for a sign but ambition and a sense of mission (they are not to be distinguished) soon drove him forward.

The army had already presented a petition of complaint to parliament in which it was recommended that miscreants in positions of authority should be replaced by 'men of truth, fearing God and hating covetousness'. This was a standard preamble based on Exodus 18:21. They listed many necessary reforms that needed 'speedy and effectual' redress. The members of the Rump promised to take such matters 'under consideration'.

Cromwell attempted to mediate between the officers and parliamentarians, although he believed that the Rump was in general guided by pride and self-seeking. He told a colleague that he was being pushed to action, the consideration of which 'makes my hair stand on end'. His practice was always to withdraw into himself, in a process of self-communing, before taking swift and decisive action.

The officers of the New Model Army had devoted the first week of 1653 to prayer and fasting, seeking for God's counsel. From this time forward the members of the Rump feared some form of military intervention. It was rumoured that parliament was preparing a bill for new elections, vetted by its own members, that would destroy the army's expectations of godly reformation; it was also claimed that parliament was about to remove Cromwell from the leadership of the army.

On 20 April Cromwell came into the chamber of the House of Commons, dressed in plain black, and took his seat; he had left a file of musketeers at the door of the chamber and in the lobby. He took off his hat and rose to his feet. He first commended the Commons for their early efforts at reform but then reproached them for their subsequent delays and obfuscations; he roamed down the middle of the chamber and signalled various individual members as 'whoremaster' and 'drunkard' and 'juggler'. He declared more than once that 'it is you that have forced me to do this, for I have sought the Lord night and day that he would rather slay me than put me upon the doing of this work'. He spoke, according to one observer, 'with so much passion and discomposure of mind as if he had been distracted'; he shouted, and kicked the floor with his foot.

In conclusion he called out, 'You are no parliament. I will put an end to your sitting.' He then called for the musketeers and pointed to the parliamentary mace lying on the table. 'What shall be done with this bauble? Here. Take it away.' He said later that he had not planned or premeditated his intervention and that 'the spirit was so upon him, that he was overruled by it; and he consulted not with flesh and blood at all'. This is perhaps too convenient an explanation to be altogether true. He had dissolved a parliament that, in one form or another, had endured for almost thirteen years. The Long Parliament, of which the Rump was the final appendage, had witnessed Charles I's attempt to seize five of its members and then the whole course of the civil wars; it had seen some of its members purged and driven away. It was not a ruin, but a ruin of that ruin. It ended in ignominy, unwanted and unlamented.

Cromwell remarked later that, at its dissolution, not even a dog barked. On the following day a large placard was placed upon the door of the chamber. 'This House to be let, unfurnished.'

32

Fear and trembling

The most powerful image of the age, after the demise of the Tudor line, was that of a society without divine sanction. In the early decades of the seventeenth century Jacobean tragedy, as we have seen, assumed a world without God where men and women struggle for survival. The civic broils of the 1640s had rendered the prospect of chaos only more acute. Out of that fear and insecurity came a book that has been described as the only masterpiece of political philosophy in the English language.

Thomas Hobbes had shown no signs of greatness. After a conventional humanist education at Oxford he became tutor and companion to William Cavendish, second son of the 1st earl of Devonshire; with that gentleman he undertook the almost obligatory European tour. On a subsequent journey, to Geneva, he experienced his moment of awakening. He happened to open a copy of Euclid's *Elements of Geometry* and was immediately impressed by the Greek mathematician's reliance on deduction through definitions and axioms; it was the method, not the matter, that inspired him. In that spirit he began to brood on the nature of human society.

He began work on *Leviathan, or the Matter, Form and Power of a Common Wealth Ecclesiastical and Civil* in the late 1640s, the volume eventually being published in 1651. It was begun at a time, there-fore, of chaotic civil war; its writing continued through the trial and execution of a king; it was completed in a period when the political experiment of the Rump Parliament was being challenged by various sects and interests. Where was certainty, or safety, to be found? Hobbes was in any case of a timorous and fearful nature. He wrote, at the age of eighty-four, that 'fear and I were born twins'.

So *Leviathan* emerged from the very conditions of the time, or what he called 'the seditious roaring of a troubled nation'. He did not read other political or philosophical accounts; he believed 'that there can be nothing so absurd, but may be found in the books of philosophers'. He followed his own bright line of thought through all of its logical consequences. He would ponder and ruminate, then jot down the phrases and conclusions that came to him. One axiom would lead to another, and then to the next, so that he was inexorably guided towards his own vision of the world.

His clarity of purpose, and his rigorous method, allowed him to cut through all the political cant of the period; his was a thorough scepticism that pierced the pious platitudes and false generalizations, the truisms and solecisms, that always attend political discourse. He would proceed only upon first principles maintained by firm definition and vigorous argument. He stated that 'words are wise men's counters, they do but reckon by them; but they are the money of fools'.

So his argument opened. Stripped of order and security, men are at enmity one with another in 'a perpetual contention for honour, riches and authority'. The goad for action and conflict is pre-eminently 'a perpetual and restless desire for power'. The strength of one man is more or less equal to that of another, leading to an eternal war of all against all. Once the dire predicament is understood, a solution may be found amid the discord. The fear of death encourages prudence and the desire for self-preservation; the principles of reason might therefore be applied to the quest for peace, and for life rather than death. A form of contract might be agreed whereby each man is 'contented with so much liberty against other men as he would allow other men against himself'. Each man agrees that he will not do to another what he would not have done to himself.

This instinct for self-preservation then becomes the key element in what might be described as Hobbes's metaphysic whereby 'man

which looks too far before him, in the care of future time, has his
heart all the day long gnawed on by fear of death, poverty, or other
calamity, and has no repose, nor pause of his anxiety, but in sleep'.
This is the foundation of his theory of the state.

The contract between men is the beginning of wisdom. How
is it to be maintained? It cannot be entrusted to the individuals
themselves. It must be transferred to 'a common power set over
them both, with right and force sufficient to compel performance'.
There must be an authority that can enforce the contract in per-
petuity; supreme authority demands supreme power and, as Hobbes
puts it, 'covenants, without the sword, are but words'. To escape
from fear and trembling, therefore, men must agree among themselves to create a system of such powerful control that no deviation
or dissension, no unrest or cause of unrest, will be tolerated. They
transfer their own prudence and reason to this other thing, this
living absolutism that he names as 'great Leviathan'. This act of
authorization is the mutual surrender of the natural rights of each
man in order to create the sovereign power which will guide and
protect them.

Leviathan will impose the religion of the state, thus avoiding
the divisions that Hobbes saw all around. There will be no such
thing as liberty of conscience, which simply created confusion and,
in the case of England, bloodshed. Justice and truth are to be determined by civil authority rather than individual choice. Justice is
simply what the law demands.

It did not matter whether this omnipotent authority was king,
or conquering invader, or magistrate; it was only important that it
existed, and that it was authorized to act and to will in place of
individual action and private will. Only thus could true order be
maintained. That is why some critics accused him of complying
with the doctrine of the divine right of kings, while others attacked
him for compounding with Cromwell's commonwealth.

In his preface to the Latin translation of his treatise he wrote
that 'this great Leviathan, which is called the State, is a work of
art; it is an artificial man made for the protection and salvation of
the natural man, to whom it is superior in grandeur and power'. By
the rigorous argument from first principles, Hobbes believed that
he had uncovered the true imperatives of civil society. He was also

convinced that he had written for the benefit of mankind, and in the last sentence of the work he concludes ironically that 'such truth, as opposeth no man's profit, nor pleasure, is to all men welcome'.

Leviathan created a sensation at the time, and it has been said that it inspired universal horror. The Commons proposed to burn the book, and one bishop suggested that Hobbes himself should be tied to the stake. It was so exact, so convincing in its logic, so simple in its argument, that it was difficult to repudiate without relying upon the political pieties and the cant that Hobbes had already attacked.

Nevertheless he was denounced as an atheist and as a materialist. Clearly he had no very great confidence in human nature, and described the character of any man's heart as 'blotted and confounded . . . with dissembling, lying, counterfeiting and erroneous doctrines'. He stated that 'the value, or WORTH of a man, is as of all other things, his price; that is to say, so much as would be given for the use of his power'. He added that 'to obey, is to honour, because no man obeys them whom they think have no power to help or hurt them'. His clarity of judgement is sometimes terrible; he has the savagery of the true moral philosopher, and *Leviathan* must rank as one of the central statements of the seventeenth century.

33

Healing and settling

Cromwell had engineered what was in effect a second revolution. He was now, by virtue of the sword, the indisputable head of state and sole source of power. The officers of the army concluded a dispatch with the encomium that 'we humbly lay ourselves with these thoughts, in this emergency, at your excellency's feet'. The ministers of Newcastle upon Tyne made 'their humble addresses to his godly wisdom'. Yet Cromwell did not intend or wish to be a dictator; he was still concerned with the constitutional niceties of his unique position.

He appointed a reformed council of state, with himself a prominent participant, but its thirteen members were in something of a quandary. They were in a situation without precedent, faced with the obligation of creating a constitution out of nothing. Some in the army wished for government by the council itself, perhaps with the assistance of a carefully selected parliament; others pressed for near universal male suffrage; yet others demanded a council of godly men on the model of the Jewish Sanhedrin.

Cromwell spent eight days locked in conversation with his councillors, and from their deliberations emerged a wholly original form of parliament. It was eventually agreed that members of the new assembly should be either nominated by the various Independent congregations or favoured by the army and by prominent individuals; those chosen were to be 'known persons, men fearing God, and of approved integrity'. One of the godly men chosen to serve was Isaac Praise-God Barebone, a leather merchant and preacher from London who, at his warehouse in Fleet Street, proclaimed the imminent coming of Jesus Christ. His colourful name and nature led to this nominated parliament becoming known as 'Barebone's Parliament'. There were 144 men who were nominees, and thus it was also called the 'Little Parliament'; it was indeed the smallest parliament to date ever to sit at Westminster.

It would be wrong, however, to conclude that all of its members were zealots; the preponderance of them held the rank of gentleman, and their number included a viscount and a baron as well as several baronets and knights. The provost of Eton and the high master of St Paul's School were among them. Yet, unsurprisingly, the radical element prevailed in their deliberations; those who burn hottest inflame the rest. No one wishes to be known as tepid or lukewarm. In his opening address to them, Cromwell remarked that 'we are at the threshold' and that 'you are at the edge of promises and prophecies'. It was supposed to mark the beginning of a new era.

The members of the new assembly were zealous and busy, but they were perhaps not worldly enough to judge the consequences of their decisions. They determined to abolish the court of chancery, for example, and drastically to simplify the law; some in fact demanded the abolition of the common law, to be substituted by the code of Moses. They voted to abolish tithes, a proposal that might have eventually led to the disestablishment of the Church and the violation of all rights of property.

The alarm and horror of the nation soon became manifest, and Cromwell realized that it was time to end an experiment that had lasted for just five months. He is reported to have said that he was more troubled now by fools than by knaves. A parliament of saints had gone to excess. He had learned that it was not possible to create instruments of power in an arbitrary manner; they had no stable foundation, and therefore veered wildly from side to side. In December the more conservative or moderate of the members were persuaded to launch a pre-emptive coup by voting in an early morning session that they should abdicate their powers; the radicals were in a prayer meeting at the time. The Speaker then took up the mace and led them in procession to Whitehall Palace where Cromwell was waiting to greet them. He professed later to being surprised by their arrival, but this is hard to credit.

A few of the godly remained in the chamber. An army officer entered and asked them, 'What do you here?'

'We are seeking the Lord.'

'Then you may go elsewhere for, to my certain knowledge, he has not been here these twelve years.'

The abrogation of this 'Little Parliament' was greeted with considerable relief by those whose livings had been threatened by it. The lawyers celebrated and, according to an Independent lay preacher, 'most men upon this dissolution take occasion to cry Aha, Aha'.

And then there was one. It was said that, in bringing an end to 'Barebone's Parliament', Cromwell took the crown from Christ and put it on his own head. One of his military associates, General John Lambert, had drawn up what was called an 'Instrument of Government' in which Cromwell would be granted power as Lord Protector of the British Republic. This 'Instrument' has the distinction of being the first, and the last, written constitution of England. Yet its system of checks and balances, including a council, did not dispel the impression that Cromwell was now an autocrat in all but name. Clarendon noted that 'this extraordinary man, without any other reason than because he had a mind to it . . . mounted himself into the throne of three kingdoms, without the name of king, but with a greater power and authority than had ever been exercised or claimed by any king'.

On 16 December 1653, Oliver Cromwell stood before a chair of state in Westminster Hall. He was dressed in a suit and cloak of black velvet, with long boots; a band of gold ran around his hat. He looked up and raised his right hand to heaven as he swore to observe all the articles of the new constitution; John Lambert then knelt and offered him a civic sword sheathed in its scabbard as a token of peaceful rule. In the proclamation of public acts he was now styled 'Olivarius Protector' in the same manner as 'Carolus Rex'. His passage through the streets was guarded by soldiers. He insisted that the series of nine paintings by Andrea Mantegna, *The Triumphs of Caesar*, should not be sold off but remain at his apartments in Hampton Court Palace. The proceedings of his court, in such matters as the reception of ambassadors, resembled those of Charles I. His son, Henry Cromwell, was greeted in the entertainment grounds of Spring Gardens with cries of 'Room for the prince'. Lucy Hutchinson wrote that for Cromwell's family to emulate regal state was as ridiculous as to dress apes in scarlet.

Many of his former supporters now railed at him for betraying the cause of godly reformation. He was accused of sacrificing the public good to ambition and was denounced as a 'dissembling perjured villain'. Biblical insults were hurled at him as the 'Old Dragon', the 'Little Horn', the 'Man of Sin' , and the 'Vile Person' of Daniel 11: 21. At the pulpit set up by Blackfriars one preacher, Christopher Feake, proclaimed that 'he has deceived the Lord's people'; he added that 'he will not reign long, he will end worse than the last Protector did, that crooked tyrant Richard. Tell him I said it.' Feake was brought before the council and placed in custody. The governor of Chester Castle, Colonel Robert Duckenfield, put it a little more delicately when he wrote to Cromwell that 'I believe the root and tree of piety is alive in your lordship, though the leaves thereof, through abundance of temptations and flatteries, seem to me to be withered much of late'.

In a sense the revolution was now over, with all attempts at radical reform at an end. Cromwell instituted a reign of quiet in which men of property might feel safe; in effect he inaugurated a gentry republic. It cannot be said that the new dispensation was received with any great enthusiasm, yet for many it must have been a relief after the disordered governance of recent years. For others, of course, it made no difference at all.

In the first eight months of their power the Lord Protector and the council, in the absence of parliament, passed more than eighty ordinances. Scotland and Ireland were to be incorporated within the commonwealth. The court of chancery was to be reformed. Duels were forbidden, and cock-fighting suppressed; horse racing was suspended for a period. Public drunkenness, and profanity, were punished with a fine or with a whipping. No more than 200 hackney carriages were allowed in London. The postal service was reformed, while the prisons and the public highways were improved. The treasury was reorganized. This was a practical administration.

Cromwell and the council were no less pragmatic in foreign affairs. The European powers were docile, perhaps in fear of a resurgent English navy that had recently challenged and defeated the Dutch. Peace was made with the Protestant nations, among them Sweden and Denmark. France and Spain vied with each other for the favour of the protectorate, in which equation Cromwell tended to incline towards the French side; he wanted to remove the influence of Charles II on the French court.

He also favoured balance in religious matters. An ordinance in the spring of 1654 established a commission of 'triers' who would check the qualities and qualifications of proposed clergymen. In the summer of the year commissioners were appointed to every county as 'ejectors' who would remove ministers guilty of ignorance, insufficiency, or scandalous behaviour. Cromwell supported religious liberty except for those who espoused pope or bishops. Anglicans were in theory no more tolerated than Roman Catholics, but in practice they were given tacit acceptance.

From a policy of benign neglect, Cromwell created a variegated Church made up of Presbyterians, Independents and Baptists. Doctrine was less important to him than spirit; dogma did not concern him as long as he could create a community that had what he called 'the root of the matter' within it. It has been described as not so much a national Church as a confederation of Christian sects. Some of the more committed Anglicans went into exile 'waiting for a day', as they put it, when Charles II might claim his throne. Yet many were not exercised by religion at all. In his diary entry for 11 May 1654, Evelyn noted that 'I now observed how the women began to paint themselves, formerly a most ignominious thing, and used only by prostitutes'.

Small groups of royalists frequented certain taverns of London, and of the provincial towns, where they engaged in plots against the protectorate. Where there are conspiracies, however, there are apt to be informers and suborners. In February 1654, eleven men were arrested at the Ship Tavern by the Old Bailey. It became clear, in the course of investigations, that a powerful group of royalists had been formed to incite a popular rebellion; it was known as the Sealed Knot. The exiled king was in constant and secret correspondence with his supporters, and seemed particularly interested in a scheme to assassinate Cromwell himself. He was to be shot after he had left Whitehall for Hampton Court on a Saturday morning.

Yet Cromwell had created a very efficient secret service under the command of John Thurloe, secretary to the council of state, and the details of the plot were known almost as soon as they were formulated. Alerted by his spy-master Cromwell took to the water on that morning and avoided an attack. Soon after the failure of the conspiracy the authorities mounted raids in London taverns and houses, in the course of which 500 people were arrested. Two of the leaders were executed, while others were transported to Barbados. An old Catholic priest was also seized and executed.

Yet the punishments did not deter other plotters, who would soon attempt to rise again. Cromwell was given a copy of a letter written by the new king in which Charles advised his supporters to 'consult with those you dare trust, and, if you are ready, agree upon a time . . .' Cromwell now always carried a gun. In a riding accident, later in the year, the pistol fired in his pocket and the wound kept him in bed for three weeks.

The occasion for a parliament, according to the 'Instrument of Government', had now come. On 4 September 1654, Cromwell addressed the new assembly in the Painted Chamber of Westminster Palace; he sat in the chair of state while the members were seated on benches ranged against the walls. 'Gentlemen,' he told them, 'you are met here on the greatest occasion that, I believe, England ever saw.' He then proceeded to speak for three hours on the various manifestations of God's providence in an oration that veered from messianic enthusiasm to scriptural exposition. He had called parliament, but 'my calling be from God'. He was thus reiterating, in his own fashion, the divine right of kings. He was above parliament. Yet he came to them not as a master but as a fellow servant. Now was a time for 'healing and settling'.

Yet the new parliament was by no means a compliant body. For some days its members had debated, without reaching any conclusion, whether they should give the protectorate their support. On 12 September they found the doors of their chamber closed against them, and they were asked once more to assemble in the Painted Chamber where the Protector wished to address them. He chided them for neglecting the interest of the state, 'so little valued and so much slighted', and he would not allow them to proceed any further unless and until they had signed an oath to agree to 'the form of government now settled'. All members had to accept the condition that 'the persons elected shall not have power to alter the government as it is hereby settled in one single person and a Parliament'. 'I am sorry,' he said, 'I am sorry, and I could be sorry to the death that there is cause for this. But there is cause . . .'

Some members protested and refused to sign, but the majority of them either agreed or at least submitted. Cromwell still did not attempt to guide the debates, but he became increasingly alarmed at their nature. He is reported to have said in this period that he 'would rather keep sheep under a hedge than have to do with the government of men'. Sheep were at least obedient. The members voted to restrict the power of the Protector to veto legislation; they also decided that their decisions were more authoritative than those of the council of state. They believed, in other words, that parliament should still be paramount in the nation. That was not necessarily Cromwell's view. From day to day they debated every clause of the 'Instrument of Government', with the evident wish to replace it with a constitution of their own. On 3 January 1655 they voted to reaffirm the limits to religious toleration; two days later they decided to reduce army pay, thus striking at Cromwell's natural constituency. On 20 January they began to discuss the formation of a militia under parliamentary control.

Two days later, Cromwell called a halt. He lambasted them for wasting time in frivolous and unnecessary discourse when they should have been considering practical measures for the general reformation of the nation. He told them that 'I do not know what you have been doing. I do not know whether you have been alive or dead.' He considered that it was not fit for the common welfare and the public good to allow them to continue; and so, farewell. The first protectorate parliament was dissolved. The larger problem, however, was not addressed. Could a representative parliament ever co-exist with what was essentially a military dictatorship?

Cromwell and the council once more reigned without challenge, but the price of power was eternal vigilance. In his speech of dissolution Cromwell had warned that 'the cavalier party have been designing and preparing to put this nation in blood again' together with 'that party of men called levellers'. The royalist supporters of the Sealed Knot had indeed survived, despite deportations and executions, and seem to have entered an unlikely association with the radical republicans who shared an interest in removing Cromwell from power. For those of a levelling tendency Cromwell was infinitely worse than Charles; he had used them, betrayed them and set himself up as a despot. Yet the royalists could not even agree among themselves. They had planned six different regional conspiracies in 1654, but the only rebellion was a short and ill-organized affair in the West Country. The spy-master, Thurloe, had done his work.

Cromwell had been considering a possible friendship or alliance with Spain, despite the fact that as a Catholic state it was one of the horns of the beast. He had said to a Spanish envoy that an alliance was possible on the conditions that the English were granted liberty of conscience within the Spanish dominions and that free trade be allowed between England and the West Indies. The envoy replied that this was 'to ask my master's two eyes'.

Without any agreement, therefore, Cromwell felt emboldened to test Spanish power in the sensitive area of the West Indies. He convinced himself that the action was part of a religious crusade against popery, and he trusted that the warfare would not spread to Europe; he was mistaken, or misguided, in both aspirations. At the end of 1654 Admiral William Penn and General Robert Venables set sail for Barbados with the order 'to gain an interest in that part of the West Indies in possession of the Spaniards'. They arrived safely enough, in the spring of the following year, but their expedition thereafter was not a success.

The English forces sailed to the island of Hispaniola with the purpose of subduing the city of Santo Domingo and taking its treasure. The men marched for four days through rough country in the burning sun with little fresh water; they were apparently untested soldiers who had no idea of the conditions they would confront. Exhausted and demoralized, they were an easy prey for a group of horsemen and cattle-herders who surprised them in ambush. The remaining members of the expedition, still under the command of Venables, managed to sail on to Jamaica where they were able to take and occupy the island. But at the time it seemed like a poor reward, with the additional risk that Spain might now declare a general war against the old enemy.

The news of the failure to rout Santo Domingo reached Cromwell towards the end of July. He locked himself in his room for an entire day. He had hoped to control the trade and treasure routes of the Spaniards, but he had been thwarted. The new republic had never suffered a military defeat before. He had seen himself as the protector and champion of Protestant interests, but the hand of God seems to have been against him. Cromwell had said, in reply to those who had originally questioned the wisdom of the expedition, that 'God had not brought us hither where we are but to consider the work that we may do in the world as well as at home'. Yet the Lord had not blessed this work in the world. This caused Cromwell the most painful reflections of his rule, and presaged the fears and doubts that would attend the last years of his protectorate. Wherein had he offended? Or was it the nation itself that had provoked God's anger?

It may not be coincidental, therefore, that soon after the disaster in the Indies a network of godly rule was established in England. The country was divided into eleven districts, or groups of counties; at the head of each was imposed a major-general of decidedly puritan inclinations. These army commanders were instructed to raise taxes and revive the local militia, to enquire into the conduct of clergy and teachers, to arrest any suspect persons and to prevent further royalist uprisings. Their costs were met by charges imposed on royalists alone. This became known as the 'decimation tax', taking one tenth of the 'malignants'' profits from the land, an injustice to which they were forced to submit without complaint. The newspapers and periodicals were suppressed, and no item of news could be printed without the permission of John Thurloe.

Cromwell was attempting that reformation of manners which the last parliament had signally failed to achieve. The major-generals were instructed 'to encourage and promote godliness and virtue' and, as a result, the pastimes of the people were largely suppressed. Colonel Pride, who had led the purge of parliament seven years before, raided the bear-garden at Bankside; he himself killed the bears, and then ordered his troops to wring the necks of the game-cocks in other parts of London. Alehouses were shut all over the country; stage plays as well as 'mirths and jollities' were forbidden.

One major-general, William Boteler, informed Thurloe that he had imprisoned 'drunken fellows' and others 'suspected to live only on the highway'; those accused of illegal brewing or of keeping a 'lewd house' were also arrested. Those who travelled on the Lord's day could be set in the stocks or placed in a cage; unmarried men and women who had 'carnal knowledge' of each other could be sent to a house of correction; those who swore or uttered profanities were heavily fined.

Public morals may have been improved by these measures, but public sympathy for Cromwell's regime was lost. The people did not wish to be governed, or corrected, by military officials with an attendant crew of spies and informers. Some of the major-generals were considered by the gentry to be low-born interlopers, and the natural leaders of the counties did not relish their loss of authority. A nation cannot be made virtuous by diktat or by government inspectors. The experience of the major-generals, with their troops of horse behind them, also helped to augment the national hatred for standing armies.

The experiment did not last for very long; the major-generals were sent to their counties in the autumn of 1655 and were summoned back to Westminster in the spring of the following year for consultation. With a great war against Spain growing ever more likely, fresh revenues were urgently needed; the major-generals seem to have persuaded a reluctant Cromwell to call another parliament rather than impose further taxation by decree. Thus they contrived their own fall. It was not likely that the representatives of the nation, however they were chosen, would tolerate a continuation of godly rule.

After the attack by Penn and Venables on the Spanish colonies in the Caribbean, Spain declared war on England as a natural and almost inevitable consequence. The West Indian adventure had become a European imbroglio with infinitely more dangerous possibilities. Spain and France were old enemies, however, and Cromwell now inclined towards the court of the young Louis XIV.

A commercial treaty was signed in the autumn of 1655, containing certain secret clauses about the expulsion of Charles II from French territory; the English king had in fact already left for Spa and Aachen. Charles then promptly fashioned an agreement with Spain that would allow him to live in the Spanish Netherlands (what is now Belgium and part of northern France); he promised that, on his accession, he would return Jamaica to the Spanish. He was disheartened, always in need of money; he was surrounded by squabbling courtiers. With no realistic prospect of regaining his throne, nothing could ease his distress of mind.

Cromwell was himself in no easy condition. The failure of the expedition to the West Indies, and the onset of war with Spain, had precipitated a sickness described by the French ambassador as 'a bilious colic, which occasionally flies to the brain'. He added that 'grief often persecutes him more than either of these, as his mind is not yet accustomed to endure disgrace'. Cromwell survived, but became even more aware of the extent to which the commonwealth relied upon his presence. Who else could preserve the unity and constancy of the state? He was showing signs of his age and of his cares; his hand trembled when he held his hat. 'Study still to be innocent,' he told his son, Henry. 'Cry to the Lord to give you a plain single heart.'

With the plans for a new parliament, and with the preparations for war, Cromwell and his councillors were hard pressed. The Venetian envoy observed that 'they are so fully occupied that they do not know which way to turn, and the Protector has not a moment to call his own'. Cromwell had no very sanguine expectations about parliament. He may have realized that, far from 'healing and settling', the rule of the major-generals had provoked fresh dissension; he must have feared in any case that the combined opposition of republicans and silent royalist supporters might produce a majority against him. He explained later, 'that it was against my judgement but I could have no quietness till it was done.'

The course of the election campaign was strenuous, and Thurloe wrote to Henry Cromwell that 'here is the greatest striving to get into Parliament that ever was known'. The call went out against the representatives of the military regime. 'No swordsmen! No decimators!' It was a further sign that the country was restless and discomposed. The council of state took measures of its own, however, and excluded approximately one hundred of the elected members for 'immorality' or 'delinquency'; it was another example of brute military power, and provoked much outrage in the country. How could this be called a free parliament?

Cromwell opened its proceedings on 17 September 1656, with a warning of the forces ranged against the country. England was at war with Spain, and the Spanish king was even then preparing to assist Charles Stuart in an invasion launched from Flanders. 'Why, truly,' he said employing his usual nervous syntax, 'your great enemy is the Spaniard. He is. He is a natural enemy, he is naturally so.' As for the enemy within, the levellers and the cavaliers were plotting to seize a seaport to welcome the king's forces.

In the course of a long and rambling speech Cromwell defended the major-generals for suppressing vice and for espousing the cause of true religion. And what of the forced taxation to pay for them? 'If nothing should be done but what is according to law, the throat of the nation may be cut while we send for some to make a law.' The tenor of this comment is similar to one he had made before, that government should be judged by what is good for the people and not by what pleases them. He was by instinct an authoritarian.

On the day of his speech, three conspirators met to take his life as he entered parliament; they hired a house that stood beside the east door of Westminster Abbey, and planned to shoot him as he left there on his way to the Painted Chamber. They were levellers who wished to return to the old form of a puritan republic. Yet, in the face of a crowd, they lost their nerve and dispersed; it was only the first attempt that the leader of the group, Miles Sindercombe, would undertake. Cromwell, meanwhile, dismissed all such threats as 'little fiddling things'. News soon came that might yet please the parliament and the nation. At the beginning of October Thurloe announced to parliament that Admiral Blake had seized several Spanish treasure ships on their way back to Cadiz; it was perhaps a sign that God was still with them. Parliament set aside a day for national thanksgiving.

A new Venetian ambassador, Giovanni Sagredo, came to England at this time and wrote that he found 'not elegant cavaliers but cavalry and infantry; instead of music and ballets they have

20. A contemporary tapestry celebrating the restoration of Charles II.

21. Charles II, the supposedly 'merry monarch'.

22. Catherine of Braganza, the wife of Charles II, who was reputed to have introduced tea-drinking to England.

23. Barbara Villiers, duchess of Cleveland, one of Charles II's many mistresses, who was described by John Evelyn as 'the curse of the nation'.

24. Nell Gwynne,
the orange-seller who
became a royal courtesan.

25. Louise de Kérouaille,
Charles's French mistress
who became duchess of
Portsmouth and who was
known by Nell Gwynne
as 'Squintabella'.

26. The earl of Rochester, rake and poet who did not mince his words.

27. Samuel Pepys, who turned the diary into an art form.

28. Sir Christopher Wren, the polymath who transformed London.

29. Sir Isaac Newton, arguably the greatest experimenter in English history.

30. Charles II in his role as patron of the Royal Society.

31. The members of the 'Cabal', a group of five self-interested councillors who ran a corrupt coalition around Charles II.

32. The duke of Monmouth, the illegitimate son who yearned to be king.

33. The duke of York, soon to become James II, with his wife and daughters.

34. A confused scene supposedly depicting the covert arrival of an infant,
'the warming-pan baby', to be passed off as James II's son.

35. The baby grows into James Francis Edward Stuart, better known to posterity as the 'Old Pretender' or the 'King Over the Water'.

36. James II throwing the great seal into the Thames as he escapes from England into France.

trumpets and drums; they do not speak of love but of Mars . . . no patches on their faces but muskets on their shoulders; they do not neglect sleep for the sake of amusements, but severe ministers keep their adversaries in incessant wakefulness. In a word, everything here is full of disdain, suspicion and rough menacing faces . . .'

Parliament was variously and continually employed with private petitions and private bills as well as matters of state. A member complained that 'one business jostled out another'. It seemed likely that, just as its predecessor, it would achieve nothing of any conse- quence. Yet the religious zeal of its members was not in doubt when the case of James Naylor was put before them. He was a Quaker whose preachings aroused apocalyptic yearnings among his disciples; he was 'the hope of Israel' and 'the Lamb of God'. In the summer of the year he had entered Bristol as Christ had once gone into Jerusalem; two women led his horse while others cried out 'Holy, holy, holy, Lord God of Israel'. He was arrested and brought before the bar of parliament where he was questioned. 'I was set up,' he said, 'as a sign to summon this nation.'

A debate of nine days followed his appearance in which it was agreed that this horrid blasphemy was more dangerous to the nation than any Spanish warship; it struck at the heart of its relationship with God, than which nothing was more precious. 'Let us all stop our ears,' one member said, 'and stone him.' It was not clear whether parliament had the judicial power to punish him, yet the members voted that Naylor should be placed in the pillory and whipped through the streets; his tongue was to be bored through with a hot iron and the letter 'B' for blasphemer branded on his forehead. He would then be sentenced to an indefinite imprisonment.

The ordeal of the tongue and forehead took place at the end of the year. A diarist, Thomas Burton, noted that 'Rich, the mad merchant, sat bare-headed at Naylor's feet all the time. Sometimes he sang, and cried, and stroked his hair and face, and kissed his hand, and sucked the fire out of his forehead.' Naylor was patient, and the spectators were sympathetic to the plight of one who had endured the wrath of this parliament. Cromwell himself wished to know 'the grounds and reason' for its assumption of judicial power, but no response was ever made for the very good reason that the sentence was both arbitrary and unjustified. Some contemporaries warned that, if parliament felt itself able to condemn and punish one misguided man, who could feel safe?

At the beginning of 1657 a debate was held on a bill for maintaining the 'decimation tax' to subsidize the major-generals. To the surprise of many Cromwell's son-in-law, John Claypole, opposed the measure; this was generally believed to mean that the Protector had withdrawn his support from the godly commanders in the field. Parliament itself was in large measure composed of people from the communities who had been subject to the strict measures of the major-generals, and the bill was rejected by thirty-six votes. The pietistic experiment was ended.

Another question of governance was raised. Should not Cromwell now become king and the House of Stuart be replaced by the House of Cromwell? This would satisfy the yearning of many people for a return to a traditional form of government. If Cromwell were sovereign, he might be able to curb the pretensions of parliament that had already gone beyond its powers. The newsletters anticipated a sudden 'alteration of government'. On 19 January 1657, one member, John Ashe of Freshford, moved that Cromwell 'take upon him the government according to the ancient constitution'.

On 23 February Sir Christopher Packe brought forward a remonstrance, under the title of the 'humble petition and advice', to the effect that Cromwell should assume 'the name, style, title and dignity of king' and that the House of Lords should be restored. The fury of the opponents of monarchy, most particularly the military element, was unrestrained. General John Lambert declared that any such reversal would be contrary to the principles for which he and his fellow soldiers had fought. Kingship had been so bathed in blood that it could not be restored. This was not a theoretical point. Cromwell was informed that a group of soldiers had bound themselves on oath to kill him as soon as he accepted the title.

Four days after the 'humble petition' had been advanced, one hundred representatives of the army visited Cromwell at Whitehall where they pleaded with him to resist the offer of advancement. He told them that he liked the title of king as little as they did; it was nothing but a bauble or a feather in the hat. He then reviewed the history of the last few years, in which he stated that he had faithfully followed the advice of the army; he said that 'they had made him their drudge upon all occasions', yet they had not met with success. None of the parliaments, none of the constitutional proposals, had worked. He told them that 'it is time to come to a settlement'. A House of Lords, for example, was needed to check the pretensions of the Commons; they left him with their fury 'much abated', and a few days later another army delegation assured him that they would acquiesce in whatever he decided 'for the good of these nations'.

The debate in parliament lasted for more than a month and occupied twenty-four sittings, some of them lasting all day. Eventually, at the end of March, Cromwell was formally requested to assume the crown. He replied that he had lived for the last part of his life 'in the fire, in the midst of trouble', and he requested more time for reflection. It was thought that he would accept the role of king, if only to unite a predominantly conservative nation, but in truth he was in conflict with himself. He knew that his senior military colleagues were passionately opposed to the change, but he knew also that this might prove his last and best chance to return the country to its traditional ways. It was in his means to provide the conditions for a regular and stable government.

It was not a question of private ambition; as he had said many times, the crown and sceptre meant very little to him. He already had more power than any English king. So he struggled. Thurloe said that Cromwell had 'great difficulties in his own mind' and that 'he keeps himself reserved from everybody that I know of'; when a parliamentary delegation came to him, in the middle of April, 'he came out of his chamber half unready in his gown, with a black scarf around his neck'. No doubt he prayed incessantly for divine guidance, hoping that as in the past a resolve or a decision would be presented to him as if by an act of grace.

He heard vital news of God's providence in England's affairs when he was told that Admiral Blake had successfully maintained a siege of the Spanish coast and had destroyed another treasure fleet, thus disabling Spain as a maritime power. England now effectively controlled the high seas, an ascendancy that was unprecedented in its history. With colonies in Jamaica and Barbados, as well as those such as Virginia on the American mainland, Cromwell was the first statesman since the days of Walsingham to contemplate a global empire. As Edmund Waller put it,

> Others may use the ocean as their road
> Only the English make it their abode.

Pepys noted, in the pusillanimous years of Charles II, that 'it is strange how everybody do nowadays reflect upon Oliver and commend him, what brave things he did, and made all the neighbour princes fear him'.

Yet on the most pressing matter of monarchy he could not, or dare not, come to a decision. On 3 April he declared to a parliamentary delegation that he could not discharge his duties 'under that title'; five days later parliament urged him to reconsider, on which occasion it is reported that he delivered 'a speech so dark, that none knows whether he will accept it or not'. He may still have been waiting for divine guidance. He knew that it was proper and expedient that he should take the crown but, as he said, 'I would not seek to set up that which providence hath destroyed and laid in the dust, and I would not build Jericho again.' In the first week of May it is reported that he told a group of members of parliament that he had decided to accept the title; yet once more he changed his mind.

On 8 May he told parliament that he could not and would not become King Oliver I. 'At the best,' he said, 'I should do it doubtingly. And certainly what is so [done] is not of faith.' The protests of the army officers had in the end proved to be persuasive; two of them, Fleetwood and Desborough, had in fact married into Cromwell's family. They had told him that, if he accepted the crown, they would resign from all their offices and retire into private life. Other officers, who had been with him from the beginning and had fought with him through fire, also registered their strong disapproval. This was decisive. He could not at this late stage abandon his comrades and colleagues; he could not betray their trust or spoil their hopes. So his final answer to parliament was that 'I cannot undertake this government with the title of king'.

The only way forward was by means of compromise. Even if Cromwell would not be king, he could accept the other constitutional measures recommended by parliament; in particular it seemed just, and necessary, to re-establish the House of Lords as a check upon the legislature. On 25 May the 'humble petition' was presented again with Cromwell named as chief magistrate and Lord Protector, an appointment which he accepted as 'one of the greatest tasks that ever was laid upon the back of a human creature'. On 26 June 1657, Oliver Cromwell was draped in purple and in ermine for the ceremony of installation in Westminster Hall; upon the table before his throne rested the sword of state and a sceptre of solid gold. The blast of trumpets announced his reign. His office was not declared to be hereditary but he had been given the power to name his successor; it was generally believed that this would be one of his sons. So began the second protectorate, which was now a restored monarchy in all but name.

34

Is it possible?

There was a time for celebration. At the end of 1657 one of Cromwell's daughters, Frances, married Robert Rich, the grandson of the earl of Warwick, and the ceremonial matched the status of the pair. Music and song echoed through the corridors of Whitehall in honour of the occasion; the orchestra comprised forty-eight violins and fifty trumpets. Guns were fired from the Tower in the manner of previous royal weddings. There was even 'mixt dancing', men and women together, that continued until five o'clock the following morning. In the spirit of the festivity Cromwell was moved to spill sack-posset, a rich and creamy drink, over the dresses of the women and to daub the stools where they were to sit with sugar and spice. He had an almost rustic sense of fun. At the subsequent wedding of another daughter, Mary, the ceremony at Hampton Court included a masque in which Cromwell played the non-speaking role of Jove. It was an astonishing return to the customs of the Stuart kings.

The French envoy reported that 'another spirit' was abroad and that 'the preachers of old time are retiring because they are found too melancholic'. When Cromwell gave banquets for foreign envoys 'rare music' was always part of the occasion and, in the great hall of Hampton Court, two organs were placed for the use of a resident organist. It is to the credit of Cromwell, too, that under his rule the opera was introduced into England. The Protector was known to be a great lover of harmony, both of instruments and of voices.

Immediately after his installation Cromwell had adjourned parliament until the new year; when it reappeared, it would be in its old constitutional form of two houses. He had named his new council; it was the same as its predecessor, with the solitary exception of John Lambert who had resigned all of his offices and retired with a large pension. He had once believed that he would be the Protector's successor but he now realized that he would be pre-empted by another, and younger, Cromwell.

One of the principal tasks of the re-established council was to decide upon the nature of the new upper chamber, but some of their proceedings took place in the absence of the Protector. Cromwell was now being called, even by his intimates, 'the old man'; his signature was no longer bold and striking but tremulous. He spent much of the summer in the healthful air of Hampton Court, but he was suffering from painful catarrh.

The second session of the second protectorate parliament re-assembled on 20 January 1658, but immediately it began to confront the military regime. The members of the new House of Lords were largely chosen from Cromwell's most loyal supporters and, as a result, the Commons became antagonistic; some of the most inveterate of Cromwell's opponents, who had been excluded from the previous session on the grounds of 'immorality' or 'delinquency', were returned to Westminster where at once they began to question the authority of the 'other house'.

Cromwell summoned both houses to the Banqueting House, five days after they had first met, and urged them to be faithful to the cause. But his intervention had no material effect, and the Commons remained as hostile as before. One of its most formidable members, Sir Arthur Haselrig, made a speech in which he scorned the actions of the House of Lords in the past. 'And shall we now rake them up,' he asked, 'after they have so long laid in the grave?' An observer at Cromwell's court noted that the assertions of the Commons, and the divisions between the two houses, threw the Protector 'into a rage and passion like unto madness'. His anger was augmented by the fact that elements of the army in fact supported the Commons in its affirmation of supremacy.

On a cold morning, 4 February, Cromwell rose early and announced his determination to go to Westminster. He could not journey down the frozen Thames, and so impulsively he took the first coach for hire he could find. When he arrived in the retiring room of the Lords, his son-in-law and close military colleague, Charles Fleetwood, remonstrated with him on learning his intention. 'You are a milksop,' Cromwell said to him, 'by the living God I will dissolve the house.' And that was what he proceeded to do.

He told the Commons that 'you have not only disquieted yourselves, but the whole nation is disquieted'. With the prospect of invasion from abroad, and rebellion from within, they had done nothing. 'And I do declare to you here that I do dissolve this parliament. And let God be judge between you and me.' To which pious aspiration some of the members cried out, 'Amen!' Cromwell's latest, and last, constitutional experiment had come to an end. It was a sign of the radical anomaly of military rule that none of his parliaments had succeeded. He was now being openly criticized. The envoy from Venice reported that the people were 'nauseated' by the present government; the Dutch ambassador similarly noted that Cromwell's affairs were 'in troubled and dangerous condition' while a visitor from Massachusetts remarked that many men 'exclaim against him with open mouths'.

A royalist agent in London, Allan Broderick, reported to Edward Hyde that the army 'is infected with sedition' and that the treasury was exhausted; he added that the countries of Europe were 'cold friends or close enemies' and that the people of England were labouring under 'an unwearied restless spirit of innovation'. Yet Broderick said of Cromwell himself that 'the man is seemingly desperate, any other in his condition would be deemed irrecoverable, but as the dice of the gods never throw out, so is there something in the fortune of this villain that often renders ten to one no odds'.

This message was designed to encourage Charles Stuart. It was reported that the exiled king was waiting in Flanders with an army of 8,000 men, ready to strike at the first favourable opportunity. Another royalist insurrection was planned for the spring, but once more the plotters were betrayed and taken; four of them were found by Colonel Barkstead, the lieutenant of the Tower, in what he called 'a desperate malignant alehouse'. Other royalists were beheaded or hanged, drawn and quartered, but the majority were consigned to gaol.

Another fortunate throw of the dice also favoured Cromwell. In the early summer of the year the forces of the French and English scattered the Spanish just outside Dunkirk in the 'battle of the dunes'; Dunkirk, hitherto held by Spain, was then surrendered to England. It was the first piece of continental territory to fall into English hands since the time of Calais. Since there was a royalist contingent in the Spanish army, victory for Cromwell was all the sweeter. The French king now hailed him as 'the most invincible of sovereigns'. Yet this praise concealed the truth that the Protector's expenditure far outran his income; the exchequer was often bare and the pay of his soldiers was in arrears. It was said that his ministers had to go 'a-begging' to the merchants of the City.

Sickness was also in the air. A malignant fever, called 'the new disease', had arisen. In the spring of 1658 the new epidemic spread, in the words of a contemporary, Dr Willis, 'as if sent by some blast of the stars'. Cromwell himself laboured under the burden of personal rule to the extent that, as one of his servants, John Maidstone, said, 'it drank up his spirits'. His private suffering was then increased by the death of his most loved daughter, Elizabeth Claypole, at the beginning of August from an obscure or undiagnosed disease; the event, though long expected, had a violent effect upon him. Thurloe reported that 'he lay very ill of the gout and other distempers, contracted by the long sickness of my lady Elizabeth, which made great impressions on him'; he became dangerously ill, but then recovered sufficiently to ride in Hampton Court Park.

When one of the leaders of the Quakers, George Fox, visited Cromwell, however, he reported that 'I saw and felt a waft of death go forth against him, and when I came to him he looked like a dying man'. In the last week of August Cromwell fell sick again with a condition then known as 'tertian ague', a form of malaria with fits every three days. It began with chills and sensations of coldness which were followed by a stage of dry heat that ended in a drenching sweat.

He was taken back to Whitehall where, as Thurloe put it, 'our fears are more than our hopes'. Prayer meetings assembled throughout the capital. His condition varied from rally to relapse, as all the time he grew weaker, but he was said to have prayed for 'God's cause' and 'God's people'. He asked one of his doctors why he looked so sad.

'How can I look otherwise, when I have the responsibility of your life upon me?'

'You doctors think I shall die.' His wife was sitting by his bedside and he took her hand. 'I tell thee I shall not die of this bout; I am sure I shall not. Do not think I am mad. I tell you the truth.' He then told the astonished doctor that this was the answer God had given to his prayers. He also questioned one of his chaplains.

'Tell me. Is it possible to fall from grace?'

'It is not possible.'

'Then I am safe; for I know that I was once in grace.'

He had always been sustained by the notion that he was one of the elect; his pride and his piety were thereby combined, giving him that irresistible power to remove all obstacles in his path. Yet there were many times when he did not know what to do, when he waited for a sign. He once said that no man rises so high as one that does not know where he is going. He had reached the height of his command through a mixture of guile, zeal and adventitious circumstance; no one could have predicted the series of measures and counter-measures that had led to his ascendancy. It did not matter that he was inconsistent, in turns pragmatic and authoritarian, as long as the force of righteousness was with him. That is why he believed above all else in 'providence' as both the cause and justification of his actions.

On Thursday 2 September it became clear that he was dying. One of his physicians offered him a sleeping draught but he replied that 'it is not my design to drink or to sleep, but my design is to make what haste I can to be gone'. Five officers, called to the deathbed, testified that he had declared that his son, Richard Cromwell, should succeed him. He died on the afternoon of 3 September which had been called by him his 'fortunate day' as the anniversary of his victories at Dunbar and at Worcester. His battles were all now over.

When in 1650 Oliver Cromwell came back to England, after his successful campaign in Ireland, he was greeted by '*An* Horatian *Ode upon* Cromwel's *Return from* Ireland'. It has been described as the greatest political poem in the English language, but it is not the most transparent. Andrew Marvell was at this time a poet of no great account. He had been educated well, and had made the obligatory tour of Europe. He might have become a clergyman or secretary to some great man; instead he lived off the sale of some lands in the north, and revolved in the circles of London literature.

He seems to have first been attached to some royalist poets or poetasters but the crucial victories of Cromwell, and the execution of the king, gave him pause. It might be time to find patronage among the new rulers of the land, and it may be that he composed his 'Ode' with some such purpose in sight. Yet his words, distilled as if in an alembic, testify to his creative ambiguity and equivocation. His mind is so finely tempered that he can become both royalist and republican at the same time; he is open to all possible opinions, and thus finds it impossible to choose between them. He is in the position of one who, on coming to a judgement, realizes at the same time that the opposite is also true. We may therefore discuss Marvell here as representative of the confusion that must have been experienced by many others in this period of change and conflict. The poem itself was composed in the interval between Cromwell's return from Ireland and his subsequent campaign in Scotland.

In the opening lines of the 'Ode' Cromwell is one who finds fulfilment not in 'the inglorious Arts of Peace' but in 'advent'rous War' through which he takes his 'fiery way'. This might not necessarily be construed as a compliment but Marvell is withholding judgement as well as praise. He goes on to declare that:

> 'Tis Madness to resist or blame
> The force of angry Heavens flame:
> And, if we would speak true,
> Much to the Man is due.

This is as much as to say that Cromwell cannot be resisted and should not in any case be censored or condemned. He may have emerged into the light as part of the inexorable movement of time, or of historical necessity, but in that respect his personal failings are of no consequence. It was his destiny (providential or otherwise) to

> . . . cast the Kingdom old
> Into another Mold.
> Though Justice against Fate complain,
> And plead the antient Rights in vain:
> But those do hold or break
> As Men are strong or weak.

Cromwell is in other words a strong man whose strength is its own reward. If justice has been sacrificed in the process, it is a necessary and inevitable consequence of change. Cromwell is in any case a creature of 'Fate' rather than of 'Justice', decisive and undeflectable. A leader may be both redeemer and despot. It had often happened in the history of the world, and Marvell's contemporaries were thoroughly acquainted with the career of Julius Caesar.

So this is a poetry of doubt and ambiguity rather than of praise and affirmation, which may thus reflect a more general distrust and uncertainty concerning Cromwell's motives in these crucial years. It can only be confirmed that he has:

> Nor yet grown stiffer with Command,
> But still in the *Republick's* hand:
> How fit he is to sway
> That can so well obey.

It can at least be said that Cromwell has not become a tyrant. Marvell does not take sides because there are no sides to take, and we may recall T. S. Eliot's remark upon Henry James that 'he had a mind so fine that no idea could violate it'. Marvell's almost impenetrable reserve and self-effacement are also evident. He utters no real opinion of his own, and seems ready to retreat at almost any moment into silence. This, too, may have been the stance of many contemporaries in the face of Cromwell's supremacy.

Four years later Marvell applied himself once more to the phenomenon of Oliver Cromwell with 'THE FIRST ANNIVERSARY of the Government under O.C.'. This is a much more positive account of Cromwell's rule, but it would be fair to say that it is a panegyric on the nature of protectorate government rather than on the Protector himself. Cromwell is compared to Amphion who with his brother raised the city of Thebes by means of music. So:

> No Note he struck, but a new Story lay'd
> And the great Work ascended while he play'd.

Cromwell is here praised for creating a structure of government that will, like Thebes, endure. He has also been able to create a unique form of leadership that was an appropriate substitute for royal government:

> For to be *Cromwell* was a greater thing,
> Then ought below, or yet above a King:
> Therefore thou rather didst thy Self depress,
> Yielding to Rule, because it made thee Less.

This polity has created a system of government that avoids the extremes of liberty or oppression:

> 'Tis not a Freedome, that where All command;
> Nor Tyranny, where One does them withstand:
> But who of both the Bounders knows to lay
> Him as their Father must the State obey.

As a result England was respected and feared by all of its neighbouring nations:

> He seems a King by long Succession born,
> And yet the same to be a King does scorn.
> Abroad a King he seems, and something more,
> At Home a Subject on the equal Floor.

This might be described as the 'party line' for Cromwell's adherents, and may or may not reflect Marvell's private thoughts on the matter. The difficulties of Cromwell's position as Protector, and the emergence of many agents of opposition to his rule, are not mentioned. Marvell is giving expression to the opinions of many people, however, who seem to have believed that the government of a Protector was more effective than the government of parliament. The poetry here is of great fluency and sophistication; it is precise but not pointed, hard but not wooden, eloquent but not facile.

The last poem by Marvell on Cromwell is also the most intimate. He had become by this time well known to the Protector's household; he had been asked to compose songs for the marriage of Mary Cromwell to Lord Fauconberg, and had been commissioned by Cromwell to write poems for Christina of Sweden. In 1657 he had been given employment as assistant to John Milton in Milton's position as Secretary of Foreign and Latin Tongues. So 'A Poem upon the Death of O.C.', written in 1658, was his last gift to an employer whom he may have come to love as well as admire. It seems more than likely that he was allowed to enter the death chamber and to view Cromwell's corpse:

> I saw him dead, a leaden slumber lyes,
> And mortal sleep over those wakefull eyes:
> Those gentle Rays under the lids were fled,
> Which through his looks that piercing sweetnesse shed;
> That port which so Majestique was and strong,
> Loose and depriv'd of vigour, stretch'd along:
> All wither'd, all discolour'd, pale and wan,
> How much another thing, no more that man?

35

The young gentleman

It was believed by some that after the death of Oliver Cromwell the fabric of the commonwealth would be torn apart; the centre would not hold. Yet the succession of his oldest son, Richard Cromwell, passed off without any commotion. No great public mourning was aroused by his father's death, and very little debate was instituted about his role or his legacy. John Evelyn witnessed the Protector's funeral where 'there were none that cried but dogs, which the soldiers hooted away with a barbarous noise, drinking and taking tobacco in the streets as they went'.

Richard Cromwell was a modest and self-effacing man with none of the natural authority or commanding presence of his father. He was, according to an appendix to James Mackintosh's *Eminent British Statesmen*, 'a person well skilled in hawking, hunting, horse-racing, with other sports and pastimes'. Allusions were made to 'Queen Dick'. He admitted soon after his accession that 'it might have pleased God, and the nation too, to have chosen out a person more fit and able for this work than I am'.

Yet almost at once he was engaged in the defining question of the moment. Should the army, or parliament, control this new gentry republic? Some of the army officers had already been demanding that they should have a commander-in-chief separate from the Protector, which meant in practice that they rejected the authority of the civil state. These officers were accustomed to meet at Wallingford House, the residence of Major-General Charles Fleetwood, who was their natural leader. Richard Cromwell, or 'the young gentleman' as he was known to some of them, did not concede their demand.

His position was strengthened in the election of a new parliament at the beginning of 1659, when a majority of the members seem to have been moderate or conservative men who supported the government of the protectorate and disliked the pretensions of the army; some of them were secret royalists, sustained by the impression or belief that the nation was with them. They demanded that all political activity in the army should come to an end, which at once aroused Fleetwood and his supporters. The soldiers refused to obey the order, and the few colonels who supported it found themselves abandoned by their men. Fleetwood, the regiments of the army with him at St James's, demanded that parliament be dismissed forthwith.

The impasse might have signalled the beginning of another war, but Richard Cromwell took fright at the prospect. He is reported to have said that 'for the preservation of my greatness (which is a burthen to me) I will not have one drop of blood spilt'. So he dissolved parliament and then, towards the end of May, abdicated his post as Protector. John Evelyn wrote in his diary that 'several pretenders and parties strive for the government: all anarchy and confusion; Lord have mercy on us!'

The leaders of the army decided against all precedent to revive the Rump Parliament that had been dissolved by Oliver Cromwell in the spring of 1653. In the beginning it had comprised some 200 members but the number had now fallen to 50. On their reappearance, however, they refused to be cowed by the authorities of the army and set about to reassert their power by granting the commission of officers to their Speaker rather than to Fleetwood. An open division between the two competing powers could not long be delayed.

A rebellion against the army, organized by a coalition of royalists and disaffected Presbyterians, was effectively put down in the summer by General John Lambert, who had returned from his retirement to play once more a leading role in military affairs, yet within two months he and eight other officers were dismissed by parliament for promoting a petition deemed to be seditious. Lambert then in turn expelled the Rump and instituted a very short reign of the army. A 'committee of safety' was formed consisting of twenty-three officers and committed to govern without the rule of 'a single person' and without a House of Lords.

The army itself was divided. One of its most senior officers, General George Monck, had been given the task by Oliver Cromwell of governing Scotland; from this vantage he looked upon the bewildering events in England with a wary and suspicious eye. He had thought of supporting Richard Cromwell but had then drawn back. He was considered by some to be a secret royalist. Now he refused to support Lambert and Fleetwood, but instead demanded the recall of the parliament so recently expelled.

It might seem that anarchy had been loosed upon the world, but the world went its own way. A contemporary, quoted in the Clarendon State Papers, observed that in London 'in all the hurly burly the streets were full, every one going about their business as if not at all concerned, and when the parliament sent unto the city to relieve them, they answered that they would not meddle with the dispute'. John Milton was not so sanguine and wrote that it was 'most illegal and scandalous, I fear me barbarous, or rather scarce to be exampled among any barbarians, that a paid army should . . . thus subdue the supreme power that set them up'.

Lambert was also forced to confront divisions among his own soldiers; they declared that they themselves would not fight Monck or anyone else, but would form a ring in which their officers could contest one against another in some form of prize fight; the troops stationed at Plymouth, and the entire fleet, then declared the Rump as the least worst alternative to unconstitutional military rule. They desired a justly established government as well as freedom of worship. On 24 December Fleetwood, declaring that 'God had spit in his face', delivered the keys of parliament to its Speaker, William Lenthall.

On that day the troopers now loyal to parliament marched to Lenthall's house in Chancery Lane, where they pledged to live and die with the assembly at Westminster. Lenthall, thus encouraged, decided to reconvene parliament on 26 December; the leading officers no longer had the will, or the support, to discourage him. On 4 January 1660, Lambert, who had made an unsuccessful attempt to march north and confront Monck, was now obliged to submit himself to the restored parliament; the members ordered him 'to one of his dwelling houses most remote from the City of London, in order to the quiet and peace of this commonwealth'. The confusion and uncertainty were the direct effect of Oliver Cromwell's inability to create a stable governance. Hartgill Baron, a royalist supporter, wrote that 'all things here at present are in so great a cloud that the most quick-sighted or wisest man living is not able to make a judgment of what may be the issue'. There were many, like him, who now looked to the king beyond the sea for deliverance from the chaos around them.

General Monck, at the end of 1659, began marching south from Edinburgh with 8,000 men. His intentions were not clear, perhaps not even to himself; he said only that he had come into England in order to maintain the commonwealth. He may have believed that the army's seizure of power had been misguided, but he was so taciturn and secretive that it is hard to be sure even of this. Pepys described him as 'a dull heavy man'.

When he arrived in London at the beginning of February many citizens called for 'a free parliament'; that meant the removal of the Rump and a return to the duly elected authority that had been purged by Colonel Pride eleven years before. Parliament responded by ordering Monck to enter the city in order to restore public order and to arrest its leading opponents. On 9 February Monck obeyed by removing all the gates, portcullises, posts and chains that were the symbols of the city's strength. The citizens believed that they had been betrayed and seem to have been beset with fear and dismay. It may have been that Monck deliberately set out to demonstrate the lengths to which parliament would go to protect its authority, and thus bring the people over to his side. No certainty is possible in the matter.

Two days later, however, the unfathomable Monck wrote a letter to the Rump with the order to dissolve itself and to call for fresh elections. The effect was immediate and profound; according to one pamphleteer, Roger L'Estrange, the people 'made bonfires very thick in every street and bells ringing in every church and the greatest acclamations of joy that could possibly be expressed'. Rumps of beef were roasted on every street-corner; rumps were tied on sticks and carried about; a great rump was turned on a spit on Ludgate Hill. Pepys reported that boys 'do now cry "kiss my parliament" instead of "kiss my arse", so great and general a contempt is the Rump come to . . .' Ten days later Monck made a short cut by readmitting all the members of the Long Parliament who had before been excluded. These had been largely Presbyterian in temper and had been removed precisely because of their willingness to negotiate a settlement with Charles I.

The newly restored parliament promptly decided to erase all the proceedings in the aftermath of Pride's Purge, which meant that it now resumed supreme authority in obtaining a settlement with the king. Lambert was sent to the Tower along with other members of the previous regime. On 6 March Pepys noted that 'everybody now drinks the king's health without fear, whereas before it was very private that a man dare do it'.

Charles II was still uncertain. He was not sure what Monck intended, and feared that the general might still set himself up as Lord Protector; there was even talk that Richard Cromwell might be asked to return to the post. Other supporters of the king did not trust Monck but believed that he would, in the old phrase, 'play fast and loose'. The king had experienced so many false hopes that now he could do nothing but wait. If he took any premature action, it might ruin everything. Monck himself was obliged to proceed very carefully. He may have surmised that the restoration of the king would be the best possible outcome for the nation but he could not yet fully support the popular mood; he had to maintain the unity of his army, and could not afford to alienate those who were still called 'commonwealth men'. He did not want to be suspected at this stage, as it was said, of 'carrying the king in his belly'. A month or two later it was reported that Monck was determined either to restore the king by his own actions, and thus reap the subsequent rewards, or to prevent Charles's return.

In the middle of March 1660, parliament dissolved itself and prepared the nation for a new assembly in the following month. The Long Parliament had finally come to an end, after a haphazard and interrupted rule of a little over nineteen years. In this month a known royalist supporter, Sir John Grenville, was smuggled into St James's Palace for a clandestine interview with Monck; Monck did not wish to write anything down but he intimated to Grenville, through an intermediary, that it might be fit and proper for the king to send him a letter setting out the intentions of the royal party. The general would then keep the letter in trust and reveal its contents at an appropriate time. By this happy subterfuge he might be able to ease the king's path to England. In another account of this secret affair Grenville had brought a letter from Charles to the general, offering Monck high office in a royal administration; the general replied that he had always intended to restore Charles. Whatever the exact circumstances it is clear that the king and the general were coming to an understanding.

At the beginning of April the king issued a 'declaration' from his temporary home at Breda in the Protestant Netherlands; no doubt he had consulted Monck's wishes or suggestions in their clandestine consultations. The king offered a free pardon and amnesty to anyone who swore allegiance to the Crown, with the exception of those who had voted for the late king's death; this was the only way of closing the chapter on the legacy of the civil war. Among other provisions was the promise of religious toleration to all peaceful Christians. Only thus could the struggles between Anglicans, Presbyterians and sectarians be resolved. Yet the king left all these measures to the final decision of parliament; this was seen by many to be a conciliatory gesture, but it also meant that parliament rather than king now incurred the responsibility of what might befall.

So all was set fair for the first elected parliament in almost two decades. It was known as the Convention Parliament since, in theory, no parliament could be called without a writ from the king to that effect. It soon became clear that many of a royalist persuasion had been elected; the king's friends had returned to Westminster. Charles's declaration was read to both Houses of Parliament and was received with enthusiasm. On the morning of 1 May the Lords, now with many royalist peers readmitted on the orders of General Monck, declared that 'according to the ancient and fundamental laws of this kingdom, the government is, and ought to be, by King, Lords and Commons'; the Commons assented that afternoon. It was now generally believed that a stable parliamentary government could only be established upon royal power. The republic had come to an end, and the aspirations of the army had been defeated.

On May Day, the once prohibited maypoles were set up all over the country. When the vice-chancellor and beadles of Oxford university tried to saw down a pole set up outside the Bear Inn, they were attacked by a crowd and beaten off. Pepys reported 'great joy all yesterday at London, and at night more bonfires than ever, and ringing of bells, and drinking of the king's health upon their knees in the streets, which methinks is a little too much'.

Charles II had removed to The Hague, where six members of the Lords and twelve members of the Commons were ushered into his presence; they presented the humble invitation and supplication of the parliament that his majesty should return and take the government of the kingdom into his hands. They also presented him with the sum of £50,000 to expedite his journey. Fourteen London citizens then came forward and offered the king a further £10,000. The city had not in previous years been wholly favourable to the royalist cause, and so its penitence was doubly appreciated. The king told them that he entertained a particular affection for London, as it was his place of birth, and knighted all of the citizens.

He set sail for England on 24 May, having embarked on a vessel newly christened *The Prince*; early on the morning of 26 May he arrived at Dover, where he knelt on the shore to give thanks. Monck was waiting for him, kneeling on the pier. The mayor of Dover presented him with a Bible; the king accepted it, saying 'it was the thing that he loved above all things in the world'. We may excuse him on this occasion of any attempt at irony.

Monck and the king travelled together to Canterbury where Charles listened to the Anglican service, according to the Book of Common Prayer, in the cathedral. Wherever he went he was surrounded by crowds. He had time to write to his youngest sister, Henrietta Anne, that 'my head is so dreadfully stunned with the acclamations of the people that I know not whether I am writing sense or nonsense'. From here the king progressed towards London to confirm and celebrate the fact of the Restoration.

36

Oh, prodigious change!

The return of Charles II was greeted with jubilation that was for the most part sincere. At Blackheath, just before entering the capital, he was met by what one newsletter described as 'a kind of rural triumph, expressed by the country swains, in a morris dance with the old music of the tabor and pipe'. It was believed that the restoration of the king would be accompanied by the revival of the old customs and traditions of the nation.

He rode in a dark suit through all the pomp of the procession, from the Strand to Westminster, raising his hat with its crimson plume time and time again. The streets were covered in flowers, and the houses hung with ornate tapestries; the sound of bells and trumpets mingled with the greetings of the crowd. John Evelyn noted in his entry for 29 May 1660, that 'I stood in the Strand and beheld it, and blessed God. And all this was done without one drop of blood shed, and by that very army which rebelled against him; but it was the Lord's doing, for such a restoration was never mentioned in any history, ancient or modern, since the return of the Jews from the Babylonish captivity; nor so joyful a day and so bright ever seen in this nation, this happening when to expect or effect it was past all human policy.'

As he passed under the gateway of the Banqueting House he glanced upwards to the site of his father's execution and at this point he came close to tears. When he was placed beneath the canopy of state such was the disorder and confusion that the king himself seemed to be in a daze. Yet he soon recovered himself. He had been greeted with such delight and enthusiasm that he remarked, with a smile, that he should have come back sooner. It was the wit of a man who had no illusions about human nature.

It was the king's thirtieth birthday, but he seemed older. His hair was already streaked with grey; men did not yet, in this period, wear wigs. The years of exile had made him lean, accentuating his height of 6 feet 2 inches. One contemporary, Sir Samuel Tuke, observed that 'his face is rather grave than severe, which is very much softened whensoever he speaks; his complexion is somewhat dark but much enlightened by his eyes, which are quick and sparkling'. With his large nose and heavy jaw, he was not handsome. He looked sad, and rather lugubrious, with a hint of dissipation and a trace of cruelty. 'Oddsfish,' he used to say, 'I am ugly.' 'Oddsfish' was a corruption of 'God's flesh'.

In this heady period he was affable to all he met, even to those whom he suspected of being his secret enemies. Yet behind this assumption of good humour he was calculating and even cunning. He had been brought up in the hard school of exile and, as he used to say, at all costs he wished to avoid 'going on my travels' once again. So his first decisions were made out of policy towards his erstwhile opponents rather than of gratitude to his friends. He believed that all men were governed by self-interest and therefore was not reluctant to consult his own.

When the king returned to his palace at Whitehall, it was much as he had remembered it from his childhood; it survived as a maze of a place with closets, cubby-holes, back staircases, corridors, corners and courtyards; it had grown piece by piece out of a variety of different dwellings and encompassed chapels, tennis courts and bowling greens. It covered 23 acres and contained approximately 2,000 rooms, some of which flooded when the Thames rose too high. The king loved the place, however, and rarely left it during the first full year of his reign. The great court as well as some of the terraces and galleries were in effect open to the public, and these areas were thronged with suitors hoping to gain the king's favour; others came simply to watch the splendour of majesty.

The king dined in public at midday, but he managed his business in the privacy of his bedchamber. There was also a secret closet beyond the chamber, to which few were ever admitted; soon enough this would testify to the king's penchant for secrecy and intrigue. The marquis of Halifax noted that 'he had backstairs to convey informations to him, as well as for other uses'; we may surmise what those other 'uses' were.

There was space enough at the palace for all of the king's principal councillors. Chief among them was a man who had been at his side for the years of exile. Edward Hyde, later to become the 1st earl of Clarendon and author of the monumental *History of the Rebellion*, was austere and assiduous even if, as he wrote himself, he was 'in his nature inclined to pride and passion'; he had a high opinion of his own judgement and rectitude, even to the point of lecturing his master on his shortcomings. His status was soon enhanced when his daughter, Mary Hyde, was married to the king's brother James, duke of York. It had been discovered that she was pregnant by him, prompting Samuel Pepys to recall how a wit once observed that 'he that doth get a wench with child and marries her afterward it is as if a man should shit in his hat and then clap it upon his head'.

Hyde, as lord chancellor, was one of a group of six confidants who formed what was called a 'secret committee' that, in the words of Hyde himself, was appointed by the king 'to consult all his affairs before they came to the public debate'. They were assisted by a privy council of some thirty to forty members, twelve of whom had carried arms against the king's father. Charles had decided to accommodate the recent past.

The king was at first diligent in his duties but he soon tired of the details of his administration. He grew easily bored at the meetings of his council and disliked the paperwork of office; it was reported by the marquis of Halifax that his ministers 'had to administer business to him as doctors do physic, wrap it up in something to make it less unpleasant'. It was also a convenient way for him to disown responsibility for certain policies. As he once said, 'My words are my own but my acts are my ministers'.

The sale and ownership of land were pressing issues. Many of the royalists had been forced to sell their estates in order to pay fines or to meet the 'decimation tax'. They now petitioned for their lands to be returned to them, but parliament decided that it was not in its power to reverse what had been in theory voluntary sales. The decision caused much resentment, and contributed to the feeling that the king had turned his back on his former supporters.

That feeling was compounded by one of the measures of the Convention Parliament in this year. An Act of Indemnity and Oblivion was passed, by means of which any crime or treason committed 'by virtue or colour' of parliamentary or regal authority over the last twenty-two years was to be 'pardoned . . . and put in utter oblivion'. All the rage of the past was therefore to be redeemed or, at least, forgotten. The measure incensed those royalists who believed themselves to have been injured by the actions of the military regime, and it was remarked that the king was consenting to an indemnity for his enemies and to oblivion for his friends.

The regicides, those who had signed the death warrant of the late king, were excepted from the indemnity. In the autumn of the year, in one of the few acts of vengeance perpetrated by the new administration, ten of these malefactors were hanged, drawn and quartered; they met their deaths with defiance and one of them had the strength, as his naked body was sliced open before disembowelling, to strike the executioner. Richard Cromwell had already fled from England to lead a life of decent obscurity in Europe. Charles was inclined to clemency, however, and when nineteen other regicides were about to be brought to trial for their lives he wrote to Clarendon that 'I must confess that I am weary of hanging except upon new offenses; let it sleep'.

It was a nice matter also to deal with the army. Under the command of Monck it had helped to place the king on his throne, but it might equally well be used to eject him from it. A poll tax was reintroduced to fund the payments of the soldiers' arrears and, by the autumn, they were retired; they returned, where possible, to their old homes and occupations. They were allowed to keep their swords, however, and the more radical of them still maintained 'the good old cause' of the republic. At the end of the year a declaration banned them from assembling in London, but in truth they posed no serious threat. Most of them melted away causing the preacher,

Richard Baxter, to observe that 'thus did God do a more wonderful work in the dissolving of this army than any of their greatest victories'.

Yet as always the cause of religion was pre-eminent, with a division of the clergy between those who avowed the Anglican persuasion and those who adopted the puritan or Presbyterian case. There was no particular example from the 'defender of the faith'. It is still difficult to write with any clarity of the king's religion. He died after being received into the Catholic Church, and it is possible that he had become a secret member of that faith even while in exile. Yet perhaps he did not have the conviction to espouse any particular creed; it was not his business to be pious but to be politic. The various forms of religion held no real interest for him and he used to tease his rigidly Catholic brother, James, about the scandalous lives of the popes. He was apt to say, of his own sexual escapades, that God would not damn a man for seeking a little pleasure. He had a light heart and an easy conscience.

Within a month of his return to England, however, Charles was busily engaged in the ceremony of 'the king's touch' whereby through the agency of God he could heal those afflicted with scrofula or 'the king's evil'. It was a signal instance of the divine dispensation that had made him the Lord's anointed and, as a spectacle of majesty, he deployed it frequently. Once a month, until the end of his reign, hundreds of scrofulous people flocked to the Banqueting House where with patience and dignity he laid his hands upon them.

The old order had been reasserted, but it had been subtly changed by the recent broils. The French ambassador, for example, wrote to Louis XIV that 'this government has a monarchical appearance because there is a king, but at bottom it is very far from being a monarchy'. The power of parliament had increased immeasurably after its success in the civil war; it was impossible for the king to raise money from his subjects, or to arrest any person, without its consent. Charles also now depended for his finances on the annual sum assigned to him by the members at Westminster.

The king's power had also diminished in other ways. The Star Chamber would not be revived. Any attempt at a large standing army would be treated with grave suspicion. The influence of the

City had also grown, and from the events of these years we may date the true beginning of a commercial and mercantile state.

The rule that had once radiated from one person, whether Stuart or Cromwell, had become more balanced and diffused. The departments of the two secretaries of state, devoted to the administration of domestic as well as foreign affairs, were established; permanent boards were also created for such business as the assignment and collection of taxation. The treasury broke away from royal control and became responsible for approving all payments. Thirty committees were soon in session and, later in 1660, a council of trade and a council of foreign plantations were at work.

Yet this was not a bureaucracy in the modern sense, since it was based upon patronage and the lavish giving or taking of 'fees' for services rendered. Many of the officials were not technically the servants of the state but were paid by more senior officials. The more important posts were considered to be private property, to be kept for life and subsequently sold to a close relative or to the highest bidder. It was not necessarily a corrupt system, since it represented the only way in which government could be made to work.

The central differences between the two epochs of republic and restored monarchy were less palpable. The people put no faith in paper constitutions, such as Cromwell had imposed; the religious dimension of public affairs was no longer as relevant as once it was, and piety eventually became a matter of private conscience. There would be no more zealotry at Westminster. Political theory more frequently became the preserve of philosophers, such as Locke and Hobbes, rather than of theologians. This may be the reason for the suggestion of many contemporaries that religious belief itself was in decline. Thomas Sprat, the chronicler of the Royal Society, noted that 'the influence which Christianity once obtained on men's minds is now prodigiously decayed'.

The certainties of the religious wars, if we may call them that, had begun to dissolve within a new public discourse that favoured reason and civility. A man might now gather his opinions from the coffee-house rather than from the church or conventicle (in the year of the king's restoration the drinks of tea, coffee and chocolate are first mentioned). The king was obliged by parliament to impose

Anglicanism upon the nation, as we shall see, but the puritans and dissenters could not in the end be silenced. Compulsion was eventually to be replaced by persuasion.

The formal coronation of Charles II was delayed until St George's Day, 23 April 1661, just two weeks before the opening of his first parliament. Charles II was the last monarch ever to ride in state through the streets of London on the day preceding the event, since he knew well enough that ceremony was at the centre of kingship. He ordered that all the ancient records should be studied so that the traditional solemnity of the occasion should be maintained; the crown jewels had been broken up and sold after his father's execution, but he ordered that a new set should replicate the old in every minute particular. He wore robes of gold and silver, together with a crimson cap of velvet lined with ermine. The first coronation mugs, sold as souvenirs, are a measure of the popularity of the occasion. The day itself was serene and fair but Pepys observed in his diary that, immediately after the ceremony, 'it fell a-raining and thundering and lightning as I have not seen it do for some years'. Some obvious prognostications were made.

Parliament met on 8 May; the proximity of the two occasions was a tribute to the notion of 'the crown in parliament', the title of supreme power in England. Since half of the new members came from families that had suffered in the royalist cause, it became known as 'the Cavalier Parliament'. They were for the most part young men but the king remarked that 'he would keep them till they got beards'; he fulfilled the promise by maintaining this parliament for a further eighteen years.

They of course supported his cause, and that of the bishops, but they were most intent on maintaining the privileges of the gentry from which they had largely come. The Presbyterians were in a small minority, and were in no position to check or obstruct what might be described as the conservative tide. In a series of Acts, over a period of five years, parliament enforced Anglican supremacy upon the nation. Two weeks after it met the 'solemn league and covenant', which had pledged the nation to a Presbyterian settlement with Scotland, was summarily burned by the common hangman at Westminster and other places in the city. John Evelyn remarked, 'Oh, prodigious change!'

By the Corporation Act of 1661, the municipal leaders of town or city were confined to those who received communion by the rites of the Church of England; the mayors and aldermen were also obliged to take an oath of allegiance and affirm that it was not lawful to take up arms against the king. The Act was designed to remove those of a nonconformist persuasion whose loyalty might be suspect.

An Act of Uniformity was passed in the following year which restricted the ministry to those who had been ordained by a bishop and who accepted the provisions of the Book of Common Prayer. These conditions effectively disqualified 1,700 puritan clergy, who were therefore ejected from their livings. It was the most sudden alteration in the religious history of the nation. Some said that it was an act of revenge by the Anglicans after their persecution during the days of the commonwealth, but it may also have been a means whereby the royalist gentry regained control of their parishes.

Some of the ejected clergy were reduced to poverty and the utmost distress. One of their number, Richard Baxter, recalled that 'their congregations had enough to do . . . to help them out of prisons, or to maintain them there'. John Bunyan, for example, was imprisoned in Bedford Prison for nonconformist preaching. He wrote that 'the parting with my wife and poor children hath often been to me in this place as the pulling of the flesh from the bones'; yet in his prison cell he dreamed of eternity.

Much popular derision was directed at the godly ministers. The dissenting preachers were mocked and hooted at in the street. Ben Jonson's *Bartholomew Fair*, in which puritans were roundly scorned, was revived with great popular success. The Quakers in particular were badly treated and, during the reign of Charles, 4,000 were consigned to prison; Clarendon had said that they were 'a sort of people upon whom tenderness and lenity do not at all prevail'.

Yet the rigour of the new law was averted in some areas. Many Presbyterians or 'church puritans' were more flexible in obeying the law; the clergy of these congregations might well retain their livings in acts of subtle compromise. Some authorities were in any case reluctant to enforce the law, and the ecclesiastical courts were not always efficient.

In two further Acts of subsequent years the attendance at religious assemblies, other than those of the official Church, was punished by imprisonment; no puritan clergyman or schoolmaster could come within 5 miles of a town or city. These measures did not reflect the king's promise of toleration for all honest Christians, as he had announced in the 'declaration' of Breda before sailing to England, but it is likely that he was being pressed by the young men of parliament; he acceded to their demands because he did not wish to lose their support in the funding of his revenues.

It would in the end prove impossible to subdue the whole body of nonconformist worshippers, now bound together by the pressure of shared persecution; but, by attempting to impose Anglican worship, the members of the 'Cavalier Parliament' opened up the great fissure between Anglicanism and dissenting faiths that would never be resolved. An informal network of meetings brought together Independents, Baptists and Presbyterians in sharp distinction to the established Church. No national religious settlement had been achieved. The days of the disputes between church and chapel would soon come.

Other measures followed in what was a series of busy parliamentary sessions. A new 'hearth tax' was passed in the spring of 1662, with a charge of 1 shilling for each hearth to be paid twice a year; the response was clamant and immediate. A saying passed through the streets of London to the effect that 'the bishops get all, the courtiers spend all, the citizens pay for all, the king neglects all and the devil takes all'. A Licensing Act was approved, by which it was ordered that no book might be published without the approval of an official censor; this was largely directed against nonconformist writings that would now come under the gaze of the bishop of London and the archbishop of Canterbury. The atmosphere of free debate that had pertained for much of Cromwell's rule came to an end.

These measures against 'toleration' came at a price. Pepys reported that all of the 'fanatics' were discontented and 'that the king do take away their liberty of conscience'; he deplored 'the height of the bishops who I fear will ruin all again'. The puritan clergy were ordered to abandon their livings on 24 August 1662, St Bartholomew's Day, and in many places the congregations came in great numbers to hear and lament their 'farewell sermons'. More spirited protest was also expected. Ever since the king's arrival in England minor uprisings by 'fanatics' had disturbed the peace, and through the spring and summer of 1662 fears rose of some concerted puritan resistance. A general rising was supposed to be planned for August, and from all over the country came reports of seditious meetings and treasonable speeches. Lord Fauconberg, lord-lieutenant of the North Riding of Yorkshire, claimed that in Lancashire 'not one man in the whole county intends to conform'; reports of the same nature came from his own county of Yorkshire and the West Country, while London was known to be the spiritual home of zealotry and sectarianism. The lords-lieutenant of the various counties were told to watch 'all those known to be of the Republic party'.

Yet these apprehensions were generally without foundation. The Anglican Church was now supreme under the leadership of the cleric who in 1663 was consecrated as archbishop of Canterbury; Gilbert Burnet wrote of Archbishop Sheldon that 'he seemed not to have a deep sense of religion, if any at all, and spoke of it most commonly as of an engine of government and a matter of policy'. The bishops, for example, had been returned to their seats in the House of Lords where they could exert a strong influence upon national legislation; yet it was also true that parliament, and not the Church, had taken control of the nature and direction of the national religion.

The actual faith of the people was no doubt as inchoate and confused as ever. One Lancastrian apprentice, Roger Lowe, recorded in 1663 that 'I was pensive and sad and went into the town field and prayed to the Lord, and I hope the Lord heard'.

At a meeting of the council, just after parliament had been summoned, Charles told his advisers that he had decided to marry the infanta of Portugal, Catherine of Braganza; he had already announced his preferences when he said that 'I hate Germans, or princesses of cold countries'. The mother of the intended bride, the queen regent of Portugal, had also offered £800,000 together with her colonial territories of Bombay and Tangier in order to sweeten the arrangement. English merchants were also to be permitted to trade freely throughout the Portuguese Empire, thus assisting England in its rivalry with the Dutch. In return Portugal wished to recruit English soldiers in its war with the neighbouring power of Spain, which was eager to take back its rebellious province. A marriage could accomplish a great deal.

Another matrimonial alliance completed what may be called the 'foreign policy' of Charles. His sister Henrietta was married off to the homosexual brother of Louis XIV and helped to inaugurate closer relations between France and England that came in the end to be too close. Louis XIV was feared and distrusted for his attempt to raise himself up as 'universal monarch' in the face of Spanish decline; nevertheless Charles admired his absolutist and centralized rule that he had some obscure hope of emulating.

The king travelled down to Portsmouth to meet his bride, and reported to Clarendon that 'her face is not so exact as to be called a beauty though her eyes are excellent good, and not anything in her face that in the least degree can shock one'. This may not amount to a ringing endorsement but, for a royal union, it was fairly satisfactory. Her teeth stuck out a little, and her hair was swept to the side in the Portuguese fashion. The king is said privately to have remarked, 'Gentlemen, you have brought me a bat.' One of Catherine's first requests was for a cup of tea, then a novelty. Instead she was offered a glass of ale.

She had arrived with what one contemporary, the comte de Gramont, described as 'six frights, who called themselves maids-of-honour and a duenna, another monster, who took the title of governess to those extraordinary beauties'. Much fun was also made of their great fardingales, or hooped skirts of whalebone beneath their dresses.

Catherine had some formidable competition. The king was known to be an insatiable and compulsive philanderer, and Pepys calculated that he had had seventeen mistresses even before the Restoration. John Dryden, in *Absalom and Achitophel*, characterized him thus:

> Then, Israel's monarch, after Heaven's own heart,
> His vigorous warmth did variously impart

To wives and slaves: and, wide as his command,
Scatter'd his Maker's image through the land.

Or, as the earl of Rochester put it more bluntly,

Restless he rolls from whore to whore,
A merry monarch, scandalous and poor.

By a previous lover, Lucy Walter, he had a son who would in 1663 become duke of Monmouth. His present mistress was Barbara Palmer, whose husband had been ennobled as the earl of Castlemaine; Lady Castlemaine soon became indispensable to his pleasure, and it was reported by Pepys that she ruled the king by employing 'all the tricks of Aretino [a poet of obscenity] . . . in which he is too able having a large—' The rest is silence. The lady was already heavily pregnant by the time that Catherine arrived in England.

The king's appetite for Lady Castlemaine was such that he appointed her to be his wife's lady-of-the-bedchamber. Catherine objected to the convenient arrangement, and her anger led to an estrangement between the royal couple. The new queen of England was receiving company at Hampton Court when her husband led Lady Castlemaine into the room; she may not have correctly heard her name since she received her calmly enough but, on being made aware of the lady's identity, she burst into tears before fainting. Clarendon was used by the king as a mediator and, in the end, the queen gave way and welcomed her rival.

In truth she had become devoted to her husband, and in no way wished to alienate his affections. She could do nothing, however, to fulfil her primary role; she seemed to be incapable of bearing children. It was not for want of trying. An Italian visitor at the court, Lorenzo Magalotti, heard that the queen was 'unusually sensitive to pleasure' and that after intercourse 'blood comes from her genital parts in such great abundance that it does not stop for several days'.

In time the king would become enamoured of another mistress, Frances Stewart, of whom the comte de Gramont said that it would be difficult to imagine less brain combined with more beauty. She was the model, complete with helmet and trident, for the figure of Britannia on British coins. Charles was always in love with someone or other. By seventeen of his known mistresses he had thirteen illegitimate children, some of whom became dukes or earls. The story of Nell Gwynn has often been told.

The royal court itself had become the object of much scandal and remark. Macaulay, in an essay for the *Edinburgh Review*, remarked of a no doubt exaggerated example that 'a dead child is found in the palace, the offspring of some maid of honour by some courtier, or perhaps by Charles himself. The whole flight of pandars and buffoons pounces upon it and carries it to the royal laboratory, where his majesty, after a brutal jest, dissects it for the amusement of the assembly, and probably of its father among the rest.'

The rule of the saints had been replaced by the rule of the sinners who seemed to compete with each other in drunkenness and debauchery. When a bishop preached in the royal chapel against 'mistaken jollity' the congregation laughed at him. When the court visited Oxford a scholar, Anthony Wood, observed that 'they were nasty and beastly, leaving at their departure their excrements in every corner, in chimneys, studies, coalhouses, cellars. Rude, rough, whore-mongers; vain, empty, careless.' And of course they took their morals and manners from their royal leader. Other royal courts were no doubt characterized by profligacy and sexual licence – the court of William II comes to mind – but never had they been so widely observed and criticized.

A circle of 'wits' emerged around the king; among them were George Villiers, duke of Buckingham, and Charles, Sir Sedley. They were accustomed to meet in the apartments of the king's latest lover or in the lodgings of the notorious William Chiffinch who became 'keeper of the king's private closet', where their most notable contribution to court life was a number of highly obscene poems and stories. Their wit was manifested in verbal extravagance and dexterity, in puns and allusions, or, as Robert Boyle put it, 'a subtlety in conceiving things . . . a quickness and neatness in expressing them'.

There was much to ridicule. In the summer of 1663 Lord Sedley appeared naked on the balcony of the Cock Inn in Bow Street where, according to Samuel Pepys, he proceeded to enact 'all the postures of lust and buggery that could be imagined, and abusing of scripture'. He delivered a mock sermon in which he declared that 'he hath to sell such a powder as should make all the cunts in town run after him'. After the recital 'he took a glass of wine and washed his prick in it and then drank it off; and then took another, and drank the king's health'. He then took down his breeches and proceeded to 'excrementize'.

On the following day he was brought before the chief justice, who asked him if he had ever read Henry Peacham's *The Complete Gentleman*. He was then bound over to keep the king's peace on a bond of £500, whereupon he said that 'he thought he was the first man that paid for shitting'. The bond was paid with money borrowed from the king himself.

37

On the road

On the course of their journey Faithful and Christian came upon Talkative, a gentleman who 'was something more comely at a distance than at hand'. Then he conversed with his fellow travellers.

> *Talkative:* I will talk of things heavenly, or things earthly; things moral, or things evangelical; things sacred, or things profane; things past, or things to come; things foreign, or things at home; things more essential, or things circumstantial; provided that all be done to our profit.

He walked out of their way for a little, whereupon Christian and Faithful began to discuss their new companion.

> *Faithful:* Do you know him, then?
> *Christian:* Know him! Yes, better than he knows himself.
> *Faithful:* Pray what is he?
> *Christian:* His name is *Talkative*; he dwelleth in our town. I wonder that you should be a stranger to him, only I consider that our town is large.
> *Faithful:* Whose son is he? And whereabout doth he dwell?
> *Christian:* He is the son of one *Say-well*; he dwelt in *Prating*

Row; and is known of all that are acquainted with him,
by the name of *Talkative* in *Prating Row*; and
notwithstanding his fine tongue, he is but a sorry fellow.
Faithful: Well, he seems to be a very pretty man.
Christian: That is, to them who have not thorough
acquaintance with him, for he is best abroad, near
home he is ugly enough.

John Bunyan's *The Pilgrim's Progress* has often been characterized
as the first English novel; it is as if he had the actual characters
before him, in imagination, and simply wrote down what he heard;
he also employed the plain speech of the time, to the extent that
we can hear the ordinary people of the late seventeenth century
talking to one another. Yet *The Pilgrim's Progress* is more than a
novel.

John Bunyan, born in Bedfordshire in 1628, gathered the
rudiments of learning while young but may have been largely self-
educated; he was thoroughly acquainted with the vernacular Bible
and with Foxe's *Acts and Monuments*, but in his youth he read the
ballads and romances of the time. He joined the New Model Army
at the age of fifteen, but it is not clear whether he saw any active
service before his disbandment three years later.

After his marriage to a poor woman he entered a period of
spiritual struggle, documented by *Grace Abounding*, in which he fell
into despair and fearfulness before being tempted by false hope. He
was still afflicted by anxiety and depression when in 1655 he joined
a separatist church in Bedford; he began his preaching before that
congregation where slowly he found strength and confidence. His
ministry widened, therefore, and he came into conflict with the
authorities. In 1661 he was consigned to Bedford Prison where,
refusing to renounce his right to preach, he remained for the next
eleven years. He wrote many books and treatises during this period,
but none more popular and significant than *The Pilgrim's Progress*.

In part it might be read as an account of any seventeenth-century
journey, over rough roads, encumbered by mud and puddles, endan-
gered by mires and ditches, pits and deep holes. The travellers must
sometimes reconnoitre steep hills where they may catch 'a slip or
two'. Sometimes they go 'out of the way' and among 'turnings' and

'windings' lose themselves; 'wherefore, at last, lighting under a little shelter, they sat down there till the day brake; but being weary they fell asleep'. We hear the dogs barking at their presence. If they are unfortunate they may be taken for vagrants, and placed in the stocks or in the 'cage'. If they are fortunate they will find lodgings on the course of their journey, where they will be asked, 'What will you have?'

They must also face the dangers of robbers waiting for them along the road.

> So they came up all to him, and with threatening language
> bid him stand. At this *Little-Faith* looked as white as a clout,
> and had neither power to fight nor fly. Then said *Faint-Heart*,
> Deliver thy purse . . . Then he cried out, Thieves, thieves!

In the face of such dangers some travellers formed a company for the sake of friendship and security.

'Then I hope we may have your good company.'
'With a very good will, will I be your companion.'
'Come on, then, let us go together . . .'
Such snatches of conversation are often heard on the road. They are eager to meet one another and, leaning upon their staves, they talk. 'Is this the way?' 'You are just in your way.' 'How far is it thither?' 'Whence came you?' 'Have you got into the way?' One will greet another with 'What have you met with?' or 'What have you seen?' 'Whither are you going?' 'Back, back.' Some travellers want 'to make a short cut of it, and to climb over the wall'. What does it matter how they reach their destination? 'If we are in, we are in.'

The vividness of the prose is derived from its immediacy and contemporaneity. 'I met him once in the streets,' Faithful says of Pliable, 'but he leered away on the other side, as one ashamed of what he had done; so I spake not to him.' Christian says to a man, 'What art thou?' and is told, 'I am what I was not once.' He tells Hope, 'I would, as the saying is, have given my life for a penny . . . this man was one of the weak, and therefore he went to the wall . . . And when a man is down, you know, what can he do?' The simplicity and vigour have been tested on the anvil of suffering experience but they also derive from Bunyan's reading of the vernacular Bible. The words seem to come to him instinctively but they have absorbed the cadence and imagery of the Scriptures.

They come also from Bunyan's identity as a Calvinist. To read *The Pilgrim's Progress* is to return to that world of fierce struggle and debate in which deeply held religious faith was the only stay against the dark. Bunyan is nothing like the caricatures of Tribulation Wholesome, Snarl, or Zeal-of-the-Land-Busy, in seventeenth-century drama. He is too desperate and determined to be that. Christian decides to embark upon his journey alone 'because none of my neighbours saw their danger as I saw mine'. This is the heart of it, this awareness of imminent destruction. It is the source of what he calls his 'dumps' that might also be expressed as despair and distraction, of melancholy close to madness, afflicting those who believed themselves to be in danger of spiritual destruction. This fear animates the life of the seventeenth century. It is the fear of what Bunyan calls 'the bottomless pit . . . out of the mouth of which there came in an abundant manner smoke, and coals of fire, with hideous noises'. To be saved by the infinite and unlooked-for grace of God, unworthy though you be, is to experience the transformation of the spirit. It is a glimpse into the heart of the fervent spirituality of the seventeenth-century world.

38

To rise and piss

The prosperous citizen of London would wear a cloth doublet, open at the front to display his shirt and lawn scarf; breeches, stockings and buckled shoes completed the ensemble. For the outdoors he donned his wig and sugarloaf hat, together with a short cloak, and a sword at his side. His wife would naturally wear a brocaded silk dress, looped to display her quilted petticoat; her neck and shoulders were covered with a kerchief and she wore the fashionable French hood of the day.

The house in which they lived, in the period of Charles I and Cromwell, would have been perhaps too dull and plain for modern taste; the floors were of polished wood, some of the walls wainscoted and the ceilings panelled with oak. The rooms were solid and well-proportioned, but a little gloomy and confined; the floors creaked under foot. Only towards the end of the seventeenth century was there a general movement towards lighter and more gracious interiors.

The houses of those who were known as 'the middle rank' contained between three and seven rooms; the household would characteristically contain between four and seven people, including servants. In the more prosperous of these dwellings the hall, parlour and kitchen took up the ground floor while above them were one or two bedrooms. Of ornament there was very little. The windows rarely boasted curtains; carpets and armchairs were not widely used. Clocks, looking glasses and pictures were still relatively scarce but they were more in evidence towards the close of the period; this was also the time when the cabinet-maker, working in walnut and mahogany, became more popular. The richer households, however, might place hangings against some of the walls.

Their furniture was not comfortable, being comprised of high-backed chairs, stools, chests and benches with perhaps a few cushions to soften the hard wood. The dining table would have no ornament, and cutlery of the modern type was not in use; the crockery was of pewter rather than of earthenware. A display of plate might be set on the sideboard, but otherwise ostentation was still slight. The rooms were heated with coals. Sanitation was of the most rudimentary, with only the occasional mention of a pewter chamber pot or a 'close-stool'. There is no evidence of any utensils for washing.

The good citizen might engage in trade as a merchant or in commerce as a shopkeeper, but there was no firm distinction between the various avocations of the city. In the reign of Charles II 3,000 merchants could be found in the Royal Exchange, and in this period foreign trade, domestic industry and shipping all enjoyed rapid growth in advance of that period that became known to twentieth-century historians as the 'commercial revolution'. In *A Discourse of Trade*, published in 1670, Roger Coke stated that 'trade is now become the lady which in this present age is more courted and celebrated than in any former by all princes and potentates of the world'. The list of imported commodities included tobacco, sugar, indigo and ginger from the colonies as well as Indian calicoes and chintzes; a large proportion of these goods was then re-exported in English ships to continental Europe.

The gentry and the local administrators of the counties must not be forgotten since in this period they exercised full control of their neighbourhoods. It was a time when the old principles of the social hierarchy were reinforced. The 'Cavalier Parliament' had extended the authority of the local aristocracy in such matters as the control of the militia and the administration of the Poor Law. The justices of the peace had almost complete possession of local affairs, from imprisoning vagabonds to fining parish officials for breach of their duties.

The gentry had resumed their role as the leaders of local society, after the unfortunate experiment of republicanism, but they seemed not to have returned to their old complacency. Many of them, for example, paid very close attention to the new methods of agricultural practice. The farmers themselves were engaged in what were known as 'improvements' that increased the profitability of the land; in this period the country was able to export grain to mainland Europe.

A large class of 'professional men' had also emerged in this period; the lawyers and the doctors were principal among them, but accountants and professional administrators of estates were also to be found. Samuel Pepys has become for posterity the master of this world, and his diary does in some degree provide a mirror for his age. He is twenty-six at the time of his first entry; living with his wife in Axe Yard, near Downing Street, he is about to be appointed as secretary to Edward Mountagu, the lord admiral. This was the period when the Rump Parliament had reassembled and General Monck was beginning his march from Scotland.

And so we read that on 3 January 1660, 'Mr Sheply, Hawley and Moore dined with me on a piece of beef and cabbage, and a collar of brawn'. Meat was the principal item in the diets of the period, and it is characteristic that Pepys should have two types; dinner was eaten at noon. On another occasion Pepys sat down to a dish of marrow bones and a leg of mutton, a loin of veal and a dish of fowl together with two dozen larks. He also had dinners of fish but, on being offered a dish of sturgeon, 'I saw very many little worms creeping, which I suppose was through the staleness of the pickle'.

He drank ale and 'strong water' that was most probably gin. After dinner there was often a 'mad stir' with games and forfeits. Sports were of all kinds including one that Pepys called 'the flinging at cocks', in which sticks were hurled at a bird that was tethered by its leg or held down by some other means; whoever rendered it unconscious was allowed to cook and eat it. He also visited a cock-fight in a new pit by Shoe Lane. Other vignettes of the period emerge from his notations. A new disease sprang up in the autumn of 1661, consisting of 'an ague and fever'.

The cleanliness of the age is perhaps in doubt. He had 'like to have shit in a skimmer that lay over the house of office'. He made a cloth suit out of a cloak 'that had like to have been beshit behind a year ago'. 'This night I had a strange dream of bepissing myself, which I really did.' He was en route to the Guildhall, 'by the way calling to shit at Mr Rawlinson's'. He had forgotten his chamber pot one night, 'so was forced to rise and piss in the chimney'. In the theatre, 'a lady spat backward upon me by a mistake, not seeing me'. He sometimes washed himself with warm water, and sometimes washed his feet, but the occurrences were rare enough to merit mention. His wife, Elizabeth, visited a 'hot-house' and 'pretends to a resolution of hereafter being very clean – how long it will hold, I can guess'. Sure enough, on a later occasion, 'she spent the whole day making herself clean, after four or five weeks being in continued dirt'. Two months later, however, 'she finds that I am lousy, having found in my head and body above twenty lice, little and great'.

He was particular about his clothes. He ordered a coat of velvet, what he called a 'close-kneed coloured suit' with stockings of the same colour together with belt and a new gilt-handled sword, as well as a black cloth suit with white lining. In the autumn of 1663 he bought a new shag-gown, trimmed with gold buttons, and two periwigs. He then decided that the wig maker should cut off his hair and make another periwig with it, and 'after I had caused all my maids to look upon it and they conclude it to become me'. Soon after he also purchased a black cloth suit trimmed with scarlet ribbon as well as a cloak lined with velvet. 'Clothes', he wrote, 'is a great matter.' He went into the street 'a little to show forsooth my new suit'. A poor fellow was one 'that goes without gloves for his hands'.

It was a society of spectacle and display, in which all the leading characters were also actors. In his bright costume and new wig he might promenade with his wife in certain select neighbourhoods, such as Gray's Inn, followed by 'a woman carrying our things'. It was quite usual to stop and enquire of a 'common' person if he or she were ready to fetch this or to deliver that for a small fee. Servants could be severely treated, even in the relatively peaceful household of the Pepyses; Pepys sometimes beat his boy until his wrist hurt and Elizabeth was obliged 'to beat our little girl; and then we shut her down into the cellar, and there she lay all night'.

His adventures with women are well enough known. When he

was observed kissing a woman in the window of a winehouse, someone in the street called out, 'Sir, why do you kiss the gentle-woman so?' and threw a stone towards the window. He decided to join the congregation of St Dionis Backchurch after he had noticed that a 'very great store of fine women there is in this church'. He was always ogling and touching. One young lady, in the congrega-tion of another church, took some pins out of her pocket to prick him if he molested her. He wrote in code about his sexual encoun-ters; 'mi cosa naked', for example, was 'my bare penis'. He 'had his way' and 'got it', as he said, on many occasions. Yet he could be less demanding. 'I got into the coach where Mrs Knipp was, and got her upon my knee (the coach being full) and played with her breasts and sung.'

Violence in the streets was not uncommon. During one alterca-tion 'I did give him a good cuff or two on the chops; and seeing him not oppose me, I did give him another'. The constable and his watch were there to prevent mischief or riot; they once found Pepys's backyard door open 'and so came in to see what the matter was'.

Pepys often 'fell to cards'. Cards, and gaming in general, were the delight of the age; gambling was endemic in all classes of the society, and lotteries were used as a method of public finance. On one afternoon he paid 18 pence to join a 'coffee club' of the Rota that met in the Turk's Head Tavern in Gerrard Street; coffee-houses had come to London eight years before, and had immediately become a success among the merchants and lawyers of London. Yet the merchants and lawyers were not alone. Roger L'Estrange complained that 'every carman and porter is now a statesman, and indeed the coffee-houses are good for nothing else'. No regard was given to 'degrees or order' but in the coffee-house, according to Samuel Butler, the author of *Hudibras*, 'gentleman, mechanic, lord and scoundrel mix'.

In a city dominated by conversation and speculation, by news and gossip, they were the single most important venue of public recreation and of public information. London was characterized by its coffee-houses, and it became common to address letters to a citizen 'at the Grecian' or 'at the Rainbow'. Macaulay said that they almost became a political institution. Yet they were not wholly concerned with 'news piping hot'. On one visit Pepys 'sat long in good discourse with some gentlemen concerning the Roman empire'. At the end of 1664 he stepped into a coffee-house to taste the new drink of 'Jocolatte', 'very good'.

And then 'after dinner we had a pretty good singing and one, Hazard, sung alone after the old fashion'; music and song were everywhere. There were 'song rounds'. While he waited for a lawyer, 'I sat in his study singing'. Before he retired to his bed, he often played the lute. In one of the rooms of a coffee-house he heard a variety of Italian and Spanish songs as well as a canon for two voices on the words *domine salvum fac regem*. When he came for recreation to Epsom Wells he observed some townsmen, met by chance, singing together in company. Pepys and his young male servant were accustomed to sing psalms and motets together. During the time of the plague he hired a boat that already had a passenger, so that 'he and I sung together the way down'.

Like many of his contemporaries he seemed to have an open mind about the vagaries of faith and devotion. On one Sunday, 'I went out and looked into several churches'; if he liked the sermon he might stay until the end, but there were times when he slept through the oration. When the inventor Sir Samuel Morland and his wife entered a church with two footmen in livery the congregation took 'much notice of them', especially on 'going into their coach after sermon with great gazing'. He observed also 'that I see religion, be it what it will, is but a humour . . . and so the esteem of it passeth as other things do'. There was always room for superstition, however. He carried a hare's foot as a charm against illness, but a companion noticed that it did not have the proper 'join' in it. No sooner did he touch his friend's charm than 'my belly begin to be loose and to break wind'.

In pursuit of his duties at the Navy Office it was a matter of routine to accept gifts from various claimants to office or privileges. On one occasion he was offered in turn a rapier, a vessel of wine, a gown, and a silver hatband, in return for 'a courtesy'. His master, Mountagu, told him that 'in the meantime I will do you all the good jobs I can' for making money. He was eager to make a profit from the hiring of some ships for service in Tangiers; he received a share of the proceeds 'which I did not demand but did silently consent to it'. When he was handed a packet containing money, he emptied out a piece of gold and some pieces of silver, all the time averting his eyes so 'that I might say I saw no money in the paper if ever I should be questioned about it'. Commerce of every kind was the essence of the state, and Pepys was keen to acquire a good wife for his brother 'worth two hundred pounds in ready money'. He noted that at court all was 'lust and gain'.

He had some interesting encounters. He recorded how one gentleman had served eight different governments in one year, 1659, 'and he did name them all, and then failed unhappily in the ninth, viz that of the king's coming in'. He was beside the king when a Quaker woman delivered a petition to him; Charles argued with her, 'she replying still with these words, "O King!" and "thou'd" him all along'. He conversed with an experimenter, John Spong, who told him 'that by his microscope of his own making he doth discover that the wings of a moth is made just as the feathers of the wing of a bird'. While he and Spong were talking, several sectarians were arrested for attending a service at a conventicle. Pepys added that 'they go like lambs, without any resistance'. It was common for men and women to weep in this period, whether out of joy or sorrow.

This was an age of much observation and experiment. An acquaintance brought to his house one evening a 12-foot glass, through which they endeavoured to see the moon, Saturn and Jupiter. He met Robert Hooke in the street by chance, and the experimenter told him that he could estimate the number of strokes a fly made with its wings 'by the note that it answers to in music during their flying'. Pepys had previously attended a lecture by Hooke on the art of felt-making. While travelling by boat from Rotherhithe to Gravesend, he read Robert Boyle's *Hydrostatical Paradoxes*.

He noticed 'a fine rarity: of fishes kept in a glass of water'. When he purchased a watch he found it so marvellous that he kept it in his hand 'seeing what a-clock it is 100 times'. He visited the country house of a goldsmith, Sir Robert Viner, where 'he showed me a black boy that he had that died of a consumption; and being dead, he caused him to be dried in an oven, and lies there entire in a box'. Black servants, slaves brought back from West Africa, had become very fashionable.

On Thanksgiving Day, 14 August 1666, in celebration of a recent sea victory over the Dutch, family and friends were very merry 'flinging our fireworks and burning one another and the people over the way'. They then began 'smutting one another with candle-grease and soot, till most of us were like devils'. They drank, and danced, and dressed up. One man put on the clothes of the serving boy and danced a jig; Elizabeth Pepys and her female friends put on periwigs. Pepys sometimes observed that, where there was no company, there was little pleasure.

Some phrases are redolent of the period. 'He talked hog-high.' 'I am with child that . . .' or 'I am in pain for . . .' meant I am anxious and impatient to be told something or for an imminent event. Someone's antics 'would make a dog laugh'. 'I did laugh till I was ready to burst.' 'As she brews, let her bake.'

As he was writing, one winter night, a watchman came by with his bell under the window and cried out, 'Past one of the clock, and a cold, frosty, windy morning.' And so to bed.

39

And not dead yet?

The early hopes for Charles's reign had now faded. It had become clear enough that he was a very poor match for Oliver Cromwell, and the erstwhile cavaliers were bitterly hostile to a corrupt court and a mismanaged government; the revenues were misused while the king himself was at the gambling table with what John Evelyn described as 'vast heaps of gold squandered away in a vain and profuse manner'. The great questions of state and of religion were left unsettled in an atmosphere of squabbling, cynicism, corruption and faction-fighting; the only thing that the king's ministers shared was mutual hatred. The king did not have the patience or the intellect to formulate clear lines of policy or enunciate the ideas that might sustain them. He was reticent and secretive, ever intent upon concealing his opinions on men or on measures. Clarendon wrote to the duke of Ormonde in 1662 that 'the worst is, the king is as discomposed as ever, and looks as little after his business, which breaks my heart, and makes me and other of your friends weary of our lives'.

Yet Clarendon himself, the most loyal and substantial figure of the regime, was also under attack. In the autumn of 1662 it emerged that he had been the prime agent in the sale of Dunkirk to the French; it had been captured by Cromwell's men from the Spanish, but the one continental possession in English hands was now to be delivered to the nation's old enemy. There were good reasons for the sale; the port was costly to maintain and was in no way essential to the national interest, but its surrender (so it was called) was considered to be an act of betrayal. Clarendon was accused of accepting French bribes, and the great mansion he was then building in London was dubbed 'Dunkirk House'. The merchants in particular feared that Dunkirk would be used as a base for privateers intent upon seizing their ships; when the mobs of London grew restless at the news of the sale, the gates of the city were shut and double guards posted in various sensitive locations.

At the close of the year the king attempted to heal the religious divisions of the nation by making a 'declaration of indulgence' in which he expressed his regret at his failure to introduce 'a liberty for tender consciences'; he proposed to ask parliament to give him the power to dispense some of his subjects from the Act of Uniformity and to begin removing penal legislation directed at those Roman Catholics 'as shall live peaceably, modestly and without scandal'. It is the clearest possible evidence that he believed parliament had gone too far in imposing Anglican orthodoxy upon the realm. For this, he may also have blamed Clarendon. The lord chancellor was at the time crippled with gout and forced to keep to his house; he was in no position to object.

Yet the king's appeal was ignored. When the fourth session of the 'Cavalier Parliament' assembled in February 1663, the Commons refused to ratify the declaration. The king therefore was obliged to drop the matter and retire from a possible confrontation. It was in truth a significant failure, since he had proved himself unable to sustain the power of his royal prerogative in religious issues. In the spring of 1663 a new Militia Act was passed that reformed the local militia and placed them under the control of the lords-lieutenant of each county; they were given adequate funds, and were thus able to recruit more men for their service. It was reported that the measure was necessary to combat the continual threat of conspiracy and sedition, but it was feared by some that the king might use the troops for other purposes.

The navy rather than the army, however, was the priority. When parliament resumed once more in the spring of 1664 one of its first measures was a declaration or 'trade resolution' against the Dutch, complaining that 'the subjects of the United Provinces' had invaded the king's rights in India, Africa and elsewhere by attacking English merchants and had committed 'damages, affronts and injuries' closer to home. It was believed that the Dutch wished to establish a trade monopoly throughout the known world, which was as dangerous as the 'universal monarchy' sought by Louis XIV.

The republic was therefore seen as a threat to English ships and to English commerce, but of course its very existence as a republic could be interpreted as an essential menace to the kingdom of England. The religion of the enemy was Calvinist in temper, and it was feared that the Dutch would support the cause of their co-religionists in England; they could thereby sow dissension against the king and the national faith. The 'trade resolution' was an aspect of the Anglican royalism asserted both by Lords and Commons. The fervour of the Commons, in particular, was matched by their actions. They agreed to raise the unprecedented sum of £2.5 million to assist the king in his prosecution of hostilities.

The formal declaration of war came, in February 1665, after months of preparation. The cause seems to have been largely popular, as far as such matters can be ascertained, particular among those merchants and speculators who would benefit from the embarrassment of Dutch trade; one of these was the king's brother, James, duke of York. He led the Royal Africa Company that specialized in the business of slavery, and he invested in other commercial ventures. The conflict has therefore been described as the first purely commercial war in English history. As one hemp merchant, Captain Cocke, put it, 'the trade of the world is too little for us two, therefore one must go down'.

A great victory was won at Lowestoft in the beginning of June under the leadership of the duke of York, when twenty-six Dutch vessels were seized or sunk. Each fleet would sail past the other firing its guns into the enemy's hull and rigging until one or more ships 'broke the line', in which case the disabled vessels would be boarded or sunk with fire-ships. The two sides 'knocked it out', in the phrase of the time, for several hours.

The sound of the guns was heard even in London, and in an essay John Dryden recalled that 'the noise of the cannon from both navies reached our ears about the city, so that all men being alarmed with it, and in a dreadful suspense about the event which we knew was then deciding, everyone went following the sound as his fancy led him . . .' The success would have been even greater if a courtier, while the duke of York was asleep in his cabin, had not called off the pursuit of the remaining ships, whether for fear of waking him, or of engaging once more with the enemy, is not known. In any case the momentum of the victory was not maintained in the wider war.

In August a squadron of English ships attacked a merchant convoy, but was beaten back. In the same month the fleet under the command of the earl of Sandwich was held off the Suffolk coast as a result of poor victualling, and then spent the next few weeks chasing Dutch ships through storm and rain. Some were captured but, when the prizes were dispersed among the flag officers, charges of fraud and theft were made against Sandwich; he never really managed to refute them, and the navy itself seemed complicit in corruption. The earl was deprived of his command and sent as an ambassador to Spain. Later in the year, when the English ships were laid up for repair, some Dutch vessels appeared at the mouth of the Thames and commenced a blockade; it was dispersed only when disease, and lack of supplies, forced them to return home. The blockade, however, had compounded the problems of high taxes and uncertain business that already beset the merchants. Overseas trade had been seriously set back by the war on the high seas, and the Baltic trade shrank away almost to nothing; woollen manufacture, the staple of England's exports, was similarly depressed. A war fought for trade had become a war fatal to trade.

Yet already a greater threat had emerged in the streets of London. In his diary entry for 7 June 1665, 'the hottest day that ever I felt in my life', Samuel Pepys noted that

> This day, much against my will, I did in Drury Lane see two or three houses marked with a red cross upon the doors, and 'Lord have mercy upon us' writ there – which was a sad sight to me, being the first of the kind that to my remembrance I ever saw. It put me into an ill conception of myself and my smell, so that I was forced to buy some roll tobacco to smell to and chew – which took away the apprehension.

The plague had come back to London; houses infected with the distemper were shut up, the victims still often within, and a red cross 1 foot in height was painted on the doors. Pepys had purchased tobacco as a medical precaution.

So began a time of peril and great fear. The first signs of the disease were 'tokens' of discoloured skin; after three or four days 'buboes' or carbuncles erupted over the body and, if they did not suppurate, death was certain. Many victims were tied to the bed in the event of frenzy.

The 'dead carts' or 'pest carts' trundled through the lanes and alleys with their burden of corpses to be discharged in one of the many pits dug for the purpose; it is reported that in their misery some of the living flung themselves among the piles of the dead. Some lay dead, or dying, in the streets. Others fled wailing to the fields around London. Some people locked themselves away, and those that ventured outside looked on one another fearfully. 'And not dead yet?' 'And still alive?' Some, desperate beyond fear, sang and danced and drank in promiscuous gatherings. Others fell into a stupor of despair. It was whispered that demons in human shape wandered abroad; they were known as 'hollow men', and those that they struck soon died.

Prophets and fanatics roamed the streets bawling out threats and warnings. One of them, walking naked with a pan of burning coals on his head, invoked the judgement of God on the sinful city. Through the searingly hot months of July and August the fury of the plague rose ever higher. The principal thoroughfares were all but overgrown with grass. In September fires of sea-coal, one fire for every twelve houses, were kept burning in the streets for three days and nights. Yet they had no effect. As many as 10,000 fatalities were listed each week in the bills of mortality. It seemed that soon enough the city would be empty. But by the beginning of December the sickness abated, and the new year witnessed a return of many London families who had fled in panic. It was estimated that 100,000 had died.

The new year, 1666, was one of ill omen. The number had long been considered significant, heralding perhaps the coming of the Antichrist; for some it signified fire and apocalypse. In its Latin form, 'MDCLXVI', it is unique for including every Roman numeral once and in reverse sequence. The solar eclipse at the beginning of July, in this year, convinced many that the end of days was coming.

The prognostications elsewhere were not good. The king of France had signed a defensive treaty with the Dutch and, at the beginning of the year, he declared war upon England. In truth he did not do much for the benefit of his new ally, but his intervention increased public anxiety about the conduct of hostilities. There was no money and the lord high treasurer, the 4th earl of Southampton, asked Samuel Pepys, clerk of the naval board, 'What would you have me do? I have given all I can for my life. Why will people not lend their money? Why will they not trust the king as well as Oliver?' The reference to Cromwell's success is interesting. The nation had received no benefit, and acquired no material gains, from these inconclusive and inglorious battles against the Dutch.

They were in any case still a formidable enemy. A battle at the beginning of June off the Flemish and English coasts lasted for four days, and at the end of it the English had lost twice as many ships and men as their rivals; the two sides had fought each other to exhaustion and, as one English commander put it, 'they were as glad to be quit of us as we of them'. It was a desperate and bloody fight, leaving 6,000 Englishmen dead. Many of them were found floating in the seas wearing their dark 'Sunday clothes'; they had previously been taken by the press-gangs on leaving church.

News then came, a week later, that the French had taken over the colonial possession of St Kitts. Louis XIV had decided to take a more active part in the maritime struggle and ordered his fleet to sea. The melancholy aspect of affairs convinced many that the government and the king were about to fall. A battle in late July was the occasion for some celebration, however, after the English fleet had pursued the fleeing Dutch over the North Sea for some thirty-six hours. The cry that had gone up before the engagement was: 'If we do not beat them now, we shall never do it!' But all of the participants were growing weary of a war that would last for another year.

London was not spared further horror. After the disaster of the plague, a small chimney fire at a bakery in Pudding Lane began a conflagration that would envelop most of the city. It was the very beginning of September 1666, after an unusually hot August had left the thatch and timber of the city bone dry; the fire was carried by strong south-east winds towards London Bridge and Fish Street.

It burned steadily towards the west, and John Evelyn noted that 'the noise and cracking and thunder of the impetuous flames, the shrieking of women and children, the hurry of people, the fall of towers, houses and churches, was like an hideous storm, and the air all about so hot and inflamed that at the last one was not able to approach it'. The molten lead from the roof of St Paul's ran through the streets, according to John Evelyn, 'glowing with fiery redness'. The Guildhall stood immured in flame like a burning coal. The people took to the water or fled to the fields in the north of the city, seeking safety from the burning drops that rained down upon them. The smoke now stretched for 50 miles. Yet not everyone ran in terror. The royal brothers, Charles and James, took an active part in exhorting, and even joining, those who were trying to contain the engulfing fires.

The fire abated after three days, having consumed five-sixths of the city and leaving a trail of destruction and desolation a mile and a half in length and half a mile in breadth. When John Evelyn clambered among the ruins, the ground still hot beneath his feet, he often did not know where he was. Yet the vitality of the city was not seriously harmed. The usual round of trade and commerce was established again within a year, and the work of rebuilding in brick and stone began; within two years of the Great Fire 1,200 houses had been constructed, and in the following year another 1,600. By 1677 most of the city was once again in place. It was said that it rose almost as quickly as it fell.

The year of ill omen, however, seemed to have fulfilled its destiny. In the month after the fire parliament reassembled in a state of gloom and anxiety. Rumours of conspiracy, by the French and Dutch, were everywhere. The Catholics, and the Quakers, were also blamed. One of those returned to parliament, Roger Pepys, cousin to Samuel, predicted that 'we shall all be ruined very speedily'. A general fast was imposed upon the nation as a penance for what John Evelyn described as 'our prodigious ingratitude, burning lusts, dissolute court, profane and abominable lives'. In the same period the king ordained that all French fashions should be banished from the court and that in their place a simple 'Persian' coat and tunic were to be worn; it was supposed to be a gesture towards thrift but it was essentially a token of his flippancy. The style was in any case soon abandoned.

After much debate, and intense scrutiny of the accounts provided by the Navy Board, the king was voted sufficient funds to fight another year of war; yet there was intense wrangling about the means of furnishing them. Should it be a hearth tax or a poll tax? Nobody seemed to know. As they talked and debated it was rumoured that the French were preparing an invasion, but this was discounted as a government ploy to hasten a decision.

The assessment was finally passed in the middle of January 1667, but of course the revenues were not collected. In the following month the Navy Board declared to the duke of York that 'we are conscious of an utter incapacity to perform what his majesty and your royal highness seem to look for from us'. The shipyards were laid up without supplies or repairs. The seamen, deprived of pay and even of the necessities of life, were provoked to riot on several occasions. The City refused to lend money, and the treasury was exhausted.

It was time for peace. The king and his council had tentatively begun the process of negotiation with the Dutch, and Charles himself was at the same time engaged in private negotiations with the French king; they had no reason to fight against each other, and it was eventually agreed that they should abstain from mutual hostilities. Charles also trusted that his fellow sovereign would be able to persuade or bully his Dutch allies into signing a similar agreement. Charles and Louis had sent their letters through Henrietta Maria, respectively mother and paternal aunt of the two men; the English king kept the matter secret from even his most intimate councillors, thus emphasizing his propensity for clandestine dealings.

In the meantime, to save expenditure, the privy council had no choice but to reduce the scale of naval operations; only a 'summer guard' of ships would be sent to sea in order to protect the merchant vessels. It was also believed that, given the increasingly futile nature of the war, hostilities were about to be suspended. This incapacity led directly to one of the most humiliating episodes in English naval history.

At the beginning of May 1667, a great conference between the warring parties was called at Breda; it soon became clear to the Dutch, however, that the English were not prepared to be over-generous in the negotiations. So they decided to try force for the final time to extort concessions and to hasten the progress of the discussions. In the following month, therefore, they launched a raid into the Thames estuary; they broke the defences of the harbour at Chatham and proceeded to burn four ships before towing away the largest ship of the fleet, the *Royal Charles*, and returning with it undamaged.

Panic ran through the streets of London. It was said that the Dutch were coming, and the trained bands were called out for the city's defence. In truth the enemy fleet could have found its way to London Bridge without much difficulty. It was reported that Harwich, Colchester and Dover were already burned. The reports were false but the events at Chatham were a symbolic, as well as a naval, disaster. One parliamentarian, John Rushworth, wrote that 'the people are ready to tear their hairs off their heads'. Sir William Batten, surveyor of the navy, exclaimed, 'By God! I think the devil shits Dutchmen!'

The Dutch now pressed their advantage and the king, humiliated at home and abroad, conceded some of their demands. The principle of negotiation was that of '*uti possidetis*', by means of which the parties retained possession of that which they had taken by force in the course of conflict. As a result, England lost much of the West Indies to France and the invaluable island of nutmeg, Run, part of Indonesia, to the Dutch. In return, however, it retained New Netherland; this was the colonial province of the Netherlands that included the future states of New York, New Jersey, Delaware and Connecticut. Yet at the time the gains did not match the loss of national prestige.

After the disaster at Chatham talk of corruption and conspiracy was once more in the air; some blamed the papists, and others even blamed the bishops. It was said that, at the time of the Dutch raid, the king was chasing a moth in the apartments of Lady Castlemaine. It was supposed by many that the nation was so mismanaged by the king that it would once more turn against the Stuarts and become a republic. Charles was the subject of distrust as well as dislike, and it was feared that he was colluding with Louis XIV in some popish plot to impose absolute rule. At times of peril and disaster, fear is contagious.

Yet opinion turned in particular against Clarendon who was,

quite unfairly, accused of mismanaging the war; he had in fact opposed it from the start, but he was a convenient scapegoat. He had always been disliked by the men and women about the king – whom John Evelyn described as 'the buffoons and the *misses*' – while an attempt to impeach him had already been made by the earl of Bristol in the Lords. But the chancellor was now in infinitely greater danger. It was being said that the king had turned against him. Charles disliked being lectured or patronized; serious men in any case made him feel uncomfortable. It was not that Clarendon annoyed the king; he bored him. He was disliked by parliament for his fervent support of the prerogative power of the king, and by dissenters for his equally vehement espousal of the established Church. Gilbert Burnet, the historian of his own time, wrote that 'he took too much upon him and meddled in everything, which was his greatest error'.

The enemies of Clarendon now gathered for the kill. His wife had died early in August, and his obvious grief incapacitated him from robustly defending himself. His absence from the privy council encouraged other councillors to speak against him; the king was told that Clarendon prevented the advice of others from reaching him and that he had denied any freedom of debate within the council chamber itself. Thus all the ills of the kingdom could, in one form or another, be blamed upon him. If he was removed, the hostility towards the administration might abate. Certainly his departure would gratify the Commons that had long despised him; it might help to lighten the mood of the next session.

In the middle of August the king sent the duke of York to the lord chancellor with the request that he resign his office. Clarendon unwisely refused and a week later, on 25 August, a more peremptory demand came that he should surrender the seals of office forthwith. Again, Clarendon refused. The affair was the sole news of the court, and it had become necessary for Charles to assert his authority against this overweening councillor. The king demanded the seals, in redoubled fury, and they were at last returned.

The king told one of Clarendon's allies, the duke of Ormonde, that 'his behaviour and humour was grown so unsupportable to myself, and to all the world else, that I could no longer endure it, and it was impossible for me to live with it, and do those things with the parliament that must be done or the government will be lost'. Yet the affair may not be as straightforward as that. Pepys was told that there were many explanations 'not fit to mention'. The king may genuinely have believed that the lord chancellor was no longer capable of service, but there are suggestions that in some way Clarendon had interfered with his love-life; he seems to have been instrumental, for example, in the sudden marriage of one of the king's mistresses. It is impossible now to untangle the myriad webs of court intrigue.

The pack was in full pursuit of Clarendon, now that royal favour had fallen away, and it was believed that the king had become very interested in his former confidant's prosecution. The charges brought against Clarendon by the Commons included illegal imprisonment of various suspects, the intention of imposing military rule, and the sale of Dunkirk to the French. Since the lord chancellor had always been an advocate of arbitrary government, the charges may have been in large measure true. The Lords, however, resolved that Clarendon could not be committed; they seem to have concluded that one of their own members should not be impeached on a whim of the lower house. The king wondered aloud why his once chief minister was still in the country, and by the end of November it was rumoured that he would pick a tribunal of peers prepared to try Clarendon and execute him. The earl now heeded the advice of those closest to him and secretly took ship for France where he began an exile in the course of which he would write perhaps the most interesting history of his times.

It is now pertinent to note that after the forced abdication of the lord chancellor the administration of the king's affairs became ever more murky and corrupt. In the absence of Clarendon the senior councillors were now Clifford, Arlington, Buckingham, Ashley Cooper and Lauderdale, whose initials spelled out 'cabal'; for ever afterwards, the word was employed to designate secretive and self-interested administration. They were an alphabetical coalition, and in truth they can now be seen as mere ciphers in the game of politics; their policies brought nothing about, and their principal object was to make as much money as they could from their period of office before the wheel turned. Clifford, in particular, was known as 'the Bribe Master General'.

They suited the king, however, because he could manipulate them. George Savile, the 1st marquess of Halifax, wrote that 'he lived with his ministers as he did with his mistresses; he used them, but he was not in love with them'. The king was now in charge of all affairs and, without the interference of Clarendon, he could bend and twist in whichever way he wished. So arose one of the most devious and inconsistent periods of English history.

In the beginning the acknowledged first minister was George Villiers, 2nd duke of Buckingham, described by Gilbert Burnet as one who was 'never true either to things or persons, but forsakes every man and departs from every maxim, sometimes out of levity and unsettledness of fancy and sometimes out of downright false-hood'. This was a fit companion for a king. He had already emerged as one of the circle of wits at court, but now he had ambitions to be a statesman as well as a satirist.

He was the son of the ill-fated 1st duke, assassinated by John Felton at the beginning of the reign of Charles I. He was thereafter brought up in the royal household in the company of Charles II, and had shared many exploits with the young king; he had fought beside him at Worcester. His rise after the fall of Clarendon was still remarkable, however, he having previously only obtained the rank of Master of the Horse. The king consulted him on all matters of importance, and the foreign ambassadors generally applied to him for advice before being admitted to the king's presence.

If Buckingham had one abiding principle, it was that of religious toleration; he had so many religious whims and fancies of his own that he was happy to allow freedom of thought to others. The nonconformists were in any case now in a more secure position than before. Fears of a papist court and of a papist queen, and a prevailing belief that the 'Great Fire of London' had been concocted by Roman Catholics in the service of France, gave sectarians and dissenters a novel air of loyalty and trustworthiness.

Quakers began to meet in London, and soon enough monthly assemblies were in place all over the country; they were safer now than at any previous time. The Baptists of Bristol regathered. The Conventicle Act of 1664 was effectively dead, and was formally abolished in 1668. Certain Presbyterian ministers prepared the ground for a separate Church if they could not be assimilated within the established one. At the sessions and assizes of the realm Catholic recusants, rather than nonconformists, were presented for judgement.

The bishop of Norwich preached a sermon in 1666 in which he declared that 'it is an honour which learned men owe to one another to allow liberty of dissent in matters of mere opinion'. That liberty was already apparent in the survival of Brownists, Fifth Monarchy men, Sabbatarians, Muggletonians, Ranters, Anabaptists, General Baptists, Particular Baptists and Familists. We may invoke the words of John Bunyan, 'I preached what I felt, what I smartingly did feel.' They were perhaps not a force to challenge the popular Anglicanism of the high-church party, but the once stringent laws against them were now unenforced or only hesitantly invoked. A contemporary tract, *Discourse of the Religion of England, 1667*, observed that nonconformists were 'spread through city and country; they make no small part of all ranks and all sorts of men. They are not excluded from the nobility, among the gentry they are not a few; but none are more important than they in the trading part of the people.' That is why London was a city of dissent.

From this period, then, we can trace the emergence of the doctrine known as Latitudinarianism that propounded comprehension and tolerance in all matters of doctrine and practice. The 'Latitude men', as they were known, emphasized the power of reason as 'the candle of the Lord' and believed that such matters as liturgy and ritual were 'things indifferent'. This might be said to be the unwritten principle of eighteenth-century Anglicanism. God, and Christianity, were no longer mysterious.

40

The true force

In the early autumn of 1664 a young scholar visited Stourbridge Fair, just outside Cambridge, where he purchased a prism; he took the instrument back to his lodging at Trinity College where 'having darkened my chamber, and made a small hole in my window shuts, to let in a convenient quantity of the sun's light, I placed my prism at his entrance, that it might be thereby refracted to the opposite wall'. By these means did Isaac Newton experiment with 'the celebrated phenomena of colours'.

In this year, too, he also experimented upon himself. He inserted a bodkin or large needle 'betwixt my eye and the bone as near to the backside of my eye as I could'; at the risk of blinding himself, he wished to alter the curve of his retina and observe the results. These were the preliminary steps to his theory of colour that would revolutionize the discipline of optics; it was he who made the discovery that white light was not some primary or basic hue but a mixture of all the other colours in the spectrum. The conclusion was so contrary to the principles of common sense that no one had ever considered it before.

So began the career of the most remarkable mathematicians of the seventeenth century and one who, more than anyone else, has shaped the perceptions of the modern world. The scientists of NASA, in the United States, still use the calculations of Isaac

Newton. The two years after he purchased the prism at Stourbridge Fair were his years of glory, during which he penetrated the mysteries of light and gravitation. The story of the falling apple may or may not be accurate but it is true enough that, at the age of twenty-three, he began his exploration of the enigma of that force which held the world and universe together. John Maynard Keynes was to call him 'the last of the magicians'.

The time came when he was obliged to enter the public world of seventeenth-century science and, at the end of 1671, he allowed his 6-inch reflecting telescope to be displayed to the Fellows of the Royal Society. Newton had made the instrument himself, fashioning his own tools for the purpose, and it was taken in triumph to Charles II, who marvelled at it. Newton was duly elected a Fellow of the Royal Society, to which institution he was attached for the rest of his life.

The Royal Society may be deemed to be the jewel of Charles II's reign. At the end of November 1660, a group of physicians and natural scientists announced the formation of a 'college for the promoting of physic-mathematical experimental learning'; they were in part inspired by Francis Bacon's vision of 'Solomon's House' in *The New Atlantis*, and they shared Bacon's passion for experimental and inductive science. They were men of a practical and pragmatic temper, with a concomitant interest in agriculture as well as naviga-tion, manufactures as well as medicine. All questions of politics or religion were excluded from the deliberations of the Fellows, and indeed their pursuit of practical enquiry was in part designed to quell the 'enthusiasm' and to quieten the spiritual debates that had helped to foment the late civil wars. They met each week, at Gresham College in Bishopsgate, where papers were read on the latest inven-tion or experiment. It was in their company that Sir Isaac Newton first propounded his revolutionary theories of light.

The last four decades of the seventeenth century in fact witnessed an extraordinary growth in scientific experiment to the extent that, in 1667, the historian of the Royal Society, Thomas Sprat, could already celebrate the fact that 'an universal zeal towards the advance-ments of such designs has not only overspread our court and universities, but the shops of our mechanicks, the fields of our gentlemen, the cottages of our farmers, and the ships of our merchants'.

An enquiring and inventive temper was now more widely shared, whereby the whole field of human knowledge became the subject of speculation. The Fellows of the Royal Society debated a method of producing wind by means of falling water; they explored the sting of a bee and the feet of flies; they were shown a baroscope that measured changes in the pressure of the air and a hygroscope for detecting water in the atmosphere; they set up an enquiry into the state of English agriculture and surveyed the methods of tin-mining in Cornwall. They conducted experiments on steam, on ventilation, on gases and on magnetism; thermometers, pumps and perpetual motion machines were brought before them. The origins of the industrial and agricultural 'revolutions', conventionally located in the eighteenth century, are to be found in the previous age. In the seventeenth century, providentially blessed by the genius of Francis Bacon at its beginning, we find a general desire for what Sprat described as 'the true knowledge of things'.

At a meeting of the society in the early months of 1684 Edmund Halley, Christopher Wren and Robert Hooke were discussing the dynamics of planetary motion. Halley put a question to them. Could the force that keeps the planets moving around the sun decrease as an inverse square of its distance? Wren and Hooke agreed that this was very likely, but no one had as yet been able to prove the point. So Halley travelled to Cambridge, where he consulted Newton on the problem of the sun and the revolving planets. Newton readily concurred in Halley's hypothesis.

'How do you know this?'

'Why, I have calculated it.'

This was a reply that, as in Halley's words, struck him 'with joy and amazement'. No one had ever done it before. By the end of the year Newton had revisited his calculations and had produced a short treatise, *De motu corporum in gyrum*, that deciphered and proved mathematically the motion of bodies in orbit. He pressed on with his deliberations and, within the space of eighteen months, had completed the treatise that would confer upon him the acclamation of the world. He formulated the three laws of motion that are the foundation of his theory of universal gravitation, a revolutionary principle that proclaims the universe to be bound together by one force that can be mathematically promulgated and understood. It was the great revelation of the seventeenth century. Newton had understood the cosmos, and made it amenable to human laws. There was indeed a force that bound the sun and all the stars. 'It is now established', he wrote, 'that this force is gravity, and therefore we shall call it gravity from now on.'

Newton was eventually chosen to become president of the Royal Society and for the last twenty years of his life governed its meetings with a somewhat forbidding dignity. He ruled that there should be no 'whispering, talking nor loud laughters. If dissensions rose in any sort . . . they tended to find out truth, but ought not to arise to any personality.' These were to be the new truths of science, objective and impersonal, as adumbrated in seventeenth-century London. One Fellow, William Stukeley, recalled that 'everything was transacted with great attention and solemnity and decency' for in truth this was the century in which science became a new form of religion with its laws and principles treated as matters of unassailable dogma. Newton himself declared that natural philosophy now 'consists in discovering the frame and operations of Nature and reducing them, as far as may be, to general rules or laws, establishing these rules by observations and experiments, and thence deducing the causes and effects of things'. This is our inheritance from the seventeenth century.

41

Hot news

The casual deviousness of the king soon became apparent when at the beginning of 1668 he negotiated a 'Triple Alliance' with the Dutch republic and Sweden to oppose the French armies that had already occupied part of the Spanish Netherlands; it was a general defensive league against the encroaching power of the French and, at the time, it was regarded as a great stroke of policy. It was considered to be better to be allied with two Protestant powers against a common Catholic enemy. It was, more pertinently, meant to prove to Louis XIV that England still possessed significant influence in the game between the states.

Yet the king wrote to his sister residing at the French court, Henrietta, duchess of Orléans, that 'I have done nothing to prejudice France in the agreement'. Even as he allied himself with the Dutch, in fact, he was preparing to move ever closer to France in a secret plan to destroy their republic. He had the ability to pursue two different, and indeed opposing, policies at the same time. Feeling great admiration for his cousin, Louis XIV, he also needed the French king's money and perhaps, in some future contingency, his men. Louis ruled the most powerful state in Europe, and it was much better to be his ally than his enemy; he was also part of the family and, in dynastic terms, family was more important than country.

Suspicion was in the air. Pepys reported that in London 'people do cry out in the streets . . . that we are betrayed by people about the king and shall be delivered up to the French'. In the 'bawdy-house riots' of the spring, the apprentices of London revised the ancient custom of attacking brothels on Shrove Tuesday. But this was no ritual performance; fifteen of their leaders would be tried for high treason, and four of them were hanged. The demonstrations involved thousands of people, and lasted for five days.

The riots began on Easter Monday when some brothels in Poplar were attacked and demolished; the insurrection spread on the following day to Moorfields, East Smithfield and Holborn. On Wednesday the apprentices, swelled by an appreciable force from Southwark, attacked the bawdy-houses of Moorfields. They did not form an inchoate crowd: they were mustered into regiments and marched behind flags; they carried iron bars and axes. Some of the more notorious prisons were also besieged.

The king himself professed not to understand the motive of the apprentices in attacking the brothels. 'Why, why, do they go to them, then?' he is reported to have asked. But in fact the brothels were a sign, or token, of what was for many a larger problem. In attacking the brothels the Londoners were attacking the perceived morals of the court and, in opposing its morals, they were disowning its principles. One of their cries was that 'ere long they would come and pull Whitehall down'.

The king's favourite mistress, Lady Castlemaine, had converted to Roman Catholicism at the end of 1663. She was a sign, therefore, of the court's leaning towards papistry and was a target of much virulent comment as a 'whore' and worse. That is another reason why the brothels were attacked. The bishops were also condemned for keeping mistresses, and the archbishop of Canterbury was rumoured to retain a prostitute; other prelates were 'given to boys'. When the apprentices called out for 'reformation' they were giving voice to the pleas of the dissenters who distrusted or hated the established Church.

So sexual laxity was associated with papistry, and papistry with treason, and treason with the king of France. It was an unstable compound of rumour and fear, but all the more potent for that. The rioters could not have discerned the king's secret purposes but, in their distrust, they were in fact close to the truth. Soon after the formation of the 'Triple Alliance' Buckingham entered negotiations with the duchess of Orléans in France. Charles meanwhile apologized to the French envoy for having entered the treaty with Holland and Sweden insinuating that he would like to establish a much closer union with Louis. In the spring of 1668 the king decided to prorogue parliament for what turned out to be the unprecedented period of seventeen months; in its absence he might more easily plot and plan.

At the beginning of 1669 he sprang a surprise. He called his brother, James, and three of his most important councillors to his private chamber where with tears in his eyes he announced his desire for conversion to the Catholic faith. His brother was soon to be received into that communion, and would remain a staunch and indeed almost hysterical Catholic for the rest of his life. The honesty and fidelity of the king are more doubtful. If Charles was preparing himself for negotiations with the devout French king, what could be better than to declare his espousal of the same religion?

A secret emissary was sent to the French court in March with the offer of an offensive and defensive alliance together with a request for men, money and ships in the event of a war with the Dutch. Charles also promised to declare himself a Catholic if, in return, Louis XIV would give him the sum of £200,000 to secure himself against public wrath. He never did make any such announcement, and it seems that he was converted only on his deathbed; he was adept at the arts of dissimulation and hypocrisy even in the great affairs of state.

Throughout this year, and the first half of the next, negotiations between the two kings continued in absolute secrecy. The English ambassador in Paris, and the French ambassador in London, were not informed. Charles's anti-Catholic ministers were not told. The king continued negotiations with the Dutch as if nothing in the world had changed. By late summer or early autumn 1669, Charles and Louis reached agreement. Louis would come to Charles's aid whenever the English king announced his Catholicism, and the two would join together in an assault upon the Dutch.

Henrietta, duchess of Orléans, arrived at Dover in the middle of May 1670, with diverse documents from the French court that she gave to her brother. Among these was a secret paragraph which read that 'the king of England, being convinced of the truth of the Roman Catholic religion, is resolved to declare it, and to reconcile himself with the Church of Rome as soon as the state of his country's affairs permit'. Charles hoped and believed that the majority of his subjects had such affection for him that they would not protest 'but as there are unquiet spirits who mask their designs under the guise of religion, the king of England, for the peace of his kingdom, will avail himself of the assistance of the king of France'. The king was still engaged in subterfuge against his most intimate councillors. He allowed Buckingham, for example, to negotiate a version of the treaty that did not contain this important paragraph concerning the king's conversion to Roman Catholicism. Instead he was asked to press on with a treaty of alliance that made no mention of the secret. He was not aware of the collusion. It is unlikely that Charles ever had any intention of announcing his conversion, however, and the commitment was in large part a ploy to bind the French king more tightly to him.

The financial reward granted to the king was not large. He was to be paid £140,000 – half in advance – as a token of the French king's favour. He was also to be paid approximately £210,000 during each year of the proposed war with the Dutch, with the first instalment to be sent to him three months before the actual declaration of hostilities. The king of England had become a pensionary of the king of France, and had in effect sold his sovereignty. Another difficulty was apparent. If the French king should ever release into the world the secret paragraph, Charles's hold over his subjects might be destroyed; so Louis had a potent weapon in any confrontation with his fellow sovereign.

The counterfeit treaty was signed towards the close of the year, while the secret agreement reached earlier in the spring was not revealed even to the king's confidants. The alliance with Louis against the Dutch, however, could not be concealed for ever. The popular sentiment against France was already very strong, and the Venetian ambassador commented that 'although the king may join France, his subjects will not follow him'. A rumour was spread that French agents were kidnapping English children to take their blood as a cure for Louis's supposed leprosy. It was clear to the king's men that, if there was to be a war with the Dutch, it would have to be very short and very successful before public anger turned against them.

Yet how was any proposed war to be financed? In the intervals between various recesses and prorogations, parliament voted only modest supplies. The French pension itself was not over-generous. The king's own hereditary revenues were all pledged to repay old debts but, as a sign of boldness or desperation, it was determined to postpone the repayment of all those loans. This became known as 'the stop', imposed on 2 January 1672. All payments due from the exchequer were cancelled, so that incoming revenues could be spent upon the preparations for war.

The principal victims were the goldsmiths operating as bankers, who in turn passed on the loss and refused to discharge to their clients the cash they held on deposit. It seemed that 'the stop' might also soon be put to trade itself. Yet another casualty, however, was the king, who at a stroke lost credibility; the financial probity of the government was severely undermined and it was not at all clear that anyone would lend to it again. One contemporary confided to his diary that the decision 'will amaze all men and ruin thousands'.

In the spring of 1672, the French declared war on the Dutch; Charles immediately followed their example, and justified hostilities by citing the attempts of the republic to supplant English trade and to harass English traders. He also mentioned the fact that he was personally insulted by Dutch caricatures and publications. Two days before the call to war, Charles had honoured another undertaking to Louis by issuing a 'declaration of indulgence' that included his Catholic subjects. The nonconformists were granted complete freedom of worship while the Roman Catholic 'recusants' were permitted to worship in their private houses. It was a signal use of the royal prerogative at a time when parliament was not in session. Licences to hold public meetings were now generously and variously distributed to the nonconformists. John Bunyan was one of those released from prison. It may also have occurred to dissenters and Catholics that their new religious liberties now depended upon royal favour.

The measure could also have been designed to assist the king's brother, who had recently been received into the Catholic communion.

James, duke of York, by his own account, had been converted after reading certain tracts for and against the Roman faith; he also perused church histories and came to the conclusion that none of the English reformers 'had power to do what they did'. His faith was a matter of conviction and principle; for his brother it was a question of expediency.

It was said by the earl of Arlington that the 'declaration of indulgence' was so intended 'that we might keep all quiet at home while we are busy abroad'. Yet hostilities had already begun. In the middle of March an English squadron attempted to detain and board a rich Dutch fleet of merchant vessels on its way home from Smyrna and Malaga. Its commander had been warned in advance, however, and was accompanied by a convoy that allowed him to elude the English enemy. It was a humiliation for Charles, who had also been deprived of the treasure he had hoped to capture. The affair did not bode well for the greater war.

The duke of York had been appointed as lord high admiral, but Charles played a large part in preparing and arming the fleet. In the early summer of 1672 an inconclusive battle took place near Sole Bay, off the coast of Suffolk, in which both sides claimed success. Since the original plan of the English was to sail across the North Sea and blockade the Dutch in their home ports, they could hardly be described as the victors. It was clear enough that this would be no easy fight for the seas. The French fleet, ostensibly present to aid their allies, had played no part in the battle and thus earned the angry rebukes of the English; soon enough, in popular opinion, the French would be far more hated than the Dutch. John Evelyn observed in his diary entry for 27 June that the inconclusive battle 'showed the folly of hazarding so brave a fleet, and losing so many good men, for no provocation but that the Hollanders exceeded us in industry, and in all things but envy'.

The armies of Louis XIV had more success. They poured across the Rhine in the first two weeks of June and attacked the territories of the United Provinces; there seemed no possibility of withstanding their advance, and some of the principal cities were obliged to open their gates to the invaders. The fires from the French camps could be seen from Amsterdam. Of the seven republics of the United Provinces, only Holland and Zealand remained unconquered. At this perilous juncture the Dutch opened their dykes and flooded the country to prevent any further French advance. The land war came to a peremptory halt.

Charles had asked for a further £1 million from the French king, for the maintenance of the war, but Louis had refused. So Charles had no choice but to recall parliament in the hope of obtaining funds. Parliament returned in February 1673. In its absence a war had been declared and a declaration of religious indulgence had been issued. It might have seemed superfluous to requirements, except that it knew its power over the raising of money. The king had hoped to meet its members after a successful campaign against the Dutch, but that possibility had been removed.

A new lord chancellor had become the king's official spokesman in the lords. The earl of Shaftesbury would soon become the most controversial man in the kingdom but, in these years, he was one of the most vigorous supporters of the royal prerogative; Charles would eventually describe him as 'the weakest and wickedest man of the age' but at this time he relied upon his judgement as an administrator and adviser. Shaftesbury had been an enthusiastic supporter of Oliver Cromwell, and even a member of the Barebone's Parliament, but by dint of eloquence and industry he had managed to exorcize his interesting past. He would in turn inspire one of the most powerful pieces of satirical verse when he was denounced by John Dryden in *Absalom and Achitophel*:

> For close designs, and crooked counsels fit;
> Sagacious, bold and turbulent of wit:
> Restless, unfixt in principles and place;
> In pow'r unpleas'd, impatient of disgrace.
> A fiery soul which, working out its way,
> Fretted the pigmy-body to decay.

Parliament met in an unsettled and fractious mood. It was angry in particular that the king had seen fit to issue a declaration of religious indulgence without obtaining its consent; his action was deemed to be unconstitutional. Parliament was not necessarily opposed to the Dutch war but, if it was to vote supplies for the continuation of hostilities, its authority must be reasserted. The Commons then passed a resolution that parliamentary statutes concerning religion could not be suspended or cancelled except by Act of Parliament, thus denying the king's power in matters of 'indulgence'.

Charles tried to resist with the help of the Lords but, in desperate need of money, eventually he submitted. After a number of rancorous exchanges he cancelled the declaration of indulgence and said that 'what had been done with respect to the suspension of the penal laws should never be drawn into consequence'. The king broke the seal of the original declaration with his own hands. Bonfires were lit in the streets of London and, by the end of the month, Charles had received the supply of funds he so badly needed.

Parliament had taken aim at papists rather than dissenters, since the Catholic recusants were still believed to pose a threat to the state. Abednego Seller, in *The History of Passive Obedience*, suggested that 'treason in papists is like original sin to mankind; they all have it in their natures, though many of them may deny it, or not know it'. Some members believed that the 'declaration' had in fact been part of a papist plot concocted by Charles and Louis to impose that religion upon England.

So in March 1673, the Commons passed a measure that became known as the Test Act. All aspirants to office or to a place of trust were to swear the oath of royal supremacy as well as the oath of allegiance, thus placing king before pope; they were also obliged to take the sacrament according to the rite of the Church of England and to swear that 'I declare that I believe there is not any transubstantiation in the sacrament of the Lord's Supper, or in the elements of bread and wine, at or after the consecration thereof by any person whatsoever'. This struck at the heart of Catholic belief. When the king gave his assent to the Test Act a 'great hum' of approval arose in parliament. Charles was heard to say that he would now purge his court of all Catholics except his barber, 'whom he mean[s] to keep in despite of all their bills, for he was so well accustomed to his hand'. The remark had a point; the king trusted the Catholic who put a razor to his throat.

The first casualty was James, duke of York, who was obliged to retire from public life. He resigned as lord high admiral and command of the fleet was entrusted to Prince Rupert, who last appeared in these pages as the leader of the royalist cavalry during the Civil War. It was therefore advertised to the world that the king's brother and heir apparent was a Roman Catholic; immediately rumour and innuendo began to surround him. It was widely believed, for example, that the lord chancellor himself, the earl of Shaftesbury, was plotting against him in an effort to exclude him from the throne. When James did not receive communion with his brother in the royal chapel John Evelyn wrote in his diary that it 'gave exceeding grief and scandal to the whole nation, that the heir of it, and the son of a martyr for the Protestant religion, should apostatize. What the consequence of this will be, God only knows, and wise men dread.'

One of the king's principal councillors and one of the original 'cabal', Thomas Clifford, also resigned all of his posts. He was a secret Catholic, and it had been suggested that the Test Act was in part formulated by his rivals precisely in order to remove him from office. He died soon after. Confidence now flowed to yet another of Charles's ministers. Thomas Osborne, soon to become the earl of Danby, was a staunch Anglican who had opposed the Dutch war; he had also been a signal success as an administrator and, on Clifford's resignation, he was appointed to be lord treasurer.

The preparation for another year of hostilities with the Dutch was not undertaken with any great enthusiasm; the discovery of James's Catholicism called into further question the alliance with papist France and the attack upon a fellow Protestant state. The king himself is reported to have been vacillating and inconsistent, ready to prosecute war on one day and ready to retire from conflict on the next. Shaftesbury said of his master that 'there is not a person in the world, man or woman, that dares rely upon him or put any confidence in his word or friendship'.

In July Charles ordered Rupert to avoid any naval confrontation unless he could be sure to win it decisively. He had already returned to negotiations with the Dutch, and simply wished to apply pressure upon them. No such clear outcome emerged from the last sea battle of the war, the battle of the Texel, when the Dutch and English vessels fought a long and inconclusive struggle that left the waters filled with wreckage and floating bodies. It was notable, also, for the inactivity of the French fleet that simply stood apart and watched. Prince Rupert wrote later of the French admiral's reluctance to become involved that 'it wanted neither signal nor instruction to tell him what he should then have done; the case was so plain to every man's eye in the whole fleet'. It was now believed by many that Louis XIV was happy to watch the two maritime nations destroy one another's navies, thus adding more fire to the anger of the English against their nominal allies.

James increased the anti-Catholic bias of the nation by taking advantage of the parliamentary recess to betroth himself to a papist princess. His previous wife, Anne Hyde, had died two years earlier, leaving him with two Protestant daughters, Mary and Anne. The new bride was of quite another nature. Mary of Modena was fifteen but already a devout Catholic, and it was reported that the French king highly approved of the match and might even provide a dowry for the occasion. The imminent prospect of a royal Catholic dynasty was not one that the English favoured. When Mary eventually arrived in England she was generally greeted with sullen silence by the populace. When she was allowed to sit in the queen's presence, the English ladies 'humped' and walked out.

When parliament reconvened towards the end of October 1673, the outcry against the marriage was immediate. Sir William Temple declared that the effort to defeat papistry with the Test Act would come to nothing 'if it got footing so near the throne' and he begged the king to forbid the proposed match. A resolution to that effect was almost unanimously approved.

A broader assault upon the administration now began. Some of the members had already stated that they would not vote a penny more for the war unless and until they had a voice in its management. A resolution to that effect was amended with the proviso that no money should be granted until the previous supply of war funds had been collected. It was also found necessary to give room for a debate on 'grievances', principal among them the French alliance and the war against the Dutch. At the beginning of November it was declared that the standing army was also a 'grievance', perhaps not the most appropriate note to be struck during a war. On 5 November the old sport of pope-burning returned to the streets, when the effigy of Pope Clement X was set on fire by the London apprentices. A figure of a Frenchman was also used for target practice.

Charles was aware that his lord chancellor, the earl of Shaftesbury, had helped to foment opposition against his brother and that he was steadily becoming the leading spokesman for the Protestant interest. So he dismissed him from his councils, and appointed Heneage Finch as lord chancellor; it was reported that the king changed his mind six times, in as many hours, over the appointment. The Venetian envoy reported to the doge and senate that 'the king calls a cabinet council for the purpose of not listening to it, and the ministers hold forth in it so as not to be understood'.

Shaftesbury did not go quietly, however, and against the king's direct order remained in London to recruit allies for his anti-Catholic cause; for the rest of his political life he would organize the opposition to the king. When parliament met again at the beginning of 1674, after a brief prorogation, the attack moved on to the king's principal ministers who were 'popishly affected, or otherwise obnoxious and dangerous'. Lauderdale had ruled on the king's behalf in Scotland, and was accused of favouring absolutism; it was resolved therefore that the king should remove him from 'all his employments and from the royal presence and councils for ever'.

The duke of Buckingham was next to be arraigned and agreed to speak before the Commons; he tried to excuse himself by shifting the blame onto the ineptitude of others, and declared that 'I can hunt the hare with a pack of hounds but not with a pack of lobsters'. It was widely believed that the lobsters in question were the king and his brother. His wit did not impress the Commons, however, and it was determined that he should also be removed from all of his employments. Buckingham later complained that 'men ruined by their princes and in disgrace are like places struck with thunder; it is accounted unlawful to approach them'.

Arlington was then in turn impeached for treason and crimes of high misdemeanour, but his case was ceded to a special committee. The 'cabal' had in any case now been dissolved. It was obvious to everyone that the king was ready to sacrifice ministers when he had no further use for them.

He was also engaged in extreme and unwise deception. Shaftesbury had opposed the king's measures in part because he had become acquainted, by one means or another, with the secret treaty whereby Charles became the pensionary of the king of France in exchange for his conversion to Catholicism. At the opening of parliament in January 1674, however, Charles stated that rumours of 'secret articles of dangerous consequence' were completely untrue and he declared, 'I assure you, there is no other treaty with France, either before or since, not already printed, which shall not be made known.' He was perceived to fumble with his notes at this point.

It had now become clear that the war against the Dutch could not be continued; the Spanish had now entered an alliance with the enemy and it was unthinkable that England would also declare war against Spain. Too much trade was at stake. So the Dutch now appointed the Spanish envoy in London as an arbitrator for peace. It could not come soon enough for all the participants. The Dutch agreed to pay an indemnity and consented to salute the English flag at sea; this was really a question of saving face, on the English side, and the outcome was hardly enough to justify a costly and bloody war of two years' duration. The king announced the peace to parliament on 24 February, and then unexpectedly prorogued the session until November. The members of the Commons looked upon one another in amazement in light of the fact that, in the words of Lord Conway, 'they had sat so long upon eggs and could hatch nothing'. Conway also observed that 'now there will be a new game played at court, and the designs and interests of all men will be different from what they were'.

Thomas Osborne, who had emerged as the king's principal minister, was created earl of Danby in the summer of the year. He was a determined and pugnacious Yorkshireman who firmly believed that the Anglican faith was of paramount importance in unifying the nation and who had as a result favoured alliances with the Protestant states of Europe. He was determined to reform royal finances, and to maintain control over parliament by any and every means possible; those methods included clandestine payments to members from secret service funds and the select distribution of various titles or offices. Danby did his best to demonstrate that the king was wholly in favour of the Anglican cause, and that Charles was determined to maintain an anti-French and an anti-Catholic stance.

As a pronounced royalist and courtier he was of course opposed by the earl of Shaftesbury and by the duke of Buckingham who, abandoned by the king, now joined together in the campaign against the court. It has been often observed that in the creation of these factions and interests we may see the modest beginnings of 'party' in the contemporary sense. From 1674 forward an 'opposition' to the royal cause began to emerge in the Commons, with the aim of imposing restrictions upon the king's power and of upholding the supremacy of parliament.

Its members did not consider or call themselves a party, because the term implied disruption or disloyalty, yet in 1673 a member of parliament, Sir Thomas Meres, could speak of 'this side of the house and that side'. The term was considered to be unparliamentary but it was observed, for example, that a cluster of members sat together in the 'south-east corner' of the chamber. The 'court' and 'country' parties were also distinguished. The former were intent upon maintaining all the rights and privileges of the throne while the latter wished, according to the parliamentarian Sir John Reresby, 'to protect the country from being overburdened in their estates, in their privileges and liberties'.

In the spring of 1675 parliament reassembled. Here was another opportunity for Danby to reassert the primacy of orthodox Anglicanism at the court of Charles II. He had recently engaged in what Andrew Marvell called 'window-dressing' by taking in hand the rebuilding of St Paul's Cathedral after the Great Fire; the first stone of Christopher Wren's design was laid in the early summer. A brass statue of Charles I was also raised on its pedestal at Charing Cross.

Now in parliament, Danby wished to reintroduce a bill that compelled members of parliament and holders of public office to declare that resistance to the king was unlawful; they were also to be obliged to disown any alteration in Church or government. It was a measure designed to please what was still a 'Cavalier Parliament' in its fourteenth year. In a 'Letter from a Person of Quality' Shaftesbury denounced the proposal as a plot by 'high episcopal men and cavaliers' to establish an absolute government. In a speech to the Lords he had questioned that 'if a king would make us a province, and tributary to France, and subdue the nation by a French army, or to the papal authority, must we be bound in that case tamely to submit'? The question was never answered. A formal battle between the Lords and the Commons, over the extent of their respective rights, meant that no business could be introduced. Danby's measure failed, therefore, and the king prorogued parliament until October.

The summer of 1675 was spent in preparation and calculation. Some of the votes in the last session of parliament had been very close; there were occasions when frustration and anger erupted in mild violence as periwigs were pulled off and swords were drawn. On one occasion the Speaker had to bring the mace crashing down upon the table in order to restore order. Danby himself had been obliged to fight off charges of impeachment made against him by some of the Commons. So he was determined to create a majority for the court by what was called 'high bribing'. Some thirty members were given pensions on the excise while others were granted minor offices.

In this same summer Charles also received another subsidy from the French king on condition that he further prorogued parliament or, in the event of a difficult session in October, dissolved the assembly altogether. Louis did not wish his cousin to be forced into measures against the French, while at the same time envoys from Spain, the United Provinces and elsewhere were busily bribing individual members of the parliament. Everyone was bribing everyone else.

The parliament of the autumn was not a success; the Commons voted £300,000 for the navy, but then vetoed the introduction of any new money bills. In the Lords the supporters of Shaftesbury and Buckingham argued for a dissolution, on the grounds that the 'Cavalier Parliament' was now old and corrupt. So on 22 November the king, without attempting to make a speech, prorogued parliament once more for a further fourteen months.

A report compiled for Danby, after the session was over, reveals the calculations of one of his managers.

Sir Nicholas Slanning. He was absent most part if not all last session. Lord Arundel should be sure to take care of him. *Mr Josiah Child*. I am loath to speak plain English, but if he were well observed he might be proved to be a capital offender. *Mr Joseph Maynard*. He seldom or never goes right. *Mr John Grubham Howe*. Your lordship knows who can influence him . . . *Sir Thomas Bide* is past cure. *Sir John Cotton*. He is a very good man, and rarely misses his vote, and then by mistake only. Some person (trusty) should always sit near him. *Sir John Newton*. I suspect he has been corrupted by Sir Robert Carr . . . *Mr Henry Monson*. Mr Cheney must take care of this gentleman, and that most particularly, for he is very uncertain unless one be at his elbow.

In the parliamentary recess Charles was angered into taking a clumsy and ill-considered measure to silence idle tongues. It was a winter of discontent at the failure of parliament and the maladministration of the king. So he agreed to issue a proclamation that closed all the coffee-houses of the city, in the knowledge that these were the places where his opponents gathered to plot and to plan. Those who followed Shaftesbury, for example, were accustomed to meet at Kid's Coffee House otherwise known as the Amsterdam. The government employed at least one 'coffee-house spy' to keep an account of their proceedings.

Some observers blamed the appetite for news and scandal on the consumption of coffee. In the days of the tavern, sack and claret created an atmosphere of gaiety; but the city chamberlain, Sir Thomas Player, complained that 'these sober clubs produce nothing but scandalous and censorious discourses, and at these nobody is spared'.

The king might also have taken the opportunity to close down the bookshops attended by the opposition which, in a memorandum, Danby described as devoted to spreading false news through city and country. The temperature of public debate and interest in the politics of the day was such that young law students flocked to the shops and stalls every afternoon, together with those citizens and gentry who were eager for the latest reports. The agents of every faction circulated among them, ready to lend their interpretation to any turn of events. The bookshops remained open, however, and such was the outcry over the closing of the coffee-houses that the proclamation was withdrawn. They had been shut down in January 1676, but were reopened ten days later. The volte-face was characteristic of the hesitation and confusion that beset all aspects of public policy.

At a later date, however, an attempt was made to exclude satires and newsletters that were composed, according to the king, by 'sordid mechanic wretches who, to gain a little money, had the impudence and folly to prostitute affairs of state'. Yet the appetite for news could not be curbed or diminished. There was only one newspaper that was granted official authorization, the *London Gazette*, but this consisted mainly of proclamations, official pronouncements and advertisements.

Everybody needed news. Everybody wanted news. News was known as 'hot'. It was a society of conversation so that rumour and gossip passed quickly through the streets. At times of more than usual excitement papers and pamphlets were dropped in the street and were eagerly snatched up and passed from hand to hand. Anonymous publications, without a printer's imprint, were also widely circulated. One owner of a coffee-house trained his parrot to squawk 'What's the news?' at his customers.

42

New infirmities

And what was the news? After the Commons had declined to pass any new money bills, Charles was once more compelled to turn to his French cousin for financial aid. It was agreed in the early months of 1676 that Louis would pay him a yearly pension, and that both kings would refrain from agreements with other powers without mutual consent. Charles told his brother about the arrangement and was congratulated for his fidelity to the Catholic sovereign. He also informed Danby, who was wholly opposed to any transactions with the French; he disapproved, and asked his master to take the advice of the privy council. Charles was in no mood to consult anyone, however; he wrote out the secret treaty in his own hand, and delivered it to the French ambassador. The king then retired to Windsor, where he supervised certain 'improvements' to the castle and went fishing.

When parliament reassembled in February 1677, after a prorogation of fifteen months, it was claimed by Shaftesbury and others that such a long suspension of proceedings was illegal; Buckingham proposed a motion to that effect and cited two statutes of Edward III, which ordained that parliament should meet 'once a year, or oftener, if need be'. This was considered to be an affront to the royal prerogative. Shaftesbury and Buckingham were ordered to retract their 'ill-advised' action and to ask pardon of king and

Lords. Both men refused and were promptly dispatched to the Tower for an indefinite period together with two other dissenting lords. Buckingham confessed his fault soon afterwards, and was released, while Shaftesbury preferred to remain in prison. 'What, my lord,' he called down to Buckingham as he departed the Tower, 'are you leaving us so soon?'

'Ay, my lord, you know that we giddy-pated fellows never stay long in one place at a time.'

France was still continuing its land war against the United Provinces, despite English withdrawal from the conflict, and in the spring of this year the French enjoyed a series of victories. The Commons reacted by reaffirming its animus against the French. The king was in any case suspect. He had in recent years acquired a French mistress, Louise de Kérouaille, made duchess of Portsmouth, thus binding his ties to the French court of which she was a prominent member as duchess of Aubigny. There is a famous story of the crowd threatening the coach of Nell Gwynn under the misapprehension that it contained the duchess; she called out, 'Be silent, good people! I am the *Protestant* whore!'

Charles was in every sense a Frenchified king. An address was issued by both Houses of Parliament calling upon him to allay the anxieties of the nation by entering appropriate alliances with the opponents of Louis. At an audience with one of the ambassadors from the United Provinces, he threw his handkerchief into the air with the exclamation, 'I care just that for parliament.'

On 23 May, however, the king invited the Commons to the Banqueting House in which he declared that 'I do assure you on the word of a king that you shall not repent any trust you repose in me'; he then proceeded to ask for a further supply of money, 'both to defend my subjects and offend my enemies'. They did not place very much faith in the king's word, however, and two days later they found themselves 'obliged (at present) to decline the granting your majesty the supply your majesty is pleased to demand'. They also called for the king to unite himself with the Dutch against the power of France.

An angry king then adjourned parliament on 28 May with a speech in which he said that 'could I have been silent, I would rather have chosen to be so, than to call to mind things so unfit for you to meddle with'. He had told the French ambassador, the month before, that 'I put myself in trouble with my subjects for love of the French king'. Soon enough he was negotiating for further supplies from his much loved cousin that would more than match the money withheld from him by parliament. He had adjourned that assembly to the summer, but in fact it did not meet again until the beginning of the following year.

In the meantime the earl of Danby endeavoured to burnish the Protestant credentials of the regime by furthering the scheme of marrying Mary, elder daughter of the duke of York and therefore niece of the king, to William of Orange. William was the leader of the United Provinces even then threatened by the French; since he was a Protestant champion, the union might have seemed unwise to a king who relied upon French money. Yet Charles assented to the match in part to placate the public clamouring for an alliance with the United Provinces, and in part with the hope that he might be able to negotiate some treaty of peace between William and Louis. He could then emerge as the saviour of Europe. He was, in short, looking both ways at once. The belief of Louis XIV that the English king was quite unreliable was amply confirmed. He suspended his financial subsidy, and rejected Charles's proposal for an extended truce between France and the United Provinces. The marriage between William and Mary was solemnized at the beginning of November, to much public rejoicing. The Protestant powers were matched.

Parliament met finally in the last week of January 1678, in a more amenable atmosphere. In his opening speech the king confirmed that he 'had made such alliances with Holland as are for the preservation of Flanders', and that he now required 'a plentiful supply'. The Commons resolved that all trade between England and France should be curtailed and that no peace could be made until France had withdrawn to its previous frontiers. In February the members proceeded to vote him £1 million for prosecuting the war against France. The money would not in fact be enough to wage a successful campaign, but Charles had in any case no intention of declaring war on Louis.

He was in a trap or, rather, by his double-dealing he had trapped himself. A period followed in which parliament was adjourned or reconvened on almost a monthly basis; the shortest session was 6 days and the longest 172 days while the recesses lasted from 10 days to 15 months. This aberrant pattern is a measure of the confusion into which public policy had fallen. Charles did not know where to turn. He wanted the French subsidy from Louis but he had also been promised by parliament £1 million to furnish the means to attack him. He was making active preparations for war against France, while at the same time assuring the French ambassador of his devotion to Louis.

Parliament was also thrown into doubt. It had voted funds to raise an army of 30,000 men, but what if the king should use that army for his own ends? Charles and Danby were consequently feared and distrusted. The French king was liberally distributing bribes to various parties, and all men complained that darkness and deep mist covered the affairs of state. Sir William Temple explained in his *Memoirs* that 'from these humours arose those uncertainties in our counsels that no man, who was not behind the curtain, could tell what to make of' the confused rumours and reports.

Towards the end of March 1678 the king instructed Danby to write to the English ambassador in Paris, Ralph Montagu, with an outline of possible peace proposals; Charles then demanded the payment of 6 million *livres* a year (more than £4,000 of gold) for three years, in return for using his influence with the Dutch to negotiate a treaty. The whole arrangement was to be hidden in the most complete secrecy and Montagu 'must not mention a syllable of the money'. In his own hand the king added that 'I approve of this letter'. It was perhaps the only way that he could have persuaded Danby to write it. Louis promptly refused the request, but Charles had left another hostage to fortune that would in time severely damage Danby himself.

Then Louis caught Charles unawares by making a separate peace with the United Provinces, leaving no room for the English king to manoeuvre himself into the good graces of one party or the other. He had in a sense been abandoned by his French cousin. This gave him pause for thought. He was walking through St James's Park on a summer morning, in the middle of August, when he was approached by a chemist who worked in the royal laboratory. Charles, ever affable and courteous, greeted Christopher Kirkby with a salutation.

Kirkby then informed him that a Jesuit plot had been detected against his life; the sovereign was to be stabbed or poisoned so that the Catholic James, duke of York, could be raised to the throne. Charles, always inclined to dismiss such conspiracies as little more than hot air, advised Kirkby to consult his confidential secretary. Some desultory enquiries followed, in the course of which a long indictment against certain Jesuits was discovered. The supposed author of this indictment, Titus Oates, was then brought before a committee of the privy council to justify his accusations. Thus began the episode that became known as the 'Popish Plot'.

Roger North described Oates as 'a low man, of an ill cut, very short neck; and his visage and features were most particular. His mouth was the centre of his face . . .' He had a low forehead, long nose, and huge chin; his voice was high, and his manner dramatic. Yet he was very plausible. He outlined the meetings and consultations of the Jesuits in confident detail, and went on to name two prominent men as the authors of the plot. He accused Sir George Wakeman, physician to the queen, of planning to poison Charles; he also cited Edward Coleman, her secretary and previously secretary to the duke of York. The Catholic heir apparent was therefore touched. One of the councillors who listened to this damning testimony, Sir Henry Coventry, observed that 'if he be a liar, he is the greatest and adroitest I ever saw'.

Then a sudden death seemed to confirm Oates's testimony. He had previously sworn an affidavit to the truth of these matters before a London magistrate, Sir Edmund Berry Godfrey; he had told Godfrey that he had attended a clandestine meeting of Jesuits at the White Horse Tavern in the Strand, where the various methods of assassinating the king were discussed. It seems that Godfrey was alarmed to see the name of an acquaintance, Edward Coleman, on the list of suspects. On 12 October Godfrey did not return to his home. Five days later his body was found in a ditch on Primrose Hill, run through with his own sword. A coroner's inquest then concluded that the body had been taken to Primrose Hill on the day it was discovered, and that multiple bruising about the upper part of it and, in particular, the neck was indication that he had been strangled. Had he been murdered by the Catholics in fear of their discovery? Had he been killed by the supporters of Oates, who feared that his lying would be proven? Had he committed suicide? The truth of the matter will never be known.

Alarms and prophecies were already circulating. In the previous year a blazing comet had hurtled through the sky, and in 1678 occurred three eclipses of the sun and two of the moon. William Dade's *Prognostication* divined 'frenzies, inflammations and new infirmities proceeding from cholerick humours' while John Partridge's *Calendarium Judaicum* predicted 'troubles from great men and nobles'. In this atmosphere of anxiety, the discovery of Godfrey's body prompted mass panic and hysteria about a possible Catholic rising. The lords-lieutenant of the counties were ordered to search the homes of Catholics for hidden weapons, and of course the more general fear of a French invasion in favour of an uprising was never far from the surface. It was also widely believed that many thousands of apparently orthodox Protestants were in fact Catholics in disguise, waiting for a sign. One contemporary observer, Sir John Reresby, wrote that 'it seemed as if the very cabinet of hell had been laid open'.

When the papers of Edward Coleman were taken it was revealed that he had written certain suspect letters to Jesuit priests, close to Louis XIV, asking for money on the grounds that he and his colleagues 'had a mighty work on their hands, no less than the conversion of three kingdoms'. It may have been a piece of bravura, and seemed to have no connection with the plot outlined by Oates, but in the present circumstances it was explosive.

The publication of this plot, together with the possible collusion of James, admirably suited the intentions of Shaftesbury who could come forward as the champion of Protestantism. He had left the Tower for his Dorset estates a few months before, after making a formal apology to the king, but he could now take up the cause of 'No Popery!' with fresh justification and enthusiasm. It had become his abiding purpose to exclude James from the throne of England. He commented later that 'I will not say who started the game, but I am sure I had the full hunting of it'.

When parliament reassembled on 21 October 1678, he and his supporters were in charge of the pack. Committees were established to secure the king's safety and to investigate the plot. Both Houses of Parliament unanimously carried a resolution that 'there has been, and still is, a damnable and hellish plot contrived and carried on by popish recusants, for the assassinating and murdering the king, and for subverting the government and rooting out and destroying the Protestant religion'. Oates appeared before the Commons on three consecutive days and, as a result of his testimony, five Catholic peers were arrested. A bill was passed that excluded Catholics from both houses. Shaftesbury proposed that the king should be asked to dismiss James, duke of York, from his council.

At the end of November Titus Oates further raised the temperature when he appeared at the bar of the House of Commons. 'I, Titus Oates, accuse Catherine, queen of England, of high treason.' This alarmed the members who voted that the queen and her household should be removed from Whitehall. The Lords were not so hasty, however, and examined the witnesses who had testified against her; they were not convinced of their veracity and suppressed the charges brought by Oates. The king had previously held a private interview with Oates during which the informer had laid the charges against his wife; he kept his temper but ordered that all of Oates's papers should be seized and that his consultations with other people should be supervised.

The king does not seem to have believed a word that Oates uttered, but he could not openly withstand the full force of Protestant rage. As one of his ministers, the marquis of Halifax, put it, 'it must be handled as if it were true, whether it were so or no'. Measures against papists were made more severe, therefore, and the five Catholic lords held in the Tower were impeached of high treason. A second Test Act was passed obliging all Catholics in the Lords or Commons to repeat the oaths of allegiance and supremacy. In the course of the debate one peer declared that 'I would not have so much as a popish man or a popish woman to remain here; not so much as a popish dog or a popish bitch; not so much as a popish cat to purr or mew about the king'. At the beginning of December Edward Coleman was dragged to Tyburn where he was hanged, drawn and quartered; in 1929 he was beatified as a Catholic martyr.

Another act of this political drama now opened with the decision of Ralph Montagu to attack the earl of Danby. It was he who, as ambassador in Paris, had received the earl's letter concerning a secret subsidy from the French king to Charles. He had lost his office in the summer of this year, for the crime of corrupting the daughter of the king's former mistress, Lady Castlemaine, and now sought revenge. Another party may also have been involved. Louis XIV, knowing of Danby's antipathy to the French cause, had reasons enough to want him removed.

On being elected to the Commons for the borough of Northampton, Montagu arranged that his 'secret letters' from Danby should be disclosed to parliament. It became apparent that Danby, with the approval of the king, had asked for a bribe from Louis at the same time as he had solicited funds from the Commons to raise an army against France. As Lord Cavendish put it, 'it will appear by those papers that the war with France was pretended, for the sake of an army, and that a great man carried on the interest of an army and popery'. In the Commons the member for Shaftesbury, Thomas Bennet, said that 'I wonder the House sits so silent when they see themselves sold for six million *livres* to the French'. The situation was rendered infinitely worse for Danby by the fact that the army itself was still in existence; the king had no money either to deploy it or disband it.

The earl could not survive. Seven articles of impeachment were passed against him, amongst them the charge of keeping up an army to subvert the government and of being 'popishly affected'. In the Lords Danby defended himself with vigour. He poured scorn upon his accuser, Montagu, for perfidy and duplicity against his royal master; he denied the charges and demanded a speedy trial.

Charles then decided to suspend the proceedings against his chief minister by proroguing parliament. At a meeting of the privy council in the first weeks of 1679 the king told his councillors that he would not seek their advice because they were more afraid of parliament than they were of him. He dissolved the assembly on 24 January. So ended the 'Cavalier Parliament' that had first met in 1661, just after the restoration of the king; it had lasted seventeen years and in that period had turned from an assembly of the king's supporters into a fractious and suspicious body ready to turn upon the king's ministers and even upon the king himself.

Yet Charles and his ministers influenced the country in ways of which they were wholly unaware. The ending of the naval war with the Dutch in 1674, for example, materially increased the volume of the country's export trade. The excise returns after that year rose markedly in such staple items as beer, ale, tea and coffee, which in turn indicates a sharp rise in consumption. The increase in revenue had a significant effect upon royal income, too, which began to rise. Contemporary reports also suggest that the 'middling classes' were now indulging their taste for imported 'luxuries' and that the labouring poor were purchasing such items as knitted stockings, earthenware dishes and brass pots. The 'commercial revolution' of the eighteenth century had its origins three or four decades earlier. The successful colonization of portions of North America and of the West Indies, undertaken in the realms of the early Stuart kings and under the protectorate of Oliver Cromwell, now found its fruit in the ever-increasing rate of trade. By 1685 the English had the largest merchant fleet in the world, and their vessels were filled with the merchandise of sugar, tobacco and cotton on their way to the great emporium of London.

Other evidence supports this picture of material advantage. By 1672, for example, stagecoaches ran between London and all the principal towns of the kingdom; it was reported that 'every little town within twenty miles of London swarms with them'. The ubiquity of the stagecoach is the harbinger of the reforms of transport in the next century, with the further development of turnpike roads and canals; the country was slowly quickening its pace while at the same time finding its unity.

It is now a commonplace of economic history that the 'agricultural revolution' of the eighteenth century in fact began in the middle of the seventeenth century. The introduction of new crops, and the steady spread of 'enclosures' designed to achieve cohesion and efficiency of farming land, were already changing the landscape of England. The abundance of grain, for example, was such that in 1670 cereal farmers were allowed to export their crop without any regard to its price in the domestic market.

John Houghton, in *Collection of Letters for the Improvement of Husbandry and Trade*, wrote in 1682 that 'since his majesty's most happy restoration the whole land hath been fermented and stirred up by the profitable hints it hath received from the Royal Society by which means parks have been disparked, commons enclosed, woods turned into arable, and pasture land improved by clover, St. Foine [a grass], turnips, coleseed [rape], parsley, and many other good husbandries, so that the food of the cattle is increased as fast, if not faster, than the consumption . . .' It is a sign that practical experiment and innovation were already proving fruitful.

Another revolution began during the reigns of the later Stuarts. The exact conditions for the whirlwind of invention, commerce and trade that comprised the industrial revolution may not yet have been present; but the atmosphere was changing. English shipbuilding reached an unprecedented and unrepeated 'peak' in the seventeenth century. From the mines of England issued more coal, tin and iron ore than ever before; the coal production of the north-east of England, for example, more than doubled between 1600 and 1685. The old trade of heavy cloths was now being replaced by that of lighter cloths made in what were known as 'woollen manufactories'. Sugar refineries, iron foundries and glass works were ubiquitous by the close of the seventeenth century. The industries of brewing and soap-boiling had already been created. The rapid growth of towns such as Manchester and Birmingham, Halifax and Shef-field, testified to the interdependence between industrialization and urbanization. Birmingham had under the Tudors been little more than a village but, by the turn of the century, it would have at least 8,000 inhabitants. The population of the whole country may have stabilized, but a larger proportion of it was now migrating from the country to the town.

The election in the early weeks of 1679, after the dissolution of the 'Cavalier Parliament', was necessarily fought on the choice between king and parliament. Since the mood of the country had turned against the king, after the revelation of the 'Popish Plot' and the disgrace of Danby, the new parliament was even more hostile to the court than its predecessor. The king himself remarked that a dog would be elected if it stood against a figure from court. Shaftesbury, the principal benefactor of this change of mood, calculated that 158 'courtiers' had been elected against 302 of the 'opposition'.

The king had to deal with two pressing matters in advance of negotiating with the new parliament. He met the earl of Danby and requested him to resign his office; in exchange he would be granted the title of marquis, and receive a large annual pension. Since most of his dependants had been voted out of parliament, his ministry was effectively already at an end. A new politics, of agitation and campaign, had emerged.

The archbishop of Canterbury had been asked to discuss with James, duke of York, the prospect of his returning to the Anglican communion; the duke refused. The king then summoned his brother and ordered him to retire beyond the seas as the only way of averting the displeasure of parliament. James fought hard against this sentence of exile but, at the beginning of March, made a lachrymose departure for the Spanish Netherlands on the pretext that he was visiting his daughter and new son-in-law, William of Orange.

Yet the new parliament would not be diverted from its pursuit of the 'Popish Plot' or the impeachment of Danby, especially after it was revealed that the earl had received a pardon from the king. A week after its assembly he resigned and in the following month he was sent to the Tower by the Lords. When Lord Halifax condemned the decision to confer a marquisate upon 'a traitor to his country' he fixed his eyes upon the king who was watching the proceedings. 'My God!' the king was said later to have exclaimed, 'how I am ill-treated; and I must bear it, and keep silence!'

In the spring of the year, just after the parliament had met, the king announced a change in the administration. He dissolved the privy council and established in its place a smaller council of thirty-three members comprising office-holders and independents. In what at the time seemed a surprising and even shocking move he appointed Shaftesbury as its lord president together with four members of parliament who had always been resolute in opposing him. His purpose may have been to tame or to corrupt these men, but the nominations may simply have afforded a screen to conceal his real intentions. Some of the new counsellors lost their former influence, in any case, and were widely regarded as having sold themselves to the king. The members of the council were soon divided among themselves, and proved to be singularly ineffective. That may also have been the king's intention. Charles distrusted all of them and confided to the earl of Aylesbury that 'they shall know nothing'. He was isolated, after

Danby had been removed from office, and he told Sir William Temple that 'he had none left with whom he could so much as speak of them in confidence'. In his fight against vigorous and well-organized parliamentary opponents, he was on his own.

Towards the end of April 1679, an address was introduced that was designed to exclude the duke of York from the crown of England; it was said that the 'Popish Plot' had been encouraged by his likely succession to the throne. It marked the formal beginning of what became known as the 'exclusion crisis', and was the cause of much partisan rancour. Pamphlets and verse satires came from the presses; the votes of parliament were published and widely disseminated. The 'exclusionists' in large part controlled the Commons, but legislation could not pass without the consent of the king and the Lords.

Nevertheless an Exclusion Bill quickly received its first and second readings; it pronounced that the duke of York had been seduced by papal agents into entering the Roman communion, and that it was the duty of parliament to exclude him from the throne. One member, Sir John Trevor, stated that 'the king's eyes are closed; he knows nothing of the danger that we are in . . .' The mood of hysteria was translated beyond the walls of parliament. It was said that the citizens slept with pistols beside them, and that their wives carried knives into the street. At the beginning of July Charles, exasperated by the proceedings, prorogued parliament. The unpopularity of his decision was such that he doubled the guards at Whitehall. Shaftesbury declared that the royal advisers should pay for the decision with their heads.

The session left only one permanent memorial in the form of a Habeas Corpus Act which decreed that no person could be unlawfully detained and that all those charged with felony or treason should be granted a speedy trial or discharge from prison. This was designed as a means of public safety in the event of James's ascending the throne. In his *Commentaries on the Laws of England* Sir William Blackstone wrote that 'the point of time at which I would choose to fix this *theoretical* perfection of our public law is the year 1679; after the habeas corpus act was passed, and that for licensing the press had expired . . .' The sudden prorogation had indeed meant that the laws inhibiting the press had not been renewed, so that the rage of party could now be fully conveyed in the public prints.

In the latter half of 1679, the terms of 'Whig' and 'Tory' became common currency. The Presbyterian rebels of Scotland, ever zealous for a stricter covenant, had been given the name of Whiggamores after the Scottish word for corrupt or sour whey; the Irish royalist Catholics, who had been reduced to banditry, had the Gaelic name of *toraihde*. Soon enough Shaftesbury's Whigs, who supported the Protestant Church and favoured the exclusion of James, would oppose Danby's Tories, who were prepared to countenance a Catholic king as part of the divine order of natural succession. The Whigs were the enemies of popery and arbitrary government, and thus wished to limit royal power; the Tories were determined to defend the monarch and the constitution against the onslaught of those whom they considered to be republicans or rebels. Various factions could of course be observed on both sides and a third group of 'trimmers', who pursued a middle course, was also evident. A sympathetic witness, the duke of Ormonde, described the 'trimmers' as using the language of 'moderation, unity and peace' combining the Whig concern for the maintenance of property and the true religion with the Tory desire for a secure monarchy and an untouched royal prerogative.

Moderation and unity were not readily apparent in a political nation violently divided. The Green Ribbon Club, perhaps the first ever political club, consisted of a variety of groups of Whigs including dissenters, lawyers and merchants; it met at the King's Head Tavern on the corner of Fleet Street and Chancery Lane, where it was accustomed to plan its strategy and to co-ordinate its tactics. As avowed supporters of Shaftesbury, its members wore green ribbons and thus identified themselves as a 'party'. They paid customary obeisance to the royal prerogative but more often than not they talked of their responsibilities to 'the people'; one phrase, '*salus populi suprema lex*', was often repeated: 'the safety of the people is the supreme law'. This would in effect have created a political revolution, albeit without the bloodshed of another civil war.

Charles believed that if his opponents managed to get rid of James he himself would surely follow. He was engaged in a battle for his survival. His opponents believed that, under increasing pressure, he would eventually submit and bar his brother from the throne; many now looked to the king's illegitimate son, the duke of Monmouth, a Protestant, as the next heir. Shaftesbury even argued that the king was pretending to oppose exclusion while all the time hoping to be 'forced' to agree to his natural son's accession. It is true that he had a low opinion of his brother. When James cautioned him from walking in St James's Park without a guard he replied, 'I am sure no man in England will take away my life to make you king.' It was unlikely, however, that Charles would deny James his lawful right to succeed.

The French ambassador observed that the king's 'conduct is so secret and impenetrable that even the most skilful observers are misled. The king has secret dealings and contacts with all the factions and those who are most opposed to his interests flatter themselves that they will win him over to their side.' The ambassador may have credited the king with too much cunning; it is possible that Charles simply moved from one expedient to the next.

The duke of Monmouth, the Protestant candidate for the succession, now covered himself with glory or at least with blood. A band of covenanters dragged the primate of Scotland, Archbishop Sharp, from his coach outside the town of St Andrews and stabbed him to death in front of his daughter; they then went on to defeat a royalist squadron sent after them. Monmouth was now dispatched to the north with a large army where, at Bothwell Bridge, he routed the covenanters. The subsequent repression of these enthusiasts became known as 'the killing time'. Monmouth became the hero of the hour, his ambitions for the throne significantly increased; as a Protestant he was Shaftesbury's preferred candidate, and James looked on in alarm from his exile in Brussels as the king's favour towards his natural son increased.

Charles had, a few months earlier, signed a document in which he explained that 'for the voiding of any dispute which may happen in time concerning the succession of the Crown, I do hereby declare in the presence of Almighty God that I never gave nor made any contract of marriage, nor was married to any woman whatsoever, but to my present wife Queen Catharine now living'. He had declared to the world that Monmouth was illegitimate, therefore, but the king was not inexpert at lying.

When Monmouth returned to London, the people assembled in the streets where bonfires were lit and toasts were drunk. He was considered by many to be the champion of the Protestant faith and, as the first illegitimate son of Charles II, the true heir to the throne. Despite the king's denial it was claimed that a 'black box', carefully concealed, contained a contract of marriage between Charles and Lucy Walters; Lucy Walters had been one of his first mistresses, while in continental exile, and had borne this particular son. Monmouth was handsome and affable, in every respect a royal boy, and on his journeys through the kingdom he was treated with as much ceremony as his father. Wherever he went he was escorted by columns of gentlemen and admirers. He was, in the words of Macaulay, 'the most popular man in the kingdom'. It is perhaps no wonder that his thoughts turned towards the crown. The shield that bore his coat of arms quartered the lions of England and the lilies of France as a symbol of his aspirations. He had even begun to 'touch' for the king's evil.

In July 1679, the king decided to turn the prorogation of parliament into a dissolution, pending a new general election; he was gambling that public sentiment had turned towards him. And indeed there were many now who questioned the wisdom and loyalty of Shaftesbury in his relentless pursuit of the duke of York. Yet at the hustings in the summer of the year the Whig Party, as we may now term it, was in full cry against the Catholic heir. When the clergy of Essex were believed to incline to the court interest, they were called 'dumb dogs . . . Jesuitical dogs . . . dark lanterns . . . Baal's priests . . . jacks and villains . . . the black guard . . . the black regiment of hell!' The Whigs were in turn dismissed by the Tories as a 'rabble' of disloyal and rebellious traitors. Lists were drawn up by both sides, noting down the names of 'the vile' and 'the worthy'. Sir Ralph Verney, soon to become a member of parliament, remarked that 'there are vast feuds in our Chilterns as well as in our Vale, occasioned by elections, and so 'tis, I suppose, all over England'.

But then all the problems of succession became more acute. Towards the end of August the king fell seriously ill, and was for two or three days in danger of death. James was summoned from Brussels to be by his brother's side, and perhaps to take the crown; he came to England disguised in a black wig. Meanwhile Monmouth's supporters began to intrigue on his behalf. The political nation was in confusion.

43

Or at the Cock?

On 12 January 1675, a conversation took place in London. It was ostensibly about china, that commodity then being the rage of the town. Lady Fidget desires some from a dear male acquaintance 'for he knows china very well, and has himself very good, but will not let me see it lest I should beg some'. The gentleman's name is Horner, whose welcome for Lady Fidget alarms her husband.

> *Sir Jaspar:* Wife! My Lady Fidget! He is coming into you the back way!
> *Lady Fidget:* Let him come, and welcome, which way he will.
> *Sir Jaspar:* He'll catch you, and use you roughly, and be too strong for you.
> *Lady Fidget:* Don't you trouble yourself, let him if he can.

Horner, having been detained in his chamber with Lady Fidget, is asked a few minutes later if he has any china left.

> *Horner:* Upon my honour I have none left now.
> *Mrs Squeamish:* Nay, nay, I have known you deny your china before now, but you shan't put me off so. Come.
> *Horner:* This lady had the last there.
> *Lady Fidget:* Yes indeed, madam, to my certain knowledge he has no more left.

Mrs Squeamish: Oh, but it may be he may have some you
    could not find.
Lady Fidget: What, d'ye think if he had any left, I would
    not have had it too? For we women of quality never
    think we have china enough.

The conversation took place on the stage of the Theatre Royal
in Drury Lane. 'China' is course a euphemism for male sperm, as
all the members of the audience knew, and *The Country Wife* by
William Wycherley soon gained a reputation for indecency. Yet, in
the 1670s, this was not considered to be a great offence. It was,
perhaps, a quality to be praised.

Two companies of players were re-established immediately after
the restoration of the king, the King's Players under the management of Thomas Killigrew and the Duke of York's Servants under
Sir William Davenant. They played at first in makeshift venues
until such time as suitable playhouses were erected. They did in any
case cater for a considerably diminished audience since the great
days of the Globe and the Fortune; the new theatrical public was
largely made up of 'the quality' or 'the fashion' as well as those
members of the middling classes who wished to emulate them.

The 'sparks' and 'wits' of the court were also in attendance and
would, in the words of Etherege from *She Wou'd if She Cou'd*, roam
'from one play-house to the other play-house, and if they like neither
the play nor the women, they seldom stay any longer than the
combing of their periwigs, or a whisper or two with a friend; and
then they cock their caps, and out they strut again'. The play began
at half past three in the afternoon, and lasted for approximately two
hours. The gentlemen brought their own wine with them and often
made more noise than the players on the stage, hectoring or
exchanging badinage with the actors.

In *The Country Wife* Horner feigns impotence in order to
deceive husbands and enter into clandestine amours with their
wives; among these is Margery Pinchwife, an innocent young bride
from the country who is fiercely guarded by her husband. The usual
complications of sexual farce ensue amid innuendo and double
meaning, with the principal women desperate to enjoy Horner's
favours by clandestine means. Lady Fidget herself does not deplore

the hypocrisy of seeming virtuous. 'Our reputation! Lord, why should you not think that we women make use of our reputation, as you men of yours, only to deceive the world with less suspicion?' As Leigh Hunt once remarked of these seventeenth-century dramas, 'we see nothing but a set of heartless fine ladies and gentlemen, coming in and going out, saying witty things at each other, and buzzing in some maze of intrigue'.

But this is the heart of the comedies of the Restoration period. They reflect a hard, if brittle, society where the prize goes to the most devious or hypocritical; they represent a world in which all moral values are provisional or uncertain; they convey a general sense of instability in which no one knows quite what to believe or how to behave. It is the perfect complement to Restoration tragedy in which fantastic notions of love or valour are pitched past the reality of life or true feeling; they are contrived and sentimental vehicles for rant and rhetoric.

The comedies, unlike the tragedies, of the period are at least set in real time and real place. The time is always the present moment, and the place is always London.

> *Sparkish:* Come, but where do we dine?
> *Horner:* Even where you will.
> *Sparkish:* At Chateline's?
> *Dorilant:* Yes, if you will.
> *Sparkish:* Or at the Cock?
> *Dorilant:* Yes, if you please.
> *Sparkish:* Or at the Dog and Partridge?

This was a world in which the participants must 'stay, until the chairs come', in which the prostitutes always wore vizards, and in which the women 'all fell a-laughing, till they bepissed themselves'. The protagonists are always those of the gentry or nobility, or at least those who aspire to be such; the playwrights were of the same mould, as were the members of the audience. Everyone knew everyone else but, in this multiple game of mirrors, we may glimpse the shape of the age.

The characters of course express themselves in prose; good conversation was considered be the medium of truth as well as of manners. Nothing was so delightfully true as that which was perfectly expressed. The notion of 'wit' is crucial here since, as Horner expresses it, 'methinks wit is more necessary than beauty, and I think no young woman ugly that has it, and no handsome woman agreeable without it'. Wit was not simply the effect of an epigram but, rather, the product of a fertile mind and keen observation. Wit was the currency of the court of Charles II.

The obscenity was also as much part of the court as of the stage. Horner apologizes to Lady Horner for bringing to her from France 'not so much as a bawdy picture, new postures, nor the second part of the *École des Filles*'. Pepys described the latter publication as 'the most bawdy, lewd book that ever I saw . . . so that I was shamed of reading it'. So the comic stage was used to strong meat. Yet not, perhaps, as strong as this:

> In liquid raptures I dissolve all o'er,
> Melt into sperm, and spend at every pore.
> A touch from any part of her had done 't:
> Her hand, her foot, her very look's a cunt.

The author, John Wilmot, earl of Rochester, was an indispensable element of the court of Charles II. At the age of seventeen, on Christmas Day 1664, he arrived at Whitehall bearing a letter to the king from the duchess of Orléans in France. Soon enough he was enrolled in the circle of wits that surrounded the king and by the spring of 1666 he had been appointed as one of the gentlemen of the bedchamber. He had all the qualities that the king admired. He was witty and he was fluent; he had a lightness of manner, and indeed of conscience, that were of paramount importance in such surroundings:

> That pattern of virtue, Her Grace of Cleveland,
> Has swallowed more pricks than the ocean has sand;
> But by rubbing and scrubbing so large it does grow,
> It is fit for just nothing but Signior Dildo.

He was sent to the Tower after attempting to abduct a lady; on his release, at the king's orders, he played a valiant or perhaps foolhardy role in one of the conflicts with the Dutch. His subsequent life at court principally consisted of liberal doses of drink and sex, interlarded with fashionable atheism or, as it was sometimes known, 'Hobbeism'. He recalled that at an atheistical meeting at the house of a 'man of quality' 'I undertook to manage the cause, and was the principal disputant against God and piety, and . . . received the applause of the whole company'. This conveys sufficiently the presiding atmosphere of Whitehall.

For five years he was, by his own account, continually drunk and was so little master of himself that he forgot many of his 'wild and unaccountable' actions. Like most of his contemporaries at court he was deeply engaged in the theatre of the time; in fact the drama can perhaps best be seen as an extension of the court itself. Rochester patronized playwrights such as Dryden and Otway; he wrote a comedy and a tragedy as well as various prologues. Yet he is still remembered principally for his satirical invectives and for his mastery of obscenity:

> Much wine had passed, with grave discourse,
> Of who fucks who, and who does worse . . .

A character in *The Country Wife* asks, 'Is it not a frank age? And I am a frank person.' The 'frankness' might have consisted principally of blasphemy and obscenity, but it was also part of a novel dispensation represented by the cogent social analysis of Thomas Hobbes and the decision of the experimenters of the Royal Society to deal in things and not in words. It was an attempt to see the world anew, after the realization that religious obscurantism and doctrinaire prejudices had previously brought England into confusion. Horace Walpole wrote that 'because the presbyterians and religionists had affected to call every thing by a scripture-name, the new court affected to call every thing by its own name'. It was time to clear away the rubble of untested assumptions, false rhetoric and standard appeals to authority or to tradition. This was the context for the ironical, cynical and materialist atmosphere of the Restoration court.

44

Noise rhymes to noise

When James arrived at his brother's sickroom in Windsor Castle he fell to his knees, and it is reported that the two men burst into tears. The king had recovered some of his strength and was already out of danger. Yet the two claimants to the throne, the dukes of York and Monmouth, were now in confrontation; each had his own band of supporters, but James for the moment had the upper hand. His sudden return to England had not caused an insurrection, as some had feared, and he had indeed been received with deference; the lord mayor and the aldermen of London, for example, had come to kiss his hand. He did not wish to return to exile in Brussels, and seems to have made it clear that he would leave England only if the duke of Monmouth also made his exit. It was agreed therefore that Monmouth would retire into Holland, out of harm's way, while James would be dispatched to Edinburgh as a kind of viceroy. He remained there for almost three years.

It had already become clear that, in the election of the summer, the Whigs had won the majority and that those who had voted against the 'exclusion' of James were generally turned out of office. Charles refused to allow this parliament to sit, however, and prorogued it to the beginning of the following year, 1680. He told his nephew, William of Orange, that he had no choice in the matter and that otherwise 'they would have his crown'; he also feared that

443

the Commons would proceed to the impeachment of his brother and his wife for their Catholic beliefs. Few expected parliament to meet again.

Shaftesbury was discharged from his office as lord president of the new council, and at once entered his true role as leader of the opposition to the court and Crown. Yet he knew well enough that he had no real power unless or until parliament was assembled. The Commons was his praetorian guard. Almost at once, therefore, he planned to launch petitions from all parts of the country for its return. His organization was such that his agents, together with notable local men, went from parish to parish collecting marks and signatures. No one, not even the poorest, was overlooked.

On 17 November the Green Ribbon Club, opposed to Catholics and to the court, organized a great pageant in London in which it was claimed that 200,000 people took part. A variety of Catholic personages were in representation dragged through the streets, and the procession eventually halted in Fleet Street just by the King's Arms, the headquarters of the club; here effigies of the pope and of the devil, as well as sundry monks, nuns and Jesuits, were hurled into the flames of a fire accompanied by a great shout that, according to a pamphlet, 'London's Defiance to Rome', reached France and Rome 'damping them all with a dreadful astonishment'. Macaulay remarks in his *History of England* that two words became current at this time, 'mob' and 'sham'.

When the duke of Monmouth arrived in London unexpectedly from exile, he was greeted with bonfires and jubilant crowds as the natural Protestant successor to the throne; he was not so warmly received by his father, however, who told him to be gone from court. His son disobeyed on the grounds that he must stay in order to preserve the life of his father from the designs of the papists.

At the beginning of December 1679, with a party of fifteen other peers, Shaftesbury stopped Charles on his way to the royal chapel and presented him with a petition for the sitting of parliament. The king was so irate that he prorogued the assembly for a further eleven months and issued a proclamation against petitioning itself. His supporters were said to 'abhor' the conduct of those who were trying to force the king's hand; for a while grew up the factions of 'the Abhorrers' and 'the Petitioners'.

After some months of impasse Shaftesbury once more raised the temperature when in the early summer of 1680 he tried to present, to a Middlesex grand jury, the duke of York as a papist and the duchess of Portsmouth, Charles's mistress, as a prostitute. The latter had already attracted the dislike and suspicion of many, and it had often been suggested that she should be sent packing to France as soon as possible. Shaftesbury's action was of course an open affront to the king, and an obvious attempt to inflame public opinion. The king hastened to London from Windsor where he instructed the chief justice, William Scroggs, to dismiss the grand jury before it heard any evidence for the charges. The damage had been done, however, compounded by the fact that Shaftesbury received no rebuke.

When parliament finally met, towards the end of October, the Commons was full from the very first session. The king's ministers, known as 'the chits' because of their relative youth, had formulated what they hoped was a consistent policy; they intended to defuse the threat of exclusion by imposing limitations on the power of a future King James, and to seek an alliance with the United Provinces against the French. It was still important to signal hostility to Louis XIV, even though Charles had been engaged in constant negotiations to obtain money from him.

The Whigs were not to be averted from their purpose, however, and at the beginning of November a second Exclusion Bill against the duke of York was introduced. It received its third reading within nine days and was then sent up to the Lords. The duke of Monmouth came back to London from a triumphal tour of the West Country in order to participate in the discussions.

The king also attended this long session of the peers, from eleven in the morning to nine at night, and listened to them with eager attention. It had been believed that he would abandon his brother, however reluctantly, for the sake of public peace; he was known to fear, more than anything else, the outbreak of another civil war. But in fact he remained firm and made his feelings known during the course of the Lords' debate. When Monmouth expressed his concern for his father, Charles called out, 'It is a Judas kiss that he gives me!' The sentiments of the king may have helped to concentrate the minds of the Lords. They voted, sixty-three to thirty, against the Exclusion Bill. Shaftesbury's measure had failed.

It was hoped that the Commons might now suggest a compromise upon which both sides might agree, but no possibility of a middle way existed. The Commons passed a series of resolutions aimed at the exclusion of the duke of York; they stated that no supply of money could be voted under the circumstances, that the councillors of the king should be removed from public employment, and that any man who lent money to the king should be called to the bar of parliament. The king was advised to prorogue parliament once again and the Commons, speedily warned of this threat, met early on the morning of 10 January 1681, to vote that anyone who offered such advice was a traitor to the king and to the realm. The king therefore issued a proclamation dissolving parliament, and ordering that a new assembly should meet in Oxford within two months.

This aroused anger, resentment and no little anxiety among Shaftesbury and his followers. Oxford was known to be the most royalist of all English cities. They would have been even more concerned if they had learned that Louis XIV had proffered another bribe to the king. Louis offered to grant him an annual pension, larger than anything parliament would provide, as long as he refrained from joining in any attack upon France by Spain or others. A ban on French imports was also allowed to expire. Nothing was put in writing, and no signatures were required; it was simply a verbal agreement, mediated by envoys, between the two kings.

The new parliament, meeting on 21 March 1681, was no more willing than its predecessor to come to any agreement. Charles appeared before the two houses with a compromise. If James ever became king, his powers would be transferred to a regent. In the first instance that regent would be James's older daughter, Mary, princess of Orange, a Protestant; and, in the event of her decease, the regency would devolve upon his other Protestant daughter, Anne. This seemed on the face of it an eminently sensible arrangement, but the Commons refused to accept it. Instead it debated a third Exclusion Bill. Charles in fact seems genuinely to have wished for an agreement in the calmer atmosphere of Oxford, no less for the fact that he feared another civil war. That was another reason for his secret alliance with the French king; he might need men as well as money.

On 28 March, Charles, with his full regalia concealed in a covered sedan chair, proceeded to the Lords, who were sitting in the Geometry School of Oxford. He was about to spring a surprise. He appeared before the Lords in his ordinary clothes, but then he ordered his attendants to dress him in robe and crown. Thus attired he summoned the Commons. 'My lords and gentlemen,' he said to the two houses, 'all the world may see to what a point we are come, that we are not like to have a good end, when the divisions at the beginning are such: therefore, my lord chancellor, do as I have commanded you.' He now told his opponents, to their faces, that they had been dissolved and must disperse. He left Oxford immediately, and they had no choice but to follow. It was reported that 'the king's breath scattered them like leaves in autumn'.

Charles now believed that he could survive without any parliamentary funds. His pension from France, and the raising of customs revenue from luxury French imports now freely admitted, would grant him room to manoeuvre; his household expenditure had in any case been considerably reduced. He had decided to embark upon a period of personal rule without an opposition to divert or trouble him. In this respect the king was greatly assisted by what seemed to be a resurgence of loyalty towards the Stuart monarchy. The intransigence of Shaftesbury and his followers, in rejecting what seemed to be a just and sensible offer on the matter of the regency, could be contrasted with the moderation of the king. They had wanted to bully him into submission, but he had remained firm. He had resisted any attempt to alter the natural succession because it was repugnant to his conscience and to the laws of England. That is how the abortive Oxford parliament could be represented.

In his declaration 'to all his loving subjects, touching the causes and reasons that moved him to dissolve the last two parliaments' he stated that 'we assure ourself that we shall be assisted by the loyalty' of those 'who consider the rise and progress of the late troubles'. The 'late troubles' were the divisions that had led to the civil wars. 'And we cannot but remember that religion, liberty and property were all lost and gone when monarchy was shaken off, and could never be revived till that was restored.' He appealed, therefore, to the instincts of loyalty and stability that maintained the traditions of the nation.

He now turned his fury upon Shaftesbury and his allies who, with no likelihood of a parliament, began to lose strength as well as purpose. Charles was determined to exclude them from all public offices; he decided to remove them from the judicial bench and from the administration of the towns. Sixty members of parliament who had voted for exclusion were removed from nomination as justices of the peace. Some of the lords-lieutenant of the counties were dismissed, together with the lowlier recorders and town clerks. Since the nonconformists had played a large role in the opposition, the laws against dissenters were executed with more rigour; they, rather than Roman Catholics, were increasingly consigned to prison. One contemporary said that it was a form of civil war, with the law replacing the sword.

At the beginning of July 1681 Shaftesbury was taken into custody and brought before the king and council where he was accused of treason; the earl denied the charge but was in any case committed to the Tower. Yet there was a flaw in the royal project. Shaftesbury had a residence at Aldersgate, and so his case came within the jurisdiction of the City. London was still in the hands of those who opposed the court; it was still, for the king, enemy territory.

When the earl's case was heard in the Old Bailey, therefore, the grand jury was packed with prominent Whigs; the foreman had in fact been an exclusionist member of parliament. It was perhaps inevitable that a verdict of *ignoramus* – 'we do not know' – was given and Shaftesbury acquitted. Four days later he applied for bail and the king's son, the duke of Monmouth, offered to act as his surety. He was released and, that night, the streets rang out with the cries 'A Monmouth! A Shaftesbury!' In many places, however, a Whig demonstration was countermanded by a Tory manifestation; or, as Sir Roger L'Estrange put it in his *Observator*, 'Noise rhymes to Noise, and Noise must be opposed to Noise'.

Two days after the verdict had been given the king launched an investigation into London's charter, asking '*quo warranto*' or by what warrant did the City enjoy the corporate privileges that it claimed; it was a protracted and expensive procedure, replete with formal and legal niceties, which could easily be turned against the City corporation. Any pretext could be found or concocted by the court lawyers to justify a forfeiture. It was easier and less expensive to ask for a new charter, but this in turn might give the king power to remove 'disaffected' members of the corporation. It was a device that Charles had already been using to great effect.

Even before the *quo warranto* proceedings had ended, the court party was exercising all its influence to elect Tory sheriffs and a Tory mayor. Various subterfuges were employed. The keepers of the alehouses and coffee-houses were told that their licences would be revoked if they did not vote for the Tory candidates; most of the Whig candidates were removed from the poll on the grounds that they were Quakers, or were non-residents, or had refused to take the oaths, or were in some other way ineligible. The campaign of trickery and intimidation was successful, and the Tory candidates were elected. On the following day Shaftesbury left his house in Aldersgate and went into hiding before taking ship to Holland. He knew now that, in any new trial for high treason, his opponents would be able to control the juries. The king would finally claim his head. He died in Amsterdam at the beginning of the next year. It was his belief that the souls of men and women entered the stars at the moment of death; the spirit of Shaftesbury would kindle, perhaps, a very fiery comet.

Some London radicals were now convinced that Charles intended to create an absolute monarchy, and began to plot among themselves to resist any such attempt. It was reported by government informers that preparations had been made for an uprising by city dissenters, who were apparently resolved to capture the king and force him to act against his brother. In November 1682, hundreds of 'brisk boys' in the East End rioted with the call 'A Monmouth! A Monmouth!' Before he left for the continent Shaftesbury had joined with the duke in discussing an armed uprising in the event of the king's death.

All this plotting and planning concluded in what became known as the 'Rye House Plot'. Certain discontented Whigs – among them William, Lord Russell, Algernon Sidney and the earl of Essex – seem to have laid plans to ambush and kill the king and his brother on their way back from the races at Newmarket. The assassins would assemble at a lonely farmstead known as Rye House in Hertfordshire, for the purpose of 'lopping the two sparks'. The plot was betrayed by one of the minor conspirators, and in the early summer of 1683 the principal agents were arrested. Even as the trial of Russell proceeded, the news came that Essex had been found dead in the Tower with wounds about his throat. It was supposed that he had committed suicide, thus presuming guilt, but it is possible that he had been murdered to prove the reality of the plot against the royal brothers. It would provide a convenient opportunity for the king to destroy all of the prominent Whigs.

When Lord Russell's family pleaded for him the king replied that 'if I do not take his life he will soon have mine'. His beheading, in Lincoln's Inn Fields, was badly managed by the public hangman, Jack Ketch, who later issued an apology. When Algernon Sidney was also sentenced to death by the axe, he made a passionate statement of his innocence. The chief justice, Judge Jeffreys, rose and rebuked him. 'I pray God work in you a temper fit to go into the other world, for I see you are not fit for this.'

'My lord, feel my pulse and see if I am disordered. I bless God, I never was in better temper than I am now.'

Russell, Essex and Sidney became known as the first Whig martyrs.

The duke of Monmouth had also been implicated in the plot, and an indictment been drawn up against him. Yet he submitted to his father and signed a confession that 'he owned the late conspiracy' but was innocent of any design against the life of his father. On the following day he withdrew the statement, for fear that he had betrayed his erstwhile associates; whereupon he was banished from the court. John Evelyn reported in his diary, the entry of 15 July 1683, that 'the public was now in great consternation on the late plot and conspiracy; his Majesty very melancholy, and not stirring without double guards; all the avenues and private doors about Whitehall and the Park shut up, few admitted to walk in it'.

The news of the conspiracy helped to rouse further anger against Whigs and dissenters, and the king published a declaration against 'the factious party' that was read out from every pulpit. This provoked the publication of innumerable 'loyal addresses' that underlined the supremacy of the king. Charles had in effect won his battle against parliament. He was also about to conquer London. The *quo warranto* proceedings had come to a conclusion, and in the summer of 1683 the king's bench decided that the liberties of the city had been rendered forfeit and returned into the hands of the king.

Charles could now govern in any manner that he pleased. The earl of Danby, once pursued by the Commons, was promptly released from the Tower. The duke of York was granted extensive powers, and it seemed to many that he was already ruling in place of the king who more and more consulted only his pleasures. In the spring of 1684, in fact, the duke was reappointed to the privy council after an absence of eleven years. In this period Titus Oates, the instigator of the 'Popish Plot', was arrested for calling James a traitor; he was convicted and fined £100,000. This ensured that he remained in confinement for the foreseeable future.

An entry from Evelyn's diaries conveys the mood and atmosphere of the triumphant court with its 'inexpressable luxury, and prophanesse, gaming and all dissolution, and as if it were total forgetfulness of God'. The king was 'sitting and toying with his concubines', among them the duchess of Portsmouth, with a 'French boy singing love-songs, in that glorious gallery, whilst about twenty of the great courtiers and other dissolute persons were at basset round a large table, a bank of at least two thousand in gold before them'.

Yet the games of Charles II were about to end. In the early weeks of 1685 he suffered from prolonged attacks of gout which left him debilitated. On the morning of Monday 2 February, he arose early after a restless and fevered night; to his attendants he seemed lethargic and almost torpid. He was also confused in speech and action. Then he fell into convulsions, or as one of his doctors put it '*convulsivi motus*', that left him speechless for two hours; cantharides, or Spanish fly, was applied to his skin to promote blisters. The letting of his blood lent him some relief, and the king recovered his power of speech. The duke of York had been summoned, and arrived so rapidly that he was wearing one shoe and one slipper. The doctors now prepared powders to promote sneezing so that the pressure of 'the humours' upon the king's brain might be relieved; he was also given a solution of cowslip flowers and spirit of sal ammoniac.

The king gradually seemed to grow better but by Wednesday afternoon he was covered in a profuse cold sweat that was a stage in the progress of dissolution. A preparation known as 'spirit of human skull' was then applied. By noon on Thursday there was little hope; he suffered several fits but was conscious in the intervals between them.

On that Thursday evening he ended the vacillations of a lifetime and formally entered the Roman Catholic communion by the ministrations of a Benedictine monk, John Hudleston. When the bishops and other attendants had withdrawn, the monk was conducted to the death chamber by the duke of York through a secret door. There seems little reason to doubt this account. James wrote, and spoke, of it. Hudleston himself left a brief description of the event. The observers had indeed been excluded from the chamber for a period, and afterwards the king refused to receive Anglican communion.

After that rite his mind was clear and his speech composed. On the following morning he asked to be taken to a window where he might see the rising sun. By ten o'clock he was unconscious. He died, quietly and without pain, shortly before noon.

45

The Protestant wind

So on 6 February 1685, the new king, James II, ascended the throne in the face of sustained and organized opposition from Shaftesbury and the Whigs. He was fifty-two years of age, and in vigorous heath. He had already proved himself to be determined and decisive; he had remained faithful to his Catholic beliefs despite every attempt to persuade him otherwise. He was more resolute and more trustworthy than his brother, but he lacked Charles's geniality and perceptiveness. He seemed to have no great capacity for compromise and viewed the world about him in the simple terms of light and darkness; there was the monarchy and authority on one side, with republicanism and disorder on the other. His manner was stiff and restrained, his temper short.

The prospect of such a monarch, however, was not necessarily disagreeable. He was known to be more diligent and more scrupulous than his late brother, with a greater concern for economy in financial matters. He was the very model of a retired naval officer of moderate abilities. The court itself acquired quite a different tone. Where before there had been music and mirth and gambling there was now, according to Sir John Lauder, 'little to be but seriousness and business'.

James's first statement maintained his support for the Church of England as the truest friend to the monarchy. Yet a little more than a week after the old king's death, according to John Evelyn, James 'to the great grief of his subjects, did now, for the first time, go to mass publicly in the little Oratory at the duke's lodgings, the doors being wide set open'. When the host was elevated, the Catholics fell upon their knees while the Protestants hurried out of the chapel. The new king was proclaiming his faith to the nation. He built his church upon the rock of Peter, but on that rock he would eventually founder.

Louis XIV had already sent a large sum of money to James as a reserve fund, held by the French ambassador, in case any insurrection or opposition should rise against him; Louis knew well enough that the English king would now favour Catholicism as far as lay in his power. James's councillors were also aware, however, that parliament would have to pass any order for new taxation. James called in the French ambassador to explain the position. 'Assure your master', he told him according to the ambassador's own account, 'of my gratitude and attachment. I know that without his protection I can do nothing . . . I will take good care not to let the Houses meddle with foreign affairs. If I see in them any disposition to make mischief, I will send them about their business.'

He need not have concerned himself. Parliament met in the spring of 1685 and was overwhelmingly Tory or royalist in composition; in his speech he gave 'assurance, concerning the care I will have of your religion and property' and in return requested revenues for life. The members proceeded to vote him the funds; given the extraordinary increase in his excise revenue as a result of growing trade, they furnished him with more money than he actually required. They may have been given pause, however, by the king's reference to 'your religion'.

The only possible threat came from his late brother's illegitimate son, the duke of Monmouth, who still harboured ambitions for the throne. Sure enough the duke left his exile in Amsterdam and, on 11 June, appeared with a small force off the coast at Lyme; he had believed that after his landing a multitude of supporters would flock to his flag, and so arrived with no more than 150 followers. Monmouth planted his blue standard on the soil of England and pronounced James to be a usurper; he also declared that the traitorous king had poisoned his brother, set light to London in the

Great Fire, and encouraged the 'Popish Plot' as part of 'one continued conspiracy against the reformed religion and the rights of the nation'. He then took upon himself the title of King James II.

Some of the natives of Dorset and Somerset joined his small army as he marched towards Taunton and Bridgwater, but there were far fewer recruits than he had originally expected. He had no coherent strategy of campaign, and he was quickly overwhelmed by James's better-trained and better-armed soldiers. The battle of Sedgemoor was the last one to be fought upon English soil. Monmouth escaped from the field and was found lying under a bush, half-asleep from exhaustion, and covered with fern and nettles for camouflage.

No mercy was shown to the defeated. Monmouth himself was taken before the king; he knelt down and pleaded for his life. 'Is there no hope?' he finally asked. The king turned away in silence. The duke was beheaded upon Tower Hill, and became the victim of another botched execution by Jack Ketch.

The consequences for the people of the West Country were severe. Judge Jeffreys was sent among them to deal out punishment. The 'Bloody Assizes' became part of the folklore of the region. Many died in prison, 800 were transported to be slaves, while some 250 were sentenced to death. Twenty-nine were sentenced to die at Dorchester but the two executioners protested that they could not hang, draw and quarter so many men on a single day. A woman was beheaded for offering food and water to an escaping 'rebel'. 'Gentlemen,' Jeffreys said to the jury, 'in your place I would find her guilty, were she my own mother.' Jeffreys laughed aloud, joked and exulted at the plight of the prisoners who came before him. He used to say that he gave the defendants 'a lick with the rough side of my tongue'. 'I see thee, villain, I see thee with the halter already around thy neck.' When he was told that one prisoner relied upon parish alms he replied, 'I will ease the parish of the burden.'

The defeat of the rebellion confirmed the king's authority; he had triumphed over his enemies, and now set about the process of building a new state based upon his absolute power. He determined to abolish the Test Act, thereby allowing Catholics to assume control of various offices; he wished to repeal the Habeas Corpus Act, thereby granting him more control over his opponents, and to maintain his standing army of approximately 20,000 men. He needed an army to safeguard himself from any 'disturbances', without or within.

In the summer of the year, after the defeat of Monmouth, some 15,000 men were encamped on Hounslow Heath; a lawyer of the time, Sir John Lowther, recollected that the standing army came 'to the astonishment of the people of England' who had never heard of such a force in times of peace. The troops were soon billeted throughout the country where, under the guise of pursuing 'rebels', they might act as James's security force. Some of their time was spent in disrupting the gatherings of Baptists and Presbyterians who, in this period, were once again some of the most persecuted of the dissenting sects. With the close assistance of Samuel Pepys, also, the king was intent upon establishing a formidable navy; this was part of his determination to consolidate and exploit the colonial territories within India, North America and the West Indies. He can be considered, therefore, as one of the founders of the commercial and imperial state that emerged in the eighteenth century.

The twin bonds of royal autocracy and the Catholic religion ensured the amity of James II and Louis XIV, and there was naturally much alarm in England when, in the autumn of 1685, the French king cancelled the Edict of Nantes that guaranteed freedom of worship to his Protestant subjects. Could James follow the same path? It was of course unlikely that James would dare to take measures against the English national Church but he might attempt to check its powers. His attitude towards the Protestant Huguenots who fled to England was not encouraging; he believed them to be anti-monarchical and was not anxious that they remain in his kingdom. They stayed, however, settling in Spitalfields and elsewhere, and were essentially to create the silk industry of the country.

When parliament reassembled on the appointed day, 9 November, much apprehension was naturally felt by the king's supporters, the Tories, who also upheld the Anglican faith. 'Never was there a more devoted Parliament,' one contemporary observed, 'but you know the point of religion is a tender point.' The members of both houses were most alarmed by the fact that, in defiance of the Test Act, the king had already appointed Roman Catholic officers to the army and navy. The king declared, in his speech from the throne, that 'having had the benefit of their services in such a time of need and danger

[Monmouth's invasion], I will neither expose them to disgrace, nor myself to the want of them, if there should be a second rebellion to make them necessary to me'. It was soon made clear to him that the members of both houses, but particularly those of the Lords, were dismayed by his illegal and unparliamentary appointments. One brave peer, Viscount Mordaunt, stated that 'the evil which we are considering is neither future nor uncertain. A standing army exists. It is officered by papists. We have no foreign enemy. There is no rebellion in the land. For what, then, is this force maintained, except for the purpose of subverting our laws, and establishing that arbitrary power which is so justly abhorred by Englishmen?'

Eleven days after parliament had been summoned, James prorogued it until the following year; it was characteristic of his rule that he suppressed the assembly before it had the chance formally to challenge his authority. It was the first sign of the growing tension between the king and the political nation. Parliament never met again in the course of his short reign.

On the strength of his prerogative alone he now began to assist his co-religionists. He issued orders forbidding the celebration of 'gunpowder treason day', in which it was customary to burn an effigy of the pope; the edict was only partly successful. Various of the religious orders were once again settled in London; the Benedictines were ensconced at St James's, the Carmelite friars in the City, the Franciscans in Lincoln's Inn Fields and the Jesuits in the Savoy. A Catholic school was established by the Jesuits in that neighbour-hood. One of James's most intimate advisers was a Jesuit priest, Edward Petre, who was placed in charge of the royal chapel and who lodged in the king's old apartments in Whitehall. By the end of the year five Roman Catholics were part of the privy council.

The king's morals, however, were not governed by strictly Catholic standards. His principal mistress, Catherine Sedley, was given a large mansion in St James's Square and soon acquired the title of countess of Dorchester. She seemed not to know the reason for his affection. 'It cannot be my beauty,' she said, 'for he must see that I have none; and it cannot be my wit, for he has not enough to know that I have any.'

The king often said that his purpose was to 'establish' or 're-establish' Roman Catholicism. He may have realized that he would not be able to impose his faith upon the nation and he knew well enough that his likely successor, Mary, was a fervent Protestant; he hoped only to put Catholicism on terms of equality with Anglicanism in the belief that the virtues of his religion would in time elicit many converts. He had hoped to persuade his Anglican and Tory supporters to accede to his wishes but instead he only managed further to antagonize them. When a Catholic chapel was established in Lime Street, a crowd of Londoners gathered to attack 'the mass house'; the trained bands were called out to disperse the crowd but demurred on the grounds that 'we cannot in conscience fight for popery'. The king's own stubborn and imperious temper did not help his cause. 'I will make no concession', he was accustomed to say. 'My father made concessions, and he was beheaded.'

His purpose was to purge the judicial bench of all those who might be disaffected from his policies or his powers. It has been estimated that in the course of his reign he replaced up to nine-tenths of the serving justices of the peace in each county; the replacements were Roman Catholics who, in the absence of a police force, became the principal agents of law and royal authority. The corporations of the towns and the lords-lieutenant of the counties were also purged. When the king subsequently relieved the arch-bishop of Canterbury of his duties at the privy council, the French ambassador observed that James had resolved to favour only those who supported his interests.

The case of *Gooden* v. *Hales* was brought forward, in the summer of 1686, as a test of power. At issue was the right of the king to dispense with the penalties of the law and to suspend their execution, with particular reference to the Test Act against Catholics. When four judges declared that any such decision would 'overturn the English constitution', he simply dismissed them from the bench. Even those once most loyal to the king were now dismayed. 'Everyone was astonished', John Evelyn wrote in his diary entry for 27 June. 'Great jealousies as to what would be the end of these proceedings.'

In this summer, too, the king established a commission for ecclesiastical causes for 'the prevention of indiscreet preaching'; it was in effect an institution designed to assert the rights of Roman Catholics. The commissioners had the power to deprive any cleric of his living or to excommunicate any layman, and, perhaps more importantly, they were given the authority to regulate the schools and universities of the kingdom.

It is not at all clear that the Catholics of England, who made up some 2 to 3 per cent of the population, welcomed the efforts of their Catholic king. He was stirring up resentment, and worse, against them. Riots against 'papists' had broken out in certain parts of the country. They were too few, in any case, to fill up all the offices that were becoming vacant. How could they become judges when they had previously been denied entrance to the Inns of Court?

James also began the scrutiny of all those in power. In the royal closet he interviewed those who held public office as well as the members of both houses of parliament; these individual encounters became known as 'closetings' whereby he demanded the acquiescence of each man in his religious policies. Those who demurred were dismissed. Lord Chesterfield reported that 'we do hear every post of so many persons being out of their employments that it seems like the account one has after a battle of those who miscarried in the engagement'. The king's proceedings created much anger and disaffection among those who, in other circumstances, would have been faithful to him.

At the same time James also decided to gain the loyalty, or at least the acquiescence, of the nation by granting religious liberty to all of his subjects. In a declaration of indulgence, issued in the spring of 1687, he suspended 'the execution of all penal laws for religious offences' and lifted 'the imposition of religious oaths or tests as qualifications for office'. Thus he materially assisted the case of his co-religionists while at the same time hoping to gain the gratitude of nonconformists. He may have believed that he could still rely upon the tacit support of the royalists and the Anglicans, even though they had been sorely stretched. In this judgement he may have been unwise. From this time forward, however, the dissenters flocked to their chapels and assemblies without the least hindrance; Macaulay observed that 'an observant traveller will still remark the date of 1687 on some of the oldest meeting houses'.

One sign of Anglican unease emerged in the king's decision to impose his will upon Oxford University. When the president of Magdalen College died, letters mandatory were sent by the king to the Fellows of that college for the election of Anthony Farmer; Farmer was in fact ineligible for the office, and was notable only for his Catholic sympathies. The Fellows proceeded to elect a Doctor Hough, in defiance of royal instructions. When the king visited Oxford in the course of his summer progress, he berated the recalcitrant Fellows and ordered them to leave his presence. 'Go home,' he said, 'and show yourselves good members of the Church of England. Get you gone, know I am your king. I will be obeyed and I command you to be gone.'

The recently appointed ecclesiastical commission then annulled the election of Hough, whereupon twenty-five of the Fellows of Magdalen resigned or were dismissed. The college now became essentially a Catholic stronghold, and Mass was performed daily in its chapel. It was a hollow victory for the king, however, who thereby managed to alienate a great number of the clergy and to lose any reputation he hoped to gain for religious tolerance. The Magdalen affair was widely reported, adding to the anger and dismay at the king's indifference to Anglican sensibilities.

It was widely reported, also, that in the course of the summer he made a pilgrimage to the 'holy well' in North Wales dedicated to St Winifred where he prayed for an heir. It was also noted that the king had knelt to the papal nuncio, Archbishop Adda, and implored his blessing. No English king had ever knelt before another man since the time of King John, and the posture was treated with embarrassment and even disgust. This was Catholicism with a vengeance. The envoy from Modena reported that 'such of the nobility as have any credit, standing, or power in the kingdom are rarely to be seen at court'. William of Orange, staunch defender of the Protestant cause, had sent an ambassador to London who held meetings with disaffected noblemen; the prince of Orange watched and waited.

William had been appointed captain general for life of the forces of the Dutch republic and, by right of his territory of Orange, he was also a sovereign prince. His mother was Mary, eldest daughter of Charles I, and his wife, Mary, was the daughter of the present king; no doubt he considered himself to be a rightful heir to the throne, on the supposition that James had no legitimate son. He was a staunch Calvinist, like the rest of his family, and the doctrine of predestination weighed heavily upon him. If he had one duty beyond all others it was to curb the power of France; he had seen Louis XIV invade his adopted country, only to be halted by the opening of the dykes. The imperial pretensions of the House of Bourbon had not been tamed, however, and William dedicated himself to the defence of the Protestant states of Europe from the forces of the French king.

By the end of 1687 James had decided to call parliament in order formally to repeal the Test Act and the other penal laws against the exercise of religious liberty. For that purpose he decided to renew the 'closeting' on a local and regional level by asking all office-holders and justices of the peace whether, if elected, they would vote for repeal; if they were not standing as members of the Commons, would they at least vote for candidates who were committed to doing so? If they answered in the negative, or were equivocal, they were to be dismissed from their posts. Over 1,000 men, for example, were expelled from the borough corporations. This was another action designed to infuriate the local gentry, as well as the corporations of the towns and cities; it also served further to alienate the Anglican Church, now confirmed in its belief that Catholicism served only to reinforce arbitrary government.

At the beginning of April 1688, government agents set out with 20 shillings a day in expenses in order to prepare the ground for the coming general election; they were to liaise with the leader of the 'court party' in each locality, arrange for the proper distribution of court literature and counter the work of the opposition. The king's aim was, in other words, to 'pack' his new parliament with his own supporters and thus clear the way for complete and uninterrupted rule. Subsequent events, however, ensured that no such parliament would ever meet.

It had already become clear that the queen, Mary of Modena, was with child. The prospect of a Catholic heir then became palpable, with all the anguish and anxiety that ensued among the Anglican and dissenting populations. The Stuart imperium might stretch on perpetually. On 7 May 1688, James reissued his declaration of indulgence, together with a promise to call parliament by the end of the year. An order followed that the declaration was to be read from the pulpits of every church on two successive Sundays. His

Jesuit adviser, Father Petre, had told him that the Anglican clergy 'should be made to eat their own dung'.

The order incited only rage and disobedience from the clergy. The archbishop of Canterbury and six other bishops printed a petition for its withdrawal, on the grounds that the dispensing power assumed by the king was in fact illegal. When the petition was presented to him the king was irate. 'This is a great surprise to me,' he told the bishops. 'I did not expect this from your Church, especially from some of you. This is a standard of rebellion!' The declaration of indulgence was in fact largely ignored. Of the 9,000 churches of England, it is estimated that it was read in 200. It was read in only seven, out of one hundred, in London. When its first words were pronounced in the church of St Gregory's by St Paul's, the whole congregation rose and withdrew. The angry will of the king now superseded any kind of caution or circumspection. He demanded that the seven bishops be consigned to the Tower and prosecuted for publishing a seditious libel.

William was watching events as they unfolded. A swift sailing boat was continually passing over the North Sea from London to The Hague, with messages and reports designed for the sole attention of the prince of Orange.

On 10 June 1688, a son was born to James and Mary of Modena. Many disbelieved the report. It was just too convenient that a Stuart heir should emerge at this particular moment. It was rumoured that a warming pan had been used to smuggle a newborn infant into the royal chamber. Five days after the birth of the prince of Wales the seven offending bishops were brought by barge from the Tower to Westminster Hall, where they were greeted with repeated cries of 'God bless the bishops!' The jury, after a night's deliberation, acquitted the bishops of publishing a seditious libel; on publication of the verdict, Westminster Hall rang with cheers and acclamations for half an hour. The news spread rapidly throughout the city, where bonfires were lit and church bells rang. Effigies of the pope were burned in the streets; in Somerset an effigy of the newborn prince was also set on fire. Most ominously for the king, perhaps, his soldiers encamped on Hounslow Heath cheered on receiving the news. When the king heard that the bishops had been acquitted, he said merely, 'So much the worse for them.'

Yet the decision had shaken the earth beneath his feet. On the day of the acquittal seven prominent men of state – among them the earls of Devonshire, Danby and Shrewsbury – sent a secret letter to William of Orange and informed him that the vast majority of the people were 'dissatisfied with the present conduct of the government' and were eager for a change. If William were to invade England, he would find the nation behind him. They told him that 'much the greatest part of the nobility and gentry' was opposed to the king and to his policies, and that on his landing they would 'draw great numbers' to his side.

Even in this extremity it is unlikely that they wished to remove James from the throne. They wanted William to act in the role of a Protestant saviour who would force the king to call a free parliament, which would then settle the religious affairs of the nation and extirpate all bias towards popery. Speed, and decision, were of the essence before the king could call a 'packed' parliament. William was in fact already making active preparations to assemble a field army and a fleet.

By the beginning of August the news of his intentions reached England. In his diary entry for 10 August 1688, John Evelyn noted that 'Dr Tenison now told me there would suddenly be some great thing discovered. This was the Prince of Orange intending to come over.' An envoy from the court of Louis XIV reached James a few days later, warning him of an imminent invasion and offering him French assistance. James refused to believe the message. Could his daughter Mary conspire with her husband to depose her father? It was not possible. Would William lead his forces on a perilous expedition abroad at a moment when his country was threatened by French power? No. It was more likely that the French were trying to frighten him into an alliance with Louis XIV, an alliance that would not be to the liking of the coming parliament.

The decision was not long delayed. On 28 September William of Orange announced the forthcoming invasion of England to the States General. On the same day James proclaimed to the nation that its object was 'an absolute conquest of these our kingdoms and the utter subduing and subjecting us and all our people to a foreign power' and that it had been promoted 'by certain wicked subjects for their own selfish ends'; the king also declared that he had 'declined any foreign succours'. He was on his own.

William then issued his own declaration in which he stated that he had been invited to come over the water by 'a great many lords both spiritual and temporal' and that he would come simply 'to have a free and lawful Parliament assembled as soon as is possible'. He did not mention any pretensions to the throne but stated only that 'we for our part will concur in everything that may procure the peace and happiness of the nation'. James wished to know who these 'many lords', inviting William to England, might be. He questioned the bishops and asked them to sign a paper declaring their 'abhorrence' of the invasion but, to his surprise and dismay, they refused to do so.

He now realized the full gravity of his position, and began to make desperate efforts to reverse the policies that had alienated his kingdom. He dismissed Father Petre from his councils. He issued a declaration promising that he would 'inviolably . . . preserve the Church of England' and bar Catholics from parliament. He pledged to restore to office those justices of the peace and other local leaders whom he had summarily dismissed in the spring of the year. He stated that he would readmit the Fellows of Magdalen College whom he had banished for disobedience, and agreed that he would terminate the ecclesiastical commission that had been responsible for their punishment. The charter of the City of London, rendered forfeit six years before, was now returned to the mayor and aldermen. Yet all these palliative measures came too late, and he was now despised for weakness and vacillation.

He was resolute enough, however, in organizing his defences. He fitted out more ships to join the squadrons already at sea; they now consisted of thirty-three large ships and sixteen fire-ships. Royal commissions were sent out for the creation of new regiments and additional men were appointed to existing ones; the militia of London and the counties were called up, and ordered to stand in readiness for the defence of their country. Battalions of infantry, and regiments of cavalry, were brought back from Ireland and Scotland to serve closer to home. Sir John Lowther, a baronet who supported the cause of William, recalled that 'nothing was left undone that might put the king in a posture to defend himself'. It was clearly within James's power to confront and defeat the invader.

William, prince of Orange, set sail in the middle of October; it was dangerously late in the season, and a gale drove his ships back. Now that he had made his decision, however, he was determined to go on. At the beginning of November he embarked for England once more with an east wind filling his sails; it became known as 'the Protestant wind'.

He did not come to 'save' Protestantism, however, except in a particular sense. His principal purpose was to find the means to contain and, if possible, curtail French power that was directed towards the United Provinces and elsewhere. He needed an English army, and English ships, for that endeavour. He could by no means be certain of the outcome. While preparing for the invasion he wrote to his principal councillor, Willem Bentinck, that 'my sufferings, my disquiet, are dreadful. I hardly see my way. Never in my life did I so much feel the need of God's guidance.' Yet he was a firm believer in predestination, and now chanced all. He could not be certain that he would be welcomed; he had been advised that the majority of the English would come to his side once he arrived, but he could not be sure of this.

It was believed that he would land in the north or in the east, and James's defences were accordingly clustered there; William himself was apprised of the decision, and determined that he would go to the relatively unprepared south-west. By the time he reached the coast of Devon, strong winds hampered the English fleet in pursuit and, at a subsequent council of war, it was determined that no attack should be made against what was considered to be a far stronger Dutch fleet. James subsequently averred that a conspiracy had been hatched among the captains, but it is far more likely that they were influenced by caution rather than treason.

The prince of Orange set foot on English soil at Brixham, at the southern end of Tor Bay, on 5 November. It was an auspicious day, the anniversary of the overthrow of the gunpowder plot and the dissolution of a papist conspiracy. The movements of William's troops, once they had disembarked, were hampered by rain and foul roads. By 9 November William had reached Exeter, where his men were able to rest, but he was not met with any enthusiasm; the citizens treated him coldly, and at a service of thanksgiving in the cathedral the canons and most of the congregation fled. William remained in the city for nine days but no one of renown or distinction came to him; he began to believe that he had been deceived about the situation in England and seemed willing to re-embark with his men. When some local gentry did enrol under his standard he declared that 'we expected you that dwelled so near the place of our landing would have joined us sooner'. The simple answer to his bafflement may have been that he had landed in a region where no one expected him. Supporters did now begin to march towards him.

Yet James II had not been able to take advantage of this interval in the conflict. He called back his troops who had been originally sent to the north but, when he joined them at their camp in Salisbury, he found both the officers and the men demoralized and divided. A strong king would have immediately launched an attack upon his enemy but James hesitated. Some of his commanders wished to press forward quickly, while others advised a retreat to London.

In this crisis the king himself broke down; he suffered from a catastrophic series of nosebleeds, tokens of his rising panic, that deprived him of rest. Some of his officers began to desert him and make their way to the prince of Orange, among them Lord Colchester, Lord Abingdon and Lord Cornbury; they trusted William's declaration that he had come to save the Protestant religion and to install a free parliament. A series of local risings, in favour of parliament and Protestantism, now increased the king's isolation; Nottingham and York, Leicester and Carlisle and Gloucester were some of the towns that declared for 'the Protestant religion and liberty'.

In an atmosphere of confusion and intense distrust the king, seized with apprehension at the news of the desertions, decided to retreat to London. He had in effect capitulated to William without a fight. Other senior officers, among them John Churchill and the earl of Berkeley, now decided to leave him and go over to William. When the king arrived at Whitehall, and an almost empty court, he was greeted with the news that his younger daughter, Anne, had also defected to the enemy. She was a staunch Anglican who had been horrified by her father's open espousal and encouragement of Catholicism. Under the protection of the bishop of London, she had escaped by hackney carriage to Nottingham.

The king did not know whom to trust or whom to believe any more. A courtier reported that 'the king is much out of order, looks yellow, and takes no natural rest'. He could sleep only with the assistance of opiates. He summoned to a council all the nobles and bishops who remained in the city; they advised him that he had no recourse except to call a free parliament. On 30 November he issued a proclamation to that effect, and combined with it a pardon to all those who had risen against him. But it was too late. He had already forfeited the trust and loyalty of many of those who had been closest to him.

William was on a slow march towards London, and the king had the choice of flight or resistance. Yet where would he find the arms and the men to withstand the invader? He sent some commissioners to treat with William at Hungerford, but this was a feint to disguise his true purpose. He had already provided for the safety of his wife and son; on the night of 9 December Mary of Modena, disguised as a laundress, escaped with her child to Calais. On 11 December the king himself fled and, with two Roman Catholic companions, he crossed the Thames to Vauxhall and there took horse. It is assumed that he threw the great seal of England into the waters, so that public order could not legally be maintained by his successor. He did not think of himself as abandoning his kingdom but, rather, finding temporary security before regaining his throne. Yet he had effectively surrendered the initiative to William, who could already regard himself as the next king of England.

On the news that the king had fled, the lords spiritual and temporal formed a temporary administration in order to negotiate with the prince of Orange for the return of a free parliament designed to restore 'our laws, our liberties and properties'. James's departure also provoked open fury against the papist enemy; the Catholic chapels of London were fired, while the residences of the Catholic ambassadors of Spain and Florence were ransacked.

Wild rumours now spread through the country that Irish troops under the command of the king had massacred the people of London and were marching to the north. It was reported that Birmingham had been fired by the papists; Nottingham and Stafford were then said to have been sacked, with Doncaster and Huddersfield following in the line of fire. When the rumours reached Leeds that the child-eating Irish were in the suburbs, Ralph Thoresby wrote in his diary that 'the drums beat, the bells rang backwards, the women shrieked and such dreadful consternation seized upon all persons'. The false alarm is a token of the hysterical anxiety into which the people had sunk. A doggerel song against the Irish came out of the consternation. 'Lillibulero' is a parody of papist sentiment and it became so popular that its composer, Thomas Wharton, declared that it had whistled a king out of three kingdoms:

> Now the heretics all go down
> Lillibulero bullen a la
> By Christ and St Patrick's the nation's our own
> Lillibulero bullen a la.

The music is still used as a signature tune by BBC Radio.

The king's departure from England was now interrupted when he was discovered on a customs boat about to sail from the Isle of Sheppey; he was disguised in a short black wig and was at first mistaken for a Jesuit. When he was brought to the port of Faversham he was soon recognized and taken to the mayor's house where he was guarded by the seamen who had found him; they wanted to claim their prize. He was by now thoroughly frightened and bewildered, at one moment pleading for a boat and at the next weeping over his misfortunes. An eyewitness, John Knatchbull, 'observed a smile in his face of an extraordinary size and sort; so forced, awkward and unpleasant to look upon that I can truly say I never saw anything like it'.

When informed of James's enforced sojourn in Faversham, no one in authority really knew what to do with him. He could not stay where he was. James himself then seems to have determined to return to London, where he might hold an interview with William; his messenger, bearing this news to the invader, was promptly arrested and consigned to the Tower. Who was the master now?

James, unaware of his envoy's fate, proceeded towards the capital; as he approached Blackheath on 16 December he was greeted by cheering crowds who were no doubt hoping for an accommodation between the two parties. They were largely comprised of the 'king and country' stalwarts among the people, but they represented a more general sense of relief. A royalist supporter noted after the event that in the streets between Southwark and Whitehall 'there was scarce room for coaches to pass through, and the balconies and windows besides were thronged'. The king himself was to write that it was 'liker a day of triumph than humiliation'.

A less enthusiastic welcome also awaited him. While resting at Whitehall that evening, he was advised that all the posts were to be taken up by the Dutch guards of the prince of Orange; he would in effect be a prisoner in his own palace. In the early hours of the next day he was woken by an order from the prince commanding him to leave London by nine in the morning and travel on to Ham House. He was to depart at that time because William himself was to enter London at midday and did not wish the people to be diverted by the sight of their king. The king obeyed the order, with the exception that he wished to remove to Rochester rather than to Ham. The wish was granted but it was still clear that the monarch was a helpless captive in his own kingdom.

William himself entered the capital on 18 December to be in turn greeted by cheering crowds, bells and bonfires. He was heralded as one who had come to redeem 'our religion, laws, liberties and lives', but a large element of the jubilation must have come from the fact that the Protestant religion had been restored without war or revolution. They had cheered the king two days before as one who had abandoned his Catholic policies; they could equally well cheer their Protestant saviour.

The king stayed at the house of a local baronet in Rochester for a few days, but every moment he was looking for a means of escape. He feared assassination or, at best, straight imprisonment. Yet he noted that the guards about him were not strict in the performance of their duties. In truth William wanted his rival to escape as the least worst outcome of their conflict. James's presence in the country caused difficulties of its own but, if it could be said that he had departed by his own wish, then he might be considered to have abdicated. On the night of 22 December he rose from his bed and departed through a conveniently opened back door; he walked through the garden to the shore of the Medway where a skiff was waiting for him.

Thus was accomplished what was variously called the great or prodigious 'Revolution' and what was eventually known as the 'Glorious Revolution'. A supporter of William, Bishop Burnet, wrote of the king that 'his whole strength, like a spider's web, was so irrevocably broken with a touch, that he was never able to retrieve what for want of judgement and heart, he threw up in a day'.

It was not a matter of a day, however, but of years. In his obstinacy and fervent piety he had miscalculated the nature of the country; he had advanced where he should have called a halt. He had pitted the power of central government against local government to the ultimate disservice of the nation. By assaulting the sensibilities of both Anglicans and Tories he had alienated his natural supporters, and by advancing the claims of Catholics he had touched upon a very sensitive prejudice. He may not have wanted to become an absolute king, but he acted as if that were his intention. The birth of an heir stretched that prospect indefinitely.

James II spent the rest of his life in France. It was said, in his court at the Château de Saint-Germain-en-Laye, that 'when you listen to him, you realize why he is here'. Thus ended the public life of the last Stuart king of England. We may leave the scene with the words of John Dryden from *The Secular Masque*:

> Thy wars brought nothing about;
> Thy lovers were all untrue.
> 'Tis well an old age is out,
> And time to begin a new.

Further reading

This is by no means an exhaustive list, but it represents a selection of those books the author found most useful in the preparation of this third volume.

GENERAL STUDIES

G. E. Aylmer: *The Struggle for the Constitution* (London, 1963).

J. C. D. Clark: *Revolution and Rebellion* (Cambridge, 1986).

Thomas Cogswell, Richard Cust and Peter Lake (eds): *Politics, Religion and Popularity* (Cambridge, 2002).

Richard Cust and Ann Hughes (eds): *Conflict in Early Stuart England* (London, 1989).

Godfrey Davies: *The Early Stuarts* (Oxford, 1959).

Kenneth Fincham (ed.): *The Early Stuart Church* (London, 1993).

S. R. Gardiner: *History of England, 1603–1642*. In ten volumes (London, 1899).

William Haller: *The Rise of Puritanism* (New York, 1938).

Christopher Hill: *Puritanism and Revolution* (London, 1958).

Derek Hirst: *Authority and Conflict* (London, 1986).

Ronald Hutton: *Debates in Stuart History* (London, 2004).

J. P. Kenyon: *The Stuart Constitution* (Cambridge, 1966).

Peter Lake: *Anglicans and Puritans?* (London, 1988).

Peter Lake and Steven Pincus (eds): *The Politics of the Public Sphere in Early Modern England* (Manchester, 2007).

John Lingard and Hilaire Belloc: *The History of England*. Volumes seven to ten (New York, 1912).

Judith Maltby: *Prayer Book and People in Elizabethan and Early Stuart England* (Cambridge, 1998).

Brian Manning: *The English People and the English Revolution* (London, 1976).

John Morgan: *Godly Learning* (Cambridge, 1986).

John Morrill, Paul Slack and Daniel Woolf (eds): *Public Duty and Private Conscience in Seventeenth Century England* (Oxford, 1993).

J. F. H. New: *Anglican and Puritan* (London, 1964).

Linda Levy Peck: *Court Patronage and Corruption in Early Stuart England* (London, 1990).

H. S. Reinmuth Jnr. (ed.): *Early Stuart Studies* (Minneapolis, 1970).

Conrad Russell: *Parliament and English Politics, 1621–1629* (Oxford, 1979).

—————— *Unrevolutionary England* (London, 1990).

Kevin Sharpe, *Politics and Ideas in Early Stuart England* (London, 1989).

—————— *Image Wars* (New Haven, 2010).

—————— (ed.): *Faction and Parliament* (London, 1978).

Kevin Sharpe and Peter Lake: *Culture and Politics in Early Stuart England* (London, 1994).

Alan Smith: *The Emergence of a Nation State* (London, 1984).

J. P. Sommerville: *Politics and Ideology in England, 1603–1640* (London, 1986).

David Starkey (ed.): *The English Court* (London, 1987).

Margot Todd (ed.): *Reformation to Revolution* (London, 1995).

Howard Tomlinson (ed.): *Before the English Civil War* (London, 1983).

Hugh Trevor-Roper: *Historical Essays* (London, 1957).

—————— *Catholics, Anglicans and Puritans* (London, 1987).

Nicholas Tyacke: *Anti-Calvinists* (Oxford, 1987).

—————— (ed.) *The English Revolution* (Manchester, 2007).

David Underdown: *Revel, Riot and Rebellion* (Oxford, 1985).

J. Dover Wilson (ed.): *Seventeenth Century Studies* (Oxford, 1938).

Andy Wood: *Riot, Rebellion and Popular Politics in Early Modern England* (London, 2002).

JAMES VI AND I

Robert Ashton: *James by his Contemporaries* (London, 1969).

Bryan Bevan: *King James* (London, 1990).

Caroline Bingham: *James of England* (London, 1981).

Thomas Birch: *The Court and Times of James*. In two volumes (London, 1848).

Glenn Burgess: *Absolute Monarchy* (London, 1996).

Irene Carrier: *James* (Cambridge, 1998).

Thomas Cogswell: *The Blessed Revolution* (Cambridge, 1989).

James Doelman: *King James and the Religious Culture of England* (Cambridge, 2000).

Kenneth Fincham: *Prelate as Pastor* (Oxford, 1990).

Antonia Fraser: *King James* (London, 1974).

S. J. Houston: *James* (London, 1972).

Robert Lockyer: *James* (London, 1998).

David Matthew: *The Jacobean Age* (London, 1938).

——— *James* (London, 1967).

W. M. Mitchell: *The Rise of the Revolutionary Party* (New York, 1957).

W. B. Patterson: *King James and the Reunion of Christendom* (Cambridge, 1997).

Linda Levy Peck (ed.): *The Mental World of the Jacobean Court* (Cambridge, 1991).

Menna Prestwich: *Cranfield* (Oxford, 1966).

Walter Scott: *Secret History of the Court of James*. In two volumes (London, 1811).

Alan G. R. Smith (ed.): *The Reign of James* (London, 1973).

Alan Stewart: *The Cradle King* (London, 2003).

Roy Strong: *Henry, Prince of Wales* (London, 2000).

Roland Usher: *The Reconstruction of the English Church*. In two volumes (New York, 1910).

D. H. Willson: *King James* (London, 1956).

CHARLES I

G. E. Aylmer: *The King's Servants* (London, 1961).

Thomas Birch and Cyprien de Gamache: *The Court and Times of Charles I.* In two volumes (London, 1848).

Charles Carlton: *Charles I: The Personal Monarch* (London, 1983).

Hester Chapman: *Great Villiers* (London, 1949).

H. P. Cooke: *Charles I and his Earlier Parliaments* (London, 1939).

E. S. Cope: *Politics without Parliaments* (London, 1987).

Richard Cust: *Charles I: A Political Life* (London, 2005).

C. W. Daniels and John Morrill: *Charles I* (Cambridge, 1988).

Isaac Disraeli: *Commentaries on the Life and Reign of Charles I.* In five volumes (London, 1828–1831).

Christopher Durston: *Charles I* (London, 1998).

J. H. Hexter: *The Reign of King Pym* (Cambridge, Mass., 1961).

Christopher Hibbert: *Charles I* (London, 2007).

F. M. G. Higham: *Charles I* (London,1932).

Clive Holmes: *Why Was Charles I Executed?* (London, 2006).

David Matthew: *The Social Structure in Caroline England* (Oxford, 1948).

―――― *The Age of Charles I* (London, 1951).

Brian Quintrell: *Charles I* (London, 1993).

L. J. Reeve: *Charles I and the Road to Personal Rule* (Cambridge, 1989).

Conrad Russell: *The Fall of the British Monarchies* (Oxford, 1991).

Kevin Sharpe: *The Personal Rule of Charles I* (New Haven, 1992).

Hugh Trevor-Roper: *Archbishop Laud* (London, 1940).

C. V. Wedgwood: *The King's Peace* (London, 1955).

―――― *Thomas Wentworth* (New York, 1962).

G. M. Young: *Charles I and Cromwell* (London, 1935).

OLIVER CROMWELL

Maurice Ashley: *The Greatness of Oliver Cromwell* (London, 1957).

Hilaire Belloc: *Cromwell* (London, 1934).

John Buchan: *Cromwell* (London, 1934).

Barry Coward: *Oliver Cromwell* (London, 1991).

J. C. Davis: *Oliver Cromwell* (London, 2001).

C. H. Firth: *Cromwell* (London, 1901).

Antonia Fraser: *Cromwell* (London, 1973).

S. R. Gardiner: *Oliver Cromwell* (London, 1901).

Peter Gaunt: *Oliver Cromwell* (Oxford, 1996).

François Guizot: *Oliver Cromwell* (London, 1879).

Christopher Hill: *God's Englishman* (London, 1971).

Roger Howell: *Cromwell* (London, 1977).

Frank Kitson: *Old Ironsides* (London, 2004).

John Morley: *Oliver Cromwell* (London, 1904).

John Morrill (ed.): *Oliver Cromwell* (Oxford, 2007).

Micheál Ó Siochrú: *God's Executioner* (London, 2008).

C. V. Wedgwood: *Oliver Cromwell* (London, 1973).

CIVIL WAR

John Adamson: *The Noble Revolt* (London, 2007).

Michael Braddick: *God's Fury, England's Fire* (London, 2008).

Charles Carlton: *Going to the Wars* (London, 1992).

Edward, earl of Clarendon: *The History of the Rebellion and Civil Wars in England*. In six volumes (Oxford, 1888).

David Cressy: *England on Edge* (Oxford, 2007).

Richard Cust and Ann Hughes (eds): *The English Civil War* (London, 1997).

Barbara Donagan: *War in England, 1642–1649* (Oxford, 2008).

Anthony Fletcher: *The Outbreak of the English Civil War* (London, 1981).

S. R. Gardiner: *History of the Great Civil War*. In four volumes (London, 1888).

Peter Gaunt (ed.): *The English Civil War* (Oxford, 2000).

Ian Gentles: *The English Revolution* (London, 2007).

Christopher Hill: *The English Revolution* (London, 1940).

Ann Hughes: *The Causes of the English Civil War* (London, 1991).

Ronald Hutton: *The Royalist War Effort* (London, 1982).

D. E. Kennedy: *The English Revolution* (London, 2000).

John Kenyon: *The Civil Wars of England* (London, 1988).

Mark Kishlansky: *The Rise of the New Model Army* (Cambridge, 1979).

Jason McElligott and David Smith (eds): *Royalists and Royalism during the English Civil Wars* (Cambridge, 2007).

Allan Macinnes: *The British Revolution* (London, 2005).

Brian Manning (ed.): *Politics, Religion and the English Civil War* (London, 1973).

Michael Mendle (ed.): *The Putney Debates* (Cambridge, 2001).

John Morrill: *The Revolt of the Provinces* (London, 1976).

———— *The Nature of the English Revolution* (London, 1993).

———— (ed.) *Reactions to the English Civil War* (London, 1982).

Jason Peacey (ed.): *The Regicides and the Execution of Charles I* (London, 2001).

R. C. Richardson: *The Debate on the English Revolution* (London, 1977).

Ivan Roots: *The Great Rebellion* (London, 1966).

Conrad Russell (ed.): *The Origins of the English Civil War* (London, 1973).

David Scott: *Politics and War in the Three Stuart Kingdoms* (London, 2004).

Lawrence Stone: *The Causes of the English Revolution* (London, 1972).

John Stubbs: *Reprobates* (London, 2011).

David Underdown: *Pride's Purge* (Oxford, 1971).

Malcolm Wanklyn: *The Warrior Generals* (London, 2010).

C. V. Wedgwood: *The King's War* (London, 1958).

Austin Woolrych: *Britain in Revolution* (Oxford, 2002).

Blair Worden: *The Rump Parliament* (Cambridge, 1974).

———— *The English Civil Wars* (London, 2009).

Commonwealth and Protectorate

G. E. Aylmer (ed.): *The Interregnum* (London, 1972).

Toby Barnard: *The English Republic* (London, 1982).

Jakob Bowman: *The Protestant Interest in Cromwell's Foreign Relations* (Heidelberg, 1900).

Barry Coward: *The Cromwellian Protectorate* (Manchester, 2002).

C. H. Firth: *The Last Years of the Protectorate*. In two volumes (London, 1909).

S. R. Gardiner: *History of the Commonwealth and Protectorate*. In four volumes (London, 1903).

William Haller: *Liberty and Information in the Puritan Revolution* (New York, 1955).

Ronald Hutton: *The British Republic* (London, 1990).

William Lamont: *Godly Rule* (London, 1969).

Jason McElligott: *Royalism, Print and Censorship in Revolutionary England* (Woodbridge, 2007).

John Morrill (ed.): *Revolution and Restoration* (London, 1992).

Robert Paul: *The Lord Protector* (London, 1955).

David Smith (ed.): *Cromwell and the Interregnum* (Oxford, 2003).

Michael Walzer: *The Revolution of the Saints* (New York, 1974).

Austin Woolrych: *Commonwealth to Protectorate* (London, 1980).

——— *England without a King* (London, 1983).

CHARLES II

Maurice Ashley: *Charles II* (London, 1973).

Robert Bosher: *The Making of the Restoration Settlement* (London, 1951).

Hester Chapman: *The Tragedy of Charles II* (London, 1964).

Raymond Crawfurd: *The Last Days of Charles II* (Oxford, 1909).

Godfrey Davies: *The Restoration of Charles II* (London, 1955).

Antonia Fraser: *King Charles II* (London, 1979).

Tim Harris: *Restoration* (London, 2005).

Tim Harris, Paul Seaward and Mark Goldie (eds): *The Politics of Religion in Restoration England* (Oxford, 1990).

Cyril Hartmann: *Clifford of the Cabal* (London, 1937).

Ronald Hutton: *The Restoration* (Oxford, 1985).

———: *Charles II* (Oxford, 1989).

Matthew Jenkinson: *Culture and Politics at the Court of Charles II* (Woodbridge, 2010).

J. R. Jones: *The First Whigs* (Oxford, 1961).

——— *Charles II* (London, 1987).

——— (ed.) *The Restored Monarchy* (London, 1979).

J. P. Kenyon: *Robert Spencer, Earl of Sunderland, 1641–1702* (London, 1958).

Anna Keay: *The Magnificent Monarch* (London, 2008).

Maurice Lee Jnr: *The Cabal* (Urbana, 1965).

John Miller: *Charles II* (London, 1991).

────── *After the Civil Wars* (London, 2000).

Annabel Patterson: *The Long Parliament of Charles II* (New Haven, 2008).

Stephen Pincus: *Protestantism and Patriotism* (Cambridge, 1996).

Paul Seaward: *The Cavalier Parliament and the Reconstruction of the Old Regime* (Cambridge, 1988).

Thomas Slaughter: *Newcastle's Advice to Charles II* (Philadelphia, 1984).

Jenny Uglow: *A Gambling Man* (London, 2009).

Brian Weiser: *Charles II and the Politics of Access* (Woodbridge, 2003).

James II

John Callow: *The Making of King James II* (Stroud, 2000).

Eveline Cruickshanks (ed.): *By Force or By Default?* (Edinburgh, 1989).

Lionel Glassey (ed.): *The Reigns of Charles II and James II* (London, 1997).

Tim Harris: *Revolution* (London, 2006).

J. R. Jones: *The Revolution of 1688 in England* (London, 1972).

T. B. Macaulay: *The History of England from the Accession of James II* (London, 1848).

John Miller: *Popery and Politics in England* (Cambridge, 1973).

────── *James II* (London, 1978).

W. A. Speck: *Reluctant Revolutionaries* (Oxford, 1988).

────── *James II* (London, 2002).

Culture and Society

I have not included studies of individual authors mentioned in the text.

Maurice Ashley: *Life in Stuart England* (London, 1964).

David Cressy: *Bonfires and Bells* (London, 1989).

Eveline Cruickshanks (ed.): *The Stuart Courts* (Stroud, 2000).

Anthony Fletcher and Peter Roberts (eds): *Religion, Culture and Society in Early Modern Britain* (Cambridge, 1994).

Ian Gentles, John Morrill and Blair Worden (eds): *Soldiers, Writers and Statesmen of the English Revolution* (Cambridge, 1998).

Johanna Harris and Elizabeth Scott-Baumann: *The Intellectual Culture of Puritan Woman* (London, 2011).

Alan Houston and Steve Pincus (eds): *A Nation Transformed* (Cambridge, 2001).

Ronald Hutton: *The Rise and Fall of Merry England* (Oxford, 1994).

N. H. Keeble: *The Restoration. England in the 1660s* (Oxford, 2002).

W. K. Jordan: *The Development of Religious Toleration in England* (London, 1936).

Gerald MacLean: *Culture and Society in the Stuart Restoration* (Cambridge 1995).

Allardyce Nicoll: *Stuart Masques* (New York, 1968).

Rosemary O'Day: *The English Clergy* (Leicester, 1979).

David Ogg: *England in the Reign of Charles II*. In two volumes (Oxford, 1934).

Stephen Orgel: *The Jonsonian Masque* (Cambridge, Mass., 1965).

Stephen Orgel and Roy Strong: *Inigo Jones. The Theatre of the Stuart Court*. In two volumes (London, 1973).

Graham Parry: *The Golden Age Restor'd* (Manchester, 1981).

R. Malcolm Smuts: *Court Culture and the Origins of a Royalist Tradition in Early Stuart England* (Philadelphia, 1987).

——— (ed.) *The Stuart Court and Europe* (Cambridge 1996).

John Spurr: *England in the 1670s* (Oxford, 2000).

Roy Strong: *Art and Power* (Woodbridge, 1984).

Blair Worden: *Literature and Politics in Cromwellian England* (Oxford, 2007).

Index